Praise for *Lost Genius*

"Even if your interest in classical music is elementary or—shame on you—merely perfunctory, *Lost Genius* offers much more than the elegance of the Vienna Philharmonic and the fun of the Boston Pops. . . . Though there will undoubtedly be some bigger biographies published this fall, it is hard to imagine a more delicious one."
—MICHAEL DIRDA, *Washington Post*

"An extensively researched, nuanced account of a spectacularly dysfunctional life." —BARBARA JEPSON, *Wall Street Journal*

"Extraordinary . . . Bazzana painstakingly re-creates a life lived mostly in obscurity and judiciously separates greatness from vainglory. The result is a balanced portrait that also often reads like a parable about the artistic temperament." —*The New Yorker*

"[Bazzana] fleshes out the details of Nyiregyházi's rise and fall, and rise and fall . . . he represented the desire for . . . a collective wish to stem the tide of time and return to an era when classical music mattered more."
—MICHAEL KIMMELMAN, *New York Times*

"In a chronicle crowded with colorful characters—a famous novelist, a prize-fighter, unscrupulous managers, divas, whores, and even Count Dracula, Bela Lugosi—the most colorful and conflicted figure of all is Nyiregyházi himself. . . . Kevin Bazzana's enthralling biography conducts us through his life with compassion, insight, humor, humanity and a proper degree of amazement."
—RICHARD DYER, former music critic of the *Boston Globe*

"A page-turner. . . . There was no modern pianist like him."
—MARK SWED, *Los Angeles Times*

"The amazing thing about this story is the inextinguishable nature of this man's genius, which kept flickering to life in recordings and odd performances, even incognito on occasion, long after the mainstream musical world had written him off." —*The Atlantic*

KEVIN BAZZANA

Lost Genius

The Curious and Tragic Story
of an Extraordinary Musical Prodigy

DA CAPO PRESS
A MEMBER OF THE PERSEUS BOOKS GROUP

Photograph, page vi: The earliest known image of Nyiregyházi,
from the cover of *Compositions d'Ervin Nyiregyházi*, Opp. 1-3, published
in 1909, when he was six (*National Széchényi Library, Budapest*).

Set in Aldus Roman by The Perseus Books Group

Cataloging-in-Publication data for this book is available
from the Library of Congress.

First Da Capo paperback edition 2008
First Carroll & Graf edition 2007
First published in Canada by McClelland & Stewart Ltd. 2007
ISBN: 978-0-306-81748-9

Published by Da Capo Press
A Member of the Perseus Books Group
www.dacapopress.com

Da Capo Press books are available at special discounts for
bulk purchases in the U.S. by corporations, institutions, and other
organizations. For more information, please contact the Special Markets
Department at the Perseus Books Group, 2300 Chestnut Street,
Suite 200, Philadelphia, PA 19103, or call (800) 810-4145,
ext. 5000, or e-mail special.markets@perseusbooks.com.

10 9 8 7 6 5 4 3 2 1

To Sharon, Sophie,
and Blossom – again

CONTENTS

Opposite: Ervin Nyiregyházi in his mid-twenties. *(Photograph by Albert Witzel. University of Southern California, on behalf of the U.S.C. Specialized Libraries and Archival Collections.)*

PRELUDE

THE STRANGE CASE
OF ERVIN NYIREGYHÁZI

One Sunday afternoon in Los Angeles, not long after the end of the Second World War, the impresario Irwin Parnes attended an open house at the home of some Hungarian friends. "I could hear through the din of conversations someone playing the piano," he recalled in his memoirs. "Strangely enough, out of the large gathering, there were only a handful of people listening. I moved closer to the piano growing more excited every minute. The pianist was playing Liszt's 'St. Francis Walking Over the Waves.' Never before and never since have I heard this work played so well. The pianist was magnificent. To my mind, not even Horowitz, Hofmann, or Schnabel in their prime could play with more ardor – with more relentless technique than this obscure salon performer. When the work was concluded, I alone shouted 'bravo' and enthusiastically introduced myself to someone whom I considered a very great artist, Ervin Nyiregyházi."[*]

---

[*] Pronounced "*air*-veen *nyeer*-edge-hah-zee." As Nyiregyházi spoke the surname, the "r" was lightly rolled and the syllable "hah" slightly (and rather musically) drawn out; sometimes the second syllable sounded like "etch." In some European sources, including

The pianist, in his early forties, looked destitute, and Parnes felt compassion as well as astonishment. He saw at once a cause he could champion: "I would revive him, ballyhoo him. I would force the world to hear and acknowledge his glory. Within a year, his fees would be astronomical. I scrawled my address upon a paper napkin and forced it into his hand. 'You must not waste your genius on this . . .' My scornful gestures swept our hostess' ample home, with its recently lauded acoustics and the now depleted buffet. 'Come and see me tomorrow and we will plan your next concert.'" But Nyiregyházi did not show up. Parnes later learned that he lived in a flophouse on Main Street – to reach him, you had to leave a message at a nearby bar – and was reputed to be "quite mad."

Parnes began to collect stories about Nyiregyházi's prodigious musicianship and prodigious eccentricity. He had cancelled a major concert because a bartender had kept him waiting a few minutes that afternoon and, offended, he had decided that he could not play in such a city. He would arrive at a dinner party with a toothbrush in his pocket and leave only when forced to do so. He had married seven times, selecting wives from among his fans backstage, and once walked offstage when he spotted one of his former wives in the audience. These stories were all false, though the truth about Nyiregyházi was no less strange: he really *was* that temperamental and unpredictable, and by the end of his life he had been married *ten* times.

Some months later, early in 1946, after Parnes had stopped trying to track him down, Nyiregyházi simply showed up at his door, and

---

the one surviving letter of Nyiregyházi's mother, the surname was spelled with a "y" at the end. In Europe, the Germanic spelling "Erwin" was common (the pronunciation is the same), while in America, both spellings, and occasionally "Irwin," "Irvin," and "Irving," were used; Nyiregyházi himself wrote "Ervin" and "Erwin," and sometimes used the American pronunciation of the latter. I have corrected the surname where appropriate in quotations from both published and unpublished sources, except where a misspelling is somehow revealing.

Parnes was amazed that he was so unlike the typical self-promoting artist. He had not had a real career for more than twenty years and had become (as Parnes had heard) terrified of performing in public; he would give a concert only when starvation loomed. If only there were some way of presenting his art to the public without presenting *himself*, Nyiregyházi mused. And so Parnes came up with a radical solution: Nyiregyházi, billed only as Mr. X, could give a recital while wearing a black silk hangman's hood to disguise his identity. He agreed.

On March 5, Parnes wrote to his new client: "The 'MR. X' concert is already being discussed all over town and I haven't even started the publicity campaign. As the concert draws near, I know it will be a temptation for you to ask your friends to attend, but please let me again emphasise the *extreme* importance of keeping the entire thing *entre nous.*" Parnes, whom one expert on the cultural history of Los Angeles describes as a "bizarre dilettante-type impresario" with a "mixed reputation," proved an adept (if shameless) publicist. "The newspapers went gleefully along with the gag," he wrote in his memoirs. "Each day I released, and they printed, another clue. Mr. X had been soloist with the Boston Symphony Orchestra, the Vienna, the London. His records had sold so many millions. He had played eight times with the Los Angeles Philharmonic. The *New York Times* critic had called him the world's greatest living interpreter of Liszt." (Only the reference to Boston was true.) Parnes knew there would be skepticism about the credentials of the anonym he was touting as the "Sensation of Three Continents" and whose picture he was plastering on telephone poles, so he announced an ambitious program of nineteenth- and twentieth-century music, and included a notice in his ads: "PERFORMANCE GUARANTEED FOR GREAT ARTISTRY: MONEY REFUNDED TO UNSATISFIED PATRONS." Tickets sold quickly, and speculation grew as to Mr. X's identity: a prisoner from San Quentin, an escaped mental patient, a citizen of a hostile nation, an actor miming to records.

The concert took place on May 13, in the Wilshire Ebell Theater, in the presence of the police, for Parnes claimed that an anonymous caller had threatened to blow up the building. Nyiregyházi offered what was indeed, as one of the newspapers put it, a "far-from-ham-and-eggs program": Schumann's *Carnaval*; Beethoven's Op. 101 sonata; Liszt's "St. Francis Walking on the Waves," *Consolation* No. 3, and *Mephisto Waltz* No. 1; Schoenberg's *Klavierstück*, ·Op. 11/No. 2; Debussy's "Clair de lune"; Shostakovich's Prelude in G-flat Major; and Rachmaninov's "Polichinelle." At the appointed time, a sold-out crowd watched as a blue spotlight illuminated the keyboard on the otherwise darkened stage, revealing Nyiregyházi already seated at the piano wearing his hood. "He played magnificently," Parnes wrote. "It was as though beneath that dark, anonymous hood, his lifelong battle with his own ghost had ended. He could address the piano as a free man, playing easily and masterfully, with only the emotion of the immediate moment to communicate." Backstage, Parnes felt assured of a triumph.

Near the end of the concert, however, when Nyiregyházi went into the wings between pieces to wipe his face, a wily reporter spotted him and shouted his name. "Mr. X rushed back to the piano like a cornered animal," Parnes wrote. "In his desperation, he seemed almost to spring upon the keyboard. His stroke battered upon the instrument as if to tear from the reluctant mechanism some ideal, unrealizable sound that pounded in his brain. There was raw anger in every note. The audience, disquieted by a sense of the disastrous struggle within him, sat on the edge of their seats. He was violent, brilliant, and terrible." The local representative for the Baldwin piano company wanted to stop the concert, fearing for his instrument, but Parnes "patted his arm, reassuringly. What was the destruction of a piano or so compared to the rebirth of a genius?"

Mr. X's identity was surely not much of a secret, at least among aficionados, for Nyiregyházi had been performing sporadically in Los Angeles for more than twenty years, and was not like any other local pianist. His long-and-lean physique and capacity for pianistic thunder were well known; many in the audience surely recognized the figure whom the music critic Isabel Morse Jones, in the *Los Angeles Times*, described as a "thin man of average height, with abnormally long fingers of steel." Jones herself wondered if Mr. X was Nyiregyházi, and she was not alone. Frederick Marvin, then a young pianist and teacher, still remembers the concert, and remembers exclaiming, "It's Nyiregyházi!" after hearing just a few notes. (He says that Nyiregyházi played so forcefully already in the first half that he broke a string or two, and a new piano was brought out for him at intermission.) Another pianist, Raymond Lewenthal, who followed Nyiregyházi's career in the early 1940s, recalled, in a 1978 essay, hearing that "when the pianist came out on the stage in his mask and struck the opening chord of his program, bringing the piano to its knees with one stroke, everyone shouted 'Nyiregyházi.'"

In any event, the audience roared its approval, no one asked for money back, and Parnes was besieged with offers for the masked pianist – from a Sunset Strip eatery and a Hollywood studio, for a Midwestern tour and a Carnegie Hall recital. Though the local critics had been intrigued, the reviews were not all favourable: Jones wrote of "soulless technique," and R. Vernon Steele, in *Pacific Coast Musician,* compared the "ludicrous" event to a prizefight: "We [have] never seen a man hit a piano so hard nor heard produced such completely disagreeable tone." Still, Parnes was confident that a major new career loomed. But the neurotic and insecure pianist, intimidated as much by success as by failure, had fled after the concert and could not be found. Parnes combed skid row looking for him; eventually, he tried to find another pianist to don the hood and fulfill Nyiregyházi's engagements, but every one he asked rebuffed him. He never saw Nyiregyházi again.[*]

In later life, Nyiregyházi discussed the Mr. X concert with regret but without apology. "I shouldn't have done that, but I did it anyway," he

---

[*] Years later, Parnes received a call from a woman who had heard a wonderful pianist playing in a bar on skid row – Nyiregyházi, obviously – and thought Parnes should try to revive his career. "I placed the receiver down, gently," he wrote. "I had heard the siren's song before, and the immunity would last my lifetime."

LOST GENIUS

said to a prospective biographer less than a year before his death. He had been in desperate financial straits at the time, as he often was. (In a 1977 letter, he noted ruefully: "I only got Seventy-five Dollars for this misadventure.") Among his papers is a note scribbled apparently years after the concert: "Mr. X is not to be scoffed at. In this case, pitied would be a truer word." Bizarre and sad, this is a classic Nyiregyházi anecdote, merely one of the stranger pages in a surpassingly strange story.

Parnes was not the first or last person to be moved by Nyiregyházi – by his phenomenal talent, his lost career and pitiable personal life, his passivity and fragility and helplessness – and to feel compelled to play the saviour. But rescue efforts were always doomed. Nyiregyházi's personality and art were simply not compatible with the music business, and he could be counted on to flee or sabotage any revival of his career, for he valued nothing more than his freedom. Parnes, like all the others, found himself saddled with a proud maverick unwilling to exploit a commercial opportunity if doing so would compromise his artistic ideals or unleash his plentiful demons – and most every opportunity did. To be fair, the Nyiregyházi story is not merely one of self-destructive temperament; he had a generous allotment of plain bad luck in his life. But however we apportion the blame between him and the Fates, we are left with a gross disparity between his potential and his achievement, and with a tattered reputation that merits repair.

In the hype that surrounded the Australian pianist David Helfgott after the release of the movie *Shine*, in 1996, there was much talk of a great pianist felled and reclaimed, for, of course, the greater his talent, the more lamentable his obscurity, the more newsworthy his rediscovery. But, in fact, Helfgott was nothing more than a promising piano student when he was lost to mental illness. In the present case, there is no need to exaggerate for the sake of a good story. Ervin Nyiregyházi really *was* a lost genius; his talent really *was* as great as his life and personality were strange. Even long after the early ruin of his career, knowledgeable listeners who chanced upon him playing were stunned by what they heard.

One of them was no less a figure than the composer Arnold Schoenberg. On December 1, 1935, early in his self-imposed exile in America, Schoenberg attended a soirée in Pacific Palisades at the home of his friend Rolf Hoffmann, a professor of German literature at the University of California at Los Angeles, for the express purpose of hearing Nyiregyházi play. The night before, Hoffmann, at the urging of two friends – the pianists Maurice Zam and John Crown – had attended a Nyiregyházi recital at a local Hungarian church. Astonished, he insisted on introducing the pianist to Schoenberg. Nyiregyházi played some of the same pieces at Hoffmann's house, and Schoenberg, also astonished, offered stilted but heartfelt praise: "You are the person most replete with genius I have ever heard."

The next day, Schoenberg wrote to Otto Klemperer, the conductor of the Los Angeles Philharmonic, who was then in New York. His letter opened and closed with news and pleasantries, but its raison d'être was a dissertation on Nyiregyházi:

> Yesterday, at Dr. Hoffmann's, I heard a pianist who seems to me to be something utterly extraordinary. I went very reluctantly, as the descriptions [I had heard] from Dr. Hoffmann and also Maurice Zam had made me very skeptical. But I must say, I have never heard such a pianist before. . . . First and foremost, he does not play in the style you and I strive for. And I believe that, just as I did not judge him on that basis, you, too, when you hear him, will probably feel compelled to set all principles aside, just as I did. They would not be proper standards for him. What he plays is pure *expression*, in the older sense. But such power of expression I have never heard before. You will agree as little as I did with his tempi. You will also find that by means of sharp contrasts he seems often to lose sight of the form: [but only] seems:

surprisingly, in its own way, [his playing] does acquire form, has sense and proportion. The sound he gets out of the piano is unprecedented. At least, I have never heard anything like it. He himself seems not to know how he draws out these utterly incredible and novel sounds (though he seems to be a man of intelligence and not just a flaccid "dreamer"). And such fullness of tone, without ever becoming harsh, I have also never encountered before. For me, and probably also for you, much too much. But on the whole, incredible originality and conviction. And above all, he is 33 years old, and so still has more stages of development before him, from which, given the foundation, the greatest things are to be expected. And that is why I believe it is crucial that he be given the opportunity to participate again in concert life. I am certain that he will have great success. And Zam and Crown, who are very enthusiastic and in any case arranged our meeting, also call him a second Liszt. If it were up to me, I would engage him immediately.... But isn't it still possible for you to find a spot for him [in one of your concerts]? He would most like to play [a concerto by] Tchaikovsky or Brahms.

I would be very happy to know that I have succeeded in describing adequately to you my impression of this man. I believe that, if you can get used to the idea that he does not follow our notions of style, and can imagine his tremendous potential, and if you come to know his unparalleled technique, of which I have not yet spoken, then you will do the right thing. Technique: it is astonishing what and how he plays: one never has the sense that it is difficult, that it is technique at all, but rather that sheer force of will permits him to surmount all difficulties in realizing an idea. – You see I'm becoming almost poetic.

Schoenberg knew that Nyiregyházi had been a great child prodigy and that the American critic James Huneker had dubbed him "a new Liszt" – an opinion that, he noted, "truly seems to be the case, assuming that Liszt was actually this good." Klemperer took the recommendation seriously, for Schoenberg was not only a great musician but a cranky iconoclast who did not bestow praise lightly.

And so, in January, again at Hoffmann's, Nyiregyházi played for Klemperer. The results were less happy. Klemperer was no fan of the excerpts he played, in his own improvised arrangement, from Liszt's oratorio *Christus*, and sat silent after Scriabin's Sonata No. 5, which Nyiregyházi, who compared a proper performance of that piece to "a cosmic upheaval," was known to play with thrilling power. When Klemperer said he could not judge a performer until he had played Beethoven, Nyiregyházi obliged with the Op. 111 sonata; Klemperer did not like *that* either. Finally, Nyiregyházi played Chopin's popular B-flat-minor sonata, in his own version: dissatisfied with Chopin's strange, slight finale, the famous "winds over the graves" movement, he replaced it with the more substantial and dramatic finale of Chopin's B-minor sonata, transposing it down a semitone. Schoenberg, who was again present and full of praise, thought the substitute finale ingenious, but Klemperer, who (as Nyiregyházi well knew) insisted on respect for a composer's score, was indignant, the more so as Nyiregyházi would not justify himself except to say that he liked the piece better his way. Klemperer concluded that this could not be a "sincere" musician, and Nyiregyházi never heard from him again.

The letter, at least, remains, and it has a special authority, given the writer's stature and objectivity as a witness (this, remember, was his report on a performer whom he had to be dragged to hear and whose style did not accord with his own). We do well to keep this letter in mind. It reminds us that, though his story reads at times like melodrama or black comedy or myth-making, our subject was a musician great enough, even at a low point in his career, to widen the eyes of Arnold Schoenberg.

The historian John Lukacs has written of the "national character fault" of the Hungarians, "excoriated often by great Magyar thinkers and writers: the brilliance of short-run effort at the expense of prudence and foresight. Their word for it is 'straw-fire nature,' since straw burns brilliantly but rapidly, leaving only a heap of black ashes." In Nyiregyházi's case, the straw burned brilliantly but rapidly twice, at the beginning and end of his life. As a prodigy, he enjoyed a sometimes sensational international career and was admitted into the highest artistic and social circles, first in his native Budapest, later in other European capitals, finally in America. (This, in fact, is the second book to have been written about him. The first, by the psychologist Géza Révész, was published in 1916, when Nyiregyházi was thirteen.) But not long after he entered adulthood, his career foundered; by the mid-1920s, he was broke, living where he could, and subsisting on musical odd jobs. For almost half a century, he only rarely re-emerged into the spotlight and invariably slipped back into obscurity. (He composed all the while, however, producing hundreds of works in a defiantly old-fashioned idiom.) As the decades drifted by, his life became increasingly messy and restless, because of his childlike psychology, because of the vicissitudes of a life of poverty, because a sheltered upbringing had left him ill-equipped to cope with either a domestic or a professional life, because he developed ruinous appetites for alcohol and sex – though he often wore his dissolution as a badge of honour, evidence of his refusal to compromise art to commerce. In 1972, at the age of sixty-nine, he was rediscovered by chance in California, and he was later, for several years, the subject of noisy international celebrity (and controversy). But by the time he died, in 1987, he had been forgotten – again. He still is.

In some ways, the straw fires that bound his life were as damaging to his reputation as the half-century of obscurity in between. His childhood career is most often cited as a cautionary tale: he has become the classic case of the failed prodigy, crushed by the pressure of great expectations and unable, in adulthood, to fulfill his promise as an artist. And his renaissance in his seventies, while it fostered some genuine appreciation of his gifts and yielded a body of work that gives posterity a taste of his art, bore the unmistakable stamp of a fad. Remembered, if at all, as a failed prodigy or aged novelty, he has left many people wondering (like Klemperer) whether he could really have been "sincere."

As a man, moreover, he could be both attractive and repellent, and was always difficult. He once called himself "a fortissimo bastard," and he did indeed, for good and ill, live his life fortissimo. Hypersensitive, he experienced every emotion in Technicolor. "I am master of my passions to some extent," he wrote to a former lover in 1929, "and yet I am torn by desires, aspirations, conflicts, memories, all playing the melody of life on the strings of my heart." This was a man for whom sentimentality and bombast were never dirty words, in life or art, and the turmoil in his life was a by-product of a tumultuous personality. He resisted all categories, rejected conventional notions of morality and sexuality, good taste and responsibility, and was a morass of contradictions. "Sometimes he's a celestial saint, and sometimes he's a wonderful old grandfather, and sometimes he's a rotten bastard," one acquaintance said; another called him "a dictionary of adjectives." He had a great capacity for adoration and devotion, yet he invariably exhausted and injured those closest to him. He was an idealistic philosopher who championed the loftiest spiritual goals, yet he demanded the satisfaction of his basest urges. He lived most of his life in poverty and anonymity, yet he always thought of himself as an aristocrat by virtue of his genius, his talent, his soul. He was convinced of his greatness as a pianist and composer, yet he was so insecure that he could be felled by a mere breath of criticism or some slight assault on his dignity. For every person who found him pitiable and cruel, another found him generous and noble. On the back of a chequebook that is among his papers, he scrawled, "I am a rotten S[on] of a b[itch] pianist, but God *does* speak throu[gh] me."

It is hardly surprising that posterity has not known what to do with this man and his art, and so has done (mostly) nothing. Admittedly, Nyiregyházi left only frustrating glimpses of his art in its prime, and a case for him can be made only by teasing often shy evidence out from a tangle of obscure sources. What emerges is one of the greatest and most individual pianists of the twentieth century, and something less lofty but no less interesting, too: one of the most singular characters, with one of the most bizarre stories, in the history of music.

Opposite: Ervin around age ten. *(Reproduced from the frontispiece of* The Psychology of a Musical Prodigy, *the 1925 English edition of Géza Révész's book.)*

PART ONE

MUSICAL WONDER CHILD

1903–1920

Beginnings in Budapest

Nyiregyházi knew little about his father's ancestry, even less about his mother's, and his family's history is spottily documented. Both sides of the family were Jewish. Among the ancestors of his paternal grandmother, born Esther Rottenberg, were some important rabbis, in northern Hungarian cities like Sátoraljaújhely and Sajószentpéter and, farther back, in Germany; the Rottenbergs, indeed, believed that they had descended from the thirteenth-century German rabbi and poet Meir ben Baruch, the "Maharam of Rothenburg," a legendary medieval authority on the Talmud. Nyiregyházi's maternal great-grandfather was a certain Rabbi Mandl, and he believed that his mother's family had originally been named Mandel and may have come from outside Hungary – perhaps also from Germany.

The Nyiregyházi family name was originally Fried (in German, "Friede" means "peace"), though Nyiregyházi did not know when it was changed. Through the nineteenth and early twentieth centuries, more and more Hungarian Jews adopted the Magyar language in preference to German and Yiddish, and took Hungarian surnames. Often they took their name from that of their hometown – the "i" at the end of such names is equivalent to the suffix in "Berliner" – and this seems to have been the case here. According to Nyiregyházi's cousin Henry Fried,[*] the family at one point left Budapest, possibly at the government's suggestion, to escape anti-Semitism, and settled in the town of Nyíregyháza, in the northeasternmost county of present-day Hungary. The family may have relocated several times, in fact: Nyiregyházi's father, Ignácz, was born in 1875 in the Carpathian Mountains town of Mezőlaborc (today Medzilaborce, in the northeastern corner of the Slovak Republic).

In March 1902, Ignácz Nyiregyházi married Mária Borsodi, who was born in 1885 in Budapest. Ervin was born on the evening of January 19, 1903, in the family's modest apartment at 79 Vörösmarty Street in the Theresa (Sixth) District, on the younger, more populous and vibrant Pest side of the city, east of the Danube. The district was one of the most crowded in Budapest – a veritable sea of cramped apartment buildings – and its population included petits bourgeois and the upper strata of industrial workers; about one-third of its population were Jews, some of them quite poor. When Nyiregyházi was a boy, several members of the extended family lived in his apartment: Rabbi Mandl's widow, whom he called "Lenke *ómama*" [Grandma Lenke]; her oldest, widowed daughter – Ervin's grandmother – Szidónia Borsodi; and his uncle Márton Borsodi, who left Hungary when Ervin was five and eventually settled in Los Angeles. The Nyiregyházis had once been very poor, but the family now belonged to the educated middle class. Among the extended family were a tailor, a pharmacist, a jeweller and clock dealer, the editor of a conservative newspaper, a government official, a tobacconist, the owner of a sausage factory, and a diamond millionaire in Johannesburg.

By the time Ervin was born, his family was not particularly devout or observant, did not keep kosher, and seems not to have been much involved in Jewish public life or causes. Still, they lived openly as Jews,

---

[*] Fried was the son of Nyiregyházi's uncle Arnold, who moved to Philadelphia in the early 1900s and reverted to the original surname.

within a mostly Jewish milieu, were on good terms with local rabbis, and attended (albeit irregularly) the middle-class Dohány Templom, the largest synagogue in the world and the main synagogue of the Israelite Congregation of Pest, a Neolog congregation that adhered to tradition while making concessions to modernism. Ervin's father and his grandfather, Vilmos Nyiregyházi, sang in the synagogue's choir; according to Henry Fried, Vilmos may once have been a cantor there. Ervin was circumcised, learned to read Hebrew, and celebrated his bar mitzvah. But though always philosophically and spiritually inclined, he usually claimed no religious feelings and had no opinions on matters like reincarnation or the paranormal. He could be inconsistent, however. He told his last wife, "I believe in God but not in the dogma of the church." And he believed that some undefined "higher power" was the source of his musical gifts and inspiration.

The half-century preceding the end of the First World War was a golden age for Hungary's Jews. The Compromise of 1867, which created the Austro-Hungarian Monarchy, brought emancipation to them, guaranteeing their civil and legal equality. In the fervently nationalistic atmosphere of nineteenth-century Hungary, the Magyarization of hundreds of thousands of Jews was generally welcomed – it added weight to the Hungarian half of the empire – and Jews became well known for their keenness to take up Magyar language, manners, and culture, and for their ardent patriotism and strong emotional ties to the country. Jews at this time were accepted and assimilated to a degree unmatched in Europe, and the *recepció* [law of reception] of 1895 defined Judaism as merely one religious denomination among others. Nyiregyházi was thus born into what the anthropologist and historian Raphael Patai describes as "the only period in the millennial history of the Hungarian Jews when *legally* no distinction whatsoever existed between the Jewish and non-Jewish population of the country."

The Jewish presence was particularly strong in Budapest, which attracted Jews from all over Europe. By 1910, there were about two hundred thousand Jews in the city – almost one-quarter of its population. (Only about 5 per cent of Hungary as a whole was Jewish.) Jews made a disproportionate contribution to the life of the city. They were over-represented among eligible voters and in higher-income jobs, particularly in the professions. The Jewish presence in cultural and intellectual life, in finance and commerce, in politics and government, in the sciences, and in many other fields was conspicuous, and essential to the formation of modern Budapest. The city into which Nyiregyházi was born was one of relative equilibrium and peaceful coexistence, where a Jew could flourish.

Anti-Semitism had not vanished, however. There were always some who resented Jewish influence and power and questioned the "Hungarianness" even of long-Magyarized, well-assimilated Jews, particularly in the city sometimes called "Judapest." Though anti-Semitism in Budapest (and Hungary) was traditionally less virulent than elsewhere in Europe, it sufficed to make a deep impression on Ervin, who was an unusually sensitive child. As a boy, he said, "I was spat at in the streets of Budapest because I was a Jew." When he was fifteen and taking a public-school exam, he was segregated from the rest of the class, and the teacher called for him by name, age, and religion – "Israelite." As he made his way to the front of the room, other boys spat on the floor without reprimand. He attributed his adult shyness and timidity in part to such experiences, and he learned that it was rarely to his advantage to admit to being Jewish; he did so only to wives and intimate friends, and not all of them. Often he claimed that like most Hungarians he was Catholic; he was still saying so to a prospective biographer at the end of his life. Yet, he was not necessarily *ashamed* of being Jewish. He took the view, even as a child, that it was merely a fact of his life, reason for neither pride nor shame. His public caution and reticence on the subject was a form of self-protection, fed by early, painful experiences of anti-Semitism.

Postcard showing the Royal Hungarian Opera (far right) and Andrássy Avenue as they appeared in the first years of Nyiregyházi's life. *(Archives, Budapest Opera House.)*

Though there was no longstanding tradition of music on either side of the family, Ervin's father and grandfather sang as tenors in the chorus of the Royal Hungarian Opera, and his mother was an amateur pianist who, he said, "played very well." His parents' interest in music provided fertile soil for his extraordinary talent. He was not yet a year old when his father witnessed him trying to imitate singing – something infants that young are generally incapable of doing. Before he was two, he could correctly reproduce a melody that had been sung to him, though his speech was still poorly developed (it did not progress until he was past two). Before he was three, his father discovered that the boy had perfect pitch: he could correctly locate on the piano any note that was sung to him, and could reproduce sung melodies on a mouth organ. When he was three, he began to play the melodies he heard on the piano, and was soon improvising his own tunes, some with accompaniment. He learned the principles of notation in a single sitting in

May 1906. His father had told him the plot of *Madama Butterfly* – Puccini was in town for a festival of his operas, including the Hungarian première of *Butterfly* – and though Ervin had not yet heard any music from the opera, he was inspired to sit on the floor in front of the toy piano he had recently been given, wearing what he remembered as "a little girl's dress," and picked out a tune. His father showed him how to write it down, and he named it *Madama Butterfly*. It was the first piece he could remember composing, yet he was already savvy enough to use a pentatonic scale to give his tune an "Oriental" flavour.

Natural talent of this magnitude could not remain a secret, and so, in 1907, at age four, Ervin was taken to the National Hungarian Royal Academy of Music, where he played some of his own pieces for two of the professors. That same year he received some sporadic instruction in piano and in reading music. His first piano teacher was the venerable István Thomán, who had studied with Franz Liszt, and whom Béla Bartók, one of his pupils, called "the great tutor of generations of Hungarian pianists." Bartók remembered Thomán as a devoted, unselfish teacher with a "loving interest" in the musical and intellectual growth of his students, who "stood beside his pupils as protector and as a paternal good friend," even outside the classroom, and belonged "to that rare breed of pedagogue who never represses the individuality of their pupils." Ervin felt a close bond with Thomán and was inspired by him, though for unexplained reasons studied with him only briefly. At age five, he was registered at the academy as a pupil of Arnold Székely, himself a former pupil of Thomán, and remained so until the family left Hungary in January 1914.[*] The academy's yearbooks reveal impressive progress. Young to begin with for such study, Ervin nonetheless worked, consistently, well ahead of his nominal level

---

[*] Nyiregyházi remembered studying with Thomán at least through age six or seven; perhaps he continued to see Thomán for a time after enrolling at the academy. (He studied privately with Thomán, who had retired from the academy in 1906.)

and earned excellent grades even when he took final exams intended for students a year or two ahead of him.

He took to the piano instinctively, and his development was astonishing, even though, he said, he never practised more than three hours a day in his life. By age six, his large repertoire included Haydn and Mozart sonatas, Beethoven's *Pathétique* Sonata, Schumann's *Kinderszenen* and *Papillons*, Grieg's *Lyric Pieces*, and short pieces by Chopin, Mendelssohn, and Liszt. As the earliest photographs show, he had unusually long fingers already as a child, though his development as a pianist still outran his development as a boy. His physical growth increased markedly at ages six and seven, during which time the development of his musical faculties temporarily slowed down, but afterward he began to apply himself more seriously and systematically to the piano, with impressive results. At eight or nine, he commanded much of the standard repertoire, including Bach's *Well-Tempered Clavier*, Beethoven's biggest early and middle-period sonatas, and many virtuosic Romantic works – Schumann's *Carnaval* and *Humoreske*, Chopin's ballades, Liszt's Hungarian Rhapsodies. On November 25, 1911, at the academy, he performed Haydn's D-major concerto, with a long, harmonically adventurous cadenza of his own composition, and he was no older than nine when he began studying the big Romantic concertos, like those of Grieg and Tchaikovsky; on December 20, 1912, not yet ten, he played the Schumann concerto in one of the academy's public concerts. One of his greatest childhood successes was in Beethoven's "Emperor" Concerto. "The audience was transfixed at the masterly lucidity of the boy's playing," the psychologist Géza Révész wrote. "They were astonished at his extraordinary finish, the fullness of his tone and the genuine beauty of his interpretation." He was already a stubbornly independent musician, too, and was not shy about challenging his teachers.

"A considerable length of time passed before he began to study harmony, this theoretical musical instruction only lasting a short time, being cut short, owing to external causes, after fifteen lessons, and not until a year later did he take it up again," Révész wrote. The external cause was probably Ervin's mother, who thought that his first theory teacher, Albert Siklós, was too indulgent, so she stopped their lessons. ("We got along too well," Nyiregyházi recalled. "I treated him as a friend.") In 1912, Mária placed her son with Leó Weiner, a prominent composer who taught theory at the academy, and for the next two years Ervin studied harmony, counterpoint, form, and orchestration under Weiner, who was full of praise for him. His progress in counterpoint was poor – already he was a committed Romantic ill at case with "abstract" music like Bach's fugues – but his grasp of form amazed his teacher, and he already knew most of the nineteenth-century orchestral works on which their lessons were based. Weiner, by all accounts, was an exceptional and popular teacher, an inspiring mentor and coach to generations of Hungarian musicians, though Ervin did not get along with him; for one thing, he did not encourage Ervin to compose, as Siklós had done. Of his theory teachers, he would eventually say, "They didn't teach me anything I didn't know already."

His artistic development was nourished by his city's thriving cultural life. When he was born, Budapest, the youngest of the great metropolises of Europe, was at its zenith – beautiful, vibrant, prosperous, modern. (John Lukacs dubbed the year 1900 Budapest's "noon hour.") In the last quarter of the nineteenth century, thanks to dynamic economic growth, Budapest had experienced a building boom, including massive public-works projects, and its population had almost tripled, to about three-quarters of a million at the turn of the century. It was now the fastest-growing city in Europe, and by the time of the First World War the population was close to a million. Once isolated by language and culture, it was now a cosmopolitan, truly European city, no longer so widely viewed as exotic or "Oriental." Its artistic and intellectual life, coffeehouse and club cultures, and nightlife had exploded within a generation, and among the literate middle and upper

Nyiregyházi's grandfather (top) and father, in portraits that still appear on a wall of the Budapest Opera House, in what was formerly a smoking corridor for the orchestra. *(Archives, Budapest Opera House.)*

classes, cultural achievement was nurtured – in music, painting, theatre, film, literature, journalism. Nyiregyházi, in fact, belonged to the first generation of notable Hungarians (a disproportionate number of them Jews) to become widely known outside the country.

Opera and operetta, orchestras, chamber ensembles, pianists – all flourished in turn-of-the-century Budapest. Some of the greatest European musicians of the day passed through the city, and Ervin heard many of them. His father and grandfather first took him to work at the opera when he was five, and he became a regular at the company's rehearsals and performances. Once, around age seven, he was deputized to conduct the Anvil Chorus from *Il trovatore* when the conductor was called to the telephone. The Royal Opera, at this time, had a wide international repertory and an excellent reputation, and Ervin was seduced by the passion and lyricism of opera; sometimes he was so overwhelmed that he had difficulty containing his enthusiasm or even suspending his disbelief. When he was seven, his father took him to a rehearsal of *Elektra*, but he had to be hustled out of the theatre when he began shouting for the police – people on the stage were being murdered! Around the same time, when he saw his father onstage in *Lohengrin*, he blurted out, "That's Papa over there, the thinnest man in the whole crowd!" Even in old age, his personal operatic canon aligned neatly with the Royal Opera's repertory, testifying to the decisive impact of these childhood experiences.

Ervin's thirst for knowledge extended beyond music. Like many gifted children, he was an early, passionate, and omnivorous reader. Through his early years, he devoured the weightiest classics – Dante, Dostoevsky, Goethe, Heine, Schiller, Shakespeare, Shelley, the ancient Greeks, as well as Hungarian authors – though he loved detective stories, too, and Jules Verne, who, he said, exerted a great influence on him. He learned German, as his family, like most educated Hungarians, was bilingual. (Though Magyar had replaced German as the first language of most Hungarians in the later nineteenth century, German remained indispensable to those seeking entry into the larger world of European culture.) Ervin acquired a smattering of other languages from his mother, who spoke French and knew enough English to read Dickens and Wilde. He became passionate about other subjects, too – philosophy, history, geography – and was mad for chess. He showed talent for it as early as age six, and some knowledgeable players considered him gifted. (He could play blindfolded.) He recalled that his forte was defence rather than attack – a neat metaphor for his personality: throughout his life he was passive and cautious and abhorred confrontation. He read books about chess and followed international tournaments, and by his early teens was so obsessed with chess that he considered devoting more time to it than to music, until his mother took away his chess set and books. "I was very bitter," he said. Thereafter, he would tell his mother he was going out to play sports but then sneak away in search of a chess game.

On the evening of December 16, 1910, Ervin's only sibling, a brother, was born. Ignácz wanted to name him Richard, after Wagner, but Mária overruled him and named him Alfred, a less commonplace name that she considered classier. Alfred also demonstrated some musical gifts, including a good memory, and Ervin was impressed by his natural appreciation of music. Alfred wanted to play the piano, but the family already had a pianist, his mother said, so he was compelled to study the violin. (Ervin also studied the violin, for about six months around age nine, but his teacher stopped the lessons because he had no aptitude for the instrument.) Mária believed that her younger son had the potential to be a fine musician, and Alfred kept at the violin for some time: a friend who knew him in his teens and early twenties remembered playing chamber music with him. In any event, Ervin adored his brother, and was not jealous of or condescending toward him. Like most prodigies, he was secure in his status.

Under the Microscope

Ervin Nyiregyházi is among the best-documented musical prodigies in history, thanks to Géza Révész, who spent more than four years closely studying him. Born in Siófok in 1878, Révész studied psychology at Göttingen and Berlin; he completed his studies in 1905 and, at the time he investigated Ervin, was a lecturer at Budapest University. The author of articles and books on the intersections of psychology, hearing, and music, among many other subjects, Révész developed interests in musical talent and the psychology of music, and was an exponent of experimental psychology – a symptom of an age confident that science could explain psychological phenomena. Rejecting what he considered the usual anecdotal approach to the subject of prodigies, he set himself the then radical task of quantifying his subject's gifts, not only to understand this one prodigy comprehensively, but to extrapolate larger conclusions about the roots and development of artistic talent, perhaps even about artistic creativity itself.

He began conducting systematic experiments on Ervin in January 1910, though he had been aware of (and tested) the boy earlier, and continued studying him until January 1914. Nyiregyházi remembered seeing Révész several days a week, except during the summer months or when he was out of town, usually for several hours before the big midday meal, sometimes in his family's apartment and sometimes at Révész's home. Révész conversed with Ervin, observed him playing and composing, and devised tests to gauge his gifts. Ervin did not mind these sessions. He saw them as outlets for his creativity, opportunities to talk about subjects that mattered to him with an intelligent, learned man who took what he said seriously. Révész administered the new intelligence tests of the French psychologist Alfred Binet and others, and determined that Ervin's general intelligence was at least two or three years in advance of his age, though he noted that these tests did not account "for precisely that quality which is most remarkable in his intellect, its brilliance." As the boy's teachers reported to Révész, "it was generally sufficient to show or explain something to him once, after which he not only understood it, but grasped it in such a manner that, when the occasion arose, he was able to utilize it." Révész did not hesitate to compare Ervin to the most famous of all musical prodigies: Mozart.

Ervin had absolute pitch of extraordinary acuteness. He could identify notes without hesitation or uncertainty, regardless of range, tone colour, or instrumentation, and could analyze wide-ranging, dissonant chords and tone clusters, in all registers, with astonishing accuracy, including chords of a half-dozen or more notes. His sight-reading was excellent, sometimes faultless. "Professional musicians who played chamber music with him were amazed at the musical feeling, precision, and artistic understanding which he showed when reading at sight," Révész reported. Ervin could sight-read scores of nineteenth-century symphonies. "It was just like reading a book," he said. He could transpose from key to key, usually with great ease; at ten, he could transpose pieces by Bach, and sonatas by Haydn and Beethoven, at sight. From as early as age four, he could improvise in various styles, with great imagination and emotional power. (His childhood performances often included improvisations on tunes of his listeners' choosing.) His memory, too, was astounding. At six or seven, he could learn a substantial piece by playing through it a few times; he learned the Schumann concerto by heart in about ten days, playing it no more than once a day. He could even play or write out flawlessly, from memory, music he had never played but had only read. (Révész saw him learn music by reading scores while humming and moving his fingers on a table.) And he did not forget. By the time he was a teenager, he was carrying whole repertories in his head – piano music, chamber music, symphonies, operas – and in his eighties he claimed to have at least three thousand compositions memorized.

For Révész, the "most conclusive evidence of his musical talent" was his creativity. He noted that at eight Ervin already had more than prodigious technique and command of the piano's resources; he played with "extraordinary musical sense," offering interpretations "not of a child, but of an artist of deep insight." This opinion was widely held. Leó Weiner once said, in amazement, that the boy played Beethoven's "Waldstein" Sonata better than Busoni did, and Nyiregyházi recalled playing that piece in a private concert, perhaps as young as age seven, and being greeted by stunned silence followed by cries of "Genius!"

Only very rarely, even among prodigies and great composers, does compositional talent show up in extreme youth, but Ervin, before he had received any instruction in composition or theory, possessed, as Révész noted, "a sound and genuine capacity to give form to thoughts and emotions." He continued to compose after that first effort on his toy piano. He would wake up at six in the morning, while the rest of the family slept, and sneak into the living room to compose at the dining table. He had a piano in his bedroom, and sometimes improvised or sketched ideas at it, but could compose in his head, sometimes while moving his fingers on the table. Later, after the midday meal, while everyone else napped, he composed some more. Before long he had compiled an impressive portfolio. At age five, his compositions included a barcarolle, a "dance of elves," and a programmatic piece titled *On the Death of a Little Bird*. Over the next six years, he wrote numerous pieces in generic Romantic forms (ballade, fantasy, nocturne, scherzo, serenade, sonata, variation), as well as evocative works with titles like *Longing, Spring Song, An Oriental Dream, Plaintive Sounds,* and *Life of a Butterfly,* some of which evolved from improvisations based on stories his father told him or scenes in movies. He tackled some very ambitious works, too – orchestral pieces with lofty titles like *The Life of a Hero* and *Proclamation of the Ten Commandments on Mount Sinai,* a symphony (unfinished) on Napoleon, an oratorio on the death of Moses.

This music was, of course, derivative, influenced by respectable models like Beethoven, Chopin, and the Austro-German Romantics. Moreover, as Révész wrote, "Erwin's compositions, as a rule, do not betray his Magyar descent"; only rarely did they draw on folk song, for instance.* And they were "almost entirely free from the influence of well-known contemporary composers," for he had little sympathy with most modern music. Indeed, his adult repertoire of twentieth-century music – the odd piece by Debussy, Bartók, Granados, Rachmaninov, Schoenberg, Strauss, and a few others – did not extend much beyond what was new when he was a child.† In any event, his childhood music does not rank with that of the greatest composing prodigies, but he did write some works of considerable imagination, individuality, and

---

* Nyiregyházi received a conservative education at the academy, where a long-entrenched bias in favour of Austro-German music only slowly gave way to the radical music of young composers like Bartók and Zoltán Kodály, who sought to forge a new style with roots in Hungarian folk music. Nyiregyházi knew indigenous Hungarian idioms the way most Europeans did: as tributaries to an Austro-German mainstream. Outside that mainstream, he was interested in the music of Italy, France, Russia, Norway, and Spain as much as that of Hungary.

† He considered Verdi, Puccini, and Grieg to be his "contemporaries" because their lifespans overlapped briefly with his own. As an adult, he knew little of the music of living composers, and liked none of it. In the 1980s, he called Krzysztof Penderecki "a phony" whose music "sounds like a streetcar collision," and called Witold Lutosławski's music "crap."

Example 2.

SERENATA.

Composed at the age of 7. (September 1909.)

The opening of a serenade Ervin composed at age six (not, as indicated here, seven) and performed often in childhood recitals. Though the piece is, to say the least, modest – just thirty-three bars long, utterly banal – Nyiregyházi insisted to the end of his life that it was a "masterpiece." *(Reproduced from* The Psychology of a Musical Prodigy, *the 1925 English edition of Géza Révész's book. International Ervin Nyiregyházi Foundation.)*

expressive power, and he explored a wide range of genres and styles and moods, often winning praise from his elders.

Révész marvelled not only at Ervin's talent but at his adult seriousness, his voracious curiosity, his industry, concentration, and willpower, his sense of purpose. The boy had breathtaking self-confidence, too; Révész noted how Ervin "smiles in a superior manner" during testing. "When I was six," Nyiregyházi said, "I thought I was greater than Beethoven." In conversation, Ervin, like many prodigies, was an impressive and often amusing blend of child and adult. He pretended to mature insights and adult sophistication, in language that was often formal and pretentious. Révész dutifully recorded Ervin's discourse, including his assessments of various composers:

> Bach is the stem of music, he stands on the highest summit of music, but not the summit of emotion. In his works only the *music* is perfect, but not the emotional idea.

> Mozart was more delicate and light in feeling than Beethoven, but he was not so subtle in music and in his part-writing. Beethoven wrote more serious music than Mozart, for he probably experienced much more sorrow and bitterness than Mozart, and that is why Beethoven's melodies speak to one's heart more than Mozart's.

> Wagner was a very fine part-writer and a composer of great verve. I cannot say that he always made *beautiful* harmonies, but his harmonies always sound *full* and sonorous.

> Bizet has composed very serious melodies, but by this I do not mean that his melodies are gloomy or too serious, but that they are well-thought-out and carefully considered. Of Schumann, one might say the same thing, but while his melodies are of a pleasantly serious, and dreamy character, Bizet's are rather dramatic.

Révész was mightily impressed by it all:

> The degree of certainty with which he expressed his judgments on
> difficult questions, and the deep truths that lay in his utterances were
> almost incredible. He analysed his own inner life in the manner of a
> trained psychologist, he talked about his observations on himself
> clearly and consistently, and that which will appear still more mar-
> vellous to many people – he expressed himself with great caution and
> in remarkably pregnant phraseology. He often asked me whether
> what he was about to tell me would get "into the book," for in this
> case, he said, "I want to express myself correctly, and you must pay
> great attention to me; for a single wrongly-chosen word may alter
> the meaning of the whole thing." It was also characteristic of him to
> search eagerly at times for the right expressions and, if words failed
> him, to convey his meaning by expressive gestures. In the end, he
> made everything clear, sometimes repeated what he had said, and
> then asked whether one had understood it correctly.

(An exaggerated precision in conversation and writing was apparent
throughout Nyiregyházi's life. In interviews and letters, even casual
conversations, he spoke sometimes to the point of verbosity and redun-
dancy in an effort to make himself absolutely clear.)

The comments quoted above, though confidently expressed, are
merely a smorgasbord of loftily expressed banalities and parroted ideas
taken for original, and of course Ervin's opinions were not informed by
breadth of experience. Still, it *is* astonishing to witness the assurance of a
boy this young in marshalling, developing, and expressing his thoughts,
and Révész was correct to note that Ervin gave much original thought to
received ideas, and often qualified his more sweeping judgments. His
comments reveal a cautious thinker with a remarkable grasp of the world
of music, already constructing a personal aesthetic in which everything
had its place and determined to remain true to himself in the face of

opposition. Already, for instance – and all his life – he insisted that the "emotional idea" of a piece was his paramount concern, and was loath to discuss music in technical terms. In his seventies, talking to a friend about Bach's fugues, he said, "Music that expresses only music is an empty shell."

Sometimes, Ervin could not resist showing off. When, at age five, he visited the dentist and was asked to stick out his tongue and say "La," he replied, "That's not 'La' you said, that was 'Fa.'" He was no older than six when, one night at the opera while listening to "La donna è mobile," he loudly declared that the tenor was "no good" while his mother frantically shushed him. Showing his disdain for school, he once played a precocious trick on Leó Weiner. He played a little-known concerto by Mozart and claimed it was his own composition; Weiner, as expected, dismissed it. A week later, he played something of his own and claimed it was a little-known work by Mozart; Weiner, as expected, praised it. When Ervin revealed his ruse, his teacher was startled, and his father was pleased that his son could fool such a man – though he said, "Don't tell Mama."

Erwin Nyiregyházi: psychologische Analyse eines musikalisch hervorragenden Kindes [psychological analysis of a musically prodigious child] was published in Leipzig in 1916. The only book ever devoted to the close scientific study of a single prodigy, it is still in print and still cited. While its scientific methods, analyses, and occasional pretensions have been challenged by some later psychologists, as have its claims to yield broad conclusions about prodigies, artistic development, and artistic creation, the book remains something of a classic in the literature on gifted children and the psychology of music. But Nyiregyházi believed that Révész had missed his essential personality, that the book revealed only his gifts, not his spiritual ideas. "I never told him what I really felt," he said. "He never suspected my real feelings." To his last wife, he was blunter: "It wasn't me. The Révész book is a counterfeit."

Prodigy's Progress

Ervin became the focal point of the Nyiregyházi household once his musical gifts were recognized. His parents permitted him to concentrate on his musical and intellectual development, apparently unconcerned about the consequences of spoiling him and denying him a normal childhood. He was not expected to play, do chores, dress himself, or cut his own food. For the rest of the family, breakfast usually consisted of rolls and butter, but Ervin, even when money was tight, got soft-boiled eggs, hot cereal with cream, and rolls with marmalade, and for the late-morning meal, perhaps a steak or veal with potatoes. He was exempted from public school; instead, he was tutored at home in non-musical subjects several times a week, and appeared at school only to take year-end exams. He did not regret missing school, he said, and it is easy to imagine what torments might have befallen him there. He had few friends. Naturally isolated by his gifts and interests, he was further isolated by his introversion, his shyness, his seriousness – he had little of the frivolity of youth. Other boys poked fun at him. As with many male prodigies, "feminine" traits like sensitivity were more pronounced than "masculine" traits like physical bravado; to make matters worse, his mother made him wear long hair, and a 1918 article noted the "girlish purity" of his eyes. Then there was anti-Semitism: many Jewish boys in Budapest were tutored at home for that reason.

Even among other musicians and prodigies, Ervin was ill at ease, and his great talent bred jealousy in his rivals. He recalled that one of his colleagues at the academy, Jenő Blau, a violinist a few years older than he, would push him down the stairs in fits of jealousy and, despite reprimands, stopped doing so only after Ervin rounded on him one day and said, "Is this how you want to prove you are a good Jew?" Some twenty years later, Nyiregyházi met his former tormentor at a party in New York, and Blau "turned crimson" when Nyiregyházi innocently greeted him by that name. Blau, who had psychological issues with his Hungarian and Jewish roots, was by that time famous in America as a conductor, under a new name: Eugene Ormandy.

Ervin's father was "his chief support in life," Révész wrote. "We owe it to his memory to record the fact that he wished to secure for the boy a quiet and undisturbed period of training. He was far from desiring, as often happens in the case of the fathers of 'child prodigies,' to exploit his son's talent as a means of subsistence for the whole family, but, on the contrary, did everything in his power to assist him to become not only a fine, but a thoroughly well-trained artist." Moreover, Ignácz had "a deeper understanding of musical matters than is usually found in chorus singers. Erwin's mother also possessed considerable musical talent and appears to have been a better musician than the father; he, on the other hand, seems to have had a more intimate inner relation to music than his wife." Nyiregyházi cherished this distinction. His father, he said, wanted him to follow his own inclinations, play whatever music gave him satisfaction, and realize his potential as an artist. His recollections of his father were affectionate; it was his father, he said, who really understood him, and with whose musical tastes he empathized.

Mária's view of music was more practical, commercial, cynical. "My father strongly leaned towards the dramatic, intense, impassioned music of mostly notable operatic composers," Nyiregyházi recalled, "whereas my mother's musical taste was more for Beethoven, Mozart, also Bach, therefore music that was more in conformity with her goal and endeavour to develop me into a concert pianist and prepare me for a concert career." Mária saw in her son a Mozart whom she could exploit to elevate the family's financial and social status, and the inevitable conflict with Ervin's burgeoning idealism left him deeply embittered. Already as a five-year-old, he said, "My mother hated me. She said, 'This boy will never make any money. He likes Puccini.'" She tried to dissuade him from playing the operatic and orchestral music he loved, because "you can't make money on love." But Ervin already considered music a calling, a mission, a way of life, not a trade, even though he was ill suited in terms of a career to anything else.

His mother prevailed. She was the stronger parental personality; her needs and desires dominated the household. Ignácz was more reflective, more easygoing, though he also had a fondness for drama ("Nothing was too wild for my father"). Mária was bossy, censorious, argumentative, narcissistic, with some classically obsessive characteristics: she was precise and punctual, and expected perfection from those around her. "My father was a complete slave of my mother," Nyiregyházi said. It was she who directed the boy's musical education. After Ignácz went off to the opera house in the morning, she hovered as he practised. She made him play Bach, Czerny studies, dreary scales and other exercises, and she selected his repertoire. Ignácz encouraged his composing; Mária merely tolerated it. While Ignácz sat with him at the piano, telling him stories while he improvised, Mária hectored in the background, lamenting this waste of time. (Ervin's teachers tended, mostly, to reinforce his mother's views.) With Mária intent on moulding a professional pianist, a joy was becoming a chore; playing the piano was becoming Ervin's job – and he resented it. By undermining his independence of mind and sense of self-direction (both typical of prodigies), Mária inadvertently taught him a lesson that would have grave consequences for him in later life: his *real* musical and spiritual views would have to be guarded jealously, and kept private, for they were not compatible with a musical career. At home, he had to fight and connive to make time for the kind of music-making he preferred. When he was no more than five or six years old, he would go into a dark room and stick out his tongue at his mother and his teachers. "I hated them," he said.

In public Mária promoted her son as a prodigy, but in private she was endlessly critical of him. She scoffed at teachers who coddled him. What he called Weiner's "loving nature" irritated her, as Siklós's indulgence had, for she believed that her boy needed stern discipline and feared that praise would swell his head. She would say that Weiner could not be much of a teacher if he could find nothing to criticize in him, and that critics who praised his playing obviously knew nothing about music. She claimed she did this for his own good, but there is little doubt that she was jealous of her son, and sought to knock him off his pedestal. She was probably living vicariously, realizing her own thwarted artistic ambitions, through Ervin, and so resenting him, too. In any event, he was obviously the key to fame and fortune for his family, so his mother made sure to maintain a tight grip on that commodity.

Ervin, alas, did not have a personality that was motivated by resistance to conflict; he needed gentle encouragement and respect. His mother's criticism did not inspire him; it wounded him – and changed him. As a very young boy, he was spontaneous and uninhibited in expressing affection, even with strangers. He told Révész, "I do not like to compose sad things, for I do not like sadness, I only love the joy of living," at which he stretched out his arms "as if he wanted to embrace the whole beauty of nature." Révész continued, "Erwin was a child in the full sense of the word; a clever, gay, friendly, charming boy. After overcoming the first shyness, which he always cast off quickly, he became friendly, confident and amiable; and he charmed every one with whom he spent any length of time. . . . He played as children play, was fond of boyish exploits, and enjoyed them very much."

This side of his personality deteriorated, thanks to his mother. "My father praised me; my mother criticized. My father liked me to be outgoing; my mother wanted me to be reserved and proper." By the time he was ten, he said, much of the child had been crushed out of him, and by the time he was a teenager he had become an introverted, painfully shy, neurotic, and deeply melancholy boy, quick to hurt, somewhat paranoid, now prone to stage fright; moreover, he carried deep-seated anger, resentment, and bitterness that sometimes exploded in episodes of defiance, and he would mine this lode of rage for the rest of his life. (As we will see, there is no "joy of living" in his later compositions.) He came to believe that if his mother loved him at all, it was for what he could accomplish, not who he was. He stopped expecting nurture, however much he desired it, and in adulthood, as a result, he was fatally insecure. Having never felt a mother's unadulterated, unconditional love, he was incapable of complete trust, and tended to sabotage even his closest relationships.

Though Mária was the dominant parent, Ignácz was not without fault. "My father told me wonderful stories," Nyiregyházi said, "but he beat me because I was so dumb with my hands." Ervin seemed incapable of doing anything except play the piano; he struggled to button his shirt or trousers or tie his shoelaces or put a stamp on a letter or open an envelope without tearing it with his teeth.[*] And so his father would spank or slap him for his stupidity and helplessness. Ignácz had a streak of anger that erupted from time to time.

---

[*] Nyiregyházi remained physically clumsy as an adult. His occasional efforts to cook, for instance, foundered on his inability to break an egg or peel a potato. He struggled with sugar packets, pats of butter, medicine bottles; even opening a door could prove troublesome, and he never drove a car in his life. He found bathing, shaving, and dressing difficult; one morning in 1980, his wife noted that it had taken him forty-five minutes to button his shirt. He was deeply embarrassed by this clumsiness, and tried to hide it even from those closest to him, though it is common enough among the musically gifted. Away from the piano, even Mozart was clumsy.

Ervin saw his father curse his grandmother, Szidónia, as "an uneducated shit-hole" and throw her cooking to the floor, and when he was eight or nine he saw a "nightmare" that "I wish I could obliterate from my memory": his father beating Szidónia. In a moment of candour, he allowed that his father, while better than his mother, was still not "good enough."

Nyiregyházi always tended to see things in black and white – beginning with the splitting of his parents into good and evil. Given that he exaggerated his father's benevolence and forgave him his faults, his demonizing of his mother may have been excessive. He lived in a home conducive to musical growth, and had he been one of those prodigies passionately committed to a career in music he might have found his mother a less oppressive taskmistress. Judging from his own recollections, her overseeing of his artistic development was not nearly as tyrannical as that of some stage parents – one does not have to read far in the literature on gifted children to see that. He said that his mother never beat him, only sometimes pinched his buttocks, and that she took his side when his father hit him. But such was his sensitivity that his mother's faults sufficed to prove devastating. Perceiving himself to be emotionally deprived, struggling with the conflicting emotions of youth, he seems, self-defensively, to have projected all of the blame for his anxieties onto his mother, making her the enemy of everything he held dear. She died in the Holocaust, and he was once (while drunk) heard to say that Hitler was a great man because Hitler had killed his mother.

His relationship with his mother had an enormous impact on his personality. In him, the grandiosity and narcissism typical of adolescence were greatly magnified; they were a kind of armour against anxiety but did not protect him from a crippling fear of criticism and a dread of the expectations of others, as though he had internalized his mother's carping, and he was terrified at the prospect of abandonment by those he loved. The powerful pride that made him insist on his artistic and intellectual superiority wrestled with his profound insecurity.

some of the praise he received as a child was merely polite
's greatest musicians *really* think his compositions ranked
en and Brahms, as they sometimes said? – but he always
ly, and to the end of his life he had an insatiable thirst
ycophantic flattery; he thought it his due, for such was
eassured of his worth. He learned to respond passively,
nflicts, preferring to withdraw or flee from rather than
"Whatever obstacles were put in my way, I just gave
ving chafed under his mother's domination, he came
ly on personal freedom. He was quick to perceive –
y check on his liberty, and so inevitably ran into
anagers, friends, lovers. He invariably bit the hands
en when receiving the well-intentioned love and pro-
craved, he resented being in debt, which he equated
er someone else's control, and so would assert his in-
ith often disastrous results. Determined never to be
ther had ruled him, he sabotaged his personal life and
d again.*

nts provided a culturally and intellectually stimulating
or him but at a terrible cost. His psychological developed; in some fundamental ways, he never grew up. He
dlike innocence, took most things deadly seriously,
le control over what was often a flood of powerful and
ons. Indeed, the bizarre trajectory of his story was an

---

c criteria for Borderline Personality Disorder listed in the fourth
Psychiatric Association's *Diagnostic and Statistical Manual of*
ast seven can confidently be assigned to Nyiregyházi: fear of
ut unstable personal relationships marked by extremes of love
aviour of self-damaging types (drinking, sex); instability of
of emptiness; inappropriate or uncontrollable anger; and
issociation. For the *DSM* IV, meeting five of the nine criteria

almost predictable consequence of his enduring the ps
burdens of childhood as an adult.

Once the four-year-old prodigy had been exposed t
world, his parents began eagerly to parade him abou
Mozart, and word of his talent spread quickly. He gave
concert at the age of six, in October 1909, in Fiume (toda
Croatian coast).[*] That same year, some of his music w
the first time, when Franz Bárd & Bruder, of Budap
Leipzig, brought out three pieces under a collecti
Compositions d'Ervin Nyiregyházi: Berceuse, Chatter
Wedding March, Opp. 1–3. The music is naive, to be su
sionally awkward – the march is particularly poker-fac
devoid of imagination. (Op. 2 was inspired by Ervin's fat
that there were too many women in his house.) All th
composed in January 1909, the month Ervin turned six
or not they pointed to an uncanny musical talent.

In those first years of his career, Ervin played regular
musical elite and for visitors who included some of th
celebrated musicians. All were quick to proclaim his g
summer holidays, he was put on display: thus he met tl
composer Karl Goldmark, played orchestral music f
Zoltán Kodály, and disputed confidently about the in
Beethoven sonata with the pianist Eugen d'Albert. H
visitor to the music shop of the publisher Rózsavölg

---

[*] Nyiregyházi's memory was not consistent as to the progran
works he cited, in different interviews, include one of the eas
Haydn; Beethoven's Sonata in G Major, Op. 49/No. 1, and tl
Sonata in A Major, Op. 2/No. 2; short works by Mendelssohn,
Lyric Pieces by Grieg; and his own *Funeral March* for cello an
another Thomán pupil).

Presumably
– did Europe
with Beethov
took it seriou
for the most s
his need to be r
helplessly to co
confront them.
up," he said.) Ha
to insist stubborr
and resent – ar
problems with n
that fed him. Ev
fessional help he
with being un
dependence, w
ruled, as his m
career again an
Ervin's pare
environment f
ment was stun
retained a chil
and had very lit
conflicting emot

---

* Of the nine diagnosti
edition of the American
Mental Disorders, at le
abandonment; intense b
and hate; impulsive beha
mood; chronic feelings
episodes of paranoia or
suffices for a diagnosis.

ychological

o the musical
t like a young
 his first public
y Rijeka, on the
vas published for
best, Vienna, and
ve French title,
 of Women, and
re, dull and occa-
ed – but it is not
her's complaint
ree pieces were
, and simplistic

ly for the local
e world's most
enius. Even on
he octogenarian
our hands with
erpretation of a
e was a frequent
yi, where he would

n on this occasion. The

almost predictable consequence of his enduring the psychological burdens of childhood as an adult.

Once the four-year-old prodigy had been exposed to the musical world, his parents began eagerly to parade him about like a young Mozart, and word of his talent spread quickly. He gave his first public concert at the age of six, in October 1909, in Fiume (today Rijeka, on the Croatian coast).* That same year, some of his music was published for the first time, when Franz Bárd & Bruder, of Budapest, Vienna, and Leipzig, brought out three pieces under a collective French title, *Compositions d'Ervin Nyiregyházi: Berceuse, Chatter of Women*, and *Wedding March*, Opp. 1–3. The music is naive, to be sure, dull and occasionally awkward – the march is particularly poker-faced – but it is not devoid of imagination. (Op. 2 was inspired by Ervin's father's complaint that there were too many women in his house.) All three pieces were composed in January 1909, the month Ervin turned six, and simplistic or not they pointed to an uncanny musical talent.

In those first years of his career, Ervin played regularly for the local musical elite and for visitors who included some of the world's most celebrated musicians. All were quick to proclaim his genius. Even on summer holidays, he was put on display: thus he met the octogenarian composer Karl Goldmark, played orchestral music four hands with Zoltán Kodály, and disputed confidently about the interpretation of a Beethoven sonata with the pianist Eugen d'Albert. He was a frequent visitor to the music shop of the publisher Rózsavölgyi, where he would

---

* Nyiregyházi's memory was not consistent as to the program on this occasion. The works he cited, in different interviews, include one of the easier C-major sonatas by Haydn; Beethoven's Sonata in G Major, Op. 49/No. 1, and the first movement of the Sonata in A Major, Op. 2/No. 2; short works by Mendelssohn, Chopin, and Schumann; *Lyric Pieces* by Grieg; and his own *Funeral March* for cello and piano (performed with another Thomán pupil).

Presumably some of the praise he received as a child was merely polite – did Europe's greatest musicians *really* think his compositions ranked with Beethoven and Brahms, as they sometimes said? – but he always took it seriously, and to the end of his life he had an insatiable thirst for the most sycophantic flattery; he thought it his due, for such was his need to be reassured of his worth. He learned to respond passively, helplessly to conflicts, preferring to withdraw or flee from rather than confront them. ("Whatever obstacles were put in my way, I just gave up," he said.) Having chafed under his mother's domination, he came to insist stubbornly on personal freedom. He was quick to perceive – and resent – any check on his liberty, and so inevitably ran into problems with managers, friends, lovers. He invariably bit the hands that fed him. Even when receiving the well-intentioned love and professional help he craved, he resented being in debt, which he equated with being under someone else's control, and so would assert his independence, with often disastrous results. Determined never to be ruled, as his mother had ruled him, he sabotaged his personal life and career again and again.*

Ervin's parents provided a culturally and intellectually stimulating environment for him but at a terrible cost. His psychological development was stunted; in some fundamental ways, he never grew up. He retained a childlike innocence, took most things deadly seriously, and had very little control over what was often a flood of powerful and conflicting emotions. Indeed, the bizarre trajectory of his story was an

---

* Of the nine diagnostic criteria for Borderline Personality Disorder listed in the fourth edition of the American Psychiatric Association's *Diagnostic and Statistical Manual of Mental Disorders*, at least seven can confidently be assigned to Nyiregyházi: fear of abandonment; intense but unstable personal relationships marked by extremes of love and hate; impulsive behaviour of self-damaging types (drinking, sex); instability of mood; chronic feelings of emptiness; inappropriate or uncontrollable anger; and episodes of paranoia or dissociation. For the *DSM* iv, meeting five of the nine criteria suffices for a diagnosis.

receive free and discounted scores, and a local piano maker sent him an instrument as a gift when he was perhaps no older than five. For Franz Lehár, who was in town to conduct his latest operetta, he played requests, some of his own pieces, and music from the new operetta, which he had heard his father's company rehearsing. An astonished Lehár declared the boy a genius, and Ervin jumped on his neck and kissed him. He met Puccini, too, and, after playing the master's requests, offered his own arrangements of excerpts from various Puccini operas, several of which he claimed to know in their entirety, by heart. The audience lasted more than an hour, and after hearing the boy's rendering of music from *Madama Butterfly*, Puccini, in broken German, praised him, noting, "You played it in the *vagabondo* style." "*Ja*," Ervin replied – he had no idea what Puccini meant.[*]

He quickly became a fixture of Budapest society. Between ages four and ten, he performed frequently in private homes, often attracting the attention of newspapers. He played for magnates and other members of the landowning aristocracy and gentry, for some of the country's wealthiest businessmen, for some of the great statesmen of the day, and counted the most venerable and powerful Hungarian families among his fans: Andrássy, Apponyi, Batthyány, Kánitz, Károlyi, Kohner, Lánczy, Tisza, Zichy. He played for officials at every level of government, for the wealthiest and most influential rabbis, for members of the professional class and the intelligentsia (doctors and dentists, for instance, treated him for free in exchange for private recitals). For a time, he and his father paid regular visits to Ignácz Goldziher, a professor at the university who was a pioneer of modern Arabic studies and Islamology (and himself a former child prodigy), as well as his son Károly, a professor of mathematics. The Goldzihers

---

[*] Nyiregyházi remembered meeting Puccini in 1909, when he was six, and Lehár a little later; however, according to all available information about these composers' whereabouts, it seems more likely that the meeting with Lehár took place in 1910, that with Puccini in 1912.

would give Ervin money and little gifts – a map of Africa, a photo of Liszt, a leaf from Chopin's grave – and the elder man may have served as a mentor: in 1984, Nyiregyházi composed a work titled *In Memoriam Dr. Ignaz Goldziher (Wise Counsel)*. Around 1912, Ervin met the legendary general Artúr Görgey, then in his early nineties and one of the last survivors of the Hungarian Revolution of 1848–49. Ervin's father had written to the general of his son's interest in the revolution – he had been captivated by a picturebook on the subject – and Görgey had invited the boy to play for him. On the spur of the moment, Ervin improvised on a popular recruiting song from the revolution, "Kossuth Lajos azt izente" [Lajos Kossuth sent this message]. The old man sobbed, and Ervin embraced and kissed him, saying "Don't cry, Uncle Artúr." Doors were opened for him outside Hungary, too. From as early as age six or seven, he performed for the musical and social elite in Vienna.

His triumphs crossed religious and social boundaries, though the closest relationships he formed were with other Jews, who were conspicuous among the professionals and businessmen he encountered. Through Goldziher, he met the wealthy banker Géza Kovács and his wife, Jozsa, who introduced him to other high-profile Hungarian Jews, including, around 1912, the industrialist and munitions manufacturer Manfréd Weisz, one of the richest men in Europe and an ennobled member of a well-connected, politically influential family. Ervin called Kovács and Weisz "Uncle," and was in the habit of kissing them familiarly on the neck. He visited and entertained both families regularly, but developed an especially close, almost filial bond with the Kovácses.

Ervin's parents now had access to the highest social circles. "I was like a calling card," he said. And there was more than glory at stake: his parents usually came away from his private recitals with money, and several of their new friends, particularly Kovács and Weisz, became regular sources of financial support. The money was always earmarked for Ervin's musical education, yet he recalled that not one of his teachers ever charged him a fee. The money went instead to elevating the social status of his family. Budapest was a class-conscious city, and

Mária, painfully aware of the family's relatively lowly position, was an ardent social climber. (Nyiregyházi remembered her begging Révész not to write that her husband merely sang in the Royal Opera's chorus.) In any event, she determined to live conspicuously above her station. Her hiring of private tutors and (after Ervin's brother, Alfred, was born) a wet nurse and maid was in part a declaration of status: in those days, a live-in servant was rare in the district in which the Nyiregyházis lived. Mária stood about five-foot-three, was a little plump, and had darkish-blond hair – pretty, Nyiregyházi recalled, though not beautiful or sexy. Perhaps she was self-conscious about her appearance, for she developed a passion for expensive jewellery, and obtaining it for her became something of an obsession for her husband.* She would invite people over to the apartment on some pretext whenever she had new jewels to show off, and she enjoyed wearing them in front of women who knew her husband's salary and wondered enviously how he could afford them. Such nouveau riche behaviour embarrassed Ervin and attracted comment. When Ignácz installed his own telephone, fellow-choristers dubbed him "the millionaire."

The extended holidays the Nyiregyházis enjoyed every summer had a social-climbing component, too. They invariably chose distant mountain and seaside spots popular with middle- and upper-class Hungarians – the farther away a holiday, the higher its status. Ervin's health, apparently somewhat fragile, was one pretext for holidays. "I had weak lungs,"

---

* A caricature of Ignácz in the archives of the Budapest Opera shows him hawking a trayful of watches, suggesting that he perhaps traded in jewellery on the side. The rhyming caption reads: "Throughout the wide world you won't find another like/Ignácz Nyiregyházi: our 'Náczi kid.'/He is an honours graduate of Hochme University,/Peddling jewellery, rings and playing at *vigécz*." The Yiddish word *hochme* means "wisdom," but can also connote cleverness, wiliness, and trickery (compare the English phrase *wise guy*). The Hungarian word *vigécz* is a corruption of the German phrase *Wie geht's?* [How's it going?]. The implication here seems to be that Ignácz had an ingratiating but not entirely sincere, salesmanlike charm, and may have had a reputation as a sharper.

he said, and among his childhood recollections were bouts of pneumonia, rectal sores, and some possible congenital weakness in his legs; he also experienced anemia around ages three through five – one reason he was fed well and, for a time, given cod-liver oil. Neither his doctors nor his parents could agree whether mountain or sea air best served his needs, so the family's holidays often included both. For mountain air, they retreated to Lake Balaton, about eighty kilometres southwest of Budapest, or to Spital am Semmering, a small town about eighty kilometres southwest of Vienna. For sea air, they headed to the Adriatic coast, to such towns as Crikvenica, Fiume, Trieste, and Abbazia (now Opatija, in Croatia). Ervin's parents used his health to solicit money from his wealthy admirers for these holidays, and sometimes swapped his talents for free room and board once they had arrived at a destination.

Mária's desire for money and status was the strongest force behind Ervin's career as a performing prodigy, but Ignácz was complicit. It was usually he alone who chaperoned the boy, and he was not shy about collecting money. And perhaps he, too, a singer who never got out of the chorus, lived vicariously through his son. Moreover, he enjoyed sexual affairs with some of his son's patronesses. Nyiregyházi recalled that when he was around six or seven, the young widow of a wealthy banker named Vasadi, a large woman with a "big derrière," was sweet on his father. They would go to Mrs. Vasadi's several afternoons a week, and he remembered seeing the couple disappear into a room together, while a maid kept him busy with, say, hot chocolate; later, his father would re-emerge looking "weak," and sometimes Mrs. Vasadi would then give him money. They stopped going to Mrs. Vasadi's late in 1910, and when he asked his parents why, each told him to ask the other. At some point, Ignácz began having an affair with Jozsa Kovács. Once, the two emerged from a room within a few minutes of each other, both looking flushed, and offered Ervin the same explanation: "I just slept a little." (Some twenty years later, Jozsa told Nyiregyházi, "Your mother never satisfied your father," and Nyiregyházi once claimed that in order to get sex from his mother his father had to bring her jewels.) Ignácz seems to have been often unfaithful, sometimes with women he met at the Royal Opera. He was tall (about six feet) and thin, balding but handsome, with a large, neatly trimmed moustache, and something of a dandy in his dress – a magnet to women.

Ervin did not fully understand his parents' behaviour, but knew enough to become cynical at their hypocrisy. By the time he was six or seven, he said, his father's infidelity and his mother's social climbing and the disparities he saw between the classes made him aware "that the architecture of social life is based on spurious, phony values." The attention he received flattered his ego but bred insecurity, making him wonder if he was appreciated only as a sort of performing pet. After his family left town in 1914, he heard that the Kovácses, who were childless, entertained other prodigies, and so he wondered, Was I merely a surrogate child to be replaced as required? And, of course, he always felt like a means to an end for his parents. His mother, he said, seemed to value her jewels more than she did him, and he could not help but notice how women would swarm around his father whenever he played. ("They should have paid attention to *me*.") His success brought him pleasure but also anxiety and a feeling of isolation, and it did not help that his parents, far from easing the burdens of his talent, were the main source of the pressure he felt.

Around early 1911, three counts of the family's acquaintance – Andrássy, Apponyi, and Károly – signed a letter to Count Albert Mensdorff-Pouilly-Dietrichstein, the Austro-Hungarian ambassador in London, recommending that Ervin be permitted to appear before the nobility in England. A trip was duly arranged, and, in preparation for it, Mária began more sternly enforcing her pianistic regimen. Ervin and his parents arrived in London around May 20, and over the next two weeks, he made at least half a dozen high-profile private appearances before British aristocrats. (It was the height of the social season. George v was to be crowned on June 22.) Only Ervin and his father attended these functions, for Mária's overbearing personality had a stultifying effect on Ervin, and Ignácz thought it likely that she would embarrass the family. "No one liked having her around," Nyiregyházi recalled. She did not play cards or other games, was not charming or ingratiating in social situations, as Ignácz was, and so agreed not to risk jeopardizing the boy's success.

Ervin made his first appearance at the Austro-Hungarian embassy, and Count Mensdorff was so impressed that he wanted the boy to play before the czar of Russia (that plan did not materialize). Later, Ervin played in the homes of Lady Léonie Leslie, the Duchess of Rutland, one of the Rothschilds, and Prince Arthur, the Duke of Connaught and Strathearn (one of Queen Victoria's sons). He played in the home of the prime minister, H.H. Asquith, too, including duets with Asquith's son, Anthony (who grew up to be a well-known film director); later he joined Anthony to watch a pre-coronation military parade. He met foreign dignitaries as well, including Arthur Nikisch, conductor of the Berlin Philharmonic and the Gewandhaus Orchestra in Leipzig. He played his symphonic poem *The Sea* for Nikisch, who was fulsome in his praise. Less happy was a visit to the *Times's* music critic. He tested Ervin by putting the just-published score of Strauss's *Der Rosenkavalier* before him, and though Nyiregyházi remembered acquitting himself well, the critic decided that his gifts had been exaggerated – a harsh judgment of an eight-year-old sight-reading the most treacherous new operatic music of the day.

Ervin's London sojourn culminated on the afternoon of June 2 in a command performance at Buckingham Palace, before a small audience that included Queen Mary, the Prince of Wales (the future King Edward VIII and Duke of Windsor, then just shy of seventeen), Princess Mary, and Prince John. The *Daily Mail*, in a report published the next day under the headline "MUSICAL WONDER CHILD," described "a frail-looking, pale child, who scarcely looks his eight years" and noted that the royals "took the greatest interest in the performance, and invited the boy to play several additional pieces, after hearing a fugue of Bach,

Ervin with his father (right) and local manager outside Buckingham Palace, just before his command performance there, June 2, 1911, in a photograph that appeared in a London news-paper. *(*Musical America *Archives.)*

Rachmaninoff's well-known prelude [in C-sharp minor], Mozart's [song] 'The Violet,' and Chopin's E minor valse." Nyiregyházi recalled playing Beethoven's variations on *God Save the King* and his own *The Snake Charmer*. The Queen, with whom he chatted in German, pronounced the performance "very beautiful," and the Prince of Wales, who "applauded wildly" after *The Snake Charmer*, noted in his diary that Ervin "played remarkably well. Lady May [one of the Queen's ladies in waiting] whistled an English tune which he had never heard before, & then he composed a theme on it" (that is, improvised on it). The *Daily Mail*'s music critic tested the boy, pronouncing him a "little genius" of "astonishing gifts." Ervin "showed the greatest delight at the high honour conferred upon him," and his success was reported in Budapest.

The Nyiregyházis left London about a week later, Ervin having scored an extraordinary musical and social success – and enriched his family. To the *Daily Mail*, Ignácz had claimed "that he had not the means to educate his son, and that was his reason for coming to England," and that Ervin, who was always thin, was undernourished. These fibs had the desired effect: sympathetic patrons contributed money. Prince Arthur, though he would sail that fall for Canada to be sworn in as the country's Governor General, remained a supporter for several years. Mária had coached her son to get gifts of jewellery by kissing ladies and complimenting their jewels, and he did indeed get a lot of jewellery this way, even when he confessed innocently that he had been put up to it. The money was put immediately to use. The family took its summer holiday on the Adriatic, and not long after moved into a more modern apartment in a better part of Budapest, farther southeast, at 22 Népszínház Street, in the Joseph (Eighth) District. Ervin now had a grand piano, a gift from the Viennese maker Ludwig Bösendorfer, for whom he had recently played.

Not long before his eleventh birthday, he played the first movement of the Tchaikovsky concerto with an orchestra of young musicians at a local music school and, in the same concert, made his debut as a conductor, in a movement from a Tchaikovsky symphony. The principal of the school told Ervin's parents, "Your son will become one of the greatest conductors. He conducts even better than he plays," though he apparently never conducted again. He would have liked to conduct, he said, but his musical ideas required an orchestra of supermen all in sympathy with his tastes, and he was frightened at the possibility of facing opposition from a hundred musicians with their own ideas. The piano had its limitations, but it did not fight back.

The prodigy was becoming seduced by the trappings of wealth. At lavish homes like those of Kovács and Weisz, he found himself in luxuriously appointed rooms, served caviar and lobster beautifully laid out by white-gloved servants. (A childlike wonder at such opulence was still evident in interviews he gave as an old man.) His hosts loved to reward him with rich treats, and he developed a taste for strawberries with whipped cream, cakes, chocolate, nuts. He was spoiled on holidays, too. Some summers at Spital am Semmering, the Kovácses would pick him up in their carriage and take him for visits to their more fashionable resort nearby. Everywhere he encountered sophisticated, refined people who treated him with respect and took him seriously, and their acceptance reinforced his elevated image of himself. Having always been the centre of his family's life was enough to give him the sense of entitlement that comes naturally to many prodigies, but now, deeply impressed by his experiences of high society, he came to identify with those who doted on him, to think of *himself* as an aristocrat – or, at least, as deserving by virtue of his gifts to be treated like one.

He found life at home increasingly frustrating. He envied the modern plumbing in the Kovács home. Only in the new apartment on Népszínház Street did the Nyiregyházis have their own bathtub (though patronizing public baths was common even for Budapest's middle-class citizens), and Ervin developed a profound shyness and squeamishness on the subject of bathrooms, especially toilets. Throughout his life, in fact, he was obsessively concerned about privacy in the bathroom, always demanding a private bath and toilet in apartments and hotels – for him this was a matter of status but also of personal dignity. He remembered an incident that occurred when he was about seven, while he was walking down Andrássy Avenue, the widest boulevard in Budapest, with his mother, grandmother, and great-grandmother. They had just been to a coffeehouse, and Grandma Lenke, then in her early eighties, paused in the street and urinated beneath her dress. A police officer was called, and the incident was even mentioned in a local newspaper, with Ervin, the well-known local prodigy, mentioned by name. He was deeply humiliated.

"I outgrew my family," he said. "I was the only cultured person in my family." There was not much elevated discourse in the Nyiregyházi home, and mealtimes were hardly elegant. Ervin was embarrassed by what he considered his family's coarse, boorish manners and their loud, petty squabbling (often about money). At home, he said, the food was plain, and the family "shoved" food around at table, dipping into common bowls. Butter was rationed like an expensive luxury. When he was about eight, Grandma Lenke indulged him by buying him a butter knife, prompting a tense exchange –

> IGNÁCZ: Are you a millionaire?
> ERVIN: No, but I want to live like one.
> IGNÁCZ: That [butter knife]'s reserved for guests. We'll use it for Count Tisza if he comes. Do you think you are as good as Count Tisza?
> ERVIN: Yes.

– at which point he received a slap.*

---

* Nyiregyházi never lost this sense of entitlement. In 1978, he told a television interviewer that he needed a woman "who gives me butter in the *real way*, the way they serve it to President Carter: with a *butter knife*. I want a butter knife – *that is imperative*. A woman who doesn't give me a butter knife – we get a divorce [the] next day. . . . No matter how poor I am, I am an aristocrat."

His parents were not so quick to rein in their own pretensions, however, and Ervin resented that they openly, even duplicitously, reaped the rewards of his celebrity. "Wherever I went, I was treated better than at home," he said, and he would occasionally complain to teachers or family friends about his parents' behaviour, enraging his mother. She would accuse him of lacking respect for his family – which, to a degree, was true. Géza Kovács "treated me with more nobility than my own father did."

"By the time I was five," Nyiregyházi said, "I realized I was in a world of strangers." Even with his beloved father he felt that he could not be wholly, truly himself. For all his public success, he experienced the early years of his celebrity as a "heartache," as "an absolute nightmare," for his high-society admirers bred desires that his family frustrated. He determined to follow genteel ways and an intellectual life and to show contempt for his family's manners; as he grew older, this determination intensified, as did his bitterness toward his family. Though he would know professional failure and dire poverty as an adult, he never stopped thinking of himself as someone whose talent, intellect, and ideals made him the equal of those Brahmins into whose windows he had been privileged to gaze as a child.

4

To Berlin – and Liszt – and Back

On the morning of January 8, 1914, Ervin was at home studying when his father suddenly began trembling, grew increasingly ill, and called for a doctor. Mária was out, so Szidónia and Grandma Lenke hastily dispatched the boy to the Kovács home, where he overheard frantic whispering. He never saw his father again.[*] On January 12, at the age of thirty-eight, Ignácz Nyiregyházi died of pneumonia. The news was kept from Ervin. His mother told him his father was in a sanatorium; only in June, on holiday at Spital am Semmering, did she tell him that his father was dead. Devastated, he could not stop crying; a doctor had to be called to administer a sedative. The impact on the eleven-year-old was catastrophic. With his father (whom he had adored despite his flaws) now dead, there was no longer a counterweight to his mother, who had become his implacable enemy. Ignácz's death surely contributed to the abandonment issues Nyiregyházi would struggle with all his life, and to his tendency to idealize his father at the expense

---

[*] Nyiregyházi remembered that his father's last words to him were a plea to "forgive me for hitting you."

of his mother. Her delay in revealing the death only magnified the bitterness he felt toward her.

He was now almost a teenager, yet she still controlled him. She infantilized him, too, at home and in public, determined to preserve the appearance of youth essential to his status as a prodigy. Well into his teens, she forced him to wear short pants and long hair, despite the taunts of other boys, who would pull his hair and compare him to a girl. Yet he was also, he recalled, "a very strong-willed little boy." With age, as his artistic ego strengthened and his public success grew, he became more defiant. But he had little real power. He was utterly dependent on his mother, and had to acquiesce to her, though he sought opportunities for petty rebellion. She wanted him to impress people by telling them that he enjoyed reading Goethe and Shakespeare and such – and he *did* revere the classics – yet because his mother had asked him to do it he refused, and took to citing Sir Arthur Conan Doyle as his favourite author. She thundered, "Now we'll lose money!"

In November 1913, two months before Ignácz's death, the Nyiregyházis had taken an exploratory trip to Berlin, arranged through well-connected acquaintances at home, to introduce their prodigy to the musical capital of central Europe and find him a new piano teacher. There Ervin gave a series of private recitals, one at the Austro-Hungarian embassy, another for an elderly woman who had been a pupil of Clara Schumann, another for the head of the piano department at the local academy of music. At tea in the home of a society woman, he gave a recital that included an étude by Serge Bortkiewicz, and, unbeknownst to him, the composer happened to be present. Bortkiewicz praised the performance, even the changes Ervin had presumed to make to the score. A few days later, at the composer's house, Ervin sight-read Bortkiewicz's just-published Piano Concerto No. 2, and the amazed composer dubbed him "the second Franz Liszt." Ervin gave a concert in the salon of a prominent music patron, too, before an admiring audience that included the composer Engelbert Humperdinck, the conductors Arthur Nikisch, Max Fiedler, and Siegfried Ochs, and no less a personage than Richard Strauss. According to the *Berliner Börsen-Courier*, Liszt had been resurrected in a ten-year-old boy.

Ervin did not want for pianists keen to teach him. His parents settled finally on a fellow-Hungarian, Ernő Dohnányi, who, greatly impressed, offered to teach him for free.

Shortly after Ignácz's death, Mária, Ervin, Alfred, and Szidónia moved to Berlin. (Grandma Lenke stayed behind and died not long after. Vilmos Nyiregyházi, Ervin's beloved grandfather, who had retired from the opera in 1911, also remained in Budapest; he died in 1919.) The family had financial support – from Manfréd Weisz and, at least until the outbreak of war in August 1914, from Prince Arthur. The family took an apartment at 20 Neue Winterfeldtstrasse, in the pleasant Schöneberg district, and Ervin began studying with Ernő Dohnányi.*

Born in Pozsony (now Bratislava) in 1877, and himself a prodigy of amazing natural gifts, Dohnányi was a musician of great versatility – pianist, composer, conductor, teacher, administrator – and a seminal figure in Hungary's musical life. He taught a whole generation of Hungarian musicians and did much to raise the country's musical reputation. A pupil of István Thomán, he made his professional debut in 1897 in Berlin, which became his home (and where he went by "Ernst von"). In 1905, he began teaching at the academy, and would accept only the most talented and interesting pupils (his star at the time Ervin

---

* The London *Daily Mail* reported on June 3, 1911, that "a scholarship at the Berlin Conservatoire had been secured through the instrumentality of Herr Nikisch," though no other evidence suggests that the family had considered moving to Berlin that early. In any event, Ervin was never enrolled at the academy in Berlin; he was a private pupil and had his lessons in Dohnányi's home.

arrived in town was Mischa Levitzki). Teaching, Dohnányi said, "means the exploitation of the possibilities that are lurking within a pupil, with the object of eventually allowing him to stand on his own two feet." He was, and wanted his pupils to be, "unfettered by any method," believing that "every student should be handled as an individual." Quiet, reserved, and gentlemanly, he liked to socialize with his pupils outside the classroom. "His pupils became attached to him as though they were his children," his third wife, Ilona, wrote, and most of them, including Ervin, became friends.

Dohnányi's impact on Ervin was more spiritual than pianistic. At eleven, Ervin was already a pianist of professional stature, and there was effectively nothing in the repertoire he could not play, though his technique and musicianship continued to develop through adolescence. Asked about scales and other technical exercises in a 1920 interview, he said, "I never do any, and never did. Dohnányi never spoke of such things and never required any." Dohnányi must have felt that Ervin was already beyond them. ("Nyiregyházi?" he once said, "He could do anything at the keyboard.") His focus was interpretation, and the direction he gave his pupils most often was *espressivo*, which sums up Nyiregyházi's approach to performance in a single word. With him, Dohnányi was content, from time to time, to forgo a lesson altogether and instead chat about, say, Verdi or Wagner, something Ervin was always pleased to do. There were some conflicts. Though Dohnányi had a vast repertoire, his tastes were more conservative than his pupil's. For instance, he wanted Ervin to play Bach's Chromatic Fantasy and Fugue from an unadulterated edition, while Ervin – no stickler for historical authenticity – preferred to "combine the Bülow and Busoni editions, with a little Nyiregyházi added for good measure." Still, Dohnányi's own playing in Classical and early-Romantic music made a big impact on his pupil; in Mozart and Schubert in particular, Nyiregyházi said, he was unrivalled. He admired Dohnányi the composer, too.

Ervin also studied theory in Berlin, with several important composer-conductors: Fiedler, Ochs, and Emil Nikolaus von Reznicek.

Fiedler was his principal instructor, in harmony, counterpoint, and form. Ervin was still composing prolifically, and Fiedler offered him some welcome encouragement – indeed, thought him a genius as a composer – and praised some of his works as worthy almost of Schumann, Mendelssohn, and Brahms. (Ervin, naturally, concurred.) The boy was tutored several mornings a week in non-musical subjects – German, French, literature, history, geography, mathematics – and was an eager student. He also studied fencing and played soccer and tennis, if not particularly well. (He played soccer with girls because he hated the roughness of boys' teams.) And he still sought out chess matches.

Berlin was itself a school, for he was exposed regularly to some of the greatest musicians of the day, including many pianists: d'Albert, Backhaus, Friedman, Godowsky, Lhévinne, Rosenthal, Schnabel. He considered Busoni the greatest of them all, and loved the monumentality and seriousness and "wonderful hardness" of his playing. He heard the most important conductors, too – Nikisch, Weingartner – in a wide range of new and standard repertoire. To hear Richard Strauss conduct Beethoven's Ninth or the première of his own *Alpine Symphony* or concertos with Busoni at the keyboard – these were heady experiences for a young musician.*

Ervin performed frequently in Berlin. He played at the French embassy, for the composer Max Reger, for Albert Einstein, in a concert with the great soprano Lilli Lehmann, and, wartime prejudices notwithstanding, in an all-Tchaikovsky program for General Hindenburg, who graciously allowed that music was universal. The pianist Moriz Rosenthal, a former Liszt pupil, pronounced the boy a genius and praised his compositions; he actually interrupted Ervin's performance to shout "Bravo!" at one particularly felicitous turn of phrase. Sigmund von Hausegger, whom Nyiregyházi considered the greatest conductor he

---

* He heard Nikisch conduct a performance of Mahler's *Das Lied von der Erde* that met with anti-Semitic hooting – not the only evidence he saw that his career in Berlin would be compromised if his Jewishness were not kept secret.

ever heard, also hailed the boy as both pianist and composer, and one of the local critics told Fiedler that he was "one of the greatest geniuses I have ever heard," wondering how a twelve-year-old could have such a profound understanding of music. Only one local musician, the pianist Emil von Sauer, seemed immune to Ervin's genius. Mária wanted her son to study with Sauer, who was another former Liszt pupil, but at his audition Ervin flubbed (defiantly?) the simple task of playing a scale with the left hand. Sauer refused to consider him, and Mária was crushed.

Ervin gave public concerts, too, including a high-profile orchestral debut on October 14, 1915, in Beethoven's Piano Concerto No. 3, with Fiedler conducting the Berlin Philharmonic. Critics marvelled at his technique and tone, his spirit and sensitivity. One of them pronounced the performance one of the most exceptional of that work he had ever heard; another compared him to the great Russian pianist Anton Rubinstein; another was enraptured by his unusually slow, poetic reading of the *Largo*. "To the musical world one should shout 'Pay attention' with all emphasis," Otto Leßmann wrote in the *Allgemeine Musik-Zeitung*. "This boy restores honour to the often abused, much discredited term 'Wunderkind,' as in him there is already a master who will someday cause a stir."

He became a minor celebrity in wartime Berlin, and was studied by at least two psychologists who confirmed Géza Révész's findings. Ervin was not the only prodigy in town, however. The Chilean pianist Claudio Arrau, also born in 1903, had arrived in Berlin in 1913 and gave his first recital there in December 1914. The press concocted a rivalry between the boys, though the only real feud was between their mothers.* He and Arrau met only once in Berlin, in a tony shoe store. They exchanged curt nods, and that was that.

---

* Nyiregyházi's parents, especially his mother, always reacted jealously toward rival prodigies. Once, when a young Russian pianist enjoyed some success in Budapest, Mária expressed the hope that he would contract diphtheria.

What Nyiregyházi considered the most momentous musical experience of his life occurred in Berlin: his discovery – or, more accurately, his first genuine appreciation – of the music of Franz Liszt. From that point on, Liszt's works and ideas formed the foundation upon which his aesthetic was built. As a young child, he knew Liszt's reputation as a great pianist, heard some of his music, and had a few of the more popular piano pieces in his repertoire. Ervin's father admired Liszt, as did some of his early teachers (Thomán, Siklós), and he attended the great festival held in Budapest in 1911 to honour Liszt's centennial. Still, before age twelve he was no great fan or champion. He did not "get" Liszt.

That is hardly surprising. Though Liszt was remembered as a pianist, his reputation as a composer was then poor in most countries, even his native Hungary. The controversy he courted throughout his life did not abate after his death, in 1886, nor the noisy partisanship of those who revered and those who disdained him. Liszt the composer strove always for what was new and original. His boldly experimental, eclectic, deeply personal, uncompromising music provoked extreme responses, and many considered him a charlatan. Much of the prejudice against him was not musical. There was widespread disgust at his heady love life, at the circus atmosphere of his early concert tours, at the (supposed) hypocrisy of his religious avocation. He was (falsely) accused of anti-Semitism, too; Ervin once saw Jewish professors at the academy walk out in protest when a student played Liszt.

The young Nyiregyházi encountered little acknowledgement of Liszt's greatness and originality as a composer, or of his fertilizing influence on later generations of musicians. Instead, he encountered violent rejection, even hatred, of Liszt – from Révész, Kovács, and Weisz, from most of the cultured aristocrats for whom he played, from teachers in both Budapest and Berlin. He took no position on the matter until May 1915, when a young Hungarian violinist in Berlin, Ferenc Vecsey, amazed at his colleague's ignorance of Liszt, convinced him to study the great Piano Sonata in B Minor. "It was the deepest, most profound experience I ever had," he said more than sixty years later. Discovering Liszt "was like discovering a new world." In the days that followed, he devoured whole volumes of Liszt, forgetting to eat or rest, often falling away from the piano "delirious and feverish." He sought out performances of Liszt's music and read Liszt's literary works. He was ripe for conversion. Already he disdained the sort of snobbery that insisted on the hegemony of the Austro-German canon of "absolute" music in venerable Classical forms, and long before discovering Liszt, his favourite composers included Schumann and Grieg, Puccini and Verdi. In a sense, discovering Liszt focused his already profoundly Romantic sensibility and made him more receptive, in his teens, to other then radical composers – Berlioz, Bruckner, Busoni, Debussy, Mahler, Scriabin, Strauss.

Dohnányi and Fiedler sought to temper his new obsession for his own good, though Dohnányi performed a good deal of Liszt himself, including some works that would have special meaning for Nyiregyházi, like the sonata and the *Légendes*. Dohnányi permitted Ervin to study major works like the E-flat-major concerto, the B-minor ballade, and the Hungarian Rhapsody No. 13, but "at that time Dohnányi was against Liszt" and derided his most adventurous music as formless. "Although he was a very kind, very generous man whose lessons were very inspiring, our relationship was strained because of Liszt," Nyiregyházi said. "I was not allowed to neglect my studies of Hummel, Dussek, Czerny, Beethoven, Bach – he made me learn the whole *Well-Tempered Clavier* so that I could transpose any part of it – and it was as if I was in prison – Alcatraz – because I wanted only Liszt."[*] He took to studying Liszt on the sly at the expense of assigned lessons, and, wherever possible, incorporated substantial piano pieces by Liszt into his concert programs, though privately he was just as content to play his own arrangements of the symphonic and choral works.

He challenged Liszt's detractors head-on, particularly those who thought the substance of Liszt's music vulgar, trite, exhibitionistic,

---

[*] In 1981, he composed a stormy piano piece with the pointed title *Individual Rebellion Against Scholastic Coercion (1915): Nyiregyházi Versus Dohnányi-Hummel*.

self-indulgent. Ervin heard "lyrical and dramatic intensity" in Liszt's music, an "emphasis on the grandiose and imperial." He admired its sophistication and naked emotionalism and heightened rhetoric; for him, Liszt was not bombastic but rather profound, noble, sublime, with a "bent toward the transcendental." Liszt's music does range from the frankly trashy to the religious, from the ostentatious to the austere, but for Nyiregyházi its range was part of its greatness – evidence of Liszt's depth of feeling and breadth of experience, of his individuality, of the fertility of his imagination. Liszt's music, he believed, contained more of *life* than anyone else's. It was ultimately the "spiritual content" and "idealism" of Liszt that Ervin came to admire. Defying conventional wisdom, he insisted that Liszt was a great ethical personality who "personified the rebellion against the superficial in music," and was moved by Liszt's elevated view of life and deep philosophical beliefs. His agnosticism even yielded to appreciation of Liszt's profound Catholic faith: "If Liszt believes in God, I believe it!"

The orchestral and choral music impressed him even more than most of the piano music: it was not Liszt the virtuoso that grabbed him, but the loftier Liszt who worked away from the piano and out of the public eye. (Of Liszt's oratorio *The Legend of Saint Elizabeth*, he once wrote, "That's not Music, that's the voice of God.") His Liszt repertoire was relatively short on the showpieces Liszt wrote for his own early concerts, and he favoured some esoteric late works that are still little known today. He never dismissed Liszt's music as prolix or formless; rather, he recognized that Liszt was inventing new forms to accommodate new and very personal thoughts, making the forms serve the content. Liszt defined music as "the embodied and intelligible essence of feeling," as "pure flames of emotion"; for Nyiregyházi, who always placed the highest value on the direct expression of "emotional ideas" in music, and valued intuition over reason, spontaneous expression over conventional forms, Liszt's music stood as an ideal. From Liszt, he learned that it was the prerogative of a creative genius to remake his art in his own image – a quintessentially Romantic premise that (as we will see) would have a profound impact on his performances and compositions.

The twelve-year-old quickly decided that there was no greater composer than Liszt and became a stubborn, vocal champion of this unfashionable cause. Max Fiedler, when the boy announced his conversion, told his mother, "Your son is finished in Berlin," and Mária foresaw doom at the box office. But Ervin was not deterred. Wherever he went, he asked people what they thought of Liszt, defended his new cause fearlessly, challenged the biases of much older musicians, and scorned "the *puny* detractors of Liszt" as well as those self-proclaimed Lisztians (including some of the former pupils) whose championship he considered thin. He tried to win converts, sometimes provocatively playing Liszt before unsympathetic listeners, including members of the conservative Mendelssohn family, and was pleased to find that some of the senior musicians he encountered – Reger, Schnabel – were not the Liszt haters they were reputed to be.

His discovery of the profundity of Liszt led him to appreciate the emotional, intellectual, and spiritual depth of other music that (like Liszt's) was widely considered second-rate. He began, for instance, to hear the seriousness of Grieg (whom many considered a mere dilettante), and where most heard sentimentality in Tchaikovsky, he now heard "the very depth of tragedy and heartrending sorrow." He developed a taste for serious, heavy, brooding music, and his piano style now became more Lisztian: he came to love deep sonorities and slow tempos, and began to plumb new depths of expression without concern for what good taste considered bombastic or sentimental. He claimed that Liszt was misunderstood and in poor repute because his music was usually badly played; revealing fully its emotional and spiritual content became one of his goals.

"Liszt knows no rules, no form, no dogma; he creates everything for himself," one of his contemporaries wrote, and Ervin saw in this personality the ultimate argument for freedom, individuality, and self-realization – in life as well as music. He saw Liszt as a hero figure –

proud, independent, self-sufficient, indifferent to acclaim and defiant in the face of criticism. He perhaps also saw a psychological surrogate for his lost father; the timing of his conversion is certainly suggestive. For a sensitive and embattled adolescent, it was a good model. Liszt, who believed that "to become noble is much more than to be born noble," provided crucial support for Ervin's aristocratic self-image. In gratitude, he forgave Liszt anything. Indeed, he came to believe that geniuses like Liszt – and himself – were due certain special privileges, stood above ordinary laws, because the fulfillment of their ambitions ultimately bettered civilization. Through Liszt, he came to see himself as one of Dostoevsky's "extraordinary" men, "people to whom everything is permitted."

Others assured him he would grow out of Liszt, but if anything he grew *into* Liszt. The more anxiety and hostility and failure he experienced in his life, the more he took refuge in Lisztian idealism and the Liszt aesthetic.

Ernő Dohnányi (left) and Frederic Lamond, Ervin's piano teachers in Berlin. *(Left: Photograph by Herman Mishkin.)*

In December 1915, Ernő Dohnányi returned to Budapest, and Ervin was placed with a new, no less prestigious teacher: Frederic Lamond. Lamond was born in Glasgow in 1868, and his mentors were some of the most committed and ardent Romantics: Hans von Bülow, Tchaikovsky, Anton Rubinstein, and Liszt, whose masterclasses he attended. He made Berlin his home in 1904, and was still at the height of a brilliant international concert and teaching career when Ervin joined his class. He was a cultivated musician, with a wide range of interests and sympathies (he had studied organ, violin, and oboe), and an accomplished composer. His repertoire ranged from Byrd and Bach to Scriabin and Fauré, and he managed to transcend the partisan bickering of late-nineteenth-century music: he saw no contradiction in admiring Liszt and Wagner and the other adherents of the "music of the future" while championing Bach and the "academic" Brahms and particularly Beethoven, of whose music he was considered the greatest exponent before Schnabel. (He even *looked* like Beethoven.) His piano style was free, dynamic, declamatory, rhythmically flexible, with a big tone and pervasive legato; there was great drama and power, great *sweep*, to his playing, and he valued bold gestures over the precise rendering of detail. Always, he held to a "poetical vision" of a piece, even when his style made him unfashionable in his later years (he died in 1948).

For his audition in March 1916, Ervin played Schumann's G-minor sonata, and an amazed Lamond declared (so Nyiregyházi claimed) that he had not heard such playing since Liszt. For his first lesson, Ervin solicited requests. Lamond asked for Beethoven's Opp. 101 and 111 sonatas, both from memory, and, as the thirteen-year-old played, Lamond chuckled from time to time in amazement. He, too, recognized that his new pupil had a finished technique and so focused on higher things; theirs became more a relationship of peers than of master and pupil, Nyiregyházi said. He studied Beethoven and Brahms but also Liszt with Lamond. Dohnányi *tolerated* Liszt, he said, but Lamond *loved* Liszt. Many of those Liszt works to which Lamond was particularly devoted become lifelong favourites of Nyiregyházi's: the concertos, the *Légendes*, "Mazeppa," the B-minor ballade, the *Sonetto 104 del Petrarca*, the Dante Sonata. (Lamond also introduced him to non-piano works like the Dante Symphony.) Ervin was already a pianist in the Lisztian mould. Lamond was astonished by his reading of the B-minor sonata, pointing out that his slow tempos in that piece were exactly those Liszt himself had advocated. A timing of between twenty-five and thirty minutes is typical for the Liszt sonata; relatively few pianists squeak over the thirty-minute mark. Nyiregyházi recalled that his own timing, even as a teenager, was usually about thirty-eight minutes, and sometimes topped *forty*. He apparently was always drawn to slow tempos; for him, intensity went hand in hand with breadth. As a twelve-year-old, he said, his timing for Beethoven's "Appassionata" Sonata was thirty-six minutes – longer by ten minutes or more than a typical performance.

Lamond was "tough," Nyiregyházi recalled, but their lessons, though they lasted only a few months, were productive, and left a deep impression. "None of my teachers taught me anything I did not intuitively know," he said, "but Dohnányi and Lamond inspired me." Lamond liked the boy, and Nyiregyházi remembered with gratitude the paternal affection Lamond showed him: "He treated me with the tenderness he'd show a two-year-old boy, and yet with the respect he'd show for a giant" – exactly what he craved.

In June 1916, the Nyiregyházis left Berlin. They spent the summer in Austria, then returned to Budapest, where Ervin's mother wanted him to study again with Dohnányi. (Though a citizen of both Hungary and Germany, Dohnányi had not been drafted by either country, and had taken a position as a professor at the academy.) Early in 1917, Ervin resumed his private lessons with Dohnányi and with Leó Weiner, and was tutored in other subjects typical of a humanistic *Gymnasium* curriculum: Hungarian, German, Latin, history, geography, mathematics, botany, zoology.* He continued to be put on display before important musicians, and wrote articles and reviews for a local music magazine. Barely pubescent, he was not yet too old to play the prodigy, and the appearance of Géza Révész's book in 1916 had only enhanced his celebrity.

Since the move to Berlin, he had been performing more and more often in public; Mariá, presumably, was keen to capitalize on the money-making potential of his youth while it lasted. By his mid-teens, he was playing recitals and chamber music and concertos throughout central Europe, and for a time was managed by one of the most powerful agents in Europe, Hermann Wolff. Sometime during the war years, he was invited by the Turkish government to give a private benefit concert in Constantinople, as part of the Red Cross's war-relief effort, and played before a glittering audience at the Austro-Hungarian embassy.

He was earning adult respect and mostly glowing, sometimes astonished reviews for his technique and sound and wide repertoire but also for depth and originality and wisdom beyond his years. Appreciation of him was hardly limited to wonder at his precociousness or potential: he was already ranked among the contemporary titans of the keyboard. Multiple-concerto evenings became a specialty of his, and were particularly impressive given his youth and apparent physical frailty. In Berlin, he played the Schumann concerto and Liszt's Hungarian Fantasy in one evening, and for his first orchestral appearance in Budapest, on December 12, 1916, he offered an astonishingly ambitious program consisting of the same Schumann and Liszt works *plus* Beethoven's C-minor concerto. (He was not yet fourteen.) "You really did something" was Dohnányi's characteristically laconic comment on the concert, which Nyiregyházi recalled as "a rather glorious success." He was ill with flu and a high fever at the

---

* In June 1918, Ervin passed his school exams with mostly excellent marks (except in the biological sciences, which he hated), though he said he never earned the equivalent of a high-school diploma.

time, but hid his illness so he would not have to cancel the concert. In fact, he was ill (with, among other things, pneumonia) throughout the early winter of 1916–17, and spent some of that time at a sanatorium in what is today the northcentral Slovak Republic.

On October 19, 1917, he gave a major recital in Budapest that included his own rhapsodic, one-movement *Grande Sonate héroïque*, which Béla Bartók, who attended, said had "dramatic power" but, at close to half an hour, was too long – a fair assessment. The reviews were bad – "mad dog" was a phrase that stuck in Nyiregyházi's mind – and he was scolded for impudent presumption, having programmed his own sonata between Beethoven's "Waldstein" and Chopin's B-minor. (His mother dubbed the event "Black Friday.") He continued to tour central Europe. In Vienna, on October 27, he appeared in another three-concerto program with the Tonkünstlerorchester – Beethoven's Fourth, the Schumann, and the Hungarian Fantasy – to great astonishment. Back in Berlin, he once more shared turf with Claudio Arrau, who was now earning much praise in the local press. In early January of the following year, the two prodigies both gave recitals, and reviewers could not resist pitting them against each other.[*] The *Allgemeine Musik-Zeitung*, for one, gave Ervin the edge, calling him a "pianist of the most exquisite kind," with "ear and soul for the finest and the most spectacular effects," a "phenomenon" such as one sees "once in twenty-five years."

Ervin was now in his mid-teens, with a brilliant adult career beckoning. But he was still under his mother's thumb, and their relationship was deteriorating. Every development in his musical, intellectual, and spiritual life made him resent her dominance and her crass commercialism more. (In 1917, he joined several artists in playing for a member of the Austro-Hungarian imperial family, in a benefit concert for the Hungarian Red Cross, and was humiliated when his mother insisted that

---

[*] Nyiregyházi had only praise for his putative rival, and admired him as a champion of Liszt. The two met several times in New York in the early 1920s, and had, Nyiregyházi recalled, "a genteel friendship" unimpeded by jealousy.

he be paid.) She saw (rightly) that his fixation on Liszt might compromise his success with critics and audiences. "I told you not to play Liszt," she might say after a bad review. "We'll go broke." She pressured him to play music that was popular and showed him off. She wanted him to play Chopin's "Minute" Waltz in less than a minute, lest anyone think he lacked technique. (He claimed that he once played it as an encore and was timed at fifty-nine seconds.) "If I received one favourable review and one unfavourable one after a concert, my mother would say that the man who wrote the unfavourable review knew more about music," he recalled. "She didn't want me to be conceited." Yet, she was not above boasting of his reviews herself. The two fought often, and Ervin ran away from her whenever he had a little money. But, unable to look after himself, he always returned.

His mother had him in a classic double bind, demanding that he be an adult (a professional virtuoso) while he was still a child, yet demanding also that he remain a child (a marketable prodigy) though he was approaching adulthood. The result could only be enormous anxiety and stunted emotional growth. Ervin's melancholy and bitterness grew, and his loneliness. He once said that as an adolescent he could associate with others his own age only if they were "terribly unusual." The normal turbulence of adolescence was magnified by his intelligence and sensitivity, and by his mother's infantilization and control. She still refused to let him wear long pants, which boys usually started wearing at fourteen or fifteen. She was apparently terrified that her son might grow up, and was steadfastly puritanical where his sexuality was concerned. Sexually, he was a late bloomer; he was not active until his twenties, though the rest of his family was less prudish. Grandma Lenke "talked about men's penises all the time," he recalled, his great-aunt Berta Borsodi enjoyed discussing oral sex, and her son György, a few years older than Ervin, used to boast of his conquests with girls. Ervin's father was fond of double entendre and would tell silly, risqué jokes – about girls who "played the flute" and such. But Mária did not even like Ignácz to sing mildly suggestive arias from operas. She sought to shield her son from any knowledge of sex – kept him away from books that might teach him the facts of life, forbade others to tell him. Still, he experienced sexual innuendo and sexual situations throughout childhood. He and his brother slept in the same room as their parents, and at least a few times he saw them having sex and heard his mother's moans. And, of course, he witnessed his father's infidelity. He was intrigued, sometimes aroused, but also confused by such experiences, and when he asked questions about sex his mother (and father, under orders) would reply, "I'll tell you later." He claimed to have had "a tremendous libido" even when very young, but throughout his childhood and adolescence he was bashful with girls, whom he perceived as a frightening enigma. By the time he experienced his first erection, around age twelve, he did not understand it. Worldlier boys teased him for his ignorance.

He was apparently something of a sexual target as a boy. He remembered incidents of flirtation and sexual touching involving older girls. When he was ten, one teenaged girl, at the intermission of one of his concerts, took him aside and said that to play Schumann he needed to feel more "romantic" – and then put her hand down his pants. When he told his father about this, Ignácz merely assured him, "In a year or two you'll be the biggest screwer who ever lived." Ervin may actually have been sexually abused. His last wife suspected that he was touched inappropriately by Jozsa Kovács, who nicknamed his private parts his "little rosebud." Ervin's mother may herself have abused him. He recalled that, after his father's death, she would "massage" his penis. The precise nature and extent of this activity are not clear, and he said it stopped when they moved back to Budapest, but if it did qualify as sexual abuse, it could only have exacerbated the problems he had with trust and with intimate relationships in later life. He also recalled that his mother once tried to reinforce a point by taking hold of his penis and saying, "When the girls get hold of this, they'll never let go" – and gave Ervin an erection. Small wonder that he approached adulthood anxious and confused about sex.

After returning to Budapest, Ervin fell in love for the first time, with a Serbian-Hungarian girl named Zdenka Ticharich. She was a year older than he, also a pianist and composer who loved Liszt, and it was something of a Romeo-and-Juliet saga, as their mothers were rivals. In November 1917, the two prodigies shared a review in a Viennese newspaper. Her playing was praised at the expense of his, but he didn't care – he was in love. They played for each other, made ardent declarations, held hands. Once, while sitting together in a movie theatre, she put her hand in his lap. He was aroused by her, but the relationship went no farther, and he allowed it to peter out; for one thing, he was embarrassed because he knew so little about sex. Only in 1918, shortly after he turned fifteen, did he find out (at his urging, from a tutor) that the stork does not deliver babies and that women do not have penises (he never saw his mother naked). He could not at first believe that sexual intercourse had produced Goethe and Napoleon and Liszt, because, as he put it, "pissing is dirty." When he told his mother what he had learned, she began screaming, denied it all, and prophesied the end of his career.

The Wunderkind on Tour

In September 1918, Ervin ended his studies to embark on a full-time career as a concert pianist. In early October, he appeared in three "piano evenings" in Copenhagen. After his first concert, a local newspaper called him "one of the most profound spirits that the history of music has ever known," and after his third he was invited out for drinks by Nina Grieg, Edvard Grieg's widow, who had been in the audience. While Ervin sipped chartreuse, Mrs. Grieg praised the "intense feeling" in his performance of her late husband's G-minor ballade; he played it, she said, precisely the way Grieg *wanted* it played. One of the high points of his childhood career came on October 20 and 21, when he performed Liszt's A-major concerto with the Berlin Philharmonic under the baton of Arthur Nikisch. Ervin admired Nikisch's "very Romantic" and "very individualistic" style, though it took some convincing to get the great man to acquiesce to his tempos. (*"That* slow?" "Yes!"*) [*] Nikisch had requested that the fifteen-year-old be permitted

---

[*] According to the diary notes of his pupil August Göllerich, Liszt advocated an unusually slow tempo at the beginning of this concerto.

the dignity of long pants, but Ervin's mother was still adamant. "No, sir, my boy will think he is grown up," she said. "He'll get ideas about girls." In any event, the press gushed over him as an already "ripe" artist with "not many rivals to fear."

Ervin also gave a recital in Berlin, on October 24, and in early November he received a telegram asking him to appear in Kristiania (as Oslo was then called) to substitute for Rachmaninov, who, on short notice, had fled to the United States. (Such a summons says much about the teenager's reputation in Europe.) On November 23 and 24, he duly played the Tchaikovsky concerto with Norway's National Theatre Orchestra, the second concert in the presence of the king and queen. The performances were triumphs.

Ervin at fifteen, in a portrait used in his publicity at the time of his Scandinavian tours, 1918–20. *(Photograph by Irén Werner.)*

One of the critics doubted that Rachmaninov could have played the concerto as well; another proclaimed the arrival of a new Liszt – a line that was becoming a Nyiregyházi cliché.

He remembered his Norwegian debut as "one of the most memorable experiences of my life," for it was at the rehearsal that he discovered the huge tone and thunderous fortissimo for which he would become famous. "When I played those first D-flat chords, I myself was surprised, and the conductor almost fell off the podium," he recalled sixty years later. "It was a sensation." Publicly, he would say only that he had tapped some well of power deep within himself, but privately, to a friend in the 1970s, he was more explicit: placing his hands on his groin, he said *that* had been the well from which the power had sprung. Throughout his life, he insisted that there was an intimate connection between his emotional life – including his libido – and his musicianship, and it is no surprise that he should have found new reserves of pianistic power just when he was feeling but not yet expressing strong sexual urges.

On November 27, he gave a recital in Kristiania, and afterward he and his mother decided to resettle in the city (he even learned to speak decent Norwegian). Neutral Norway must have seemed tempting. In the last years of the First World War, Hungarian society and the Hungarian economy were collapsing, and Budapest was under siege. There was some unrest and deprivation in Kristiania, but the city was still a mecca for foreigners fleeing the war. Ervin and his mother lived as guests of local friends, and were supported by his earnings and by wealthy patrons back home. Through the political influence of Manfréd Weisz and of some Norwegian friends, Ervin's brother and grandmother received permission to leave Hungary for Norway during Béla Kun's short-lived Communist régime in the spring and summer of 1919, at which time the borders were mostly closed.

Ervin performed frequently throughout Scandinavia. In Kristiania, he appeared at least five times in a one-month period in February and March of 1919, and gave a handful of concerts between January and April of 1920; the king and queen still attended regularly. In Stockholm, he played at least eight times between January 1919 and January 1920, including four concertos with the Orchestral Society. (In a 1980 interview, he recalled playing Busoni's monumental piano concerto in Stockholm in December 1919, though no documentation of this concert has been found.) He made at least one return visit to Copenhagen, in the fall of 1919, and toured smaller Norwegian and Swedish cities: Bergen, Drammen, Gävle, Göteborg, Lund, Malmö, Norrköping, Uppsala. He continued to appear elsewhere, too, notably Berlin. That fall, he undertook a three-week tour of the Netherlands, and after a performance of Liszt's A-major concerto in The Hague, one writer described him as "a small, brave, and daring David" with the virtuosity to slay "many Goliaths of technique."

He became a fixture of Scandinavian musical life and continued to impress local and visiting musicians and dignitaries, even, by one account, arousing jealousy among his colleagues. He became a friend and champion of Norwegian composers including Halfdan Cleve, Gerhard Schjelderup, and Christian Sinding. Irwin Parnes recorded an anecdote from the Scandinavian impresario Helmer Enwall, about Ervin's first concert in Stockholm. One day after lunch, according to Enwall, the pair stopped in a downtown music shop. The shopkeeper produced some demanding new piano music by Bartók that had just arrived in that morning's mail. Ervin glanced through the score while the men talked, then put it back on the counter. That evening, according to Enwall, he played the piece as an encore, from memory.

The Scandinavian concerts reveal that Ervin, in his mid-teens, had a vast repertoire studded with musical landmarks and liked to offer mammoth programs incorporating two hours or more of serious, difficult music. His adult repertoire was now effectively set. He played pre-Romantic works only very selectively: Bach's Chromatic Fantasy and Fugue and Liszt and Busoni transcriptions of Bach; a little Scarlatti and Gluck; Mozart's C-minor fantasy and A-minor rondo. His was at heart a nineteenth-century repertoire: big sonatas by Beethoven, Weber, Schumann, Chopin, Brahms, and Tchaikovsky; Schubert's "Wanderer" Fantasy (in Liszt's edition); Schumann's *Carnaval* and *Symphonic Études*; Brahms's Handel Variations; a seemingly bottomless supply of Chopin and Liszt groups; smaller works by Brahms, Debussy, Grieg, Mendelssohn, Rachmaninov, Saint-Saëns, Schubert, Scriabin, Sibelius, and some comparatively obscure composers (Leschetizky, Rubinstein, Rummel, Sinding). He played Liszt's B-minor sonata and Dante Sonata in several recitals, but also some of Liszt's flashier, more popular arrangements and paraphrases, to please his mother and his managers. He played the major Romantic concertos, too, and occasionally one of his own compositions.

He gave some of his most satisfying concerts in Scandinavia, he said near the end of his life. His Scandinavian reviews – some of the best of his career – noted large (often sold-out) audiences who sat spellbound and then erupted in wildly enthusiastic ovations, and critics called him

"a new Liszt" (yet again), even "the greatest of all pianists." Let one
review from Stockholm stand for many:

> When one first sees this thin figure of a boy, one can only wonder
> how he will succeed in playing physically straining pieces, but there
> is no trace of this doubt after he strikes his first chord. From that
> moment on he is a mature man, whose large and firm tone is aston-
> ishing for his age. Apart from this deeply rooted sound one also notes
> his glimmering passagework and octaves, which were strong enough
> to be heard over the orchestra even at forte, his springy staccato (one
> must look far and wide for so nimble a wrist), the sober, noble plastic-
> ity, the passionate temperament and the poetic expression, together
> with his simple and unassuming stage presence as an added bonus.
> Only one objection could be raised: the somewhat profuse use of the
> pedal. But this is a mere quibble when one considers the merits, and
> his interpretation of Tchaikovsky's concerto in B-flat minor can
> deservedly be labelled a masterpiece.

Not *everyone* thought this boy was mature enough to play, say, late
Beethoven, and there were occasional comments of the all-technique-
and-no-feeling variety. Mostly, however, his listeners marvelled.

He continued to compose prolifically in his teens, and in 1920 he used
his earnings to subsidize the publication of some of his works, most of
them composed in Scandinavia within the previous year. He had tried to
interest a venerable Berlin publisher, Schlesinger, in several piano
pieces, but was told that they were too old-fashioned – the influence of
Liszt was now front and centre in his music – so he paid to have them
engraved and printed in Leipzig.* He thought very highly of these

---

* Of these pieces, I have seen the scores only of the six discussed here. A seventh, the
clangorous, Lisztian *Mephisto Fantasie*, I have seen only in a manuscript that
Nyiregyházi wrote out from memory in old age. He claimed that in 1917 he composed
and orchestrated a four-movement symphony in B-flat minor, though it was not published and was apparently lost.

pieces all his life, though they are conventionally Romantic concoctions, some of them lyrical pieces with titles like *Dolcissimo, Chanson passionée,* and *Valse mélancolique,* pieces of genuine feeling – portraits of emotional states – but with little sophisticated development of ideas. The music seems more improvised than calculated. The *Grande Sonate héroïque* is more ambitious, demanding great bravura and thundering cascades of sound – Ervin was now in love with Lisztian bluster – but it is also prolix; a reviewer in 1917 found it repetitious, immature, derivative, and boring. At least two works were intended for orchestra, though published for piano: *Mephisto triumphiert!* and *Triumf!.* Both reveal Lisztian piano techniques and reflect a Lisztian fascination for the macabre and diabolical. In all of these pieces, Ervin channelled Liszt unashamedly, spurning conventional forms and importing Liszt's harmonic language and fondness for grandiose, melodramatic gestures and massive sonorities, often thickly scored in the low register, sometimes conjuring up brass and percussion instruments.

In Scandinavia, the tension between Ervin and his mother continued to mount. She wanted him dependent, exploitable; he desperately sought independence. The more she forbade Liszt, for instance, the more he wanted to play it. Girls, too, were a point of contention. Ervin, with his brooding, dark good looks, was proving attractive to the opposite sex. The composer Halfdan Cleve, who may have become a kind of surrogate father, had four daughters, and Ervin fell in love with the oldest, Astrid, who was a year younger than he, though it was her sister Signy, an especially beautiful, more sexually provocative, less sentimentally romantic girl (and a fine pianist) who stole him away. Ervin's playing sometimes had a Pied Piper effect on women. One reviewer in Stockholm noted that in the audience "ladies were definitely in the majority"; another noted that Ervin, like Liszt, could seduce the ladies with his singing tone. (A review of a recital in Szeged, Hungary, in 1918, noted his magnetism and his mastery over his public.) He recalled several concerts, in his mid-teens, during which he caught sight of a pretty girl in the audience and, fancying himself in love, directed his playing toward her. Defiantly, he would tell his mother about these incidents, and furious arguments would ensue. Girls, Mária said, would ruin him.

It all came to a head in November 1919, on a street in Berlin, during one of their frequent quarrels. Ervin was booked to play Rachmaninov's Piano Concerto No. 2 in Kristiania on January 5, but now declared that he would cancel the concert if forced to play in short pants, and would never perform again unless he was allowed to live on his own. Mária, enraged, broke an umbrella over his head, but perhaps even she now realized the hopelessness of trying to pass him off as a prodigy – he was almost seventeen.* (In the spring of 1920 he would begin to shave.) In April, Mária returned with nine-year-old Alfred and Szidónia to Berlin, though she eventually resettled in Budapest. Before leaving Ervin, she decided finally to tell him about sex. Among her insights, according to her son: "A man makes children with what he pisses with." "Your wife is the first woman who should make you come." "If you masturbate, you will die." Perhaps, for her, this counted as nurture.

Ervin spent the spring and summer in Kristiania with two spinster sisters related to the composer Schjelderup, living off money he earned giving concerts and piano lessons and support he still received from patrons back home. "I was then drunk with the idea I was on my own," he recalled. One of his first acts as a liberated young man was to buy a cane. Somehow, for him, acting the part of a debonair gentleman represented freedom.

Ervin's mother had her eye on the United States at least as early as 1915, when, after his orchestral debut in Berlin, he played for an

---

* In a 1978 interview, Nyiregyházi recalled an incident early in 1920 when, for the first time, he rather than his mother was handed his fee backstage after a concert (she had stepped out of his dressing room). He pocketed the money and fled to the nearest train station. Perhaps it was this incident that precipitated their final physical separation.

American impresario who was scouting new talent. He offered a tour of thirty concerts at a hundred dollars apiece, but Mária sought a far vaster fee – five or ten times as much.* That was Paderewski money, and the impresario, taken aback, replied, "Do you want the whole ocean?" Anyway, America's entry into the war in 1917 made an overseas tour unlikely. But the subject came up again in 1920, when it appeared that Ervin may have saturated the Scandinavian market. (A reviewer in Göteborg that January noted that a smaller hall was booked for him at the last minute, as the audience was not large enough to fill the one originally chosen.)

Returning home was not an attractive option. The defeat of the Austro-Hungarian Empire in the war had devastated Hungary. The country was invaded by foreign powers, the social order was upset, the economy was nearly bankrupt, there were shortages of food, clothing, fuel, and raw materials, and poverty was widespread even among the middle class. Budapest, one of the cities most devastated by the war, was rife with destitution, crime, and general turmoil. Politically, the country was convulsive. It experienced three radical changes of government in less than a year, yielding finally, in the fall of 1919, to a counter-revolutionary administration backed by the newly formed Hungarian National Army. In the Treaty of Trianon, signed at Versailles on June 4, 1920, Hungary lost about 60 per cent of its population and about 70 per cent of its territory to its neighbours.

For Hungarian Jews, it was a terrifying time. Rifts between Jew and Gentile, kept in check for a generation, had exploded during and after the war, causing the worst wave of anti-Semitism in Hungarian history. Jews were made scapegoats for social and economic problems, and, because of the strong Jewish presence in Béla Kun's Communist

---

* A surviving contract shows that for playing concertos in two concerts in Stockholm, in January 1920, Ervin was paid the relatively modest fee of one thousand kronor – equivalent to a little more than fifteen thousand kronor (about three thousand Canadian dollars) today.

régime, subsequent anti-Communist wrath extended to Jews generally. The counter-revolutionary government provoked a virulent "white terror" of ruthless pogroms throughout the country. The widespread Jewish influence in the arts and sciences was no longer tolerated and admired, and new laws imposed restrictions on Jews for the first time in decades. Hungary now became notorious internationally as a hotbed of anti-Semitism, which was widespread among musicians, too. Music was in a dire state after the war, in most quarters effectively paralyzed, with one great exception: Dohnányi, who almost singlehandedly kept classical concert life alive in Budapest.

For the seventeen-year-old Nyiregyházi, Budapest was out of the question, Scandinavia had been fully mined, and Berlin – well, that was where his mother now lived. America must have seemed the logical next step. Many musicians in postwar Europe saw it as a sort of El Dorado, a safe haven where money flowed freely. And so Ervin joined the thousands of Hungarians, many of them prominent figures, many of them Jews, who fled their country after the war. In the summer of 1920, Mária, through a relative in America, arranged a contract with a New York concert agency and took the necessary legal steps to have Ervin declared of major age. Everyone predicted an illustrious adult career for him, and he had every reason to expect both greater professional success and greater personal fulfillment now that he was independent. Instead, as he told a friend more than half a century later, going to America would prove to be "the beginning of the end."

Opposite: Nyiregyházi at Ellis Island, having arrived in America for the first time, October 11, 1920. *(Photograph by the Keystone Photo Co.* Musical America *Archives.)*

PART TWO

A YOUNG LISZT OF THE PIANOFORTE

1920–1928

A King in New York

On October 11, 1920, Nyiregyházi arrived at Ellis Island aboard the Danish ship *United States* and was met by Carl von Laurenz, who was to handle him on behalf of the Wolfsohn Musical Bureau, one of the most important concert-management firms in New York. His three-year contract called for twenty concerts per season, at $200 each, and Wolfsohn had offered $1,500 up front. According to von Laurenz, it was the first time Wolfsohn had offered an advance to an artist without an audition; indeed, the bureau's late founder, Henry A. Wolfsohn, was known to demand money from new clients to cover promotional expenses. Nyiregyházi had been asked to audition but had proudly refused.

Considerable publicity preceded the Wunderkind's arrival. Photographers were waiting for him at Ellis Island, and he turned heads as he stepped off the ship, especially among women. "That's good," von Laurenz said. "Women rule this country. They like you. You'll be a success." Von Laurenz simplified the surname in deference to American tongues – to "Nyredghazi" – though it remained the subject of much mangling and ribbing. Nyiregyházi moved into the Hotel Grenoble, which would remain his home until the fall of 1924, and on the evening of October 18, in Carnegie Hall, he gave his first American recital. He drew a small but eager audience "crowded with the aristocracy of the pianistic world, awaiting the appearance of the youth of whom such remarkable stories had been told," according to Harriette Brower's flattering profile, "Nyredghazi: A Young Liszt of the Pianoforte," in the December 11 *Musical America*. Everyone was struck by his youth, his exotic appearance, his demeanour. He was tall and slim – "mostly arms and legs," as one critic would describe him: he weighed just 125 pounds, though had not quite reached his full adult height of five-foot-eleven. His wrists, hands, and fingers were, Brower noted, "delicate as a young girl's," and his

Nyiregyházi at seventeen, sporting the Lisztian long hair that aroused so much comment during his first New York season, 1920–21. *(University of Southern California, on behalf of the U.S.C. Specialized Libraries and Archival Collections.)*

slender fingers were so long that he could span a twelfth on the keyboard. He had a long, oval, boyish face; his complexion, one critic would write, was "so white that it seemed as though a breath of out-door air never struck him." There was something mysterious and affecting about his impassive, melancholy expression, broken only rarely by a "wan and diffident smile." His drooping mane of dark hair, parted in the middle, was old-fashioned enough "to make him appear to emerge out of an old daguerreotype" (and, he said, to make policemen suspicious). Much was made of his resemblance to the young Liszt, and his prowess at the piano and passion for Liszt's music fuelled fresh talk of a "new Liszt."

He was awkward on stage, acknowledging the audience only with stiff bows. One critic wrote that he "walks unseeing to the piano";

another noted that "he was obviously painfully ill at ease before an audience"; another thought his manner "ridiculously studied." He insisted on carrying himself with dignity on stage, partly to conceal concert nerves, from which he suffered greatly, though once playing he seemed oblivious to his surroundings, lost in the music. "At the piano he seldom looks at his hands or the keys, but gazes up at the nearest electrolier," wrote one critic after his debut. He played straight-backed, without flamboyant movements, and performed the most virtuosic music seemingly without effort. The effect was uncanny, a little demonic.

His long debut program consisted of some of his favourite works: the Bach-Busoni Toccata in D Minor; Schubert's "Wanderer" Fantasy; the Sonata No. 4 and *Poème satanique* by Scriabin (whose music, then widely considered indigestible, he had recently discovered); Chopin's Barcarolle; the "Notturno" from Grieg's *Lyric Pieces*, Op. 54; Leschetizky's "Étude héroïque"; and Liszt's *Sonetto 104 del Petrarca* and *Mephisto Waltz* No. 1 – all supplemented generously by encores.*
After the concert, he was taken to a nightclub to listen to jazz and drink "ginger ale" (that is, bootleg whisky) and stayed up until the wee hours to catch the first reviews.

In the *Evening Journal*, he was pronounced "the seventeen-year-old Paderewski," "the sensation of the new season," and, less happily, "a thumpingly interesting pianist." But many of the reviews, particularly those of the senior critics, were filled with qualifications of a kind he had rarely encountered in Europe. The pre-concert hype had ill effects, too: some listeners seemed determined not to be too impressed by this prodigy. The dean of local critics was the venerable Henry E. Krehbiel

---

* Nyiregyházi perceived American audiences to be less sophisticated, less spiritually inclined than those in Europe, and when it came to Liszt he leaned more heavily than before on showpieces, at least in his first seasons. "I would have been reluctant to expose Liszt's greatest works to ridicule," he said. In New York, he was once disgusted to witness an audience cough with boredom as Rachmaninov played the B-minor sonata.

of the *Tribune*, a genteel and erudite writer of German parentage and conservative tastes, who hated hoopla, could be prickly or caustic when provoked, and proudly defended the New World's musical culture against the supposed superiority of Europe's. After admitting that the whole Nyiregyházi phenomenon had disturbed his critical equilibrium, he wrote:

> Last night we were bidden to Carnegie Hall to listen to a genius. . . .
>
> What we heard was a pianist of marvellously fine technical acquirements and undoubted gifts for his chosen vocation, but so obsessed with individualism that its manifestation frequently, indeed, generally, stood in the way of our enjoyment of his music. . . .
>
> [Nyiregyházi] is too indulgent in sudden tempo changes and makes rushes in speed and sonority like the musical gypsies of his native land, who are as little Magyars as he is a Magyar by race. . . .
>
> It is long since we heard the like.

Other critics heard something impressive yet wayward:

> He has a brilliant technical equipment, great strength of arm and fingers, remarkable dexterity, a fine feeling for piano tone, and in these matters he is not unique among pianists. His conception of some of the most familiar compositions for the piano is often erratic and misleading. (Richard Aldrich, *New York Times*)

> Young as he is, he has had the misfortune of having a book written about him, and this has evidently given him an erroneous idea of his importance, urging him to try to be different from all other pianists so as to convey the impression that he is original, if not a genius. Now, originality is a great thing, but when the striving for it leads to arbitrary disregard of the obvious intentions of great composers it is not to be commended. (H.T. Finck, *Evening Post*)

He can thunder, he can whisper and he can woo the keys, too, producing a singing tone of ravishing beauty. Undoubtedly he was nervous. There were, it seemed, too many rhythmic and dynamic eccentricities all through the program; the big line was too frequently lost sight of in the accentuation of details, unimportant in themselves, but affording the pianist opportunity for technical display. (*Musical Courier*)

. . . a freakish prodigy, a kind of wild, irresponsible talent, that at its best comes near to compassing genius. If young Nyredghazi could be trained up artistically in the way he should go and the mad impulses of his gifts curbed and bridled, he might emerge a potent personality. At present he is anything you will but a performer of musical legitimacy.
(H.F.P., *Musical America*)

The young Nyiregyházi already commanded technical and tonal resources impressive enough to make him stand out in a crowded field. "There is something uncannily gigantic about Nyiregyházi," noted *Musical America*, "even in these days of super-pianists." His approach to the piano was orchestral, and he stunned listeners with "his amazing power to begin a fortissimo climax where most of the thunderers of the day leave off." One critic wrote that he "ruthlessly and savagely assaulted the keyboard," and even an admirer wrote of "that peculiar hard brilliance that is Nyiregyházi's own."* It all brings to mind the Promethean young Liszt, whom reviewers likened to a conqueror astride the shattered hulls of vanquished pianos, leaving listeners bewitched and amazed by the onslaught. Yet one senior critic, William James Henderson of the *Sun*, noted significantly that Nyiregyházi also

---

* Already in 1915, a reviewer of his concerto debut in Berlin found his tone "somewhat hard" in loud passages. Nyiregyházi said he preferred pianos that had a "brilliant" and "gushing" tone.

"aroused admiration and astonishment by his exquisite pianissimos." His approach to expression – his love of vivid colours, bold contrasts, extremes of emotion – was at odds with contemporary tastes, at a time when progressive composers, conductors, and performers were increasingly casting off the perceived excesses of Romanticism. Everything about his playing hearkened back to a bygone era. "Lightness and spontaneity were conspicuously lacking in his playing," wrote one critic, but Nyiregyházi did not aspire to them; he sought Wagnerian heaviness, deliberation, mass. He loved thick, noisy sonorities in the low register, sounds that seemed to well up from some great, deep source, and what critics heard as overpedalling was his effort to blur edges for the sake of weight and expression. Rhythmically, his playing was flexible ("he contrasted exaggerated retards with mad bursts of speed," wrote one critic), and in this he followed Wagner, who had disdained "time beaters" and had considered expressive tempo changes not exaggeration or sentimentality but "a positive life principle of all our music."* Most sacrilegiously of all, Nyiregyházi had a highly subjective approach to interpretation; he was willing to tamper with the scores of even beloved canonical works, in deference to his own temperament and ideas.

Such a style, forgivable perhaps in an aged artist left over from another time, was in Nyiregyházi's case widely perceived as immaturity or self-indulgence. The origins of American classical-music culture, in the mid-nineteenth century, owed much to transplanted Germans and musicians of mostly German training or sympathy; in the 1920s, Germanic tastes were still deeply entrenched among composers, performers, critics, and the public. Many associated Nyiregyházi's hot-blooded style with his nationality – hence the patronizing clichés about his "Magyar" or "Gypsy" temperament, about "the fire, the

---

* When it came to conductors, Nyiregyházi loved the Romantic subjectivity of Willem Mengelberg and Wilhelm Furtwängler, and the latter's slow tempos. "Both gushed," he said, in praise, but "Furtwängler gushed more."

wildness, the impulsive flashes of passion, the untamed nature of a race of beings born to the road under the open stars." It was not generally known that he was Jewish.*

While many critics adopted a skeptical wait-and-see approach, the public did not. Nyiregyházi sparked such excitement that two more Carnegie Hall recitals and an orchestral appearance were hastily squeezed in on weekend afternoons to meet the popular demand. On October 30 and again on November 7, he offered big new programs,† and again the public was wildly enthusiastic: after – even *during* – both concerts, he was compelled to give many encores. Increasingly, the critics heard not just a thunderer with fingers "tipped with fire and flame," but a pianist capable of "melting tenderness," too. A critic in *Musical America* wrote: "Never since de Pachmann has the present writer heard such Chopin and there were things about it that even de Pachmann never did, a vague faery-like quality, virile yet *decadent*, an Edgar Allen Poe-esque atmosphere without which so much of Chopin is as Czerny." That was extraordinary praise, for the Russian pianist Vladimir de Pachmann, then still active in his seventies, was widely regarded as the greatest and perhaps most authentic Chopin player of his day, renowned for a whispery pianissimo and a tone of uncommon delicacy, refinement, and seductive colours.

---

* On the ships' manifests for his arrivals at Ellis Island in 1920, 1923, and 1924, his ethnicity was recorded as (respectively) "Germany Magyar," "Hungarian, Magyar," and "Hungary, German." In the 1930s, he said, he travelled with a Hungarian passport that gave his religion as Catholic; presumably he was doing so already in 1920.

† The October 30 program included Saint-Saëns's Toccata, and after the concert Nyiregyházi received a letter from the local agent of a French publisher, demanding a fee of $10 for performing the copyrighted piece. With typical contempt for authority ("To hell with the publisher!"), he addressed his payment directly to "M. Camille Saint-Saëns, Paris, le grand compositeur." Saint-Saëns received the cheque and cashed it.

On November 11, Nyiregyházi made his first appearance outside
New York, as a last-minute replacement for an indisposed baritone
recitalist in Dayton, Ohio. Even in the Midwest it was reported that
"the learned musicians objected to the many liberties Nyredghazi took
with his scores," but the concert was a huge success. (There would be a
few other concerts outside New York that fall – in Louisiana,
Tennessee, South Carolina.) On November 21, he performed for
the first time with an American orchestra: the Tchaikovsky concerto,
with the New York Symphony. The piano, it was noted, sometimes
swamped the orchestra, and Nyiregyházi received such an ovation that
he took seven curtain calls. One critic wrote: "Mr. Nyredghazi's dis-
regard of accepted tempi, observed at his recitals, was a stumbling block
in attempts of Rene Pollain, the conductor, to keep orchestra and
pianist together." Still, this was proclaimed one of the most note-
worthy debuts of recent years.

The controversy Nyiregyházi aroused was sufficient to warrant an
article in *Musical America*. He "has caused considerable excitement," it
began. "Opinions about his precise place appear to differ. One musician
who heard him told me that he was the loudest pianist he had ever
heard, and it seemed as if Carnegie Hall was too small for him. Another
said he was unquestionably a genius but in the raw. A third told me
that he was a freak and reminded him of Leo Ornstein gone wrong,
while a fourth informed me that he thought he was unquestionably a
very great talent and if not a genius, mighty close to it." Another critic
that December wrote, in *Musician*: "Few pianists who have come to
New York within recent years have given the critics so much to think
about," and of an iconoclastic seventeen-year-old on his first American
tour, in a city awash in great pianists, that was saying something.

He became a local celebrity and, of course, not just his talent but his
personality made him a publicist's dream. His impact was plain to see
in an article by Prosper Buranelli published in the December 5 *World
Magazine*. Excepting some biographical inaccuracies probably abetted
by von Laurenz, it deserves to be quoted in full:

NOTHING BUT A PIANO PRODIGY
Nyredghazi Has Practised Intensively Since He Was
Two Years Old, and Now at Eighteen
Is a Hero of the Keyboard, But Otherwise Helpless.

I FOUND the most competent and incompetent man in New York. Ervin Nyredghazi is a piano-playing prodigy of recent New York appearance. Hands on keys, he is the figure of masterful capability. In any other posture he is a monster of incompetence. He does not know how to tie his shoes. He cannot put on his collar. Knotting his necktie needs a whole corps of assistants. He cannot carve his food. Soup is a dreadful affair with him. And he owns a collection of crochets, whims and eccentricities that are arresting even among musicians – to whom crochets, whims and eccentricities are conventional.

Ervin is a tall, stringy youth, dark, and with heavy black hair greatly in need of a cutting. His face is long, narrow at top and full at jowls, and melancholy. He sat at the piano in his uptown hotel apartment, full of strength, confidence and pride, and hammered out the Liszt "Mephisto Waltz" with a display of technique and rattling octaves. He left the piano and sank into an easy chair, listless, ill at ease, an image of dejected, apologetic unfitness. His mentor looked at him with mingled admiration and contempt.

"See him there. What is he good for? Nothing, except to play the piano," said the mentor, with broad drollery. Nyredghazi while in America is in his charge. He is an American, von Laurenz by name, and himself a pianist, but a capable fellow who might lead a march through the wilderness.

"When I met him at the boat," he related, "I saw that I had a job on my hands. That night at dinner he had a pork chop on his plate. He took the knife and looked at it, and looked at the chop. He began jabbing at it gingerly, as though he were afraid it would jump out of the plate and bite him. I asked him what was the matter. He informed me with all dignity that his mother had always cut his food for him. And now I have to sit at every meal with him and cut his food.

"The next morning I went to his room. He was trying to tie his shoe laces. He couldn't do it. His mother had always tied his shoes. I do it now. He nearly choked himself trying to get his collar on, and I thought he was going to hang himself with his necktie. I found that he was as helpless as a child of two.

"He is so weak that he can scarcely raise the cover off the piano – but look at those hands and forearms."

The young pianist's hands were abnormally long. The muscles stood out like sections of wash line under the skin. The forearm was heavy and powerfully muscled, but the upper arm was emaciated and undeveloped.

Nyredghazi's case was explained as one of specialization pushed to freakish lengths – of an infant prodigy developed unhealthily. . . . He has learned to do literally nothing, save play the piano.

"He took up a new big concerto the other day," von Laurenz jibed, "and memorized it at one playing. But I don't think I shall ever succeed in teaching him how to put a pair of cuff buttons in his sleeves."

Nyredghazi does not trust himself to try talking English, but he understands most of what is said. He sat doubled up in his chair and listened to the fun poked at him. He smiled dubiously at one remark, looked grave at a second, nodded his head thoughtfully at a third.

"Look at that fuzz on his face," von Laurenz went on. "It looks like feathers. Before his first recital I said I would take him down and get him shaved. 'No, no!' he said. I shouldn't get him shaved. He wouldn't let any knife come near his face. I said I wasn't going to get him shaved with a knife, but with a razor. He replied sagaciously that, according to true definitions and the principles of mechanics, a razor was a knife. Then I said I would put a safety razor to his jaws. He was too wise for that. He said he knew there was a blade in the safety razor. You can't fool him. I asked him how the deuce he was going to get that fuzz off his face. How do you suppose he does it? He's got a pair of horse clippers."

Von Laurenz produced an old black box, and from it an antiquated pair of clippers – ordinary barber's clippers.

"He puts these on his face, and pulls half the hair out and leaves the other half there. I took him down to the barber, and after he had successfully resisted all attempts to put a razor to him, I bribed the barber to shave him with the clippers. It took an hour.

"He has an old, shabby, back-country soft hat. He won't buy a new one. Hats cost too much in America. But the other day he saw a flivver [car] price-tagged at $700 or $800. He said he was going to buy it. He was stubborn about it.

"He certainly knows what he wants. I asked him whether he thought he could ever learn to drive a Ford. He said no, but that he would engage a chauffeur. I told him he would have to pay a chauffeur as much as $15 a week. He said he would pay it. I told him he could not get a self-respecting chauffeur to drive a Ford. That puzzled him. And then I showed him that if he got a Ford and a chauffeur, he would have to buy a new hat to go with them. He dropped the Ford idea.

"He is always bored, but he likes to go walking. I introduced him to a pretty girl, a friend of mine. I told her to invite him to go walking. She did. But he wasn't walking that day. He hasn't even learned how to talk to the girl."

The raillery went fast and rough. The young musician listened to it with sheepish amusement. Finally he had enough. He went to the piano and began Scriabine's "Poeme Satanique." He played with flame and fantasy, with a dazzling technique and with a profound comprehension of the irony and diabolism of the music. He sat there a master. His face was set with the pride of an adept at his craft, who knows he commands the respect of all about him.

Carl von Laurenz and the Wolfsohn Musical Bureau were thrilled by the publicity Nyiregyházi generated, though the star himself was not satisfied. He was disturbed by the way he was portrayed in the press.[*] His dignity, earnestness, and idealism were not easily reconciled with the hucksterism and ballyhoo that had long characterized classical-music culture in America; he was not the first visiting European musician to feel debased, like a commodity. He liked the "bravado and toughness" of Americans, but not their provincialism and commercialism, and he hated the hype needed to keep one's name before the public in the consumer culture of the 1920s.

Nyiregyházi's management did not share his idealism. (Henry A. Wolfsohn had once persuaded Richard Strauss to conduct at Wanamaker's department store during business hours.) He was proving to be a difficult artist to wrangle: temperamental, constitutionally averse to authority, he was showing with his manager the defiance he had shown with his mother. For his third Carnegie Hall recital, von Laurenz insisted that he program Anton Rubinstein's Barcarolle in G Minor instead of the work he wanted to play, the "Sérénade" from Borodin's *Petite Suite*. The printed program was duly changed, but the night of the concert Nyiregyházi simply played the Borodin anyway. Few in the audience knew the difference, including von Laurenz, yet Nyiregyházi, typically, insisted on revealing the ruse. Moreover, von Laurenz was outraged that of the six or seven encores Nyiregyházi was routinely playing two or three would be numbers like "Smiles" or

---

[*] Years later, of the Buranelli article, Nyiregyházi said, "They exaggerate[d] these things beyond measuring, and then I was known as an imbecile." He admitted that the pork-chop story was true, but put the blame on a phobia. He said he had morbidly feared knives ever since, as a young child, he had watched a scene in a movie in which someone was killed with a knife. And yet, he was seen fumbling with utensils and eating largely with his hands throughout his life.

"Dardanella," or *Stars and Stripes Forever.*[*] "How dare you play jazz in Carnegie Hall?" he thundered. But Nyiregyházi was adamant: he noticed that popular songs made the girls swoon and the ladies cry.

More decisive was their dispute over piano rolls, which were then a very big business: by the end of the First World War, production of player pianos outnumbered that of regular pianos. The player piano was a veritable "musical epidemic," the pianist Arthur Rubinstein recalled, in his memoir *My Many Years.* "Suddenly in New York musicians spoke of nothing else. The most interested ones were, of course, pianists; there was a lot of money to be earned." Nyiregyházi's contract demanded that he make rolls for the American Piano Company, a conglomerate formed in 1908 that eventually had many piano firms under its umbrella, including Mason & Hamlin. (Wolfsohn had an arrangement with Mason & Hamlin, whose instruments Nyiregyházi played in his first season.) American's Ampico player-piano mechanism, launched in 1915, enjoyed great commercial success, which peaked in the early and mid-1920s. Still, Nyiregyházi refused to make rolls, and refused to give a reason. Years later, he admitted that he did not want to make rolls – or recordings – because he did not want people to discover his wrong notes, though, ironically, the piano roll was the one contemporary recording technology that permitted the correction of fingerslips.

In December 1920, von Laurenz decided that his prodigy's intransigence was outweighing his profitability. He deemed Nyiregyházi to be in breach of his contract, and cancelled it, though it meant taking a financial loss. As a result, Nyiregyházi lost some high-profile bookings in major East Coast cities, and an appearance with the Chicago Symphony. Von Laurenz angrily told him, "You can spit blood now." No less a figure than

---

[*] In one concert a few years later, he improvised, for an encore, a sort of miniature symphonic poem that incorporated "Dixie" and "Yankee Doodle."

Rachmaninov offered to pay his way back to Europe,[*] and had conditions there been more inviting for a Hungarian Jew he would have been wise to take up the offer. His $1,500 advance lasted only a few months. He sent some of the money to his mother, used some to subsidize the printing of his compositions in Leipzig, spent some indulging the taste for gourmet meals he had developed as a pampered child. By the turn of 1921, he was broke.

He sought respite from poverty in New York's Hungarian community. He found a saviour in a colourful middle-aged Hungarian named Imre Szopory, who styled himself "Baron Szopory." Short and white-haired, impoverished but well mannered, he had contacts across the social spectrum (he apparently did a little bootlegging), though Nyiregyházi was not surprised to learn that he affected the title "Baron" because "the girls liked it." Szopory, in exchange for a cut, introduced his countryman to rich Hungarians for whom he could play private concerts for a few dollars. In January, he gave at least one public concert, in a Hungarian hall (and was already so poor that he had to borrow the $100 fee in advance). Szopory also persuaded the Hungarian embassy in Washington to send Nyiregyházi money, but when it arrived he demanded more than his agreed share and, when Nyiregyházi refused, hit him with a cane and called him "a goddam Jew." Still, Nyiregyházi remembered him fondly. "He was a bunco artist" – and a mooch, and a welsher – "but he had a heart."

Socially awkward at the best of times, Nyiregyházi, now on his own, was hampered by his indifferent command of English (he had been

---

[*] Rachmaninov had attended all three Carnegie Hall recitals and (Nyiregyházi was told) had declared that he could not make up his mind about the boy's playing, which he found interesting but problematic. Nyiregyházi took this to mean that he was beyond conventional notions of good and bad – a compliment. He greatly admired Rachmaninov as both a musician and a man, yet apparently the two met only once, in New York, to shake hands backstage.

able to speak to von Laurenz in German). In the spring of 1921, he purchased a copy of Oscar Wilde's novel *The Picture of Dorian Gray* and an English-German dictionary, and after immersing himself for a week in them had mastered the language. (Plays and movies helped, too.) He eventually developed a precise, formal, baroque brand of English that to some ears sounded pretentious but suited his aristocratic self-image. For him, speaking and writing clearly was a matter of dignity, and of sensitivity toward the person being addressed. He could not abide bad grammar and slang, though he retained certain old-fashioned endearments and idioms ("They're full of prunes!").

Reading Wilde, he found not only a new language but a new hero. Wilde "became a god to me – like Liszt." He admired Wilde's "razor-like mind," his reverence for beauty, his satire, his wit. But he saw beneath the glittering surface of Wilde; he saw elevated sentiments, refinement, sophistication, spirituality; he saw an ultimately pessimistic artist not afraid to reveal the "dark side" of life. Moreover, he considered the Wilde of Reading Gaol a martyr to individual freedom crushed by a tyrannical society. From Wilde, as from Liszt, he learned that "real greatness lies in opposition to the rules of the world." He read Wilde's plays, poems, and essays, but *Dorian Gray*, in particular, became a touchstone for him; its ornate style and strong contrasts appealed to him. In Wilde's defence of the importance of art, of putting one's whole self into one's art, in his celebration of amorality and hedonism without guilt, of youth's mad passion and greed for experience and sensation, the young Nyiregyházi saw reflected his own Romantic yearnings. Shortly after discovering the novel, he began composing a symphonic poem based on it, in a piano arrangement; by the time it was finished, in 1947, it was some two hundred pages long and required two hours (or more) to play. (It was quicker to read the book, he said.) He considered it his greatest work and described it with relish. "The murder scene," he told a friend, with a menacing growl and a twinkle in the eye, "that's *really* something!"

Under New Management

Private concerts, Hungarian friends, charity, and Oscar Wilde tided Nyiregyházi over until March 1921, when he found a new manager: Robert E. Johnston, who operated out of an office at 1451 Broadway, near Times Square. Arthur Rubinstein, another client, quoted him as saying, "I'd sooner drop dead than pay advance money," though Johnston was so keen to sign Nyiregyházi that he offered him $200 up front. At once he set about making changes. He switched his client's allegiance to Knabe, another division of the American Piano Company. Nyiregyházi would be paid $50 each time he used a Knabe in concert, Knabe would promote his concerts and put a practice piano in his hotel, and he would allow ghostwritten testimonials to be published over his signature.[*] Then there was his long hair. The novelty of it had worn off, critics disapproved of it, and he got teased about it, not only in

---

[*] Sample: "The perfection of that noble instrument was apparent at all times. The tone was very large and very beautiful and the action gave instantaneous response. The Knabe helped my success greatly." Though the Knabe company was courteous to him, its pianos, he said privately, ranged from "superlative" to "not good at all."

the streets: at his concert in Dayton, he recalled, a boy in the front row had shouted, "Mommy, he looks like a girl!" So his hair was cut into the neat banker's trim then fashionable, and such was his celebrity that the haircut was reported in the press. Johnston was not shy about publicizing "the outstanding sensation of the year." One of his ads declared: "A new name has flashed suddenly into the pianistic heavens, a name that logically follows the great line of Liszt, Rubinstein and Paderewski. It is not an easy name to spell or to pronounce, but it is worth the effort. The name is Nyiregyházi." (With Johnston, he insisted on restoring the spelling of his surname.)

He returned to Carnegie Hall on October 1 and 23 (the latter would be his last appearance there – he was just eighteen), and he continued to draw large, adoring audiences. He had to give encores after every set of pieces, and at the end fans crowded the stage and the lights had to be turned off to induce them to go home. Some critics suggested that he had taken to heart the previous year's criticism. One wrote that he now performed "with a view of regulating and modifying certain vagaries of his piano playing." Before he had "played like a genius-smitten freak, in whom the freak outstared the genius and the genius seemed unaware of his own identity. Today persuasion or some manner of restraint has demonstrably curbed and corrected him and invested his work with a sobriety previously alien to it." But he was also now found to be a less "exalted," more "deliberate" performer. He couldn't win.*

During his first season under Johnston, he made several more high-profile appearances. On December 4, he participated in a "Hungarian program" with the Detroit Symphony Orchestra (repeated in Ann Arbor

---

* In a 1978 interview, he denied that he had modified his style at all. "They condemned me for excess and sought a more temperate approach. Then they heard for themselves what they had wanted to hear and praised themselves for hearing it. But I played no differently." He said he may have changed his programs a little – that was all. Still, the unanimity of the reviews in October 1921 is striking enough to make one wonder – and he *had* been stung by the mixed reviews in 1920.

Nyíregyházi during his second New York season, 1921–22, now sporting the short hair demanded by his new manager, R.E. Johnston. *(Photograph by Herman Mishkin. University of Southern California, on behalf of the U.S.C. Specialized Libraries and Archival Collections.)*

on December 12). On March 26, 1922, he received top billing in a concert of orchestral pieces and operatic arias at the Metropolitan Opera House. In May, he appeared at the annual music festival in Spartanburg, South Carolina. (On all three occasions he played Liszt's E-flat-major concerto.) For the most part, however, Johnston could not maintain the momentum of that sensational first season. Neither within nor outside New York did he secure the most prestigious bookings; concerts in smaller cities were his specialty. His circuit particularly favoured New England (especially New Jersey), and Nyíregyházi found himself saddled with the drudgery of playing, sometimes repeatedly, in cities like Bath, Elizabeth, Jersey City, Madison, Meridian, Morristown, Mt. Vernon, Newark, Paterson, Pt. Pleasant, Waterbury . . . A music magazine announced in the fall of 1922 that he "has left New York for a tour of twenty concerts which will keep him occupied until the holidays. He will play in Memphis, Nashville, Wooster, Milwaukee, Dayton, Greencastle, Indianapolis, Columbus, Cleveland, Hartford, Bristol, Montreal, Quebec, Syracuse, Chatham, Boston, and concerts on the Pacific Coast." Johnston had him playing at a women's club in Bridgeport, in a private home in Plainfield, at a high school in the Bronx, at a testimonial dinner for New York's police commissioner, and at a public exhibition of a piano that had belonged to Wagner. When a disenchanted Rubinstein complained of a similar diet of low-status concerts, Johnston replied, "There are too many goddamn pianists in this city and the managers are clamoring for Hofmann and Rachmaninoff. Here only the box office talks."

In truth, Johnston was relatively uninterested in pianists; he represented mostly singers, and they were the focus of his attention. According to an ad published in the fall of 1921, he represented only two pianists (Nyiregyházi and Rubinstein) and a couple of violinists, but a stable of singers including Titta Ruffo ("The World's Greatest Baritone") and the lyric soprano Anna Fitziu. (Most of the Metropolitan Opera's singers were represented by Johnston for their concert work.) He did not cultivate Nyiregyházi's career so much as put him to work serving his singers. Nyiregyházi was often compelled to appear as an "assisting artist" in what were principally vocal recitals – Johnston specialized in such mixed programs.* His first concert under Johnston, on March 23, 1921, was not auspicious: a mixed bill in Trenton, New Jersey, with a contralto and a glee club. Many more concerts as an assisting artist followed,

---

* An assisting artist was not an accompanist, but a soloist who performed short sets of pieces in a concert that focused on another principal performer, who had his or her own accompanist.

often with Fitziu or Ruffo,* also with the tenor Benjamino Gigli and the baritone Giuseppe De Luca. Nyiregyházi, Fitziu, and Ruffo spent much of that fall on tour, in Connecticut and New Jersey and as far afield as Denver and Kansas City.

Johnston also organized "The Biltmore Friday Morning Musicales," biweekly concerts (usually eight per season) held in the Hotel Biltmore, on Madison Avenue. Musicales featuring several artists in varied programs of serious and light music (and, often, a luncheon) were then popular with New York society – they gave rich women a break from shopping. In addition to his own artists, Johnston attracted some important singers and instrumentalists to these musicales (Geraldine Farrar, Percy Grainger, Wanda Landowska, Jacques Thibaud), and Nyiregyházi, who did one per season, shared programs with singers including Ruffo and Rosa Ponselle. Other hotels offered similar events, and Nyiregyházi appeared in some of them, too, and performed for the Beethoven Association and other New York musical societies.

He was almost always rapturously received, and in many cities the impresario wanted to rebook him at once. As an assisting artist, he generally received equal billing with singers, and was frequently singled out by reviewers; he could take the lion's share of the applause even from an artist of Ruffo's stature before a mostly Italian audience. (He remembered one headline: "HUNGARIAN PIANIST TRIUMPHS. RUFFO ALSO SCORES.") Still, of his work as an assisting artist, and of what Rubinstein called "those damned musicales," he said, "That was enough to kill any reputation. Audiences would think, 'My God! He's not a real star if he does not give solo concerts.'" Johnston's bookings, in short, were chipping away at his stature.

---

* Nyiregyházi had played for Ruffo in Budapest as a child, in 1912. Ruffo greatly admired him and was kind to him. When the two began working together in 1921, Ruffo wanted him to compose an opera for him on the myth of Prometheus. Nyiregyházi began working on the overture, but could not find inspiration and dropped the project.

LOST GENIUS

It was mostly in New York that Nyiregyházi earned hedging notices; elsewhere, he earned superlatives of the sort he had been accustomed to in Europe. Some of his greatest American triumphs were in New York's more musically cultivated rival city, Boston. On October 14 and 15, 1921, he made a sensational local debut with the Boston Symphony, in Liszt's A-major concerto. After the first concert, according to press reports, he was recalled five times, and audience members were abuzz. The concerto was repeated on October 20, at Harvard University, to satisfy public demand. The critics were overwhelmed. Olin Downes of the *Post* tracked Nyiregyházi down for a chat at his hotel after the first concert, and though known for an aversion to overly subjective or "sentimental" interpretations that strayed from the score, he was plainly dazzled by the eighteen-year-old:

> Mr. Nyiregyházi (pronounced as spelled!) had not only physical resources to play the concerto, but he had something rarer: as beautiful a singing tone, as noble and poetic a concept of the passages which demanded such treatment as any pianist the writer ever heard. . . .
>
> His rhythm, however capricious the rhythmic changes might seem, was never at fault. The orchestra rested on it, and [the conductor] Mr. [Pierre] Monteux exulted in it. His understanding of the structure of the rhapsodic virtuoso piece was so sympathetic and so clear that it had an unprecedented unity of effect. His technic [*sic*] is unnecessary to discuss. He has an apparently unlimited supply of it. The crowning fact was an interpretation all poetry, imagination, fire-youth.

In Boston, as everywhere else, the critics were astonished by Nyiregyházi's precociousness and virtuosity, but now there was no talk of immaturity; indeed, the critic for the *Transcript* defended Nyiregyházi's audacity, adding, "There is overmuch reticence, caution and repression among the young pianists of the day." He was praised for revealing the nobility and poetry and melancholy beneath the glittering surface of the concerto, and his "youth and individuality," his "large and rhapsodic" approach to interpretation, his "bardic sweep and clangor" were treated as rare, to be treasured, especially in Liszt. He made a much-heralded return to the Boston Symphony on November 27, 1922, again in Liszt's A-major concerto, this time in Hartford, Connecticut. Yet, though Johnston took out full-page ads in trade publications quoting the Boston reviews at length, the only recitals he arranged for Nyiregyházi in that city were in the role of assisting artist to another singer in 1922 and 1923.

It was in Boston, on New Year's Eve 1922, that Nyiregyházi also had the momentous experience of first hearing the Polish pianist and statesman Ignacy Jan Paderewski, who was making a triumphant comeback tour of the United States after five years away from the concert hall. He heard him shortly thereafter in New York, too, and was overwhelmed by Paderewski's power (including his ferocious fortissimo), his rich, operatic melodic tone, slow tempos, rhythmic freedom, and unapologetic changes to the score. He cared not a whit for Paderewski's legendary deficiencies of technique; he admired "the Romantic spirit, the abandon, the temperament," the monumentality and nobility of his conceptions, the naked emotionalism – the *soul*. In Liszt's Hungarian Rhapsody No. 2, he said, Paderewski "gave me a new idea of the terrible passion, inner fire, and abandon of the Gypsy," adding, "I don't think Liszt could play it better."*

In 1923, Nyiregyházi met with even more sensational success in California. He was managed locally by Merle Armitage, a multifaceted character who had had several careers before going into the concert

---

* "Strange," he said, "the two greatest interpreters of Liszt – Paderewski and Busoni – never studied with Liszt." He considered them more loyal Lisztians than Liszt's own pupils. He said, with his usual modesty, that the pianists on record who were the closest to the style of Liszt (and of Liszt's great contemporary Anton Rubinstein, with whom Nyiregyházi was often compared) were Paderewski, then Busoni, then himself.

business; the baritone John Charles Thomas called him "the most unlikely manager ever to enter the game as an impresario." Though he had enlightened tastes in literature and the arts, he was a clever and resourceful manager not shy about stirring up publicity. Having seen photos of Nyiregyházi with his long hair, he was dismayed to see less newsworthy short hair alight from the train. "Something had to be done," he recalled in his memoir *Accent on America*. So, with help from friendly newsmen, "we concocted a story which had a lot of human interest and was basically true. 'What does a prodigy do the first time he gets away from his mother?' our story inquired. 'Why, he gets a haircut, of course, so as to appear like a man.' Nyiregyhazi, free from the influence of his parent, had gone to the barber on the *20th Century Limited*, to be shorn of his youthful locks before the train reached Albany! We re-photographed Nyiregyhazi and all papers carried the story with 'before and after' pictures. This device, more effective than we had hoped, was largely responsible for a sold out house."

Nyiregyházi's scheduled recital in Los Angeles, on January 8, was followed by another added by popular demand, and he appeared in several nearby cities. Local critics reached for superlatives. The *Times* dubbed him "the musical sensation of the Coast," even though, as the *Examiner* carefully noted, "Los Angeles is not prone to rhapsodize over its musical visitors." Admittedly, the reviews leaned heavily on his athletics at the piano, his youth, his frailty; the *Evening Express* noted a "boyish modesty, quiet style, and sweetness of disposition" that made him "one of the most lovable personalities on the concert stage." From this tour dates Nyiregyházi's first brush with Hollywood. He was photographed with the silent-film comedian Harold Lloyd, who had invited him to the Hal Roach Studios in Culver City, where Lloyd was filming *Why Worry?*; later, he attended a star-studded party thrown by Lloyd, and played while guests danced. (A local columnist reported hearing him play jazz at another private function.) Frank Lloyd Wright attended one of Nyiregyházi's concerts, and later the two met and talked philosophy.

On January 30, Armitage wrote a letter to R.E. Johnston, which Johnston reprinted in his ads:

> I should like to write every concert manager in America about Erwin Nyiregyhazi, because every local manager is looking for just the thing this young man has.
>
> Nyiregyhazi gave six concerts under our management in Southern California, each one, including the Los Angeles appearances at Philharmonic Auditorium, to capacity audiences.
>
> To relate the facts sounds wild enough, for I have never seen such excitement at a recital of music for the piano. At his first concert he played fifty minutes of encores, and at his second concert, fifty two minutes of encores were demanded by three thousand people who cheered this lad like a foot-ball hero. The newspaper reviews were uniformely [sic] sensational; that is the only word to use.
>
> Nyiregyhazi is almost painfully modest; [he] knows the value of co-operation with the local manager. We know, because he was photographed with High-Powered motor cars, movie stars, and prominent club men during his stay in Los Angeles, and was the center of a dozen receptions and affairs of that sort.
>
> You can assure every local manager that a piano recital by Nyiregyhazi is about two hours of thrills.

8

Re-enacting

Nyiregyházi was now ready to compromise on the matter of Ampico piano rolls – the memory of the poverty he had endured after his disputes with the Wolfsohn Musical Bureau was still fresh – and to the American Piano Company he was still a desirable commodity. Indeed, its staff was taken aback by his gifts and by the stories that attended him; their nickname for him was "Nearer-My-God-to-Thee." The popular-music pianist Adam Carroll, a prolific Ampico artist, had some bizarre recollections of the "wild-looking" boy. "I remember Nyiregyházi who was born in a tree. During pregnancy, his mother was told she was going to give birth to a messiah so she climbed up into a tree and lived there. . . . One of our scouts who was looking for him, asked someone in a bar in Budapest if they knew about the boy who lives in a tree – can't talk – all he does is play music. That's how they found him." Wherever Carroll picked up this absurd tale, it says much about the sort of rumour that Nyiregyházi inspired. Nevertheless, the company viewed him as a major pianist; Carroll, for one, believed that, in terms of technique, "he put Horowitz to shame." But his fee was meagre: he was paid $50 per roll (of which

R.E. Johnston took 25 per cent), and earned no royalties. (The biggest pianists were paid in the hundreds.)

Twelve Nyiregyházi piano rolls were ultimately issued, though the first, which he recorded soon after signing with Johnston, almost ended his Ampico career:

> Sinding: "Prélude" in A-flat Major, Op. 34/No. 1 (issued in November 1921; catalogue number originally 111011K, later 60131H).

The company received complaints about this roll from several pianists, who pointed out that Nyiregyházi's interpretation often strayed from Sinding's score. And it did: he improvised freely on Sinding's ideas, playing fast and loose with arpeggios and other figuration and with accompanimental parts. The company was so concerned that his marketability might be compromised that he had to audition for its directors before being permitted to make new rolls; presumably he also had to pledge to behave in future. In the summer of 1922, he dutifully auditioned, and the directors loved what they heard. He recorded four more rolls in short order, and, a year later, his first rolls of music by Liszt:

> Tchaikovsky, arranged by Percy Grainger: Concert Paraphrase on the Flower Waltz from *The Nutcracker* (January 1923; 61613H).
> Leschetizky: "Étude héroïque," Op. 48/No. 3 (August 1923; 62281H).
> Kowalski: *Salut à Pesth (Marche hongroise)*, Op. 13 (November 1923; 62543H).
> Brahms: Rhapsody in B Minor, Op. 79/No. 1 (January 1924; 62703H).
> Liszt: Ballade No. 1 in D-flat Major (June 1924; 63253H).
> Liszt: "Mazeppa," No. 4 from the *Transcendental Études* (November 1924; 63703H).

He recorded three more rolls, all in one day, early in 1925:

Glazunov, arranged by Wladimir Stcherbatcheff: *La danse de Salomée*, Op. 90/No. 2 (April 1925; 64283H).
Cleve: Ballade in E-flat Major, Op. 8 (June 1925; 64603H).
Granados: "Quejas ó la maja y el ruiseñor" [laments or the maiden and the nightingale], from *Goyescas* (September 1925; 64953H).

His last two issued rolls were likely recorded in 1926:*

Grieg: *Lyric Pieces*: "Notturno," Op. 54/No. 4 (September 1926; 66523H).
Blanchet: "Au jardin du vieux serail (Adrinople)" [in the garden of the old harem (Adrianople)], from *Turquie*, Op. 18/No. 3 (May 1927; 67583H).

The Ampico, an electrically powered pneumatic mechanism that was fitted into a sliding drawer attached beneath the keyboard of the piano, created a "reproducing piano," a more sophisticated creature than the ordinary foot-pumped player piano. Its aim was to play perforated paper rolls that would automatically reproduce not just the notes the pianist played when he made the master roll, but the expressive effects – or, as the publicists liked to put it, the "soul" of the performer. Ampico's own term was *re-enacting piano*: the goal was to re-enact, as closely as the technology permitted, a particular performance on the owner's own piano.

The re-enacting piano was a roaring success. Ampico's January 1923 catalogue, the first in which Nyiregyházi appeared, was three hundred pages long and listed 188 classical artists, a who's who of great pianists and composers of the day. Like other Ampico artists, Nyiregyházi was

---

* He recorded four more rolls of works by Liszt early in 1926, but, for unknown reasons, they were never released, and the master rolls have never been found.

required to sign testimonials written by publicists,[*] and to allow demonstrations during concerts in an effort to persuade listeners that one could not tell the roll from the real thing. (A pianist would play an instrument fitted with an Ampico mechanism and at certain points in the performance would stop and allow his roll of the same piece to take over, ideally with no discernible break in musical continuity.) Like many of his colleagues, he found such events demeaning, and he came to believe that the company was interested more in money than in music.

Nyiregyházi with the silent-film comedian Harold Lloyd, in Culver City, January or February 1923, during his first tour of Southern California. Lloyd is holding Nyiregyházi's just-released Ampico piano roll of the Flower Waltz from Tchaikovsky's *The Nutcracker. (Reproduced by Joel Moran, from the April 1923 issue of Screenland.)*

An Ampico roll was as much a construction as a recording. Through most of his tenure at Ampico, Nyiregyházi recorded on the company's Model A system, which captured notes, tempos, and basic pedalling, but expressive nuances like dynamics and half- and quarter-pedalling had to be added to the master roll by an editor. Sometimes, the editor made notes in a score while the pianist played, though often enough the editor relied on his memory of the performance, or guesswork, or

---

[*] Sample: "In perpetuating my playing for the generations to come it was but natural that I should desire to have my playing re-enacted with absolute fidelity. I satisfied myself that the Ampico alone could do this, and for that reason I record exclusively for the Ampico."

his own musical initiative, when putting expression into the roll. A performance could be "improved" – the tone made warmer, wrong notes corrected, sloppy rhythms and textures clarified, though certain effects could only be mimicked using technological trickery. As a rule, the artist was consulted in order to ensure that the final roll accurately represented his interpretation, but a roll could represent the editor's thinking as much as the pianist's. Even where it had the artist's blessing, it was less a faithful reproduction of a particular performance than an idealized representation of how the artist (or editor) wanted the performance to sound. Nyiregyházi rarely recorded a selection more than once in the Ampico studio, and was not involved in the editing of his rolls. He was dismayed by the limitations of the system. It could not replicate his volcanic fortissimo, for instance, and editors were known to quieten extremely loud playing in deference to living-room acoustics.

His evaluations of his rolls were inconsistent – it depended on whom he was talking to. Some acquaintances recall that he praised his rolls when he heard them played by a pristine restored mechanism; others recall that he dismissed *all* of his rolls as "not representative of my playing." The more tempered views he expressed in private interviews with his last wife are probably more reliable: with some consistency, he pronounced the Sinding and Cleve rolls to be decent reproductions of his playing, the Tchaikovsky and Glazunov good to excellent, the Granados best of all. But none of them, he said, captured the peculiar tone and "fervour" of his playing with the fidelity of a recording.

Still, the rolls do offer some insights into his playing. They corroborate, first of all, contemporary accounts of the breathtaking ease with which he commanded the resources of the piano. (The pianist Moriz Rosenthal told him that his roll of "Mazeppa" was "magnificent" – and he had heard Liszt himself play it.) Even taking into account the constraints that bound him after the Sinding episode, the rolls also reveal his impulsiveness, his fluid approach to rhythm and texture (he often let his hands fall subtly out of sync), his ardent melodic playing, his

A Young Liszt of the Pianoforte

fondness for revealing counterpoint, and, finally, his bold underscoring of expressive nuance.

As radio and disc-recording technologies improved through the 1920s, the popularity of the reproducing piano declined, and the whole business was devastated by the stock-market crash of 1929; Ampico produced its last rolls in 1941. Nyiregyházi's rolls proved popular enough to continue selling over the years, and to be prized by some aficionados. All twelve were still available in the last Ampico catalogue, published in 1940, but by then Nyiregyházi himself had been largely forgotten.

9

Decline and Fall

Around the time of his success in California, Nyiregyházi's public-ity was at its height, and his first concert in New York in more than a year, on February 27, 1923, was a triumphant return. A large and receptive audience filled Aeolian Hall, and the reviews were full of praise and even awe. "If one permitted oneself the free use of superla-tives, adjectives would run riot over the available space," the composer Deems Taylor wrote in the *World*. "For surely no piano rendition more titanic and stupendous than Mr. Nyiregyházi's performance of the opening [Bach-]Liszt Fantasia and Fugue has been heard this season." His playing was still improving. He had recently turned twenty, and even the New York critics were now hearing interpretive wisdom to match his technique. The critic for the *Musical Courier* wrote:

> Technically, from a purely mechanical point of view, he appears to have reached the transcendental class. Any further development in this matter would appear to be impossible. And whatever technical difficulties the music may present are overcome with perfect ease and with a variety of nuance that admits of every detail of expression

being brought to the foreground. This is remarkable enough, but, after all, many a pianist has had technic [*sic*] without having anything else. But Nyiregyházi has everything else. Down to the finest details of staccato, legato, rubato, balance of tone, tasteful and musicianly use of the pedals, he seems to be guided by a deep-felt instinct that forces him to do the right thing at the right moment and raises his playing into a class with the best of artists, even those most mature in their art. There are rare moments, indeed, where his youthful exuberance and enthusiasm seems to run away with him, but that only makes his playing all the more charming, spontaneous and appealing. . . . One does not hesitate to say that Nyiregyházi is a great pianist.

Yet, for all this, the recital was only cursorily noted in some of the major papers, like the *Times*. It was a bad sign – evidence that R.E. Johnston's indifferent management was undercutting his reputation. The April 19 *Musical Courier*, under the headline "NYIREGYHÁZI IN DEMAND," noted: "Day by day, in every way, Erwin Nyiregyházi, the extraordinary young pianist, is becoming more and more popular. To prove this one need only glance at his list of engagements during the month of April: Philadelphia, 2; Brooklyn, 4; Albany, 6; Boston, 8; Dover, 11; Plainfield, 13; Wilmington, 16; Baltimore, 17; Reading, 19, and New York, 21." But many of these appearances were as an assisting artist. Admittedly, on April 26, at a musicale with two singers in Atlantic City, it was Nyiregyházi who, according to a local paper, swept listeners off their feet, provoked applause in the middle of a piece, and had to play many encores. But who cared about a musicale in Atlantic City?

Nyiregyházi's mother, brother, and grandmother were still living in Berlin, and he had kept in touch with them, sending money when he could. Johnston goaded him often to write to his mother, and even wrote to her on his behalf – beautiful letters, Nyiregyházi recalled. He

Nyiregyházi in New York, March 8, 1923 – at the cusp of his fame and on the threshold of his decline. *(Photograph by the Bain News Service. University of Southern California, on behalf of the U.S.C. Specialized Libraries and Archival Collections.)*

was anxious to see his family and old friends again, and to exploit his American successes in Europe. He spent most of the summers of 1921 and 1922 at a resort in the Catskill Mountains, but decided to spend the next summer in Europe. He arrived in Berlin at the end of May, with only two dollars to his name, and had to solicit help at once from his mother (Johnston also sent him a monthly allowance). The May 3 *Musical Courier* had announced that, after a few more concerts in New York State, he planned to tour Germany, Hungary, Norway, France, and Italy, but it appears that he performed only in Kristiania, where, in September, he gave one orchestral concert and two recitals. The public was enthusiastic, though the critical response now was mixed, and the concerts were not well attended. Already in Europe he was beginning to be forgotten. By the time Géza Révész's book came out in English, as *The Psychology of a Musical Prodigy*, in 1925, a reviewer in the *Musical Times* in London could write: "But what and who is E.N. now? He is said to be following the career of a pianist in the United States, and he is twenty-two. If he were a second Mozart we in Europe should probably have become acquainted with his name before now. He may be successful in the U.S.A., but so far as musical Europe is concerned, he is obscure." In October, back in the United States, Nyiregyházi took part in the annual Maine Music Festival, and was by all accounts a phenomenon unequalled in its history. People sat literally on the edges of chairs, applauded furiously, stamped their feet; his special affinity with Liszt's E-flat-major concerto provoked comparisons with Liszt's own playing. After a concert on October 6, a critic in the *Bangor Daily News* wrote: "Nyiregyházi has no rivals. Others are pianists. He is a magician – a god, who has given the machine capacities it had not previously possessed, a Piper of Hamelin, who draws the wondering crowds after him by his magic art." He made a side trip to Montreal, to give a joint concert with a baritone on October 11 – now, at least, it was the *singer* who was referred to as the assisting artist. His prowess (especially in Liszt and Scriabin) took everyone by surprise, and his adoring audience demanded more than an hour's worth of encores. The critic of the *Montreal Daily Star* actually praised the *piano* – for surviving the onslaught. By popular demand, he performed (with an assisting singer) twice more in Montreal that same season, on December 2 and April 13, always in huge programs replete with encores that left some listeners exhausted.

In New York, he had the pleasant task of judging a beauty contest overseen by Rudolph Valentino, who, it was reported, said that his hundred-man jury "would be incomplete without the name of Nyiregyházi." (He was the youngest judge.) At the time, Valentino was off movie screens because of a contract dispute, and to pay the bills he undertook a personal-appearance tour with his wife to endorse a line of beauty products. Throughout 1923, they toured dozens of North American cities, where Valentino often oversaw contests organized by the Beauty Foundation of America, and local winners from eighty-eight cities were gathered in a "pageant of pulchritude" at Madison Square Garden, on November 28.

Nyiregyházi returned to California in January 1924, for more concerts in Los Angeles and half-a-dozen nearby cities, to the usual acclaim. While he was there, he celebrated his twenty-first birthday.

Sensational successes like those in Maine, Montreal, and California were still being outweighed by musical drudgery. Returned from California, Nyiregyházi faced a fresh lineup of undistinguished gigs: recitals on Long Island and in Sandusky, Ohio; a Shriners convention in Kansas City; a concert of the Rubinstein Society at the Waldorf Astoria; and, in May, an eight-concert tour of New England. He should have been a star. During his first American seasons, on the basis of only a few appearances, qualified critics were willing to describe him as "a leader among the new pianists of the day," for whom "it seems safe to predict an unusually brilliant future." But now, in the spring of 1924, handed mostly trivial, poorly publicized, spottily reviewed bookings, he was becoming increasingly desperate.

Soon after signing with Johnston, he realized he had made a mistake. A former travelling salesman, Johnston was not a person to inspire confidence. As Arthur Rubinstein described him, "He was broad-shouldered and had the face of an alcoholic: big teary eyes, a large nose of indeterminate color, clean-shaven, with a shock of blond and gray hair. He must have been in his sixties." He had a wooden leg, which he was not shy about removing for shock or comic effect, was missing fingers, sported a toupee with a will of its own, and, according to the pianist André Benoist, had a "screechy soprano voice" and "wore very obviously artificial teeth that rattled when he spoke." Rubinstein portrayed him as ill-mannered and scrappy, with a thick New York accent ("This boy's got poisonality, I tell ya") and a penchant for hardboiled, curse-strewn conversation – like a character out of an old boxing movie. He went by "R.E.," and seems to have fancied himself a man of the world. Rubinstein remembered him as "a full-blooded Irishman" well acquainted with New York's Irish contingent, including the police. The Biltmore's bar was a second office for him, and he appears to have been a loud, sloppy drunk. Rubinstein wrote that "R.E., good and drunk, had to be helped to his apartment more frequently than not" from the Biltmore, and he expressed surprise, once, to encounter him sober.

Nyiregyházi hated Johnston's coarse personality, his philistinism and commercial motives, his use of undignified colloquialisms like "What's the diff?" He felt demeaned by Johnston, who (shades of his mother) treated him more like a child than like a mature artist. He was compelled to play flashy music on an upright piano to entertain Johnston's secretaries, and after a while came to dread going into the office. Moreover, Johnston interfered with his repertoire. Johnston preferred virtuoso showpieces with commercial appeal – he derided Brahms, for instance, as a "beer composer" – and Nyiregyházi had to give in to a degree. ("I let myself be pressured. It's my nature.") When he was not under Johnston's thumb, he broadened his repertoire. His January 7, 1924, recital in Los Angeles, for instance, opened with his arrangement of Tchaikovsky's *Francesca da Rimini*, a "symphonic fantasy" after Dante's "Inferno," and his January 19 recital opened with Scriabin's Fifth Sonata, a then radically modern piece.

The final straw was that he felt slighted financially. Rubinstein, after signing with Johnston, had been warned by several friends that "he does not have the best reputation for honesty in his dealings with artists" and "was sometimes untrustworthy," and Benoist, though he acknowledged Johnston's "heart of gold," noted that in business matters he was "the most unscrupulous blackguard imaginable" and "would have fleeced his own grandmother." Nyiregyházi soon found this out for himself. In May 1921, he was paid $100 to entertain Prince Albert of Monaco at a private function, but later discovered that Johnston had been paid $500, and so had pocketed 80 per cent. Their contract for the 1923–24 season specified that Nyiregyházi was to receive 50 per cent of the gross receipts of his concerts, with Johnston guaranteeing that that sum would not be less than $12,500 (out of which Nyiregyházi was to pay his own travel and hotel expenses). Nyiregyházi claimed that by the end of the season he had honoured his contract but had been paid only $6,824. Johnston offered to settle the matter for a thousand dollars, but Nyiregyházi refused, and sued Johnston for the amount owing – $5,576 – plus interest and court costs.

Money may not have been the only issue. Nyiregyházi claimed that, around this same time, Johnston discovered that he was Jewish, and confronted him, saying that if he *was* Jewish, they were finished; this was apparently a shadow motivation for the lawsuit. He had been warned to keep his religion a secret in America, and did so. The warnings proved valid. Carl von Laurenz, for instance, was rabidly anti-Semitic; Nyiregyházi saw him rant and curse and spit at the mere mention of Jews. It was commonplace for closeted Jews to be blackmailed, and Nyiregyházi was threatened with exposure several times in the early twenties, though he always refused to pay up. Some of the threats were anonymous, but, according to a note left by his last wife, on at least two occasions he may have been blackmailed by his own American relatives.

In June 1924, perhaps fleeing the coming legal dust-up, he sailed again for Europe, to visit the Cleves in Kristiania and his family in Berlin. (He never saw his mother or grandmother again.) He briefly entertained the mad idea of moving to Brazil, but returned to America in August.

His lawsuit, in the Supreme Court of the County of New York, now moved forward. His original complaint, dated July 21, set forth his claims. Johnston's answer, dated September 8, stated that the American Piano Company had agreed to arrange twenty concerts for Nyiregyházi in 1923–24, and to pay a fee of $300 for each; the company further agreed to pay $50 for every concert (up to a maximum of fifty concerts) in which Nyiregyházi used a Knabe piano. Nyiregyházi did receive the $50 bonus for thirty-seven concerts – a total of $1,850 (of which Johnston's share was 50 per cent). However, Johnston stated that American failed to arrange the promised concerts, and thus failed to provide fees totalling $6,000. Johnston claimed that he and Nyiregyházi had agreed verbally that Johnston would not be responsible for this money should American fail to arrange those concerts – and thus, by his reckoning, he was required to guarantee Nyiregyházi only $6,500 for the season, and had met that obligation. Johnston also claimed that he and Nyiregyházi had amended their original contract on March 1, 1924: for the balance of that season, Nyiregyházi would keep *all* of his fees and pay his own expenses, and would further agree to a new contract for 1924–25, whereby he would continue to keep all his fees, pay all his own expenses, and pay Johnston a 20 per cent commission; in exchange, he would waive any right to a guaranteed income. Moreover, in an amended answer dated October 15, Johnston accused Nyiregyházi of bad faith, claiming that his client had agreed to all the stated provisions while knowingly intending not to abide by them should American breach its offer of concerts – in essence, that he procured his original contract with Johnston by fraud. (The notion of a wily Nyiregyházi duping a naive Johnston can only be described as rich.)

The surviving court filings hint at missteps on the part of Nyiregyházi's lawyer. For one thing, he got the amount owing wrong by $100 – he should have been suing for $5,676. Nyiregyházi had the impression that his lawyer was venal as well as incompetent. "My lawyer and [Johnston's] lawyer were in cahoots," he claimed in 1978. "They double-crossed me." In any event, the case dragged on through the fall and winter. There was petty wrangling over the spelling of Johnston's name and his legal status as an individual or corporation, and over each other's legal strategy. Nyiregyházi's lawyer's claim, in February, that Johnston was using "questionable defenses" in order to delay judgment rings true. Johnston probably figured that dragging out the suit would impoverish Nyiregyházi and render him desperate to settle.

That is precisely what happened. Reported in the press, the lawsuit made him less attractive to other managers – and Johnston, after all, was not the first New York manager with whom he had quarrelled. His pride, too, was a hurdle. "I had to try to find other managers, and I was asked to make auditions," he recalled. "I, who had played with Nikisch and Monteux, to audition for silly ladies! I would not do it."

He was hopelessly incompetent as his own manager, and his upbringing had equipped him poorly for the assumption of adult responsibilities, but he worked where he could. A friend at Knabe arranged with a San Francisco piano dealer for Nyiregyházi to spend October participating in Ampico demonstration concerts in various Bay Area cities. On October 1, he introduced himself to local music critics in a private recital, with a heavy program that included Liszt's sonata (he no longer felt bound by Johnston's taste in programming). Redfern Mason, in the *Examiner*, wrote of "a rhapsodic magnificence about the performance," and called the playing "stunning" in both senses of the word. "Technically, he has arrived," he wrote. "When he grows in lyric grace, he will probably be one of the small group of eminent pianists." (He was still just twenty-one.) Ray C.B. Brown, in the *Chronicle*, was less reticent: "His technique is amazing in its Lisztian virtuosity. I doubt if there is a living pianist of his age comparable to him in power and swiftness of execution. One has to go to a veteran master like Rosenthal for a likeness. And he has a rushing fury of speed at times that even Rosenthal does not attain." Thereafter, Nyiregyházi gave eight concerts a week in the Bay Area.

He returned to New York, in early November, with most of the $800 he had earned still in hand and confidently rented an apartment on West End Avenue, near Eighty-fifth Street, that had a telephone and maid service. (Knabe still provided him with a practice piano.) But the money soon ran out, and he returned for a time to the Hotel Grenoble. Through the spring and summer of 1925, with his lawsuit still pending, his life was unsettled. He was often broke, and slept where he had to – in a rooming house, on the floor of a flophouse, occasionally on the subway (he liked the shuttle between Times Square and Grand Central Station), or, when he could not afford that, on a park bench. Invited for dinner one evening at the home of the violinist Mischa Elman (he dated one of Elman's sisters in the early twenties), he donned his formal wear and walked the five miles there and back. "I didn't have the five cents for the subway and was too proud to ask for money," he said. Some days he had little or nothing to eat.

He still found concert work around New York; sometimes he was even busy. On April 16, he gave a joint recital with a tenor at the Plaza Hotel. On April 19, he was the assisting artist in a vocal concert at the Metropolitan Opera House. On May 5, he was the pianist in a "memory contest" for young musicians. Private concerts increasingly provided the few dollars he needed to keep going. His recollections from this period include performances in private clubs, in the homes of wealthy patrons, in the basement of an apartment building where a good piano happened to be stored. Knabe still paid him $50 whenever he used one of their pianos, even for a private concert, and the company found some work for him: they sponsored the memory contest, and, on April 4, 1925, he played at a dance and musicale at Knabe Hall.

He gave concerts for the Hungarian community, too. One country-man, a disreputable-seeming fellow named Rasko (or possibly Rosko), found Nyiregyházi some work at this time. Usually he made just $10, though he made $15 playing at a Republican benefit banquet, where he was praised by Coolidge's vice-president, Charles G. Dawes, and $20 playing for a large gathering at Harry Houdini's house. A few hours before the latter performance, he announced that he did not feel like playing, at which Rasko, he claimed, "horsewhipped me across the face," taking the attitude, "Who the hell are you to break an appointment with Houdini?" And so he went to the party. Houdini was greatly impressed. "How can you play the piano as you do?" he said. Nyiregyházi replied, "You don't tell me your secrets and I won't tell you my secrets."

It was Rasko who, sometime around the fall of 1925, arranged for Nyiregyházi to perform for a large audience at Sing Sing prison. He accepted enthusiastically, claiming to empathize with the sufferings of prisoners, and he treated the audience with respect, offering a serious, substantial program. Through music, he thought, he could speak to the prisoners' plight and offer them solace and hope, accomplishing (as he characteristically put it) "a great task in the unending fight for the cultural progress of the human race and the unending endeavor to help the downtrodden and disadvantaged." He was received with cheers that bordered on pandemonium; afterward, some prisoners wept and embraced him. Later, invited to dine with the warden, he insisted on being served the same food as the prisoners. He earned just $25 at Sing Sing, but described the event as more satisfying than his Carnegie Hall recitals. Honest, direct responses from "sincere" listeners not "poisoned" by musical education always meant more to him than the praise of critics and the plaudits of "phonies all dressed up like monkeys."

He had pleasant memories of playing for New York gangsters, too, including henchmen of Al Capone and John Dillinger. He admired the impeccable manners, grooming, and dress of the gangsters he met, and sported derby hats in homage to them. They called him "Herr Professor" and treated him with honesty and respect, he said, and genuinely appreciated his music. In the mid-1920s, he encountered gangsters regularly at his favourite haunt, Beefsteak Charlie's, and some of them arranged private concerts for him – they were too sensitive to his pride, he said, merely to give him a handout. He remembered these events fondly. (Sometimes the gangsters were joined by politicians, judges, lawyers, businessmen – such was Prohibition society.) For gangsters, "it had to be lyrical, sweet melodies," so he usually played Chopin or excerpts from popular Italian operas. "The more sentimental the better. These were very dangerous men crying tears. I think Chopin reminded them of their mothers." At the end of a concert, he would be thanked extravagantly, handed money discreetly in an envelope, and chauffeured home. A collection after one such concert netted him $2,000, enough to support him for months. Through a gangster friend he met Jack Dempsey, who developed great affection for him. He remembered playing Chopin on Dempsey's piano, surrounded by girls, while the boxer slung a beefy arm over his shoulder and wiped away tears.

Artistically, Nyiregyházi was still at the top of his form, but without proper management he had no career. He was never better than temporarily out of poverty. He resorted to giving piano lessons – something he never enjoyed – and had to accept charity from time to time. But when he did scrape together some cash, he did not always husband it cautiously. "I was idealistic and would go to the Ritz Carlton for a superb lunch as soon as I had five dollars," he said. "I loved luxury, although I was the Count of No-Account. And in those days five dollars was a lot of money!" The worse his straits, the more determinedly he tried to maintain some little contact with the aristocratic life to which he felt entitled. He filled his days however he could. He composed prolifically, and when he had the money he would go to the movies, sometimes several times a day. Often, though, he was bored, lonely, frustrated, and depressed.

On May 19, 1925, his lawsuit against Johnston was discontinued by mutual consent, and, as a kind of settlement, he made a new arrangement with R.E. for the 1925–26 season. He was desperate for any kind of management, and Johnston probably saw an easy way to be rid of an irritant while making a little money. The new terms, for Nyiregyházi, were appalling: for a fee of $3,000 (plus some expenses), doled out as a monthly allowance, he agreed to give an unspecified number of concerts over seven months – to play wherever and whenever and as often as he was asked to do so. (Johnston guaranteed an additional $2,000 for advertising and for his own cut.) Nyiregyházi estimated that he gave some fifty concerts from October 1925 through the following April, most of them in small cities around New England (he got as far west as Milwaukee, where he played for a week in a movie theatre). He averaged two concerts a week, earning about $60 per concert – more than enough to put him back in good clothes and food, but insulting as a concert fee. A few decent jobs came his way: on December 20, he played Liszt's Hungarian Fantasy with the State Symphony Orchestra, before an audience of about ten thousand, in a benefit concert at the new Madison Square Garden. Among the featured performers were

Rosa Ponselle, the young Isaac Stern, and a visiting Ernő Dohnányi (Nyiregyházi had not seen him since 1918, and never saw him again). An appearance in April, with Albert Vertchamp's string quartet, in a Dvorak quintet, also got some press.

By June, the contract with Johnston having run its course, he was broke again. He returned to playing private concerts – at the Harrow Club and the Camera Club, in the home of a French nobleman – though he was also beholden to friends for money. It was at this time that he held, for a few months, the only non-musical job he ever had: carrying fabric from one room to another in a silk factory.

10

Love and Marriage

"You know what my biggest problem has been in life?" Nyiregyházi said in his seventies. "My pecker!" But when he arrived in America, he was still a virgin, having had limited, mostly confusing and frustrating experiences of sex. Through his teens and early twenties, the subject was more and more urgently on his mind. (He actually worried about finding formal attire that would hide an erection during a concert. He tried a jockstrap but found it too uncomfortable.) Not long after his arrival, he began to have serious girlfriends, including one of R.E. Johnston's secretaries, Maria Adele Király, whom he called Adele. She fell in love with him after hearing him play, wanted to marry him and have children, and admired him as a strong, reasonable, and honourable – though too-bashful – young man.[*] In the fall of 1922, they became engaged, though they did not even kiss until the following spring. Her family's reaction, typically, followed gender lines: her mother and sister were crazy about him, her father disliked him. Johnston discouraged the

---

[*] These were comments he recalled reading in Adele's diary, which she showed to him. She also wrote, "He should take care of his teeth." (He didn't.)

union, saying that women's musical clubs would not engage a married artist, though, according to Nyiregyházi, Johnston, a married man, was himself interested in Adele. Nyiregyházi's mother, too, predictably, registered her disapproval, by letter from Berlin.

His affection for Adele competed with his growing love for the daughters of the Norwegian composer Halfdan Cleve, Signy and Astrid. In Kristiania, in the summer of 1923, Signy got him under the piano and "squeezed me in the right spot" – yet he retained affection for Astrid, too. When he returned to America, he wrote jointly to the sisters declaring his love for both of them; their father later told him that while his letter had been wonderfully idealistic it had sown confusion and jealousy in the girls. In December 1923, he broke off his engagement with Adele, and continued what he called "a very hot correspondence" with Signy – already he was behaving as though he had no control over his romantic feelings. The following January, while visiting San Francisco, he impulsively proposed to a girl who worked in a music shop, just minutes after dispatching a transatlantic telegram to Signy professing his love. In March, he wrote to Cleve: "Anyone who would doubt the genuineness of my love for Signy – which I do not at all pursue for the purpose of seduction or abduction – would injure and offend me in the extreme." But when he returned to Kristiania that summer, she told him they were finished; he, in protest, briefly grew a beard.*

At this point, his sexual experience consisted of kissing and foreplay. On tour in New England in 1924, he recalled, he masturbated for the first time, and thereafter began doing so several times a day. His frustration intensified with time, and as he slipped into poverty he despaired of ever forming a fulfilling sexual union with a woman. Finally, around his twenty-second birthday, he lost his virginity to the twentyish Gertrude Schultheiss, who was estranged from her family

---

* Other of his reassurances to Cleve make amusing reading in light of his later behaviour: "[I] never drink alcohol, never smoke, I behave honourably, like a true 'gentleman' . . . thanks to my colossal self-control: 'sensuality' has not yet gobbled me up."

Signy Cleve. *(Sven Oluf Auguste Cleve Sørensen.*
Reproduced by Jørn Fossheim.)

in New Jersey, wealthy brewers of German descent (there is still a
Schultheiss brewery in Berlin). She had had many love affairs and
may have worked as a call girl. Nyiregyházi was never sure – she
never charged *him*. He called her "sort of a semi-prostitute" whom
various men supported. For the experienced Gertrude, this naive
young foreigner was a cause: in her mind, by sleeping with him she
was saving his soul – from masturbation. She shared an apartment on
the Upper West Side with a young friend named Marie, a chubby,
buxom divorcée who worked as an exotic dancer in a Hawaiian joint
that was a front for prostitution. (He remembered playing the girls'
upright piano for Gertrude while Marie serviced a sailor in another
room.) Soon, he was having sex with both women.

He was shy, crushingly insecure about women, poor and with limited prospects, not extravagantly endowed physically (he described his penis as "refined"), yet women were always drawn to him, and he was often a passive recipient of sexual attention. In the summer of 1923 in Berlin, for instance, after he had had his tonsils removed, a nurse had masturbated him. (His mother had told the nurse that he was ignorant of sex, and later asked him if the nurse had been "nice" to him.) That sort of thing happened to him all the time. Women were drawn by his genius and temperament and often offered themselves to him. The woman had to make the first move, or at least make her willingness known, he said, to encourage him and overcome his native reticence. He never lacked for women willing to do so.

His long-delayed introduction to sex threw open a floodgate. Sex became a consuming passion in his life, as important to him as music, a quotidian need like food or drink. He came to view sexuality as the key to his – anyone's – personality, and as a performer and composer he insisted on finding room for the expression of explicitly sexual feelings. Like every other aspect of his psychology, his sexuality was writ large. He would fall in love with hopeless passion, fall out of love with intense bitterness. Yet whatever comfort and reassurance and companionship sex brought him did not last. He was surely, to some degree, trying to fill the emptiness where his mother's love should have been – a hopeless task, as his chronic womanizing attests. In satisfying his sexual urges, he once more displayed the psychology of an adolescent or child – or, it often appeared, a toddler, demanding instant gratification. Women of any age, race, or social stratum, un-attached or married, beautiful or plain, were available and desirable to him. In this respect he was a true democrat. "For me to say no," he said, "is very difficult."

As a "great soul" – a peer of Liszt and Wilde – he felt entitled to all honest expressions of his sexuality, even if it meant loving several women at the same time, and pursuing relationships with all of them, while still having anonymous, purely physical encounters where required, too. When he sought mere sexual release, he justified it as a business transaction; when he sought a loftier union, he justified it as an expression of his highest spiritual aspirations. Of course, others often saw him as simply a lecher, and he seemed oblivious to the hurt he caused. He claimed to be sanguine about infidelity on the part of his women as long as they did not lie about it – for him, duplicity was worse than infidelity – though he was hardly immune to jealousy.

He insisted on the nobility of sex, hated the hypocrisy that surrounded it in America, and saw no contradiction between his high ideals and his sex mania. Sex, for him, was an expression of the "life force," not something base or unrefined or merely playful. "Sex is not vulgar!" he insisted. "When I screw, it is sublime!" His love letters were ardent and flowery,* and he insisted that "a woman's body is holy to me," though his and others' recollections suggest that, for all his adoration, he was more selfish than attentive as a lover.

His attitude toward sex was a recipe for a lifetime's muddle and torment, and his juggling of relationships was complicated by all sorts of predictable problems, from venereal disease to blackmail. He followed his sexual whims and appetites apparently blind to the consequences, and he enraged many men by the effect he had on their wives and girlfriends. (Of his infidelity, he quipped, "You know I can't adhere to the score!") Furthermore, he often relied on the women in his life

---

* In one typical letter from 1961, he looks forward to when "I shall again *see you* – behold the *wonder* of your Darling face – touch it – touch your Darling skin – and any and all parts of your *adorable* Body the most wonderful, *spiritualized* body in the World – touching it – with understanding – is like coming in contact with a wonderful, tremendous, delicate and exquisite, *ineffable* creation of a great poet-genius, such as *Oscar Wilde, Liszt, Chopin, Puccini,* and some of the other great ones – *not* excluding . . . well, *who* could *that* be?"

for material support; Adele, already, was occasionally lending him money. Even in poverty he could attract wealthy, high-born women, though he was also a keen explorer of the sexual underworld – street prostitutes, call girls, sexual massage, porno movies. He saw nothing wrong with a great artist standing in line, like a soldier, at a whorehouse, and he thought ill of people who looked down on prostitutes, whom he considered noble.

He flirted from the start with certain sexual predilections – a taste for black women, a sado-masochistic side (he was fond of a punishing kind of sexual massage). And he could draw sexual satisfaction not only from women. Many people assumed he was homosexual, and he was as attractive to gay men as to women. He was often the recipient of male advances, which he tended to accept with his usual passivity. He told his last wife about standing on a crowded streetcar and discovering that the man he was facing had begun to grope him, to which he responded with surprise but nothing like outrage. Once, in his twenties, when looking for sex, he inquired with a cabbie, who drove him to a male brothel. "I preferred a female to a male," he said, but in terms that implied that he cared little one way or the other. He noted that he had more inhibitions with women, whereas "at a male whorehouse they know what I want." His friendships with men sometimes seemed to have a romantic element even where they were not overtly sexual. He was known to hold hands with male friends, and address them as "darling," "baby," "angel."

He never identified himself as homosexual, and in fact took pains to assure people he was not gay. He professed to admire the "toughness" of a "real man," and insisted that he was, in his own way, "a terribly masculine man" (and a "masculine" pianist). But he protested too much. His deep insecurity about his masculinity (surely another legacy of his mother's infantilizing him) led him to cover up whatever sexual ambiguities he may have entertained. He rarely discussed the homosexual encounters in his life, and then never with the same relish as he did his heterosexual affairs. At the end of his life, to a prospective biographer, he insisted that he was "one-hundred-percent straight" and had never had a gay affair; he said he had nothing against homosexuality on principle, but found it "disgusting" and did not want to associate with homosexuals. The tone of his interviews with his last wife, however, does not suggest that he was exactly ashamed of homosexual leanings or experiences; perhaps, with homosexuality as with Jewishness, fear rather than shame was the operative rationale for covering up. In any event, the deep, long-term sexual relationships he sought were always with women and, according to every evidence, were genuine. But that his sexuality might also have been multifaceted is hardly surprising.

Through the summer of 1926, Nyiregyházi lived with Gertrude Schultheiss, but that fall he was tempted into marriage by a woman who offered him a way out of poverty: Mary Margaret Kelen, a Hungarian and a newspaperwoman – she worked at the *Daily Mirror*, a scandal sheet. The following year, when the marriage had gone sour, he recalled their meeting in court papers quoted in the New York *Daily News*:

> "I met her at a party on Sept. 29, 1926. On Oct. 3 she told me that unless I married her I couldn't visit her at her home. I told her I had no money and she forced me to accept a check for $30.
>
> "Only four days after I met her she proposed. She said she was in good circumstances – had upwards of $50,000 – and said she would spend it all to gain me universal recognition in my career.
>
> "I begged for two weeks to think it over. She gave me one day. The next day we went to the Municipal building and she filled out the marriage license application. Then I learned she had been married three times before. I asked an explanation.
>
> "'Don't worry,' she said, 'I'll explain to you later,' and she patted my hand. We were married and she took me to her home."

"Lady," gasped her husband's custodian to Mrs. Mary Kelen Nyireghazi, "Hhe says you locked up his trousers so that he couldn't go out and he made up his mind to fool you. He says he's a great artist and that he's liable to do anything."

While the policeman had to leave without the true explanation for

Erwin Nyireghazi   Mrs. Mary Nyireghazi

Discord in their romance.

the performance that had s⟨t⟩ startled his Irish eyes, Mrs. Nyir⟨⟩ eghazi gave it yesterday, she swears in affidavits submitted b⟨y⟩ former Judge Leonard A. Snitkin 299 Broadway. Her suit for sep⟨⟩ aration is pending before Suprem⟨e⟩ Court Justice Louis A. Valente.

Nyiregyházi and his first wife in photographs that appeared in the New York *Daily News* on October 29, 1927, in an article on their separation.

They were married around noon on October 5, and they intended, at first, to keep the marriage a secret. That same night, at the routinely wild party Mary threw every week at her apartment, Nyiregyházi felt ill from too many drinks and went into the bedroom to lie down. A male colleague of Mary's came in and began to unbutton Nyiregyházi's pants – at which point Mary walked in and announced that that was her husband. It was an appropriately inauspicious launch of a fractious union. More than ten years her husband's senior, Mary was intelligent, calculating, strong-willed, but, as the actor Bela Lugosi would later tell Nyiregyházi, also "dangerous." Lugosi had known Mary and one of her previous husbands in Budapest, where they had had a reputation for blackmail and other unsavoury activities.

Nyiregyházi, in later life, insisted that he did not marry her strictly for money, but a promise to use her connections to revive his career was something she brought to the table. The *Daily News*, again:

> "My wife said she wanted to be my concert manager. She became domineering and abusive and I signed."
>
> In this contract Mrs. Nyireghazi [sic] agreed to supply her husband with food, clothes and lodging and he was to pay her back out of his earnings with interest.

In marrying an older, domineering, somewhat vulgar and materialistic woman, Nyiregyházi seems unconsciously to have replicated his relationship with his mother and his parents' own marriage.*

Mary did arrange a concert, on January 21, 1927, in Aeolian Hall – Nyiregyházi's first major New York recital in years – and drummed up some interest in this comeback. His audience was as enthusiastic as ever, though the critics still had reservations; only the virtuosic showpieces, like Godowsky's arrangement of Johann Strauss's waltz *Artist's Life*, really pleased them. According to an unsigned *Times* review, his subtler, more serious performances, in works like Beethoven's Op. 109 sonata, Chopin's Polonaise-Fantaisie, and Liszt's *Légendes*, appealed only "to the taste of a minority of his listeners." He was still a thunderer, and a musician in the audience that evening was quoted as saying, "It's a wonder that the piano company trusts him with an instrument." One company, in fact, did not: Steinway & Sons. Alexander (Sascha) Greiner, of Steinway's Concert and Artist Department, attended the recital and made an entry in a book he kept containing notes on pianists who auditioned to be Steinway artists:

> NYIREGYHAZI, Erwin. Piano recital Aeolian Hall, Jan. 21, 1927. Decidedly bad pianist. His pounding of the piano took at times proportions making one fear the piano would burst in two. His efforts at originality made him drag tempi to an extraordinary extent. He knows only fortissimo and piano, nothing between. I would not let him use the Steinway piano if he pays double cartage rates as the instrument sounds disadvantageously under his fingers. AWG
> Applied repeatedly for Steinway service. Refused.

---

* It is suggestive that his first wife bore something very close to his mother's name (in Mária as in Mary, the accent is on the first syllable). His first fiancée Adele's first name was Maria.

Nyiregyházi himself, years later, said that his performance at Aeolian Hall was one of the best of his career. Now that he was twenty-four, his deeply personal and furiously passionate playing could no longer be put down to immaturity; this, obviously, was the *real* Nyiregyházi at his most considered and representative. But the critics were skeptical. In Beethoven, Chopin, and Liszt, one wrote, he "seems increasingly given to violent alterations of tempo, especially to an exasperating deliberation, which gave a 'slow-motion' effect to his playing." Had Nyiregyházi continued to enjoy a real concert career, it is difficult to imagine that he could have escaped growing opprobrium, for he was an idiosyncratic artist out of step with contemporary musical trends. No wonder he found the whole business of giving concerts increasingly dispiriting.

Mary lost money on the Aeolian Hall concert, but the couple made an important social contact: the novelist Theodore Dreiser, then at the height of his fame with the sensational success of *An American Tragedy*, published in 1925. Nyiregyházi greatly admired the novel, so much so that he wrote a long essay about it (now lost), and ranked Dreiser with Dostoevsky and Wilde. He admired Dreiser's critique of the hypocrisy and puritanism of American society, his willingness to tackle controversial subjects like money, power, religion, and sex, to the enmity of prudes. And Dreiser's dense, lugubrious, dignified prose suited his own tastes perfectly. (The literary critic Irving Howe wrote that Dreiser "had a weakness, all too common among the semieducated, for 'elegant' diction and antique rhetoric." So did Nyiregyházi.) The society at which Dreiser takes such deadly aim in *An American Tragedy* was precisely that against which Nyiregyházi's career had foundered. Perhaps he read the book as a cautionary tale, for the values that entrap Dreiser's hero, Clyde Griffiths, are basically those of Mária Nyiregyházi: money, status, power, a craving for luxury and ease. Sacrificing spiritual values to materialistic ambition,

Clyde is suffocated by the unwritten laws and institutions of a heartless society; his hankering for wealth leads only to corruption, scandal, and ruin. (Admittedly, both Nyiregyházi and Dreiser still loved the trappings of wealth.) Moreover, in Dreiser, as in Liszt and Wilde (and himself), Nyiregyházi saw a great man who could live unashamedly like a roué while championing the highest ideals, and not be troubled by the contradiction.

Mary cannily sent Dreiser complimentary tickets to the concert, noting her husband's admiration for him, and Dreiser attended with Helen Richardson, his mistress since 1919. (Dreiser lived openly with her; she would become his second wife only in 1944.) He was overwhelmed and fascinated by Nyiregyházi's playing, and the two became fast friends. Not having a suitable piano at his disposal, Nyiregyházi asked to practise on Dreiser's Steinway grand, and Dreiser agreed. He loved music, especially "sweet melodies," Nyiregyházi said; the burly author would ask him to play sentimental pieces like "Clair de lune" over and over, and weep. The friendship was such that, not long after, when Nyiregyházi left Mary (briefly) for the first time, after one of their many fights, he stayed with Dreiser.

Alas, no sooner was the friendship cemented than Nyiregyházi began an affair with Helen Richardson, who wrote a breathless but heavily censored account of the relationship in her memoir *My Life with Dreiser*, referring to Nyiregyházi as "a young, introspective, philosophic musical genius, whom I shall call Jason."[*] His playing captured her first, for "he had the power of transporting his audience to another element." The first time he arrived to practise, "I heard the most heavenly music pouring forth on the still air," she wrote. "The gentleness of the lighter tones as they poured forth found their way to my innermost being. It

---

[*] In Vera Dreiser's memoir, *My Uncle Theodore*, the affair, "one of the tidbits of family gossip," is also briefly recounted. Nyiregyházi is now "a young Hungarian musician named Kovacs," and Vera suggests that he loved Helen but that she did not reciprocate.

was as if a nebula of light, in which he dreamed and projected his thought forms, had spread over the entire atmosphere." She was moved to write a ghastly poem, "Heavenly Infant," which begins:

> *You stand –*
> *Fragile, pale –*
> *You bow –*
> *Stiffly –*
> *As a child,*
> *Or some automaton, aloof,*
> *Or robot, weird.*
>
> *And then –*
>
> *Your hands run over the keyboard,*
> *And with your touch,*
> *The heavens open,*
> *And*
> *Showers of filtered stardust*
> *Rain upon the keys*
> *As you caress them lightly,*
> *With supernal tenderness.*

Clearly, they were meant for each other; her emotional and spiritual pretensions and neediness matched his own. She had artistic aspirations – she had had bit parts in silent movies, took singing and dancing lessons – and may have seen in Nyiregyházi (as in Dreiser) a way to realize them vicariously. And though nine years older than Nyiregyházi, she was still stunningly beautiful – tall and full-figured, with gold-and-chestnut hair. She loved the outdoors, and could be bawdy, vain, and materialistic, though Nyiregyházi saw in her only a delicate, romantic creature, so unlike the cynical Mary. Helen was torn. She was devoted to Dreiser, but, as she wrote, "I was young, attractive,

Helen Richardson and Theodore Dreiser at Iroki, Dreiser's country house near Mt. Kisco, New York, summer of 1929. *(Theodore Dreiser Papers, Rare Book and Manuscript Library, University of Pennsylvania.)*

pulsating with an energy that only health and youth can radiate," and Dreiser often neglected her for long periods of time. In her memoir, she implied that while physically attracted to Nyiregyházi she resisted an affair, but to a confidant she confessed that the relationship did indeed become a "short (so terribly short) intimacy." Nyiregyházi said that the relationship was passionately sexual, and Helen was by all accounts a seductive, sexually dynamic woman. Dreiser described her as having a "lymphatic sensuality," the aphrodisiac effect of which could drive him to "quite maddening" passion and fits of jealous fury (he wrote graphically of her carnality in his diaries).

The affair was interrupted in February and March 1927 by another successful concert tour of Southern California, arranged for Nyiregyházi by Mary. He did not receive quite the attention he had just a few years earlier, though in Los Angeles, where he gave two recitals, he was invited by the Philharmonic to play solo numbers during one of their orchestral concerts – a rare honour. When he returned to New York near the end of March, Helen met his train, and he did not at first tell Mary he was back. He hid out for two weeks in a rooming house, and returned home only when the affair with Helen began to curdle. They had exchanged passionate letters while he was on tour, but in late March, according to her memoir, she confessed her feelings to Dreiser "before becoming too involved with Jason." She asked Dreiser if he minded if she formed "a constructive emotional attachment to help me live through the time you leave me so much alone." Dreiser, though himself a notorious womanizer (he was openly involved with three or four women at this time) and a public advocate of sexual freedom, replied, "Do as you please! But when you do, I'm out!"

Confused, despairing, she identified her lover and vowed to drop him. In her account, she called Nyiregyházi to break up, getting only "ominous silence" on the other end of the phone. A few days later, she found an enraged Dreiser at his typewriter, and he hissed at her, "I'm

Helen Richardson in Hollywood, around 1920. *(Photograph by Nelson Evans. Theodore Dreiser Papers, Rare Book and Manuscript Library, University of Pennsylvania.)*

copying a letter. It's from Jason, and it finishes you, I can tell you that!" The next day, he showed her the letter, in which, he said, the affair was described in the "most evil & shocking way." Finally, Helen wrote, Dreiser "told me that while he had no sympathy for me, he thought much less of Jason. 'Imagine, you wasting your affections on a man like that!'" He called Nyiregyházi a "cad" and broke off their friendship, and Helen's own relations with Dreiser were now strained, her life with him lonelier and more frustrating than ever. Nyiregyházi lamented the loss of Dreiser, whom he loved; indeed, he may have seen in the fifty-five-year-old writer another surrogate for his lost, beloved father. Astonishingly, he blamed Helen for the end of his friendship with Dreiser – he typically projected blame in such situations onto anyone but himself.

The letter Dreiser copied has apparently not survived, and Nyiregyházi's account of the incident differs slightly. According to him, Mary found out about the affair when she discovered a copy of a letter he had written to Helen from California. This, presumably, is the four-page letter of February 28, on Los Angeles Grand Opera Association stationery, that survives among Dreiser's papers. Addressed to "My Darling Baby Girl," it is a revealing document of Nyiregyházi's emotional life, written in his usual purple style and blending the highest spiritual aspirations with swooning, adolescent ardour:

> You are to me a wonderful baby, one who seems to be in well-nigh perfect harmony with me and whose belief in me and appreciation of my intellectual and spiritual capabilities strengthens my self-confidence incalculably. It is my conviction that you could be of very material assistance to the realization of my intellectual aspirations, besides giving me intense emotional joy by reason of your, to me fascinating personality and individuality. I think that you could make me supremely happy. Among the few important wishes that I have none is more powerfully latent in me, than the wish to be constantly and permanently with you, free from those at present unavoidable molestations and interferences. If the will toward this end is strong enough in you it is quite within the realm of possibility, nay, probability that all obstacles now in front of us will be surmounted and that we will be happy ever after. The question is: are you quite certain about the identity of your desires? Are you a good fighter, willing to receive unescapable punishment, and able to bear it? I realize that at times you must be swayed by conflicting desires, and that the "competition" I am up against, is strong, "massive and compact." A veritable army of Attilla [*sic*]. And yet – if the belief, that I am an exceptional individual, a powerful thinker, a great artist and what not – is fully

synonymous with your innermost conviction, than [sic] my hope that
I will defeat the competition of my extraordinary opponent, as well as
the hope that all difficulties confronting me now will receive a death-
blow, by a force immeasurably superior to the one possessed by the
petty, intriguing politicians of life, – is by no means unjustified.

. . . I have not written to her [Mary] at all (although she has written
me super-sweet and super-shrewd love-letters). Of course I will have to
give her an accounting of the box-office receipts, for the purpose of
which I will write her some letters. Aside from that – nothing. All I can
say is: that I do not love her, do not even like her. She is to me an
intensely unsympathetic woman. I wish I were divorced. And then –
Oh, my darling baby girl! I think of you much! – So much! Words
cannot express the strength of my emotional reaction toward you. And
my reasoning mind is so completely in agreement with my emotions!
– if it comes to you.

From this point dates the final decline of Nyiregyházi's marriage, the
end of Mary's efforts on behalf of his career, and her first threats of
reprisal – for she, constitutionally jealous, did not take betrayal with
equanimity. He regularly betrayed her with other women, one of his
excuses being that she refused to perform oral sex on him. Helen had
introduced him to oral sex, which became his preferred form of sexual
gratification. ("Do you do it French?" became one of his lines.) Now
Mary threatened to have him deported for adultery – no idle threat in
those days. In fact, he was actually interviewed by immigration officials,
though, by his account, he told them he had invented the letter in question as the basis for a musical composition, and was left alone.

In April 1927, they separated again, and Nyiregyházi moved into a
dingy rooming house on Fifty-eighth Street, near Dreiser's apartment
building. He described those days two years later, in a letter to Helen –
days spent "brooding, crying, despairing day in and day out over you,
Dreiser, fate, the cruelty of life, the blows of destiny and longing,
longing, longing after you, after Dreiser in vain. In vain! Absolute

hopelessness, despondency. Oh, what days they were!" After a month or so he reconciled with Mary, but the marriage remained tempestuous; over the next few months he moved out of her apartment often. He wanted to resurrect the relationship with Helen, to whom he was ardently attracted, and continued to see her, though their sexual relationship was over. He looked for ways to end his marriage – he was not just disenchanted but *bored* with Mary – while she continued to punish him for his adultery. Once, when he was half an hour late turning in his portion of the rent (he paid six dollars a week), she locked him out of his room, forcing him to stay in a hotel.

That summer they managed to stay together, but in October he moved out again, and Mary sued him for separation alimony and legal fees in New York Supreme Court. According to Nyiregyházi, she introduced his letter to Helen as evidence, even leaked it to one of the local papers. On October 27, he submitted affidavits to the judge, and on October 28 and 29, the suit was reported, in lurid prose, by Joseph Cowan in the *Daily News*. The headline of the first article, "SLAVE MAN BATTLES SUIT," and the opening lines, set the tone for the coverage:

> Three husbands? Well, one can always use a fourth!
>
> So, when Mrs. Mary M. Kelen decided the open hearth in her studio apartment at 152 Madison ave., looked awfully cold and barren without a man's ankles draped around the andirons, she just took Erwin Nyireghazi, youthful concert pianist, by his little hand and led him to the marriage license bureau.

Cowan noted that Mary was older and supposedly weighed 185 pounds to Ervin's 132. Their marital troubles, he reported, had begun just three days after the wedding, when she attacked him with a kitchen knife, causing him to flee to the fire escape. The reason? "She sent me out for a newspaper, and I returned with the Times instead of THE NEWS." There were more stories of marital woe:

"She treated me as if I were her slave," says Erwin, "and reprimanded me in the vilest terms when my opinion differed from hers. She hit me, kicked me, scratched me and slapped me."

Sometimes she locked up his trousers so he couldn't go out and wouldn't give him anything to eat for a whole day, he charges.

"Then I was dismissed from her home and I went, not knowing where I could eat or sleep. I spent one night sleeping in the subway. For twelve days I practically lived in the public library while friends gave me the little I had to eat."

His wife came to the library and asked him to come back to her, he says. She promised not to kick or scratch him any more, or to lock up his trousers, so he went back.

Mary denied it all, portraying herself as a good woman devoted to her husband's genius and trying to cater to his whims. *He* had proposed to *her*, she claimed; he abused and "frequently choked her"; she spent all her money on his career, even soliciting aid from displaced European aristocrats of her acquaintance, while he contributed nothing. A former manager of his, she said, induced Ervin to leave her and took him in, and so she reportedly sued *him* for $100,000 for "alienation of Erwin's affections." For good measure, she denied weighing 185 pounds, and stepped on a scale for Cowan, weighing in at 170. She had weighed 156 when they married, she said, but had put on pounds trying to fatten up her undernourished husband with rich food ("I spent a small fortune on caviar for him because he loves it so"). In the October 29 *Daily News*, under the headline "PIANIST IN PAJAMAS STROLLED FOR KISS," was another bizarre story:

He looked like a purple sunset, strolling down Madison ave., in his resplendent pajamas and bathrobe. A burly guardian of law and order almost dropped his nightstick in his astonishment as Erwin Nyireghazi – for it was none other than that youthful genius of the piano – nonchalantly crossed his beat.

·

Two minutes later the officer had him back in his wife's apartment at 152 Madison ave., demanding explanations.

"Lady," gasped her husband's custodian to Mrs. Mary Kelen Nyireghazi, "he says you locked up his trousers so that he couldn't go out and he made up his mind to fool you. He says he's a great artist and that he's liable to do anything."

While the policeman had to leave without the true explanation for the performance that had so startled his Irish eyes, Mrs. Nyireghazi gave it yesterday, she swears in affidavits. . . .

"Only a few days after we were married," states the pianist's wife, "Erwin said he was going to call on one of his former sweethearts.

"Two days after the ceremony he tried to kiss a girl he used to know, so I locked up his trousers to keep him in the house.

"While I was in another room he left clad in the pajamas and bathrobe."

Neither Mary's allegations nor her husband's recollections seem implausible or out of character; neither was an innocent bystander in this absurd, doomed union. Mary felt legitimately wronged. Among Nyiregyházi's papers are the last two pages of a letter she wrote to him, presumably in late 1927 or early 1928. It ends, "I may be all that you try to make others believe I am, – though you yourself will never believe it – yet I hope to God to be able to continue speaking of you as it becomes a wife. Outside the Courts no one will hear of your terrible, vicious self."

Nyiregyházi interpreted his wife's suit as vindictive, since she had money and a job while his own prospects were poor. According to him, she won her case, but the judge declined to order maintenance from him because he was unemployed. After the suit, the couple once more reconciled for a time, but before long he was moving out and in again, enduring bouts of homelessness and dire poverty.

This was the nadir. Nyiregyházi called the period from mid-1927 to mid-1928 "the worst year of my life" – and that was saying something. Musically, he was now little more than a dim memory for most of the public. His disputes with his managers and his musical and personal eccentricities had already blackened his name in the music business; now he had been made a laughingstock, his name and picture splashed across the pages of a tabloid that sold more than one and a quarter million copies per day. With his reputation in tatters and Mary no longer working on his behalf, he had little chance of securing proper management or serious bookings. He continued to give private recitals, including one in the home of the impresario Florenz Ziegfeld, and to depend on the charity of Hungarian friends. He was often reduced to playing popular music, including several weeks in vaudeville, something he had previously refused to do. According to the *Daily News*, he played in a hotel orchestra, and for a time he worked with a violinist and cellist in a trio that played both classical music and jazz. Early in 1928, he landed a regular gig, at a decent salary, with an integrated jazz band, which performed in a club in Greenwich Village. Customers occasionally asked him to play some popular classical number; one who asked for Liszt's Hungarian Rhapsody No. 2 was surprised to find out that the pianist had once played it in Carnegie Hall.

By January 1928, he had convinced Mary to file for divorce. The reason was to be adultery, for which she needed evidence, so the loyal Gertrude Schultheiss agreed to act as co-respondent. But when, as arranged, Mary and her accomplices, two private investigators, burst into Gertrude's apartment, they found only a chaste tableau: Nyiregyházi playing for Gertrude on her piano – appropriately, a composition of his own entitled *Don Juan Triumphant*. Mary was frustrated and angry, but she took Ervin back (they went home, had sex, and made up). Of course it didn't last. Not long after, she appealed to the court and won separation maintenance of $10 per week; this time, the judge felt that Nyiregyházi was able-bodied enough to find work and support her. He did not appeal the decision, as he could no longer afford legal fees, but the sum was later reduced, by gentleman's agreement, to $7.50. Mary continued to punish him. At one point, she threatened to institutionalize him for mental incompetence, citing his lechery, and even the way he played the piano, as proof that he was "not normal."

Feeling cornered, he decided to flee to Europe, and by early 1928 he had saved $465 for the purpose. He would not keep the money in a bank, fearing that Mary would claim it, so he kept $300 in cash in his shoe. One morning he awoke to find the money gone. Another boarder at his rooming house had stolen it after getting him drunk. So he sent some of what remained to his mother and moved back in with Mary.

The final straw came on March 15. Mary found out that he had once more been unfaithful. Old arguments (adultery, oral sex) were dredged up, and finally she threatened him with a knife. He determined to leave New York once and for all, and with Europe now out of the question he settled on Los Angeles, where he had had so much success. He smuggled out a packed suitcase while Mary was at the market, checked it at Grand Central Station, gave a performance with his jazz band, snuck away at intermission, and, still wearing his tuxedo, took a cab to the station. Leaving most of his possessions behind, he travelled to Chicago. Only when he had arrived there the next morning did he send word to Mary, who by this time had told her tale of abandonment to the press. (Nyiregyházi recalled reading, in newspapers in both Chicago and Los Angeles, that he had mysteriously disappeared, leaving his wife "destitute." In at least one story, in a New York paper, it was alleged that he had been known to frequent whorehouses, and may have been murdered in one of them.) He had no success at arranging a concert in Chicago, so after two weeks he continued west. Along the way, after their bus broke down in a snowstorm in rural Nebraska, he and his fellow-passengers repaired to a nearby farmhouse, where he played Liszt's *Rigoletto* paraphrase on an upright piano for his startled companions. "I'd rather play there than Carnegie Hall," he later said, though in truth Carnegie Hall was no longer an option.

During the first week of April, Nyiregyházi arrived in Los Angeles hoping to put his personal problems behind him and reanimate his career. He had six dollars in his pocket.

Opposite: Nyiregyházi, probably at age thirty-three, in a photograph published in various Los Angeles newspapers to promote his concerts in the 1930s and 1940s. *(Photograph by the Federal Music Project. University of Southern California, on behalf of the U.S.C. Specialized Libraries and Archival Collections.)*

PART THREE

A SOLDIER OF FORTUNE

1928–1972

Down and Out in L.A. and Abroad

The twenty-five-year-old Nyiregyházi resettled in a thriving, fast-growing city of about a million people that, if not as vibrant and cosmopolitan as New York, could already boast of cultural achievements extending well beyond the film business, including a busy, wide-ranging classical-music life, which would only expand and deepen in the 1930s and 1940s with the influx of many émigré European musicians and other artists, writers, and intellectuals. He reintroduced himself to Los Angeles on May 10, 1928, at Philharmonic Auditorium, with a hefty recital program "aimed at interesting the most sophisticated music lovers" and featuring "a number of works not yet heard in Los Angeles," according to one newspaper. (It included rarities like Liszt's *Mephisto Waltz* No. 3, Il'insky's "Orgy of the Spirits," and, of all things, Liszt's symphonic poem *Hamlet*, in Nyiregyházi's arrangement.) He drew a large and enthusiastic audience – he still had admirers in town – but he could not live off the proceeds of an occasional high-profile concert in one city. Before the recital, it was announced that he had "just returned from a tour embracing the principal cities of Europe," and in December it was announced that he "leaves soon on a tour of the United States prior to returning to

Europe," but these were lies presumably cooked up by his manager, Merle Armitage. Outside L.A., his career was effectively lost. By summer, short of money, he was taking whatever paying work he could find.

Over the next two years, under various managers, he appeared with a string trio outdoors at the Argus Bowl, in Glendale; played on a Monday afternoon to open a week-long "Pageant of Music"; gave recitals for the Pleiades Club, the Ebell Club, the Spanish Club, the Woman's Lyric Club, an astrological society; gave a joint recital with the Yucatan Quintette, a vocal ensemble; performed the Schumann concerto with the Women's Symphony Orchestra of Los Angeles.* He had some success. A recital at the Hollywood Conservatory of Music and Art, in March 1930, was so well received that a second was arranged for April. The critics were divided. "He caused occasional panic among the orchestral players," Patterson Greene wrote of the Schumann in the *Examiner.* "He galloped when he should have walked. He idled in unsuspected places. He sentimentalized fulsomely. And with it all he revealed a native talent, a grasp of keyboard mechanics and a tonal variety that could, rightly directed, place him among the important pianists." But many also heard an artist more mature and disciplined than the firebrand who had taken the city by storm in 1923.

During his first years in L.A., most of his income came from the movies.† In November 1928, he auditioned for the head of the music department at United Artists, the Viennese-born Hugo Riesenfeld. He had admired Riesenfeld's conducting, and Riesenfeld had been another of

---

* He performed only occasionally out of town. On November 12, 1928, for instance, he gave a twenty-minute radio recital for "Musical Moments with Famous Pianists," a program on the Washington, D.C., station WMAL, and in the spring of 1935, he travelled to Boston to perform the Tchaikovsky concerto with the People's Symphony Orchestra.

† He had loved movies since early childhood, and cheerfully admitted that his cinematic taste was lowbrow – "the worse the better." He especially liked gangster movies and crime dramas featuring such characters as Sherlock Holmes or the masked Gypsy criminal leader Zigomar.

Rudolph Valentino's "pulchritude experts" in the 1923 beauty contest, but the two had never met. As Nyiregyházi told the story, they were introduced, but Riesenfeld, distracted, did not catch the name, merely plunked him down at a piano and asked him to sight-read some difficult music. Astounded by what he heard, he declared, "There is only one man who can sight-read like that: Nyiregyházi." Riesenfeld, it turned out, had attended a private musicale in New York at which Nyiregyházi had done some sight-reading to general incredulity. He was hired on the spot, and at a salary of $4 per hour became a full-time employee of United Artists.

His main task was to sight-read orchestral scores and play through standard repertoire for studio composers and for such producers as Samuel Goldwyn, Howard Hughes, and Joseph M. Schenck. He worked on some silent-movie scores, but had arrived in town in the midst of the furor over the talkies, which would dominate the industry by 1930. It was a time of explosive expansion in Hollywood – new records for film attendance were set in the boom years 1929 and 1930 – and there was plenty of work for Nyiregyházi. Soon he was doing other odd jobs for Riesenfeld – for instance, helping to arrange and orchestrate music by Romantic composers for Mary Pickford's first sound film, Coquette, released in 1929. Nyiregyházi admitted that the prolific Riesenfeld knew his job and had excellent musical taste – everyone in the business thought so – though he scoffed at the pretensions of "Dr. Riesenfeld" and disapproved of his habit of cribbing themes from Liszt, Wagner, and anyone else not protected by copyright (arranging borrowed material was, in fact, his specialty). He sometimes played his own compositions for Riesenfeld, who stole from them, too. "A great Jew!" he concluded.

Nyiregyházi performed in several early talkies, including Lummox, released by United Artists in January 1930. Based on a lachrymose novel by Fannie Hurst, it tells the story of a servant girl – the "lummox" of the title – who is seduced by a reprobate poet, the son of her wealthy employers. She bears a son whom she gives up for adoption, and the boy grows up to be a great pianist; toward the end of the film, she stands at the back of Carnegie Hall and watches him perform. Hurst herself, after hearing him audition, requested Nyiregyházi for this latter sequence, for which he was filmed playing part of the Grieg concerto to the (unscripted) cheers of the extras, who were mostly women. *Lummox* was received with derision in most quarters, lambasted for its sentimentality, lethargic pacing, absurd situations, stagey acting, and bad, awkwardly recorded dialogue. Nevertheless, Nyiregyházi earned $400 for his trouble.

He worked for some other Hollywood studios. He performed in the Paramount production *Fashions in Love*, based on Hermann Bahr's play *The Concert* and released in June 1929. Adolphe Menjou, in his first talkie, played a temperamental pianist who is almost unable to take care of himself and is addicted to pretty women – a scenario that must have struck Nyiregyházi close to the bone. He performed several pieces for the film: Liszt's *Liebestraum* No. 3, Mendelssohn's "Spinning Song," and Chopin's "Black-Key" Étude. He also performed on the soundtrack of *The Lost Zeppelin*, released that December by the smaller studio Tiffany-Stahl. This time, to underscore a developing love triangle during a banquet sequence, he played the *Liebestraum* and a bit of Liszt's Hungarian Rhapsody No. 12; for a few seconds, he can be glimpsed in the background at the piano, surrounded by adoring women. None of the films in which he performed could pass for notable, though their soundtracks have the distinction of including his earliest true recordings, and corroborate contemporary published accounts of his ardently Romantic style.

Nyiregyházi had hoped to start fresh in Los Angeles, but he was the same person, with the same proclivities and flaws. His life now was little different, and no better, than it had been in New York. He continued to reside in cheap, shabby hotels and apartment buildings, or with friends, living hand to mouth and changing lodgings as the fortunes of his career dictated. (His most reliable mailing address was "General Delivery.") And no sooner was he resettled than he became entangled in complicated affairs with women, two of whom were mother and daughter.

Elsie Swan was born in Finland in 1893, came to the United States as a teenager, and had been married twice. She supported herself by various means – rented out rooms, was an expert tailor, and for a time operated a restaurant in Beverly Hills, where she would cook paprika chicken for Nyiregyházi and let him eat for free. Standing about five-foot-six, chubby, buxom, and blond, with blue eyes and a kindly face, Elsie was a soft but also a strong woman. She was bubbly and extroverted, and collected friends. She often rented to starstruck young people trying to break into the movies, and was a flexible, forgiving landlord. The shy, introverted Nyiregyházi, by contrast, preferred private conversation to parties, and was constitutionally precise; he always knew exactly how much money he had, and was annoyed that Elsie could not keep track of her rents. Still, she offered him understanding and companionship, and while not musically literate she admired his idealistic, highly emotional approach to music, and did not push him to give concerts. Though the relationship was sexual by the end of 1928, it was a primarily spiritual kinship. Over the years she helped him in many ways, sometimes with money and a place to live, and her concern for his well-being extended to bloodying his nose in fights over his womanizing and other self-destructive behaviour. He often asked her to marry him, but she, fearing the loss of her benefits as the widow of her second husband, a disabled veteran of the First World War, always declined.

Marie Pergain, born in 1911, was the oldest of Elsie's three daughters by her first husband. She was a pianist, and though not physically imposing she played, according to Nyiregyházi, "like a female Paderewski." No one played Liszt's sonata better (or slower) than she, he said – "except me." (She played only for pleasure, however, not in public.) She did some acting – her name appears in the credits of several silent comedy shorts released in the late 1920s – and Nyiregyházi claimed to have once chanced across a pornographic film in which she appeared. She was still a teenager when they met, but sexually experienced; in fact, she had already been married, to a shiftless Russian prince. Their sexual affair, which began soon after they met, would be complicated by infidelity on both sides (her lovers apparently included the conductor Arthur Rodzinski and the film director Ernst Lubitsch). She was taller and slimmer than her mother, a platinum blonde with bee-stung lips and a slinky walk – he compared her to the young Joan Crawford. "I was sex-crazy for Marie," he said. "With Elsie, it was something deeper." But he genuinely admired Marie's musicianship and intellect, her knowledge of literature and philosophy. At some point the two planned to marry, in Mexico, but Elsie prevented them from doing so.

As in New York, serious relationships were supplemented by other affairs. He remained a magnet to women, and reported having as many as ten or a dozen sexual encounters a week at this time. During his first years in L.A., his amours included Armitage's secretary, Riesenfeld's daughter, a seamstress who worked with Elsie, an actress, and a wealthy heiress. He once fell for the receptionist in his doctor's office, and she agreed to go out with him even though he was being treated for gonorrhea. He had an affair, too, with the German pianist Elly Ney, whose playing he had long admired. (He called her the most idealistic person he had ever known.) They met one evening in November 1929, when they played for each other in the home of Marie's piano teacher, with whom he was then living. Though Ney was more than twenty years his senior, they had a brief affair that began the next day.

Nyiregyházi had an extraordinary memory not only for facts but for emotions, which seemed to endure, to remain fresh in his mind. ("Halfdan, I am so sentimental!" he wrote to Cleve in 1929. "Memories (good and bad) cause me pain!") His love for one woman did not replace his love for another; both resided in independent compartments within his mind, more or less permanently. No wonder his love life became more complicated with time: past loves accumulated, and haunted him. Having once loved, say, Helen Richardson, a love for her lingered, always available for renewal. Helen, indeed, was still on his mind. In April 1929, he wrote to her:

What are you doing? What are your plans? If I obtained a divorce, would that mean anything to you? One of the most powerful and irrepressible of my desires is to have you, to be with you, next to you, soul and body, always. . . .

Why should I not be rewarded? For my greatness of soul, spiritual achievements, for all the sufferings, tortures, agonies. When I think of reward apart from creation [i.e., composition] it is your picture that appears before me. No one but you. You, the incarnation, the embodiment of my aspirations, the amorous summit of my existence to which – in spite of all – I, in my imagination am still ascending to. Will it be realized? Yes! No! Yes! No! Yes! No! Yes! No! The hammer of fate! The roulette! The roulette macabre! The elements! The elements! The elements! Fate! Fate! Fate!

His swooning rhetoric did not win Helen back. He would see her and Theodore Dreiser in L.A. in the spring of 1930, but was hurt by their new indifference to him. (A composition resulted: *There Are Tears in the Affairs of This Life*.) He wanted to continue an idealistic friendship of peers with Dreiser while reanimating his affair with Helen, and could not understand why the couple might demur.

Early in 1930, Nyiregyházi quit his job at United Artists and set his sights on Europe. He had long planned to return to Europe, and believed that he was more suited temperamentally to life there; he found America philistine, and had come to feel that his concert prospects might be better abroad. Marie Pergain was there, studying piano in Germany, and he had made plans to meet Elly Ney that summer at the Wagner festival in Bayreuth. American friends secured him introductions to prominent persons in London, where he arrived on July 5, but he was no longer the attraction he once had been. When, innocently, he approached the secretary to Queen Mary and offered to play for her, as he had as an eight-year-old, he was gently rebuffed.

He travelled to Bayreuth, but Elly Ney did not show up; in fact, he never saw her again, and never knew why she broke off contact with him. He continued on to Budapest, where he reconnected with family members and old friends, colleagues, and teachers. (The Kovácses offered him accommodation and financial support.) On November 17, he gave a recital, in advance of which he granted an interview to a local newspaper. It would be his first concert in twelve years in his hometown, yet in his interview he made no compromises for the sake of good press. He derided American sexual mores, and cheerfully offered details of his own sex life, including his fondness for prostitutes. "To me it is a greater joy to go to a whorehouse than to see the Queen of England," he said, though he failed to disclose that the Queen had recently declined to see him. His recital, in any event, won the ringing approval of a full house, and a review, in the *Pester Lloyd*, that dubbed him an "expression pianist" whose playing communicated "the roar of his soul."

True to his publicity, he had many sexual encounters in Budapest. He met a "very experienced" eighteen-year-old named Emma, and after they were caught in flagrante delicto in the Kovács house he took his own apartment. The affair lasted only a few months, after which he took up with another, more intellectual eighteen-year-old, Éva Kepes. Moreover, according to one unequivocal interview note in his last wife's hand, he had sexual contact with his great-aunt Berta Borsodi – the aunt who enjoyed talking about oral sex (and, apparently, not just talking).

But even Nyiregyházi, like an athlete, abstained from sex before his concert on February 10, 1931, so as not to spend his strength, for he was just recovering from a serious bout of flu. It was an astonishing program of three massive concertos – the Brahms D-minor, the Tchaikovsky, and Liszt's *Totentanz* – and the response was tumultuous. The pianist György Sándor, then a teenager, remembered the concert more than seventy years later. In the *Totentanz*, he said, Nyiregyházi took the repeated-note figures in the fugato with a single finger, with what must have been a brittle, piercing tone; Sandor described the effect as "shocking," Nyiregyházi's gifts as "freakish." A relapse of his illness sent him to the same Czech sanatorium he had stayed in as a thirteen-year-old, after which he travelled to Vienna, where he gave a recital on March 26. He had last played there at age fourteen, but he still received glowing reviews; one critic compared his reading of Scriabin's Sonata No. 5 to an orchestra playing Berlioz. Elsie Swan joined him in Vienna, where she consulted with Sigmund Freud about some personal problems. (Freud was a friend of Jozsa Kovács, who was a native of Vienna.) The nature of those problems is unclear, though Freud's conclusion, predictably, was that they were sexual in origin. In April, Nyiregyházi gave concerts in Amsterdam and The Hague, and, for the first time in years, saw Géza Révész, who had left Hungary after the war and settled in Amsterdam to become a professor at the university and director of the Psychological Laboratory. He met up with Elsie in Budapest,* and, in July, returned to the United States.

He was feeling unsettled, uncertain what to do or where to live. Los Angeles, New York, Europe – all attracted and repelled him for various reasons, none promised real personal or professional satisfaction. While in the sanatorium he had composed a work titled *Longing for America*, for he was discovering that he was increasingly uncomfortable with life in postwar Europe. America, if only by default, was becoming home.

For a time he stayed in New York, where his life was complicated by another romantic triangle involving Dreiser, who was now himself having an affair with Marie Pergain. Marie had met Dreiser early in 1930 en route to Germany; in fact, Nyiregyházi wrote the letter of introduction that brought them together. Dreiser was now renting an apartment for Marie, and she appeared openly with him in public.

---

* Did he perhaps travel still wider? In 1977, a friend quoted him as saying, on the subject of a 1932 composition, *The Third Degree*, "I was arrested in Istanbul for being drunk. You know, the Turks aren't very nice!"

When he and a committee of writers made a high-profile trip to Pineville, Kentucky, in November 1931, to investigate the abuse of coal miners in Harlan County, Marie travelled with him, provoking a public scandal and even a grand-jury indictment for adultery. (John Dos Passos described her as elegant in her manners: "Her neatly tailored gray suit gave off that special Chicago chic I so appreciated.") When a tabloid reporter tracked her down in New York, she declared, "My life is my own to live as I see fit; I really don't care what people say." No wonder Nyiregyházi loved her.

He took to visiting Marie in New York, and Dreiser became increasingly hostile and threatening. At one point that fall, he ran into one of his old gangster friends on the street, and when he poured out his tale of romantic woe his friend offered to "take care of" Dreiser; admirers of the writer's later works should be grateful that Nyiregyházi declined. Marie soon broke with Dreiser – among other things, he beat her and bragged of their affair to Helen Richardson – and took an apartment with Elsie at the Ansonia, a hotel on Broadway that had a bohemian clientele and was a hotbed of cultural gossip. Dreiser and Helen also moved to the Ansonia that fall, and for a time Nyiregyházi was visiting all three women while trying to avoid Dreiser's wrath. The situation resembled a Feydeau farce, though Nyiregyházi took it deadly seriously. A composition from this period is titled *Dark Days of 1931*.

He gave several private and public concerts, including, in January, recitals in Newark and New York as assisting artist to Paul Robeson. (They may have met the year before in London, where Robeson was playing Othello.) Nyiregyházi described the response to his solo groups, from the large, mostly black audience in New York, as "pandemonium" – indeed, claimed that Robeson's manager fired him because his playing took too much attention away from the star. Still, to the public at large he was now little more than an anonymous musical journeyman. In a pre-concert announcement in the *Times*, his name was given as "Edwin," and in a *Times* ad the morning of the New York recital Robeson's accompanist was named but not Nyiregyházi. Below the ad, in large block letters, was "HOROWITZ," and below that, "MENUHIN." More than a decade had passed since the seventeen-year-old's sensational American debut, and New York was now celebrating new stars and new prodigies.

He moved back to Los Angeles in February; Elsie and Marie also returned and helped to support him. Elsie arranged for a major recital in Philharmonic Auditorium, in April, but despite an ambitious program and a receptive audience, the event lost money. When he did find well-paying work, it was usually humiliating. For two weeks in the spring of 1932, for instance, he performed in movie theatres in L.A. and Pasadena – though at least one prominent Angelino took notice. "I must put Nyiregyházi, famous pianist, above all else on the Paramount Theater program," Louella Parsons wrote in the June 3 *Examiner*. "He is delightful and well worth a visit to the theater to hear his masterly playing." He took home some $500 from these jobs – enough, at the height of the Depression, to live on for more than half a year.

In May 1933, still restless, he returned to Budapest. This time his way was paid by a wealthy Hungarian-born widow with whom he was involved, but that did not stop him from pursuing other women. Marie joined him there, though in August she herself found a new man, and Nyiregyházi decamped for Paris ánd Rome before returning to Budapest. (Fleeing conflicts in his romantic life was always one of his principal rationales for travelling.) For all the infidelity, he and Marie were still ardently attracted to each other and wanted to marry. They *did* marry, in a way, in November, in a "commitment ceremony" that they took seriously though it was not legal, and they lived in Budapest as husband and wife. He continued to perform there. He gave a radio recital on July 23, a public recital with a violinist on October 24 (he was compared favourably with Horowitz, who had played there three days before), and recitals on February 9 and 14. The latter, in the palatial home of the violinist Jenő Hubay, was broadcast,* and the former was devoted to his own music, which the critics found heavy, monotonous, formless, and derivative. One, he recalled, said his music was so pessimistic that it made him want to vomit, though the dean of Hungarian critics, Aladár Tóth, heard a great sensibility and tragic passion that called out "sobbingly" in the music.

Back in the United States, Nyiregyházi spent two months in New York. He sought out Dreiser, who slammed the door in his face.† He tried but failed to find a concert manager. He gave some piano lessons. In Los Angeles, in May, his "marriage" to Marie Pergain unravelled. She was frustrated by his shy, passive manner and would taunt him, saying she wanted burly, brutish men who would all but rape her. His poor prospects turned her off, too, and she found him dull. The loss was painful – no one could replace her sexually, he said – though they stayed in touch (she died in 1951). The affair with Elsie, too, ended in 1934, and she would not be a part of his life again for twenty years.

Through the 1930s, Nyiregyházi, on the rebound, proposed to several women, and the parade of affairs continued. "I was in love with them all," was his helpless explanation. It was inevitable that he would marry again, for he wanted secure companionship, and needed looking after, though he was hardly a candidate for happy marriage. Consider his

---

* Afterward, Hubay wrote to Eugene Ormandy, then conductor of the Minneapolis Symphony Orchestra, recommending that he engage Nyiregyházi as a soloist, but Ormandy – Nyiregyházi's former tormentor at the academy – declined.

† Still, he wrote casually to Dreiser in December 1932 seeking permission to reproduce one of his poems on the title page of a composition. "Kindly answer and don't be pigheaded," he wrote. In the fall of 1942, fortified by drink, he dropped in on Dreiser and Helen, in Los Angeles, and effected a reconciliation of sorts, though the old warmth and intimacy were lost. As late as 1946, he wrote to Helen requesting a meeting.

program note for his 1933 composition *Man Versus Woman*: "The man's lot is portrayed as a sad, melancholy one. He is brooding. The woman – frivolous and light-hearted – tempts him and tries to subjugate him by undermining his 'dignity.' After soul-tearing conflict the man yet clinches victory by reason of indomitable spiritual strength." A man who could not help feeling oppressed in a marriage was obviously doomed as a husband, no matter how ardently he entered into the union.

In Juarez, Mexico, in July 1934, he was finally granted a divorce (in absentia) from his first wife, Mary.* Not long after, he met Xandra Lucille Caplin, who was born in Vancouver in 1913 and was variously described by L.A. newspapers as a dramatist, actress, and aviatrix. She was attractive and sexually experienced, and knew literature and music – a fit replacement for Marie. He pursued her eagerly for more than a year, but their wedding was not auspicious. An aunt had pressured her to marry, and at the ceremony she did not say "I do" but impatiently shouted "Yes!" Nyiregyházi found her little interested in traditional duties like cooking; she preferred drinking, flirting, and entertaining, and could be cruel to him, deriding his "greatness." After his audition for Otto Klemperer, she took Klemperer's side over Schoenberg's in the debate over Nyiregyházi's substitute Chopin finale, apparently because Klemperer was the taller and better-looking of the two men.

Their marriage was short-lived. Xandra left him in February 1936. "Three months of married life was all that she could tolerate with her 'famous and temperamental husband,'" the *Examiner* reported, on March 4. "Soon after their marriage last October 28 he demanded she give up her drama and aviation, and made insulting remarks about her friends." Once, she said, "he objected so violently that she became nervous and fainted." (One can guess what his reaction would have

---

* Through the marriage to and divorce from Mary, he said, he spent time in libraries studying matrimonial law, and he claimed, in 1978, that his many divorces had made him a legal expert: "I am the only known lawyer who can make a Mexican divorce recognized in New York and California."

been had she expected him to give up, say, composing, or prostitutes.) He let her instigate divorce proceedings on mutually agreed grounds, his cheapness and mental cruelty, but later claimed that the *real* reason for their separation was otherwise: though she was Jewish, he never told her that he was, too, and when she found out she called him a "lousy little hypocrite" and threatened to expose him.

He consoled himself immediately with another woman: Xandra's flying instructor, Genevieve Haugen, whom he had met in the fall of 1935 when she piloted them to Santa Barbara for their honeymoon. Born in Seattle in 1911, to Norwegian parents, Genevieve, a slim and attractive woman with auburn hair, was a celebrated aviatrix who had just published a novel, *Women with Wings.* Their friendship blossomed into a sexual relationship shortly after Nyiregyházi separated from

Nyiregyházi's second wife, Xandra, in March 1936, when their separation was reported in Los Angeles newspapers. *(International News Photo by* The Evening Herald and Express. *Herald Examiner Collection, Los Angeles Public Library.)*

Nyiregyházi and his third wife, Genevieve, filing notice of their intention to marry, in a photograph that appeared in the *Los Angeles Examiner*, May 11, 1937. *(University of Southern California, on behalf of the U.S.C. Specialized Libraries and Archival Collections.)*

Xandra, though there was another man in her life who was helping to support her. Nyiregyházi didn't mind – he considered it admirable that she was cheating on him with only one other boyfriend. On May 15, 1937, the day his divorce from Xandra was granted, and just days after Genevieve's return from a stunt-flying trip to Europe, they married.

Nyiregyházi later said that he did not greatly care for Genevieve, and that by the time they had become engaged he had fallen in love with someone else. He married her, he said, so as not to hurt her feelings, and for companionship, but their sex life was poor. Though she had been married before, she "didn't know her stuff," he said, and (unlike Xandra) would not perform oral sex or even masturbate him. "It's not natural," she would say. "A real man doesn't need help." Her independence, too, rankled. She was no homemaker, she wore pants (which he hated on women), she could be vulgar (she smoked during sex), and she sometimes embarrassed him in public. (He seemed to want a woman who was a duchess in the parlour and a whore in the boudoir – who behaved correctly but was sexually voracious, someone he could adore as well as ravish – but usually ended up with women who were bound to disappoint in one or both rooms.) Moreover, Genevieve drank. In fact, it was with her that he first became a serious, chronic drinker. She encouraged it – drink made him more aggressive. "I drank a lot before then, spasmodically," he said, but "Genevieve made it a system with me."

She knew little about music. Shortly after they married, the couple visited the Hungarian violinist Duci de Kerékjártó, a former prodigy who had had his American debut at Carnegie Hall just two weeks after Nyiregyházi's own. (They had known each other as children.) While Nyiregyházi and Kerékjártó played Beethoven's "Kreutzer" Sonata, Genevieve yawned, and she later compounded the gaffe by opining that Beethoven was no greater than the milkman. For Nyiregyházi, that was enough to end the relationship. In August, he went to Las Vegas, where he had arranged some concerts to raise the money for a divorce. When the presiding judge declined to grant a divorce on the grounds of yawning during Beethoven, Nyiregyházi declared that Genevieve was a Communist – and that sufficed. On September 20, 1937, the divorce was granted, though the two remained friends for years.

12

Pianist for Hire

Through the 1930s and into the 1940s, Nyiregyházi performed with some frequency around Los Angeles, under various managers. He had not yet lost all hope of a sustained and meaningful career as a pianist, though lowlier appearances in small halls, churches, clubs, hotels, and private homes now greatly outnumbered high-profile concerts. (He performed only occasionally out of town.) Admittedly, the odds were now against him. For one thing, he suffered greatly from stage fright – increasingly so, indeed, as years' worth of criticism and failure exacerbated his native shyness and anxiety about putting himself before the public. He rarely had regular access to a piano, but, as he liked to say, "A truck driver does not live with a truck in his room." His technique required little maintenance, and anyway he could practise at a table, he said, by thinking about music while feeling the corresponding sensations in his unmoving fingers. When money was especially tight, he gave piano lessons, though he hated it. "If I could teach how Liszt, Paderewski, and Busoni played, I'd teach, even without pay, but it can't be taught," he said. "That comes from God." His young, mostly female pupils were usually without talent, but he had good relations (and affairs) with some of them. He was at least a kind teacher, dispensing praise but never criticism. He accepted other hackwork, too. A singer once paid him $6 to rehearse with her and accompany her at an audition at MGM, where the woman hearing the audition, the great soprano Mary Garden, had to be reminded that the accompanist whom she pronounced "wonderful" had performed with her at a musicale in New York fifteen years before. Sometimes, his pride asserted itself. The president of a women's club made him audition for a concert, then made him wait several days for an answer, so wounding him that he refused to perform. Merle Armitage once insisted that he appear as an intermission act for a magician, but he refused; Armitage threatened to drop him and advertised him anyway, but he never showed up – he went to a gangster movie instead. His ego needed to know, periodically, that there was *some* limit to his abasement.

By his own admission, Nyiregyházi did some of the most artistically satisfying work of his career for the Works Progress Administration (WPA). Established by congressional legislation in April 1935, the WPA was one of Roosevelt's "New Deal" programs, intended to replace the irregular relief efforts, during the first years of the Depression, of private, union, and governmental agencies. Among those supported by the WPA were artists, under Federal Project Number One ("Federal One"), which opened its first units that fall. Its musical arm was the Federal Music Project (FMP), whose stated goals were "to give employment to professional musicians registered on the relief rolls" and "to establish high standards of musicianship, to rehabilitate musicians, and to educate the public in an appreciation of musical opportunities," in part by promoting American composers. California boasted one of the busiest and most musically sophisticated programs of the FMP. In January 1938, according to the state's report, the FMP employed almost two thousand Californians, and operated (among many other musical groups) eleven orchestras, a majority of them in the L.A. area. (Records indicate exactly one FMP employee in the category "Soloists." Was it Nyiregyházi?) The FMP was accused of elitism, and its director, the Russian-born violinist and conductor Nikolai Sokoloff, had conservative tastes and a bias in favour of "serious" music, but this only worked in Nyiregyházi's favour.

An avowed admirer of Roosevelt, Nyiregyházi was devoted to the FMP, and worked enthusiastically for both its concert and education divisions. He agreed, for instance, to give recitals in local high schools as exercises in music appreciation and "grass roots" audience building, and on one occasion, in a small town, agreed to play the Tchaikovsky concerto on an upright piano (he was still able, he said, to make the instrument "roar"). In return, he was given free rein to play whatever he liked. His first documented FMP concert was on June 19, 1936: Liszt's *Totentanz*, with the Los Angeles Federal Symphony Orchestra. (For what it's worth, Genevieve Haugen initiated their sexual relationship after hearing this performance.) At least a dozen more orchestral appearances and recitals are documented; he was a favourite with the orchestras in Southern California.* Thanks to the FMP, he had for a time a small but regular salary – $94.08 per month was the figure he remembered.

---

* Many FMP concerts were broadcast, though no off-the-air recordings featuring Nyiregyházi have come to light. His last wife's notes include references to Liszt's E-flat-major concerto "and other recordings," and the International Piano Archives, in a circular to its supporters in the mid-1970s, sought "the November 1936 Standard Hour broadcast of the Liszt First Piano Concerto with pianist Ervin Nyiregyházi. Acetates of many of these broadcasts have been donated to the Stanford [University] Archives [of Recorded Sound], but the Nyiregyházi is not among them." (He did indeed perform this concerto with the Los Angeles Federal Symphony on October 21 and 24, 1936.) The FMP made a series of fifteen-minute discs for use by radio stations, only one of which featured Nyiregyházi: Program No. 76, recorded in 1936, in which he joined the Federal Symphony, conducted by Modest Altschuler, in "Before the Dawn," from *Deserted Garden*, by the L.A.-based composer Cameron O'Day Macpherson. The movement, an exercise in brooding faux-Rachmaninov, is less than five minutes long, and the tame piano part reveals little about Nyiregyházi's playing.

Reviews of his FMP work were not all favourable, and in some circles he was developing a burdensome reputation as a pounder obsessed with sheer sound. "I am always afraid I'll disappoint them," he lamented to a newspaper reporter in 1936. "They think of me as a man who breaks pianos and they want to see me do it." But this opinion was hardly unanimous. After he played Liszt's E-flat-major concerto in October 1936, the *Examiner* called him an "artist of brilliant power, fine reserve and unquestioned musicianship" who "has won an enormous following in recent appearances." An *Examiner* review of his performance of the Tchaikovsky concerto on September 23 that year noted that three thousand people had to be turned away from the auditorium, and that the audience "sat spellbound" and then "sprang to their feet with wild acclaim at the end." The pianist Frederick Marvin still remembers the Liszt performance, which he heard as a teenager: "It was wild."

Through the later 1930s, with relief efforts less and less a priority for the federal government and hostility toward the WPA growing in Congress, employment quotas slackened and budgets were tightened in Federal One, though the music program did continue, and Nyiregyházi stuck with it to the end. Isabel Morse Jones called him "a phenomenal prodigy, who has never lost his ability to excite an audience," in her *Times* review of a concert on Christmas Day 1940, in which he had played the Tchaikovsky concerto. "Nyiregyházi is hard on pianos but his sense of drama and his control of rhythms carry his listeners along with him. . . . The audience applauded between every movement and many rose to cry bravos and demand two encores at the end."

He gave his last FMP concerts in 1941, at least two joint recitals with singers and a program, in November, of Liszt's *Totentanz* and A-major concerto – the last performances he would ever give with an orchestra. By this time, war preparedness was consuming more and more of the federal government's resources, and the FMP was focusing on building morale and selling war bonds. The bombing of Pearl Harbor that December effectively ended all Federal One projects except those related "directly to winning the war." By the spring of 1942, the WPA was inactive in L.A., and in June 1943 it was formally terminated.

Nyiregyházi's success with the WPA was a blip within a downward-sliding career, and his fortunes struck many people as greatly out of proportion to his talent. Nyiregyházi, Tom O'Connor wrote in an *Evening News* portrait in the fall of 1936,

> is one of those seldom-found people who are just sensitive enough, and just independent enough, not to care a great deal about more money than is necessary for food, clothing, and shelter. When you look at his tremendously high forehead, his full, sensitive lips, his big brown eyes, his long thin face and almost emaciated frame, his straggling unruly hair, you think of some of those early Christian martyrs, children in their faith. When you talk to him, draw out his slow, shy smile, watch his brave attempt not to be embarrassed at talking about himself, his evident desire to be obliging and his wary distrust of strangers, you know a little better what he is: a giant in his music, a naive child in his relationships with the workaday world.

An anecdote related by Donna Perlmutter in the *Herald Examiner* in 1978 is even more touching. She spoke to a Hungarian woman who had heard Nyiregyházi play in 1937 at the Sisters of Social Service Convent. "The massive sound and passion I heard that day so contradicted what my eyes saw," the woman recalled. "Here was a man trembling as he walked onstage, horrified with embarrassment. A nun begged me to visit him, knowing I could speak his native tongue. When I arrived at his miserable hovel, he was like a little boy. He wore only one shoe, laced as though by a two year old. His sweater was buttoned incorrectly and his long nails clattered on the keys of a decrepit upright."

With public outlets for his creativity restricted, and much time on his hands, he did what he could to exercise his teeming brain, his

A Soldier of Fortune

intellectual life having in no way slackened. He still composed prolifically, still read widely. From this period dates a passion for philosophy
that came to match his passions for music and chess, Liszt and Wilde.
(He particularly admired recondite philosophies, like those of Kant and
Hegel, that dealt with transcendental questions.) He also wrote music
reviews occasionally for publications including the *B'nai B'rith
Messenger* and *Californiai Magyarság*. He was always writing, in fact.
His papers reveal a compulsion to set down ideas on subjects he was
passionate about, even if only for private satisfaction. Killing time in
New York, he had toyed with the idea of writing a novel: a pianist with
no talent, making his debut, sells out Carnegie Hall at high prices, but,
though he plays so badly that "even the critics know it's bad," he
refuses to refund the money – "and blood flows."

Around 1935, he began to compile a long, motley book of essays,
which, with his usual grandiosity, he titled *The Truth at Last: An
Exposé of Life*. He worked on it for more than a decade, sometimes dic-
tating to women friends who typed, eventually producing more than a
thousand pages. The longest (book-length) essay, "The Liszt Problem,"
took up the issue of why Liszt's music was not widely loved, and
included detailed philosophical, spiritual, even sociological and political
analyses of the meaning of many works, touching on issues like social
class and notions of "good taste." Another essay, "The Libido Must
Have the Way Out Whether in the Bedroom or the Concert Stage,"
dealt with his approach to musical interpretation, though, more broadly,
"was an article about myself, what I like and don't like in music, sex,
food, hotels, etc." Yet another essay was titled "The Way They Murder
the English Language in the United States," and there were others on
Wilde and Mahler, on Dreiser's *American Tragedy*, on prostitution and
American hypocrisy about sex. He devoted an essay to a criminal case in
Connecticut that had intrigued him in the late 1920s, in which a man
had been sentenced to death for killing a policeman in the course of a
robbery. Nyiregyházi argued that killing the policeman was somehow
less dastardly than killing a bystander because the policeman was

threatening the robber's spoils – a perverse position surely aggravated by a poor man's fear of the instruments of power. There was an essay on Chaplin, too, whom he insisted on calling "Charles"; he described it as an indictment of a society that "laughs at the downtrodden." Chaplin's comedies, he said, "are tragic as hell, as tragic as anything Dostoevsky ever wrote." But *The Truth at Last* was never published.

Bela and Gloria

Nyiregyházi was a fixture of the Hungarian community in Los Angeles. He frequented Hungarian restaurants, clubs, and churches, and sometimes saw visitors from home. His Hungarian friends included artists like the painter Emery Gellert and the multifariously talented Willy Pogány, who drew a serenely beautiful portrait of him. He was also a regular guest in the homes of distinguished countrymen like the tenor and singing teacher József Diskay, whose studio was a meeting place for artists and movie people, and he gave small private recitals in the home of the architect József Bábolnay. Hungarian supporters sometimes organized public concerts for his benefit, at which he often found receptive audiences and real artistic satisfaction. Among his most devoted patrons was a priest, Mátyás Lani, who presided at St. Stephen's, on Woodlawn Avenue, a Catholic church with a largely Hungarian congregation. Over the years, Father Lani gave him financial support and promoted him as a pianist. At the recital he arranged on November 30, 1935 – the first of many at St. Stephen's – the church was packed, and among those present were the two acquaintances who, the next day, introduced Nyiregyházi to Arnold Schoenberg.

Charcoal portrait of Nyiregyházi by Willy Pogány. Nyiregyházi signed it on March 26, 1941, adding, "In memory of the days of 1933 with Willy Pogány." The artist himself offered "my belated signature," in the lower left-hand corner, only in 1946. *(Reproduced by Mark Nicholls.)*

In those days, the de facto leader of the Hungarian community was Bela Lugosi. Lugosi's temperament was effectively defined by his deep emotional bond with his homeland, yet he never returned to Hungary, because the Hungary he (like Nyiregyházi) knew had vanished with the First World War. He preferred to cultivate his nostalgia in exile, and distance only increased his desire to surround himself with all things Hungarian. He generously patronized Hungarian restaurants, clubs, churches, businesses, sporting franchises, cultural events. He had a soft spot for countrymen in need, and would give away money when he himself was destitute. He preferred fellow Hungarians to the "beautiful people" of Hollywood, and his home was open to Hungarians of any age, trade, class, or religious or political persuasion.

He had also been deeply involved with the Hungarian community in New York, after emigrating (escaping, really) in 1920, but he and Nyiregyházi did not meet until 1929, when Lugosi, now resettled in L.A., called him up out of the blue. (He still remembered the thirteen-year-old prodigy's three-concerto concert in Budapest in 1916.) The two men formed a deep bond that survived the vagaries of each other's careers. Lugosi, too, knew all about the fickleness of fortune: in Hollywood, he knew fame and wealth as well as obscurity and bank-ruptcy, to say nothing of the ruinous typecasting in horror movies that followed *Dracula*, in 1931. He and Nyiregyházi had much in common, despite the twenty-odd-year age difference. Both were tall, thin, and elegant, with the manners of a European gentleman, but also passionate, temperamental, and prone to melancholy, and both drank heavily, often releasing a tortured, bellicose side of their personalities. Both were particular to the point of obsessive, and spoke precisely in a carefully modulated, heavily accented voice. Both were loners, yet powerfully attracted (and attractive) to women and obsessed with sex. (Lugosi, between marriages when they met, offered to get girls for his new friend.) Lugosi and Nyiregyházi also shared democratic sympathies that admittedly clashed with their fascination with aristocracy and wealth.

Lugosi's home was an enclave of Old World culture. He lived grandly and spent freely, regardless of his financial state. "Live for today and the hell with tomorrow," he used to say. "We'll eat caviar and drink cham-pagne today and we'll go on bread and water tomorrow." His home was always full of people, and he entertained lavishly. He liked painters, dancers, writers, but had special affection for musicians. Nyiregyházi often performed at his parties, though he was always treated as an honoured guest, not as the entertainment. But even in such congenial surroundings, he had to be fortified in order to overcome his shyness.

After arriving at Lugosi's, he needed several stiff drinks in the kitchen before he could even face a roomful of people, never mind play for them. With his inhibitions loosened, though, he might play long into the night – always serious music, sometimes his own works or improvisations. Lugosi's biographer Robert Cremer described one performance at a party in 1935:

> His gaunt frame swayed to the cascading rhythm of his fingers on the keyboard as he opened his concert with Rhapsody in Blue, Bela's favorite piece. After that, he drifted into some of his own compositions, which reflected his own frenetic personality and suited an evening with the master of horror. Concerto in Blood rolled across the room like a fog across the moors and then rose the full two stories to the beamed ceiling. Imperceptibly, Ervin's spirit became lost in his music as it reached a crescendo. His hands were like flashes of lightning, globules of perspiration beaded his forehead, his body writhed in an uncanny choreography to his music. Mercilessly, his fingers pounded out the anguished notes until the faintest traces of blood appeared on the keys; Ervin had reached communion with his musical soul, his concentration measured by the intensity of the red splotches across the ivory keyboard. Bela sat with his eyes closed, his head swaying to the musical madness coming from the concert grand. He saw the blood-stained keys as the sign of a genius that he shared with few other artists.

While overwrought, the anecdote captures the sometimes terrifying intensity of Nyiregyházi's playing when he felt inspired. Bela G. Lugosi, the actor's son, born in 1938 and today a lawyer in Los Angeles, still remembers sneaking out of bed and peering down from upstairs as Nyiregyházi played at the bottom of the winding staircase, and remembers, too, the blood on the keys. Duci de Kerékjártó's ex-wife Marie told Cremer, "Bela adored Ervin, because he considered Ervin a man of intense concentration and dedication like himself. They were really kindred spirits, because each had a touch of true genius. Even the blood on the keys of the piano was a sign to Bela that Ervin had a rare gift of inspiration like himself. It was something you had to see to believe, though. Very unsettling."

Lugosi developed great affection for Ervin, and often invited him for intimate dinners at his house or at local Hungarian restaurants. He defended Nyiregyházi's drinking and carousing as prerogatives of a genuine "character" and a great artist who had endured much suffering. Lugosi once actually expressed shame that he had so much fame and money while his friend, a much greater artist, had so little. He helped organize concerts for Nyiregyházi,* shared his fondness for lugubrious, melancholy music, and loved his compositions ("Once more," he would often say after hearing one of them). While Nyiregyházi played, Lugosi might sing along in his deep baritone, or sob.

Nyiregyházi's talent often won him entry into Hollywood society. In the later 1930s, he became friendly with the screenwriter Frances Marion – and, inevitably, fell for what he called her "sexual induce-ments." He often played at her house and elsewhere in Hollywood, where he met movie people like Nelson Eddy and Jeanette MacDonald, Frank Capra, George Cukor, Hedda Hopper, Fredric March, William Powell, and Edward G. Robinson, and writers, too, including James Hilton and Upton Sinclair. Marlene Dietrich, at one of Frances's parties, announced to the company, "This young man is a great artist." He often found himself leaving his cheap lodgings in evening clothes and taking the bus (or, if he was broke, walking) to a glamorous party in Beverly Hills, where celebrities would cheer his talent and welcome him as a peer. For him this was no irony: in his mind his material circumstances had no

---

* After meeting the theosophist Manly B. Hall through Lugosi, in 1939, Nyiregyházi was invited to perform at a local theosophy meeting, where his playing was considered "too loud for a spiritual society."

bearing on his artistic or intellectual merit. But not everyone treated him with the respect he believed he deserved.* For a time, the actress Doris Kenyon paid him $10 a month to entertain her guests occasionally, but only *after* dinner, to which he was not invited. He keenly remembered the hurt and humiliation of sitting and waiting while hearing, in the dining room, people talking and laughing. He was still proud. While he was visiting New York, Jack Dempsey invited him to his restaurant and insisted that he eat for free. He was touched, but would not return to the restaurant: "I didn't want him to think I was a freeloader."

In April 1936, at a private recital at Frances's, he met Gloria Swanson, who pronounced his playing "godly," and later he performed at Swanson's home. The two became friendly, Swanson having recently ended a serious relationship with the actor Herbert Marshall. They developed a spiritual kinship: in his first letter to her, Nyiregyházi offered flamboyant thanks for her gift of a copy of Kahlil Gibran's *The Prophet*.

That September, he signed a two-year contract with a manager named James V. Petrie, but Petrie secured only a few concerts – a benefit concert at Shrine Auditorium, an appearance at a women's club, and one very successful recital, on November 13, at Trinity Auditorium. The concerts brought in a pittance, and in a letter to Swanson he complained, "The situation here, for me, seems quite hopeless. Mr. Petrie doesn't seem to be able to do anything, nor does it seem at all likely that he ever will." Finally, Swanson herself arranged a concert for him, ostensibly as a benefit for two local charities, and she threw herself into promoting it. Among her papers is a three-page list of more than eighty names, indicating the number of tickets each person had agreed to sell, and it reads like a *Debrett's Peerage* for the Hollywood nobility: Mrs. Adolph Zukor, Mrs. David Selznick, Mrs. Ernst Lubitsch, Mrs. Boris Karloff, Mrs. Frank Capra, Mrs. Cecil DeMille, Joan Crawford, Mrs. Harold Lloyd, Paulette

---

* He witnessed anti-Semitism, too, and so kept his Jewishness a secret in Hollywood. He recalled that a local contingent of Nazi sympathizers, not aware that he was Jewish, admired his playing, followed his concerts, and encouraged him to tour Germany.

Goddard, Howard Hawks, Mervyn Leroy. The concert took place on December 15, at the Wilshire Ebell Theater, and Nyiregyházi's program proved a great success. He received $500 for the concert, from Swanson herself, though even with her personal intervention Petrie would not waive his contracted commission. Nyiregyházi recalled, "That was the only time I heard her cuss."

By now, the relationship was deepening. On Christmas Eve, he wrote to Swanson that he was thinking of her constantly, though, of course, he was married to Xandra and involved already with Genevieve:

> My greatest wish for the coming year is: that you and I may go to some distant land, or, perhaps, to a place not so distant, but sufficiently secluded, and live for our Ideal – for a certain idea, dear to both of us.
>
> You will remember one afternoon you and I were discussing certain problems of life, plans – and you've said: that I should find an "intelligent woman" – and I've said: "yes, if I found the right one." But what I didn't say at that time was that I *have* found that woman, and that *that woman* is you.
>
> The realization of this dream is amongst the most supreme objectives of my life.

At some point, he proposed marriage. In October 1937, he wrote to her, "I have a little while ago returned from Nevada where I have obtained my divorce [from Genevieve]. I mention this merely 'apropos'." Six months later he wrote, "Please, in any event, send me a cable to notify me of your decision. I make a pretty poor show of myself – I know – but perhaps you know from your own life that such things at times are inevitable." She was reluctant – how was he going to support her? – and he understood. She had been married four times, and had supported all of her husbands, but now she was worried about money. In 1938, her net worth was about a quarter of a million dollars, a fraction of what it had been in her heyday in the silent era, and she could no longer support herself as an actress. (By this time she had made only a handful of sound films, the last in 1934.) "Four's enough," she told a friend, and she refused proposals from better-placed men, too, like her friend Gustave Schirmer, heir to a major international music-publishing firm.* Though she needed security, she "couldn't be dishonest when it came to love." (She would marry again only in 1945.)

In the summer of 1937, Swanson arranged another concert, on December 11, at the Hollywood Conservatory of Music, at which Nyiregyházi performed seven of his own works. The hall was half full (it rained hard that day), and the event lost money. Isabel Morse Jones, in the *Times*, heard deep yearning, foreboding, and bitterness in the dour music, and acknowledged its depth and authenticity, though one other critic later told Nyiregyházi that the review he had wanted to write was too "blasphemous" to be printed.

In February 1938, Nyiregyházi accompanied Swanson, Schirmer, and Douglas Fairbanks, Jr., on a train trip to New York. Swanson, now almost forty, fed up with Hollywood, and realizing that her prospects in the film industry were poor, had decided to move to New York to pursue business opportunities. En route, Nyiregyházi recalled, the train stopped in Chicago, and Swanson learned that photographers had gathered at the station. "No photographs," she said – and was humiliated to learn that they were actually there to meet Mae West. The decline of her own career probably made her sympathetic to Nyiregyházi's plight. She had invited him to New York in an effort to interest the Schirmer firm in publishing his compositions, which she admired, but they were rejected – too old-fashioned.

---

* Nyiregyházi recalled that, in 1938, Schirmer made an acetate-disc recording, in Swanson's home, of him playing Liszt's "Les jeux d'eau à la Villa d'Este." The disc was not among the artifacts from her estate auctioned in 1983, and is not in the collection of her effects at the Harry Ransom Humanities Research Center at the University of Texas at Austin; it is presumably lost.

She gave Nyiregyházi money regularly and induced friends to do likewise, and though she did so graciously, without conditions, she was dismayed that he would often spend it on liquor and prostitutes, then insist on telling her he had done so. It was his pride and defiance, once again: he had to assert his independence, had to dare his benefactor to drop him, lest her support seem like control. Moreover, he had noticed that the staff on the train had treated him royally only when they found out he was travelling with Swanson. Such hypocrisy, which humiliated him, perhaps made him resent and want to lash out at her generosity. His drinking and womanizing troubled her, too – alcohol and unresolved issues with an estranged wife having undermined her relationship with Herbert Marshall.

Still, the relationship probably evolved into a sexual affair, in New York if not earlier; that, at least, seems to be implied in one of his recollections, which paints a homey scene of Swanson serving him scrambled eggs one morning in March in her apartment in New York while he plays his own works to her on the piano. Anyway, the relationship did not last much beyond their first few weeks in New York. He was deeply attracted to her, though one senses from the available evidence that her feelings were not so strong. (She did not mention him in her autobiography.) Perhaps he was something of a "project" for her, in which case his flouting of her generosity might have led her finally to give up on him.

14

Restless

Adrift in New York, where he had been effectively forgotten and had no prospects as a musician, Nyiregyházi, now thirty-five, determined to marry again and so flipped a coin: he would either return to Los Angeles, where he was considering proposing to one of several women (including his ex-wife Xandra), or travel to Europe to marry Eva Kepes, the young woman with whom he had briefly taken up in Budapest in 1930 and had lately been corresponding. He felt that he had done all he could do in America. In April 1938, in a letter to Gloria Swanson, he wrote: "I feel that the situation for me in New York – for the present at least – is hopeless. Also, I am spiritually very unhappy here. I feel utterly alone and do not see a way for any substantial betterment, either spiritually or materially. I feel that my whole life could take on a more felicitous aspect if I were in Budapest." He asked her for money, and she gave him $100 (he solicited funds from other women, too). On April 13, he sailed for Europe, and, advised that it would be dangerous for him to travel to Budapest, stayed in Paris, where "everything was cheap: food, drink –

massage!"* Eva met him there, and agreed to marry him, though he was already being distracted by other women.

In June, he travelled to Oslo, to visit Halfdan Cleve and his daughters, whom he had not seen for almost fifteen years. Signy was now married, Astrid was a widow, and both had children. His old feelings for Signy had dimmed, but Astrid apparently made a brief attempt to rekindle a relationship, and may even have considered marrying him. They had what he described as two "dates" – that is, bouts of oral sex – but she broke off the affair, and he, to get even with her, turned to a young, blond masseuse named Ella Petersen. While in Oslo he secured two concerts: Brahms's B-flat-major concerto, on October 6; and a recital, on October 13. When he first mentioned that he was considering playing the technically forbidding Brahms, Signy replied, "You can't play *that* – it takes muscles!" The remark enraged him. He quit drinking, practised madly, and, by all accounts, played the piece like a demon.† Reviews of both Oslo concerts reported electrified audiences that demanded many encores. He had not lost his power to amaze:

> The slender young virtuoso made the pianoforte sing so ecstatically and forcefully that its tone mounted like a frothing crest over even the most powerful efforts of the orchestra. . . . Nyiregyházi played the Brahms concerto with a virtuosity that passes all limits though with a ruthlessly personal interpretation which made it, from first to

---

* Though he was permitted to re-enter and permanently reside in the United States, and had had a Social Security number since 1937, he was still travelling on a Hungarian passport, and feared that if he visited Hungary he might not be allowed to leave, having never served a term in the Hungarian army (the country had recently tightened regulations on passports and military service). He became a U.S. citizen in August 1940.

† On a program that found its way into the Norwegian National Library, someone in the audience noted approximate timings for the concerto's four movements: seventeen, seven, eight, and seven and a half minutes, for a total timing of just under forty

last, a wonderful and passionate musical self-revelation. (*Dagbladet*, October 7)

. . . superhuman and far beyond anything one has experienced in pianoforte playing for a long, long time. (*Dagbladet*, October 14)

He is in many respects an incomparable pianist. (*Aftenposten*, October 14)

Nyiregyházi has an amazing perfection of technique and a virile power which at times is almost terrifying in its intensity. He summons from the pianoforte a body of sound that one might imagine to come from a whole orchestra; the instrument is an irresistible torrent under his hands, and his passionate temperament gives a living and rich tone to this mighty output of energy. (*Morgenbladet*, October 15)

He returned to Paris, with Ella, and by the time she returned to Norway, in early November, they were engaged; he joined her early in the New Year. He gave an all-Liszt program on Norwegian radio on February 6, 1939, and on February 24, he and Ella were married at the courthouse in Oslo. He admitted that she was "very ignorant" and not interested in music, but he was still motivated by a desire to hurt Astrid Cleve, and by sexual attraction. Soon after their brief honeymoon in Drammen, he decided to return to the United States. He was running out of money, his prospects were poor, and he was appalled by the growing anti-Semitism in Europe (he had to pass even with Ella, who told him she would never marry a Jew). He wrote again to his "Savior," Gloria Swanson, now begging for money to return to Los Angeles: "It is still the best among many bad things." He did not *like*

---

minutes. These timings do not reveal Nyiregyházi's usual slow tempos; rather, they suggest a *driven* performance.

the city, but there he at least had friends and was able to cope financially. And in America, he said, you could at least get what you wanted when you wanted it; he had come to rely on North American conveniences: late-night buses, bars and all-night restaurants, Sunday shopping, and (most prized of all) private toilets and baths in even the meanest hotels. Early in March, he sailed alone to New York. He fell in love with one woman on the ship, another after he had returned to L.A. – he was incorrigible – yet he genuinely wanted to bring Ella to America, and tried to do so for more than a year before giving up. She agreed with him that a divorce was their only option, and he obtained one in Mexico in March 1941. They were never in touch again.

"I am a total son of a bitch – a soldier of fortune," he said decades later, marvelling at his own caddish behaviour, which he seemed unable to control. But if he was a cad, he also suffered. His trip to Europe, he came to realize, had been a mistake: "I paid for it both in money and in emotional suffering." In the spring of 1939, he was at one of the lowest points of his life, despairing of ever finding lasting professional or personal satisfaction. The woman who would become his sixth wife noted in her diary, around this time, that he was so despondent he spoke of wanting to "end it all."

As usual, he sought solace in companionship. In September, he met a waitress named Olga Karolyi, and on May 15, 1941, in Yuma, Arizona, she became his fifth wife. She was the same age as Nyiregyházi, born in New York, to Hungarian immigrants, in 1903, and though she had never visited the mother country she spoke the language and loved all things Hungarian. (Her maiden name was Gross, and her family was Jewish on at least one side; others in her family had changed the surname to Cross, and she had had a nose job in order to appear less "Jewish.") He described her as "frail and delicate," a nervous and high-strung woman. The relationship had tenderness and an emotional connection but no great passion. When he had sex with Olga, he said, "I always imagined a prostitute in Amsterdam."

Alas, she, too, was a heavy drinker, and their union was fractious. They argued over petty things. He was enraged that Olga wore pants, even to one of his concerts, and that she wanted him to send his laundry out, which he found embarrassing. After one quarrel, in 1942, he got drunk and tried to enlist in the army (they told him to go home and sleep it off). She was very much in love with him – when they first met, she would look at him adoringly and say, "Can a cat look at a king?" – but was insecure about his feelings. When, in the summer of 1940, he spent more than a month visiting wealthy friends in Massachusetts (including the heiress Barbara Hutton), she became almost hysterical worrying that he would not return to her.

Olga's young son by her previous marriage, Nicholas, was a major point of contention in the marriage. "That's a real hell," Nyiregyházi said on the subject of stepsons. "The woman with sons thinks more of her sons than she does of me." Having himself the needs of a child, he could not abide having to compete for Olga's attention. When Nicholas was living with them, Nyiregyházi began to grouse that the boy got served first, and got a bigger, rarer portion of meat; moreover, Nicholas hated classical music, and took to ridiculing Nyiregyházi. There were in-law troubles, too. Toward the end of the war, he had a year-long affair with Olga's sister-in-law Mildred Cross, who apparently expected him to leave Olga for her. In the end, Mildred and her husband turned against him and conspired to break up the marriage.

On a visit to Las Vegas in the summer of 1943, the couple quarrelled drunkenly, and he threatened divorce; she retaliated by lying that he had beaten her, and he spent a night in jail. They separated, and on October 25 the *Examiner* reported that he had sued for divorce; her cross-complaint alleged "cruelty and non-support" and sought monthly maintenance. (She claimed to be "unable to work because she is in need of a surgical operation.") The suit was withdrawn, but the following August he sued again for divorce, and again withdrew. Finally, in May

1945, they separated for good, and Nyiregyházi obtained a divorce, in Las Vegas, on August 7. And then they made up again. In fact, he continued to visit Olga regularly, for dinner (and sex?), during his *next* marriage; for a time, he was actually living with her, because his sixth wife did not then have a private bathroom. Finally, in the early 1950s, the relationship petered out, and Olga, who died in 1970, never got over her bitterness toward him.

❦ 15 ❦

That Strange Romance

From the first summer after his arrival in Los Angeles, there was an important (if sometimes remote) presence in Nyiregyházi's life: the woman who became his sixth wife. Their relationship is documented in hundreds of pages, in her hand, that survive among his papers. The earliest of them is dated June 28, 1928, just days after the two met; the last was written a few weeks before her death in 1955. They include a few letters, but mostly comprise entries in what she called her "Little Book" (or "L.B."), a sporadic series of diary entries the purpose of which was precisely to document what she called "that strange romance."

Her name was Ethel Vivian Grey, though Nyiregyházi disliked the name Ethel and always called her Vivian. She was born in San Francisco in 1899, of English and Swedish parentage. She played the piano, and worked in the music department at the main branch of the Los Angeles Public Library. Nyiregyházi described her as a smallish woman with auburn hair, "scholarly" and somewhat homely. Her papers reveal a young woman who was decent and proper, sincere and often sweet, but also passionate, emotionally turbulent, romantic to the point of melodrama. She had already been captivated by his playing when they first encountered each other at the library shortly before his recital in May 1928. (She would continue to be captivated. Years later, after hearing him play Beethoven's Op. 111 sonata, she wrote, "I did not hear E. I heard the sounds on one of those distant planets.") They met again at a party on June 16, and by June 19 she was ready to declare that she was in love with him.

Nyiregyházi's sixth wife, Vivian. *

By her own admission, her thoughts would revolve around Nyiregyházi for the rest of her life. Widely read in philosophy, morals, and religion (including Eastern religions and mysticism), as well as literature and music, she was impressed by the "bigness" of Nyiregyházi's artistic and philosophical vision. Her papers are full of passionate declarations – variously dreamy, touching, pretentious, pitiable – attesting to the effect Nyiregyházi had on her. One of them reads like a sort of Mediocrity's Lament:

> Oh God, why am I so stirred when I come in contact with a mind like N's?
>
> I can only utter one wish, one prayer, one longing, that when I come again to this earth, when I continue my soul's existence, make me have the spark of genius. I worship genius, I reverence it – the creative in anyone. I cannot tell you now of last night – of all the

things N. said – of how it affected me. Tonight I feel only that I want to get on top of a lonely mountain and shout to the winds until the Universal Spirit shall hear me – that I want this gift, if not in this world, in this life, then in the next incarnation, surely.

I hate commonplace-ness, I hate ordinary-ness, trivial-ness, small-ness of mind, intellect, soul and spirit. Oh, why should I have been given – why blessed or cursed with the intense capacity for admiring and understanding the great spirits, the great minds, and not been given any power within myself to create?

She felt schoolgirlish excitement at encountering Nyiregyházi. Seeing him approach the music desk at the library, she "shook as with a chill." She recounted every moment of physical intimacy – holding hands, kissing – breathlessly. She was thrilled to be the genius's escort to one of his concerts, and reported "shaking with inward tremor" as he played. She wondered sometimes if he thought her merely a silly young girl with delusions of grandeur, but his letters suggest that he felt a real intellectual, emotional, and spiritual connection to her: "Perhaps you know without my telling you so, how deeply I am in sympathy with your intense longing after greatness and self-expression," he wrote to her late in 1928. "And I cannot reject the conviction that someone who was so deeply affected by such a music as I played and someone who loves Bach and Verdi at the same time so intensely as you do, is really a person quite out of the ordinary, fully deserving of love and admiration." They enjoyed long, intense, weighty conversations, and she became a trusted musical confidante.

But the relationship was always turbulent: there was something mad, obsessive, dangerous in her love for Nyiregyházi. From the beginning, "caught by his world-famous name and genius," she was tempted to "leave everything for him," yet they had known each other barely a month before she realized that his companionship was both a blessing and a curse. The "forbidden fruit" of his "great mind" stirred up a "turgid," "dark," and "uncertain" love, she wrote – a kind of "fever," which she found exhilarating but also frightening. She yearned to see him again, yet wished he would go away so as not to "undo all my good resolutions."

There was much in his personality that she despised and that wounded her deeply. As early as June 11, 1929, she could write,

> N. has just left. And I am sick. He has made me physically ill. By the thots [sic] which he put into speech. Such a feeling of revulsion has swept over me. It is almost unbearable. Could I ever have thot in these last few days that I might again feel the same for him as I did last year at this time? He killed that delicate undescribable emotion. Which I almost thot might grow into – perish the thot, into love. When E wants to be attractive he can *be* that more than anyone else I know. But when he lets one glimpse – even ever so little – into his other nature, then it is so repellant, so abhorrant [sic] to me that there sweeps over me a sensation of absolute physical illness. And such I feel tonight.

She was tempted by the ordinary connubial life that other men offered her, yet was drawn to Nyiregyházi as to a drug.

His derision about religion rankled, for Vivian was Catholic and devout, and despaired at having to hide the part of her she held "most dear." (He suspected her leanings, forbade talk of it, yet sometimes made blasphemous comments in her presence as though to draw her out.) Her papers are rife with ecstatic declarations of faith, disquisitions on religious questions, quotations from sacred texts, passionate appeals to God, Biblical analogies to her lot (the Old Testament prophet Jeremiah was a "bulwark" for her). In fact, she believed that she had received some sort of prophecy or "illumination" to the effect that she and Nyiregyházi were fated to be together, that he was destined to love one woman and, with her support, to compose great music. She was confident that his creative "spark" would take him eventually from "bitterness" to "victory," that he would conquer Europe and America and had the potential to be a great composer or philosopher – a Beethoven or a Kant – if only he would believe that "it was God who commanded him." She wrote, "Those compositions of his – bitter, cynical, banal – have *no* divine inspiration," and in this she considered him a figure to be pitied – a notion that would have enraged him.

Vivian's papers reveal many misunderstandings and quarrels, periods during which they kept their feelings hidden and barely acknowledged each other, but also periods of openness and joy in each other's presence. His visits to the library filled her with emotion, even when the relationship was strained and he was merely asking politely to hang up a poster for a concert. For her, each encounter was charged with meaning. She suffered in his presence but missed him when he was away. She made feeble efforts to assert her independence – refusing, for instance, to attend some of his concerts – and declared, again and again over the years, that the relationship was over. But she never stopped loving him, thinking about him, dreaming about him, and always renewed contact. She gave him money, though she had very little to give, and fretted over his prospects. "What *is* going to happen to him?" she wrote in December 1939. "My poor little five dollars can't last him. I can't spare it but I can't see him starve." She did not resent giving him money – indeed, claimed that *she* owed *him* for having had the opportunity to know him.

When the relationship was "on," there were long walks and regular Friday-evening dinners at Vivian's house. Nyiregyházi would play for and read to her, and they would go out to restaurants, concerts, and movies. She wanted to marry him, and admitted that she had longed to hear him propose since they met. The half-heartedness with which she occasionally pursued other romances only proved that she was, in essence, waiting – stoically, but with some bitterness – for him to come around, even through his marriages to Xandra, Genevieve, Ella, and Olga. In 1940, she bleakly described her principal memory of the past twelve years as one of "pain," though took solace in the cliché that "great love means great suffering." She inevitably spoke of her ordeal in religious terms – "I have carried the cross he made me bear" – and, addressing God, wrote, "Thru E. I have served thee." Perhaps her belief that destiny, not chance, was behind the relationship gave her the willpower to be a martyr to his genius.

Their "strange intellectual romance" seems to have remained platonic until they married, despite his persistent sexual solicitations. In her diary on December 19, 1939, she recorded that they had kissed for only the second time in eleven years. From the first she suffered because of his promiscuity, for despite her best efforts she was jealous of the other women in his life. (He, too, was jealous when another man showed interest in her.) She expressed disgust at his escapist hedonism and commitment to the "sex instinct," and endured his drunken tirades about women and marriage and sexual freedom. She worried that he would tire of her because she spurned his overtures, but she considered sex outside marriage tawdry – a betrayal of their spiritual union. She would not even visit him at his hotel except in the company of others.

Vivian's papers include some brutally honest insights into his personality. She wrote of his sensitivity and insecurity, of "his tremendous ego or vanity so easily wounded and causing *cosmic* upheavals in his temperament." She saw how easily his self-confidence could collapse. Once, in anger, she said something sarcastic about his compositions, hitting him (she knew) in his sorest spot; the next time he came over, he announced, "I will never play any of my compositions on this piano again." He was hurt whenever she skipped one of his concerts, and when she once let slip some praise for Vladimir Horowitz, he reminded her of it again and again, in hurt, accusing tones. All of this was typical – his quickness to perceive (or invent) slights, his desperate need for reassurance in matters great and small. His confidence in his status as a titan was like a great dam that needed constantly to be shored up, for the tiniest hole could blow it apart.

Vivian wrote of his passivity, too, which, for her as for so many others, was a lure: she felt compelled to look after him. Despite his poverty, he was more likely to wait for relief than to make something happen on his own initiative. ("In some ways E. has the mentality of a dullard," she wrote of his helplessness.) She knew that his passivity was a species of selfishness, and felt used by it. In 1942, she wrote,

> E. is not the type to give – he wants to be served. He thinks always of his own comfort. His greatness to him is a reason why always he is the recipient of kindness, never the donor. He wants me now, he regrets his marriage, he is not happy with O[lga]. He longs to be with me at least for some moments so that we can have again those evenings of dinner & music & discussion. But as for me – what has he ever done for me! He wants them again because he knows at last I and only I can make him happy! He realizes that now – but must he not realize something beyond that before our living together could be perfect? Must he not want to make me happy, do a few things for me, serve me as well as I serve him. Such thots I could swear have never entered his tremendous brain.

Of course, the ready availability of women willing to do his bidding only encouraged this selfishness. "[I]t has been too easy for him," Vivian wrote in 1939. "He has had to make no effort. Nor has he."

She wrote of his pessimism and volatility, too. One week at dinner he was wonderful and attractive, the next he was a stranger spewing rage. But she also wrote of the sweet and charming and childlike sides of his personality, of his tenderness and courtliness, of his touching physical frailty (she saw him white-faced and white-knuckled – "frightened to death" – during the "Buggy Ride" at an amusement park). And she wrote of his fun-loving side, which very few people ever saw. More than once the two were "dizzy and weak from laughing." On one of their walks, they "laughed so hard that we would stop in the middle of the street and hold our sides and be almost doubled up from the exertion. We literally laughed ourselves sick. I was weak when we reached Grace's house & so was he. And this was Nyiregyházi, the gloomy, tragic, morose genius who never was known to smile." Nyiregyházi himself said in a 1978 interview, "I feel I am a tragic personality given to melancholy. But I am not so full of melancholy that I can't have a wonderful time. I have been known to laugh. . . . I must admit that I seem to either have a very good time in life or a very bad one. Unlike most people, there does not seem to be a lot of in-between."

When Nyiregyházi flipped that coin in the spring of 1938, Vivian was one of the women he was considering proposing to, though she did not know it, and he knew he was "a damn fool," leaving a "wonderful woman who adores me," when he decamped for Europe. By 1940, he was expressing a desire to marry her. "My other marriages meant nothing," he now told her. "It was always only you." Her response was typical. "Oh – thrice declared happiness!!" she wrote. "For I love E. always have & always wil[l;] no [other] man can ever satisfy me." He proposed in March 1941, but could not afford a ring, so, touchingly, he slipped off one of her rings while she closed her eyes, then put it back on while popping the question. The wedding plans foundered almost immediately. He had no money, his personality still troubled her, they fought. In fact, it was after one of their fights, just two months into the engagement, that he married Olga – a characteristic response. Still, he insisted that Vivian was his "inspiration," his "salvation," that his ability to do creative work depended on her becoming his wife, and she knew his devotion was genuine, though he could still be "cruel" and "overbearing." Finally, in August 1945, he summoned her to Las Vegas, where he had obtained a divorce from Olga, and Vivian became his sixth wife.

Not surprisingly, marriage did little to improve their relationship. The Entitled One was, of course, no help in domestic matters, and made little effort to earn a living, while Vivian, struggling to keep her vow to make him happy, poured time and energy and money into the relationship, undermining her mental and physical health, all the while keeping her feelings mostly to herself and fearing collapse from the strain. Sometimes she would resolve anew to break with him, and they were occasionally estranged. For the first few years they did not live together. She had tenants in her house – she needed the money – and he resented their presence, mostly because he refused to share a bathroom. He moved in around 1948.

One anecdote recorded in Vivian's "Little Book," from 1948, says much about what she endured as Nyiregyházi's wife. On Christmas Eve, she stayed up excitedly until the wee hours decorating, and on Christmas Day, exhausted but happy, she ate nothing after breakfast in anticipation of a big dinner at six or seven. At five o'clock, Nyiregyházi arrived and announced that he was in the mood to talk and play, which he proceeded to do for hours. One of his compositions alone lasted an hour, and Vivian was expected to turn pages ("I couldn't leave the piano for fear of offending 'his majesty'"). When she rushed into the kitchen to turn off the oven, he called out, "Come right back!" When he finished playing, he sipped sherry and expounded. Finally, a little after midnight, he announced, "Now you can prepare the dinner. I am hungry now." Vivian, weak with hunger, exhausted, and "utterly disgusted," then served the ruins of her meal. This, apparently, was a pattern in their domestic life. She would come home after a day's work and be expected to serve as a worshipful audience for his liquor-fuelled performances and monologues late into the night, when she was allowed to serve dinner before collapsing into bed. To maintain a household while working a full-time job and catering to his needs wore her down. At the same time, she acknowledged many happy times, and continued to be "warmed by the rays" of his genius.

They did not have much of a sex life. According to an interview note in his last wife's hand, they attempted intercourse on their wedding night but "it didn't fit": Vivian had some unspecified gynecological problem, and an operation in 1952 failed to correct it. Moreover, she thought oral sex a crime against nature. (He said he masturbated more during this marriage than at any other time in his life.) But sex was never at the root of their union. For all their problems they had an enduring emotional and intellectual connection, and in his own way he repaid her support and companionship. Sometimes, he expressed surprise at his own feelings for her. The relationship, he said, proved to him that there were forces stronger than sex – and that, for him, was a revelation indeed.

He still needed sex, though. He continued to have sexual encounters outside of the marriage, and as always his feelings for old flames complicated his life. He had homosexual encounters, too. In the 1940s, he befriended the pianist Shura Cherkassky, who was gay, and recalled an evening on which the two went to a sexually charged party ("orgy," in one version of the story) at the home of a Danish baroness in the Hollywood Hills. At one point, a woman sat in Nyiregyházi's lap, kissed him, and declared her love; he kissed her back, declared *his* love, then realized that his partner was a man – one of many transvestites at the party. He was "confused," he said, but not alarmed or disturbed, and admitted doing his share of flirting. A pianist active in Los Angeles in those days remembers an incident that took place while he was visiting the home of a wealthy local music patron. When the subject of Nyiregyházi came up in conversation, the patron placed a call to him, and though it was late and Nyiregyházi was in bed, the patron ordered him to come over, which he did. Plied with drink, Nyiregyházi, on command, played Liszt for about an hour. Later, the pianist, retrieving his coat, found Nyiregyházi and the patron in bed together. The patron, unfazed, got up, took out his wallet, and gave Nyiregyházi several hundred-dollar bills, which he accepted.

Through it all, Vivian pampered and tried to please him. In May 1952, a quarter-century after their first meeting, she left him a note that read, in part, "I don't see how my love for you could become greater, it is already so all engrossing – yet such expressions from you would – if it were *possible* – make me love my Darling even more because he is so great in *all* ways and so wonderful to me these times past. I can not imagine a more wonderful life than to be always with a *Genius* and that *Genius* to be my own *darling Ervin!*" For all its problems, the relationship sustained them both, through often difficult times.

Swan Songs

Nyiregyházi performed in Los Angeles through the 1940s and into the 1950s, occasionally attracting large audiences and some press attention (his concerts were often stacked with friends, lovers, fellow-Hungarians). But the momentum of his career was irretrievably lost; now he was simply drawing on his one marketable skill in order to make money, and only because his concerts brought in little did he play as often as he did. He found performing increasingly nerve-wracking. Alcohol helped. When Shura Cherkassky told him that even one drink made him unable to play, Nyiregyházi replied, "If I have one drink, I can't play either – I need six or seven." It was essential to find the right balance: "I have to be sober enough to be able to play, and yet drunk enough to *want* to play." He now had a reputation locally as an un-reliable eccentric, a drunk, a womanizer. Arnold Schoenberg tried to arrange a concert for him at UCLA, where he had been teaching since 1936, but encountered only resistance in the music department.[*]

---

[*] Nyiregyházi and Schoenberg saw each other from time to time until 1950, the year before the composer's death, and Schoenberg (politely?) pronounced Nyiregyházi's own music "unique."

A Soldier of Fortune

Nyiregyházi had some musician friends, and Vivian, in her "Little Book," noted the couple's occasional visits to a composers' club, but many colleagues were wary of him, and he stayed mostly aloof from the thriving local music scene. "I had my own thoughts about music, and they had theirs," he said, "and we simply did not see each other."

In September 1939, he gave a concert under the auspices of Lazar S. Samoiloff, a Russian-born voice teacher who maintained a small hall for his pupils, which he rented to Nyiregyházi for a few dollars, and over the next year and a half he gave about a dozen concerts there, often for overflow crowds. He continued to perform sporadically elsewhere – a ticket survives for one recital, on April 6, 1941, at the odd admission price of $1.01 – but his career did not take off anew. Managers came and went,* and his pride continued to interfere with his prospects. One manager asked him to audition before agreeing to represent him in a concert in a casino; after waiting two hours for his audition, Nyiregyházi, indignant, went home. In 1956, he said, the film composer Miklós Rózsa wanted him to perform in one of his scores, but Nyiregyházi thought the fee ridiculous and the music "crap."

Even within the Hungarian community, he was no longer the draw he once was. For one all-Liszt recital in 1940, only about two dozen people – effectively just the concert's sponsors – showed up, and he netted barely $20. Father Lani and Bela Lugosi arranged a concert at St. Stephen's on October 14, 1940, to celebrate the twenty-fifth anniversary of his orchestral debut in Berlin; with a second pianist accompanying, he played the first movement of Beethoven's C-minor concerto, the work with which he had made his debut. Lugosi sold tickets – admission was thirty cents, ninety if you wanted goulash – and gave a pre-concert speech in which he hailed his friend as one of the greatest artists in the history of music. This time, Nyiregyházi cleared a little more than $60.

---

* A friend interested in investing in his career contacted the legendary impresario Sol Hurok, in New York, but Hurok, though interested, worried that Nyiregyházi was "too individualistic" and demurred.

197

Occasionally he found work out of town. There were concerts in San Francisco and Oakland in 1940, and one for the USO at an army hospital in Denver in 1942. He gave several more concerts in Denver the following year, including a recital on October 29 presented by the Franz Liszt Foundation. In August 1942, he joined the entourage of his friend Roland H. Wiley, the Democratic district attorney of Clark County, Nevada, who was running for governor, on a whistlestop train tour of the state and gave concerts in Reno, Las Vegas, Boulder City, · Winnemuca, and Elko in support of the campaign. Wiley lost the election, but Nyiregyházi was a hit. In Elko, he played for miners who attended his concert under orders but liked it so much that they stood him drinks in a saloon afterward. Inevitably, he compared himself with Wilde, who had addressed miners, with great success, on a lecture tour of America. Genuine appreciation from lay audiences always meant a great deal to him. He remembered fondly a concert he once gave in a Las Vegas cocktail lounge, not because the city's leading citizens were present, but because prisoners in the jail across the street overheard the music and joined in the cheers.

"My activities as a pianist can be said to be in a constant state of stagnation," Nyiregyházi wrote in a 1943 letter, yet in his thirties, forties, and fifties he was in his prime as a pianist and still growing as a musician. No longer nurturing a real career, he felt liberated artistically; he played only what he wanted to play, how he wanted to play it. He continued to add to his already enormous repertoire. His ambitious recital in Los Angeles on January 29, 1941, was typical in featuring some relatively esoteric fare, including Liszt's *Weinen, Klagen, Sorgen, Zagen* (after Bach); Anton Rubinstein's Sonata in E Minor; Musorgsky's *Pictures at an Exhibition*; and Schoenberg's atonal piece Op. 11/No. 2. He was drawn to what in those days was off-the-beaten-track repertoire – sonatas by Brahms, Tchaikovsky, and Scriabin, unfamiliar works by Albeniz, Bartók, Debussy, Godowsky, Il'insky, MacDowell, Respighi. He thought nothing of entertaining a women's club with Scriabin's weird, forbidding Ninth Sonata, the "Black Mass." And the loss of orchestral opportunities did not wrest concertos from his grasp: he simply performed his own solo arrangements of Liszt's *Totentanz*, the Grieg concerto, Rachmaninov's Second, *Rhapsody in Blue*.

He did not limit himself to piano music either. He played orchestral and choral music by Schumann, Liszt, Saint-Saëns. He opened one recital in 1943 with the first movement of Bruckner's Ninth Symphony (at his tempos, it ran some twenty-eight minutes); in another concert that same year he played the entire *Symphonie fantastique* of Berlioz. He performed operatic music, too – the *William Tell* overture, part of *Cavalleria rusticana*, the last scene of *Elektra*. There was, he admitted, not just personal preference but fear of criticism in such programming – he had no competitors among pianists in Bruckner and Berlioz – as well as naughty-boy defiance: "I like to get away with it!"

Some people, hearing his uncompromising programs and very individual piano style in these years, thought he was crazy; others were astonished and moved. "I've never heard anything like it" – some variant of that remark appears again and again in the comments of those who heard him play, cognoscenti and lay listeners alike (Schoenberg said as much in his 1935 letter). The American pianist Raymond Lewenthal, born in 1926, heard Nyiregyházi many times in his teens, and, in 1978, left valuable recollections of Nyiregyházi's "colossal technique" and "colossal personality." Of the reading of Beethoven's Op. 111 sonata he heard at one of the Samoiloff concerts – "one of *the* great musical memories of my life" – he wrote:

> After forty years I still remember that granitic performance of the first movement, the immense power heightened by Nyiregyházi's immobile demeanor at the piano; and I remember the metaphysical beauty of sound of the second movement, emerging from those white slender hands with the blue veins showing through the fine skin. The fingers produced the tone by a sort of plastic, controlled

tension. And I remember the handsome face, which remained so quiet and concentrated that a drop of perspiration at the end of the nose stayed poised there indefinitely, as though frozen.

Lewenthal claimed to know no other musician as talented as Nyiregyházi and, by way of conclusion, placed him among "the demon-driven poets, artists who have seared their way into my heart . . . the evokers of passion and tenderness, of the epic, the strange, the mysterious, of great darkness and brilliant light."

When nothing else was available, Nyiregyházi fell back on private recitals in the homes of friends.* He derived some satisfaction from these concerts. As he wrote of one series, in a letter to Ayn Rand, "It seems to me that the 'atmosphere' on these occasions is 'right.'" The purpose of these concerts "is to put me on my 'tottering' feet, and help me a tiny-weeny-bit financially," he wrote. "The situation is a bit embarrassing to me. But nothing can be done about that."

Yes, *that* Ayn Rand. The newly famous writer and philosopher had attended one of his private concerts,† and Nyiregyházi was wildly enthusiastic about her best-selling novel *The Fountainhead*, which had been published in 1943. He was enthralled by Rand's individualism-at-all-costs philosophy, and by her protagonist, Howard Roark, an idealistic and highly original architect who willingly accepts the ruin of his career rather than compromise the integrity of his creative work. Roark knows the folly of living by the opinions

---

* As early as the 1940s, record cutters and tape recorders were sometimes observed to run at private gatherings at which he played, though none of the resulting acetates or tapes have yet come to light.

† According to one of his last wife's interview notes, he and Rand first met at a concert of his in 1935, she "loved Ervin's music," they became friends, and he visited her at her home, though none of this is corroborated.

of others, refuses to be used or controlled, never changes his mind, hates hypocrisy, and defines "the creator" as "the man who stands alone." His maxims, especially those in his climactic speech to the jury, surely resonated with Nyiregyházi: "The first right on earth is the right of the ego . . . Great men can't be ruled . . . There is no standard of personal dignity except independence . . ." Roark's mentor, at one point, says, "Architecture is not a business, not a career, but a crusade and a consecration to a joy that justifies the existence of the earth." Read "music" for "architecture" and you have the credo of Ervin Nyiregyházi.

Rand, like Nyiregyházi, identified proudly as a Romantic in the nineteenth-century mould, and her happily highfalutin, overwrought prose was no flaw to a man who could write of "attendant circumstances fairly contributory to a satisfactory unfoldment." He wanted to play more for her, and talk with her. In April 1944, he wrote her two long letters. In the first, he wrote, "The stand you take is great and exceptional and will, I believe, remain a monument to the powerful expression of a powerful, and rigid, and for that reason great Credo." In the second, he offered more praise that revealed much about his own values and about his mind in the throes of intellectual excitement. "You are the greatest, the most deadly satirist since Oscar Wilde," he wrote, and after comparing specific Wilde and Rand characters, he continued: "You and Oscar Wilde seem to have forced a difficult issue through by creating that hardly definable spiritual 'aura' emanating from, and vibrant around, the mordant, and only *so-called* witticisms of these characters. It is this 'aura' that is the thing."

There is no evidence that Rand replied or that Nyiregyházi ever encountered her again, and anyway it seems unlikely that the author of *Capitalism: The Unknown Ideal* felt much honoured to be so ardently lumped with the author of *The Soul of Man Under Socialism*.

During the Second World War, Nyiregyházi lost contact with most of his family and friends in Europe, and twenty years would elapse before he found out what happened to them. Jozsa Kovács died in 1939, Géza Kovács committed suicide in 1942, and some other members of the Kovács family, and other of his Jewish friends, perished in Nazi concentration camps. Through most of the 1930s, his brother, mother, and grandmother lived in Berlin. Alfred, who never married, worked for the travel department of American Express (Nyiregyházi last saw him in the early 1930s). Szidónia died of natural causes, at the age of eighty, in 1937, and afterward Mária and Alfred moved back to Budapest, where Alfred continued to work for American Express. He was drafted, and died in 1944, fighting with other Hungarians alongside the German army on the Russian front. Mária became a victim of the Holocaust, shortly after the Arrow Cross Party, which cooperated with the Nazis in persecuting Jews, came to power in Hungary in October 1944. As Nyiregyházi was told, his mother had managed to obtain a passport from Brazil (a supporter of the Allies), which was supposed to ensure that she could be taken to the border and released, but because she was Jewish, and moreover owned expensive jewellery, the passport was ignored. When, in a confrontation on the street in front of her building, a Brazilian representative insisted that Mária was under his country's protection, Nazi officials just laughed. Her property was confiscated, and she was sent to a concentration camp. Years later, Nyiregyházi saw her last postcard, in which she lamented the loss of her beloved jewels.

Over the years, Nyiregyházi's friends and acquaintances among the Hollywood elite occasionally sought work for him as a pianist – and even as a composer – in the movies; a few promising projects did come his way, but none of them, in the end, were realized. Only during and just after the war – ironically, when he had effectively stopped socializing in Hollywood – did he become involved, quite by chance, in several movie projects. And with his concert career now all but over, he was glad to have the work.

The first of these projects was a forgettable horror film, *The Soul of a Monster*, released by Columbia Pictures in August 1944. Nyiregyházi got the job by answering an advertised call for pianists, and claimed that he was selected from the line-up of applicants because Columbia's president, Harry Cohn, thought him talented but also "an ugly son of a bitch" – meaning he had just the diabolical quality they were looking for. Here is the plot synopsis of the film in the *Fantastic Cinema Subject Guide*, in which the film appears just below *Sorority Babes in the Slimeball Bowl-o-Rama*: "A noble doctor, a good and kind man, is dying, and his wife makes a desperate plea to any force which can make him live. Her plea is heard by a mysterious, sinister woman – the agent of evil, a demon, perhaps even the devil himself (or herself) – who miraculously cures the doctor, then exercises an evil influence over him. He is changed, however – his soul blackened, and he must engage in a monumental struggle to free himself from this evil." Dismissed by the *New York Times* as "a preposterously foolish film," it includes Nyiregyházi's only credited appearance in a movie. He plays "Erwin" in a scene in which several friends gather in an apartment. It begins with Nyiregyházi playing the end of Liszt's *Spanish Rhapsody*, rising from the piano, with that stiff dignity the critics always noted, and joining the other guests. (One of them, a young woman, chirps, "I've always loved the *Spanish Rhapsody*! Somehow it never sounds Spanish to me!") Outside, a storm rages, and the doctor says, "It's Nature's music, so why shut it out? It ought to make a wonderful background for the *Mephisto Waltz*." Nyiregyházi, in his heavy accent, replies, "Perhaps it would," and plays a few pages of the piece (brilliantly) before the scene changes.

In the mid-1940s, he had a brief career as a "hand double" in several films that featured piano playing. "Only in sentimental novels do pianists have hands with long, tapering fingers," the critic Harold C. Schonberg observed. "Your average pianist has a broad palm and spatulate fingers." But Nyiregyházi (like Liszt) did have precisely the long, tapering fingers of legend, and they were ideal for Hollywood's purposes. His hands were featured in *A Song to Remember*, another Columbia film, directed by his fellow-Hungarian Charles Vidor and released at the start of 1945. A fanciful biography of Chopin – frankly, something of a mess, dramatically and historically – the film was a big-budget production in garish Technicolor, and was a huge success, though it was received with both acclaim and derision, especially for its manhandling of Chopin's music.[*] In close-ups of Chopin's hands at the keyboard, the hands are Nyiregyházi's – including the famous sequence in which the consumptive composer, bravely undertaking one last concert tour, coughs blood onto the keys. But Nyiregyházi was bitter that José Iturbi was hired to perform (uncredited) on the soundtrack, for such was the popularity of the film that Iturbi's subsequent RCA recording of Chopin's Polonaise in A-flat Major sold more than a million copies.

The box-office success of *A Song to Remember* inspired a host of classical-music films, among them *Song of Love*, a big-budget MGM production that explored the relationship of Robert and Clara Schumann (Paul Henreid and Katharine Hepburn) and their friendships with Brahms (Robert Walker) and Liszt (Henry Daniell). The film was recognized as whitewashed, sentimental, and historically inaccurate when it was released, in October 1947, though its casting made it an interesting novelty. Arthur Rubinstein (uncredited) supplied the soundtrack, and Nyiregyházi doubled for Daniell during a soirée sequence in the middle of the film, in which Liszt, before a glittering crowd, plays the *Mephisto Waltz* No. 1 and a paraphrase on Schumann's "Dedication" – the "song of love" of the title. During this sequence, Nyiregyházi, in costume, bewigged, and made up, appears

---

[*] "A strange film," Robertson Davies wrote, through his alter-ego Samuel Marchbanks, "brightly coloured, sweet and gassy, like a fruit salad." The film, incidentally, made a deep impression on many a young pianist of the day, including Van Cliburn and Liberace, who stole his trademark candelabrum from it.

repeatedly in hand close-ups and in face and body profiles. (His impassive face, calm demeanour, and high, erect posture are all evident.) He bore a striking resemblance to Henry Daniell, who was also tall and thin, with a long face, big, dark eyes, long, thin lips, and a melancholy air.

Nyiregyházi's most whimsical cinematic turn was in the classic horror film *The Beast with Five Fingers*, released by Warner Brothers in the last days of 1946. In a village in northern Italy, a concert pianist who has the use of only his left hand dies, but the disembodied hand comes back to life, leaves the crypt, and begins a murderous rampage against the pianist's relatives, nurse, secretary, and friend. It was all a dream, it turns out: the secretary, played by Peter Lorre, imagined the whole thing. (As one of the characters helpfully observes, "There's no such thing as a hand cut off and walking around.") In sequences in which the hand scuttles crablike over floors and bookshelves (and people), the director, Robert Florey, used his own hand, but Nyiregyházi was deputized in several sequences at the keyboard, playing a left-hand arrangement of Bach's famous Chaconne in D Minor. This time, Nyiregyházi himself (uncredited) is on the soundtrack.

His two weeks' work on *A Song to Remember* allowed him to put a $500 down payment on a house for himself and his fifth wife, Olga, on Wesley Avenue, just south of the Memorial Coliseum, and to pay for furniture, an ice box, and a piano – though he would soon have to sell the piano to finance their divorce. These movies did nothing for his career, however. In fact, the film and concert work he did during the war – including the Mr. X concert of 1946 – was a kind of last hurrah professionally.* In the 1950s, he stopped teaching piano, and gave only

---

* Around the late 1940s, Nyiregyházi made private tapes occasionally for a wealthy friend, Ernie Bysshe, who would pay him $10 – or pay him in liquor. He recalled recording the "Appassionata" Sonata, and perhaps Chopin's B-flat-minor sonata, but the tapes are presumably lost. Around 1960, he taped the Liszt sonata for Elsie Swan. After giving

Nyiregyházi sporting the black silk hood he wore in his Mr. X concert in Los Angeles, May 13, 1946. With him is the impresario Irwin Parnes. *(Reproduced from* Irwin Parnes Takes the "Bull by the Horns," *by Joy and Irwin Parnes.)*

a few sporadic public performances – concerts for women's clubs and Jewish groups, a free recital for The Humanists in a school auditorium, some benefit concerts on behalf of a black congressional candidate.*

what he said was one of his most inspired performances of it, he discovered that Elsie had forgotten to turn on the tape recorder. She did so, and he played the whole sonata again, less well. A note in his last wife's hand, probably referring to the 1960s, reads, "Carl Negake has Ervin's tape of Schumann's Carnival [sic]." Another reads, "Ervin recorded Grieg nocturne for Elsie & [his eighth wife] Margaret & Elsie gave it to Mark Fabean in the late 60's – 67, 68, or 69." None of these recordings have come to light, however.

* One of Nyiregyházi's sketchbooks, from 1956, includes a draft of a letter to the Liszt Society in England, in which he offers to give all-Liszt recitals in London and perhaps elsewhere in Europe. Nothing came of this idea.

A recital for the Hungarian community in Patriotic Hall, on July 27, 1957, was apparently his last public appearance for more than fifteen years.

He claimed that the "debacle" of his career did not crush his spirits, that he faced it philosophically. "Of course financial trouble is never welcome," he said in 1978. "But I never regarded concertizing as a glorious occupation. I always preferred music as a way of life, not as a profession." (He liked to call himself "a talented amateur.") He always thought of himself as a great man, and longed for others to agree, but he was not so concerned to be renowned as a great pianist. "I am first a human being, second a philosopher and composer, thirdly a pianist," he said. His anxiety about performing in public had only increased as the fortunes of his career had waned and criticism of his playing had mounted, and he knew that he could never reconcile his artistic tastes and ideals with the demands of the musical market-place. No wonder he expressed so little regret about abandoning the whole business of being a professional pianist, which he had always associated with life under his mother's thumb. But he did not abandon *music*. He continued to work privately, contentedly, and pro-lifically, without compromise, in the sphere of music that gave him the most satisfaction: composition.

17

An Uncompromising Rebel

MY MUSICAL CREDO

The composer regards music, or at least his musical activity, as a means of expressing a particular view of life or attitude toward life, and his compositions seek to express the various aspects of his spiritual and intellectual nature.

Consequently, the composer wholly subordinates the "laws" and "requirements" of music – as determined by the so-called authorities – to the performance of the aforementioned task.

It is, for instance, the accepted belief that there "must be" a display of counterpoint in a composition, and also that a musical piece "must" manifest a variety of moods. If, however, these are not conducive to the accomplishment of the ends previously mentioned, he will not adopt such methods just because it is the "custom" to do so. For one thing, he questions the soundness of "that" which keeps this "custom" in power.

His purpose is not that his works furnish "entertainment," but that through them an intensified awareness of certain facts and phases of life be created in the consciousness of the audience.

All his works are based upon deeply personal experiences, far more so than is usual with other composers. In other words, what is meant here is that he is more intent upon communicating to the audience the most personal of his idiosyncrasies than other composers have been. This composer does not separate his musical expression from his life, nor does he believe that such a separation is at all necessary, desirable or the "thing to do." Quite the contrary. He wants that his life go down on record – gloriously or ingloriously, as the case may be – and for the achievement of that end he finds music a particularly helpful medium.

The titles of his works are not superimposed externalities, but form intrinsic parts of his conceptions.

The view of life expressed in this music is essentially tragic and grim, though the seemingly humorous titles and character of some of his works might easily mislead people.

Furthermore, his individual reactions and what he sees in life do not permit him to be "objective" and "detached" – as is, apparently, the great vogue of today.

As for his titles, he knows that they will give rise to some "fun-making." This he does not object to. The tragic conception is heightened and its validity is verified by the fact that what should be regarded as a deeply serious issue is, instead, taken for a joke.

Not only is music to him a medium of expressing his sorrows, heartaches, etc., but also his aversions, his dislike of certain groups and institutions.

He is an uncompromising rebel, but not in the sense that he wants to be "original" at all costs. Quite the contrary. He does not believe in the "traditional" value of originality, though he condemns the unscrupulous appropriation of musical material belonging to others, as is being practised today by certain groups.

He believes in the romantic musical idiom and in complete freedom of the choice of subject matter.

He is fully and wholeheartedly both an eclectic and an iconoclast.

This statement appeared in the program for the concert of his own works that Nyiregyházi gave in Hollywood in 1937, and though remarkable – and convenient – it does not tell the whole story of him as a composer. From the age of three he thought of himself as primarily a creator and only secondarily a performer. Coercion and need forced him into a career as a virtuoso, but temperamentally he was always better suited to the private life of a composer. Composition, he believed, was his calling, and with the decline of his concert career it became his principal creative outlet: he composed almost every day, sometimes six, seven, eight hours at a time. To be sure, there were times when he had difficulty concentrating on creative work – the mid-twenties, for instance, when he was, as he put it, "hounded by sex and starved for food." Nevertheless, at the end of his life he could boast of a compositional career that had lasted more than eighty years.

Composition was many things to him: autobiography, escape, solace, protest, plea, testament. It was vital to his sense of artistic self-worth, and like alcohol and sex it filled a need to express pent-up thoughts and feelings. He took composing very seriously, and his music had profound meaning for him – no wonder he rarely risked putting it before the public. To share his music was tantamount to confessing, and his closest, most trusting relationships were invariably with those who loved his music and encouraged him to write it.

Nyiregyházi's compositions have never been catalogued or even counted. In 1979, he estimated that he had completed eight to nine hundred works, with some five hundred more still unfinished, and he continued to compose – indeed, was especially productive – in his last years. He wrote piano music primarily, some chamber music (mostly for violin, cello, or double bass with piano), and many songs, most in Hungarian or German, some in English, a few to his own texts. He conceived some works for orchestra, though preserved them only in a

piano arrangement or short score.* Sometimes he conceived or completed a work years before writing it down. There were periods in his
life when, though composing prolifically in his head, he had little time
or energy for writing works down; some were lost altogether for this
reason. His memory for his own music was astonishing. Around age
seven, he saw a silent movie the piano accompaniment to which drew
on a Serbian folk song; in 1938, he remembered that song and began
composing a piece based on it; in 1985, he finally wrote the piece down.
The title, appropriately, was *A Diary of My Life*.

Music was always in his head. He composed while reading, convers-
ing, walking, taking the bus. Alcohol helped to release musical ideas,
and some compositions came to him in dreams (in one, he was playing
the piece in question for Saint-Saëns). Some works came to him almost
fully formed; others he laboured over. Some of his sketchbooks
survive, along with many loose sketches on odd bits of paper – letters,
bills, flyers, pamphlets, concert programs. A sketch from 1973 for
a work grandly titled *Fate Inexorable* is scrawled on hand-drawn staves
on an Occidental Life of California envelope. When struck by a
musical idea, he might first write, in his own shorthand, what he called
a "memory sketch," which might be no more than a bit of melody or a
bass line with perhaps some indications of key and harmony. More
detailed "working-out sketches" might follow, and "constellation
sketches," in which he decided on the order of musical ideas and other
matters of form. When a piece was finished, he copied it out neatly,

---

* I have seen no orchestrated music by Nyiregyházi, and he admitted to having no training or skill (and little ambition) when it came to orchestration. Some of his pieces require
as many as six staves, the results being unplayable by a single pianist; these were probably
intended as short scores for orchestral works, though they include no clues to instrumentation. His piano music always tended to be "orchestral." Géza Révész already noticed
that, sometimes, "Erwin is so obsessed with the desire to express his musical ideas orches-
trally that he oversteps the limit of technical possibilities on the piano."

signed it, and dated it. Beginning in 1947, he occasionally microfilmed batches of his compositions, and stored the microfilms in bank vaults. The pristine state of his manuscripts, and the care with which he preserved them through a peripatetic life, says much about the high value he placed on his compositions.*

As a composer, Nyiregyházi followed a strictly private agenda. His goal was not to contribute to a repertory or canon, to carry on a tradition or found a school, to breathe new life into established genres and forms, to address a community. He sought only to give voice to the thoughts and feelings that teemed within him. All composers do that, of course, but Nyiregyházi's music is distinguished by the particularity of the extra-musical impulses that inspired it. His pieces almost always had subject matter in the sense of being motivated by something specific and identifiable in the real world or in his mind: a person, place, or thing, an emotion, a memory or dream, a concept or belief, an incident in history or in his own life, a scene in a movie or something he read – hence the eccentric and seemingly whimsical titles of many of his works.† His music was the ultimate expression of his belief (influenced by Liszt) that all of life is properly the domain of the composer. *All* of his compositions, really, might be considered entries in a diary of his life.

---

* Some of his music did fall victim to his poverty and wanderlust. For instance, sometime in the 1920s he stored a suitcaseful of compositions at Penn Station, in New York, but did not have the three dollars needed to retrieve them. He said he did not write down many pieces at one point in the 1970s because the table and chair in his hotel room wobbled, and he could not fit in (or afford) new ones.

† Some of his works, especially from his later years, are untitled, but most bear a title in English, Hungarian, or German, some a title in Latin, Italian, French, or some other (or more than one) language. (What determined the choice of language is not always clear.) With a few exceptions, I give titles in English only – his own English, where available.

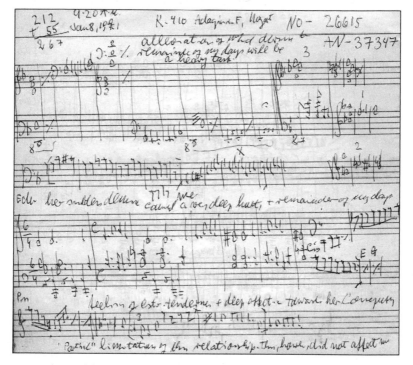

A page of musical sketches dated January 8, 1971, showing at least two stages of work, in blue and (beginning at the end of the fourth and fifth staves) red ink. Some keys are indicated in shorthand according to the German system – for instance, "E dur" (E major) at the start of the fourth stave, and "Cis" (C-sharp, presumably minor) six bars later. The reference at the top to Mozart's canonic *Adagio* in F major for two basset horns and bassoon, K. 410, appears to be unrelated to the music being sketched. As this page shows, Nyiregyházi's sketchbooks doubled as notepads and diaries for the recording of phone numbers, accounts, and other quotidian data, as well as passing thoughts. *(International Ervin Nyiregyházi Foundation.)*

The subject matter that inspired his music included his profoundest feelings, as he revealed in a letter to Helen Richardson in 1929:

> What sufferings I have gone through on account of you! Oh, God! No wonder that I was able to compose a musical work which in regard to somberness, gloom, despair, soul-crushing sadness and consuming passion is without paralell [*sic*] in musical literature. It is a work of tremendous intensity, power and expressiveness. I shall entitle it: "The Tragedy of Life". It is a grandiose title and I do believe that the music is quite worthy of it and the expectations connected with it. Yes indeed, if not for the heart-tearing suffering caused by the relation between myself on [the] one hand and yourself and Theodore Dreiser on the other hand, I should never have been able to create such a work.

Yet, the pettiest quotidian events, the basest thoughts, the tiniest annoyances – these, too, inspired compositions. He once said that "if my scrambled eggs are not fixed right I compose to make up for the fact that I don't get what I want," and he was not kidding: a single bad lunch one day in 1984 inspired *two* compositions – his reward for what he called his "suffering." His sketchbooks, which doubled as notepads and diaries, include many, wide-ranging marginal comments that often seem to bear on the music: "This is *not* Government music[;] this is music of the people that beheaded Marie Antoinette, & brought about the French, the Russian, & the Chinese Revolution[s]." . . . "Throw caution to the 4 winds – the Motto of the successful drinker." . . . "I advertised for sex and all I got was the double negative. 'It don't make no difference'." . . . "A shitpot tells the great piano player what to do." . . . Under one sketch from the mid-1960s, he wrote, "*These* shitty sons. *These* Sons-of-Bitches," flagging the emphasized words to join them to particular bars of music.

Nyiregyházi could not think of music, his own or anyone else's, abstractly. To make sense of a piece, he had to find some personal extra-musical content in it. Musical ideas were constantly simmering within him, accompanying his life like a soundtrack, but apparently could be tapped and brought to light only through the intercession of some incident or idea that gave the music a "story." Anything might do. Once, walking down Hollywood Boulevard, he dropped and shattered a bottle he was carrying, and the jolt caused a new piece to pop into his mind. The ostensible subject matter of a piece was not always its "real" or sole meaning, however; some pieces had both literal and symbolic meanings. *Orgy of the Desperadoes: Mutiny in Singapore*, ostensibly about pirates, was also about his rebellion against authority and convention, in which sense he regarded himself as a "desperado." (He described it as an hour and a half long and "very much like Spanish bullfight music.") In the end, he admitted he did not really understand the subconscious sources of his musical ideas. They came to him, he said, from "the Lord God."

Whatever its extra-musical impetus, his music was not programmatic or picturesque. "Purely descriptive music is just trash!" he said. "Dead sound. Nonsense." One finds only the mildest tone painting in his music; for instance, *The Bottomless Pit* (after Poe) begins and ends with the lowest note on the piano. Géza Révész noted that the young Nyiregyházi was more concerned to convey emotional responses than to depict things or people in tones, and that remained true. In his "mood pieces" (as he called his works), he depicted not the extra-musical subject matter itself but his feelings toward it – a crucial distinction. Those feelings were invariably dark; trivial subjects and whimsical titles never meant light-hearted pieces (he said he sought out the cosmic within the seemingly trivial). What went into his composing, he wrote in that letter to Helen, was "the indescribable suffering and tortures of my soul," his "sadness and tragedy, overmastering, tornading passion and sinister determination," his "so far bitter fate, the disappointments, the heartaches," yielding music that was "an everlasting monument to those emotions, those agonies of the soul, to life which is inculcated with the spirit of Tragedy." His musical idiom remained (to recall his credo) "essentially tragic and grim," throughout his life and across his *oeuvre*, and, as a result, in his pieces, for all the variety of the subjects that motivated them, one hears the same few compositional attitudes again and again, whether the ostensible subject matter was the tragedy of life or one of his wife's cats.

Nyiregyházi had an almost infallible memory for the titles and subjects of his compositions, wrote down from memory several lists taking in hundreds of his pieces, and talked about many of his works in interviews. The range of subject matter is astonishing. He often took his own personality as a subject, and his grandiosity is apparent in titles like *Caesar, The Hero, The Sultan,* and *The Titan.* ("You know who this is!" he said of the latter title, adding, unnecessarily, "Me!") The circumstances of his life inspired many pieces – hotels he lived in, streets he walked, his financial problems, the minutiae of his daily life (hence *The Installation of the Telephone* and *The Mailman Makes His Weary Rounds*). He wrote pieces about his career too, some of them very specific (*The Terror of Playing Beethoven's "Appassionata" in Concert*).

His sexual life inspired many pieces, some with self-explanatory titles like *A Night of Love with Lisolette. Red Menace* was inspired by a redheaded waitress, *So Near and Yet So Far* by nothing more profound than "a big derrière on a streetcar in L.A.," and *Happy Tom Cat* was presumably a self-portrait. His wives provided much creative fodder. *My Ships Are Coming In!* referred (with irony) to his hopes about his second marriage, though Xandra, along with Genevieve, also figured in a later composition titled *My Gallivanting Wives.* Encounters with prostitutes, too, figured in his music. The melody for *Tired, Tired* came to him as he rested on a bench on a street corner, having walked from one massage parlour to another, with only a few dollars in his pocket, looking for one he could afford. Some works were downright pornographic. On the manuscript of *There Are Tears in the Affairs of This Life,* he wrote of one passage, "H[elen] R[ichardson] squats on EN and gets him an orgasm." In 1978, he discussed what he called one of his most extraordinary works: *The Massage*. Written down in the middle of the night in a state of sexual excitement, it depicts the sort of punishing erotic massage he liked to solicit from a large Scandinavian masseuse.

Composing helped him to express his powerful feelings of nostalgia – hence the dozens of pieces with titles like *Amongst the Ruins of the Past, The Good Old Days, The Past Has Vanished Forever, Voices from the Distant Past*. He wrote pieces inspired by specific memories, some from earliest childhood – pieces in memory of his father and other members of his family (though never his mother), his teachers, friends and champions like the Kovácses and Weiszes. Many of his "memory" pieces bear titles like *In Memoriam January 5, 1939, Copenhagen*, or *Fifty-seven Years Ago (March 15, 1928)*, or *Arriving at the 125th Street Railroad Station in New York City, March 1927 (Sad Vista)*. His travels inspired many pieces too, some dealing with specific journeys and places, some with minutiae (*The Refusal of the Dutch Consulate to Grant Me a Visa*).

History and politics figured in many of his compositions, including memories of the First World War and the Hungary of his childhood. He kept up with current events throughout his life, and drew many pieces from the news. He wrote pieces about FDR, Truman, and various later presidents, about the Second World War, about the execution of the Rosenbergs, about other political figures (Walter Mondale, Daniel Ortega), even about the Supreme Court. *The Calling Card . . . We'll Be Back* was inspired by the failed American attempt to free hostages in Iran, in 1980 (Nyiregyházi applauded President Carter's decision to sanction the raid: "No real man should be a milquetoast"). First Ladies were not spared. Deeply affected by a televised image of Richard Nixon's wife crying after his loss in the 1960 presidential election, he composed *Phantasmagoria of Pat Nixon*. What inspired *The Beheading of Nancy Reagan (Like Marie Antoinette)* is not known, and is anybody's guess.

Nyiregyházi's philosophical bent, too, influenced his composing: *Before the Tribunal of Transcendental Judgment* was based on Kant's *Critique of Pure Reason*. Many works hint at a spiritual or mystical impetus: *The Hereafter, Journey into the Unknown, Message from Beyond, The Unsolved Riddle*. Despite his lifelong agnosticism, he often composed on religious subjects, invariably Catholic ones (Liszt's influence, no doubt) – hence *Crucifixion of the Lord at Golgotha, The Holy Trinity, Judas and Jesus*. His bitterness about religion also emerged in ironic works like *Onward Christian Soldiers* and *The Father, Son, and (Un)Holy Ghost*, and he composed some sinister and explicitly "satanic" pieces.

He drew inspiration from a lifetime's reading of great literature – Dostoevsky, Dreiser, Goethe, Heine, Hugo, Poe, Shakespeare, Strindberg, Verne, Zola, and other authors (including many Hungarians). Wilde, naturally, inspired many pieces; besides *The Picture of Dorian Gray*, they included *Oscar Wilde in Cheyenne* and *Work Is the Curse of the Drinking Classes* – the latter a "very solemn work, terrifically majestic like a religious credo." He wrote tombeaux for some of his heroes – literary figures like Wilde as well as composers, including Brahms, Chopin, Cleve, Reger, and Wagner. Liszt inspired many pieces, including dozens of works titled *Mephisto* and at least one piece that was a reply to Liszt's "puny, contemptible detractors."

Given his temperament, it is no surprise that a great deal of Nyiregyházi's music deals with death and grief, melancholy and loneliness, despair and boredom, the brevity of life. In much of his music he seems intent on exposing the wounds in his psyche. The sheer volume of works with morose or pessimistic titles is revealing, and what follows is but a sampling from dozens of works: *Enveloped by the Dark Shroud, The Erosion of Hope, Life Is a Valley of Sorrows, The Mills Grind Slowly, My Heart Hurts Terribly, On the Road of Loneliness, This Short Span of Life, To Celebrate Life's Defeats, We Live in Hope and Die in Despair*. He was particularly drawn to "dark" themes: *Dark Days, Dark Fate, Dark Foreboding, Dark Journey, Dark Mood, Dark Streets*.

But then there is the unclassifiable four-page manuscript, received by the Library of Congress in 1934, bearing the title *Sweet Memories*. It is a convincing pastiche of a popular song from the 1920s (though without words), the sort of number that Nyiregyházi liked to play as an encore in his American recitals. The way he signed the piece –

Composed by ERVIN NYIREGYHAZI
Pen name: THOMAS GORDON

– raises a tantalizing question: Did Nyiregyházi, he of the musical vision "essentially tragic and grim," once consider a second career as a Tin Pan Alley tunesmith?

As a child, Nyiregyházi wrote some music in conventional genres (sonatas, symphonies), and he did so occasionally in later life. In the 1930s and 1940s, he said, he wrote a piano sonata, a violin concerto, a piano concerto (in the unusual key of A-flat minor), and an unfinished symphony in D minor (the first movement was "sort of a half-brother spiritually to Bruckner's Ninth," he said, "very powerful, very majestic, very intense, sort of a symphonic *Götterdämmerung*"). But the vast majority of his music, especially from the 1930s on, is *sui generis*, like Liszt's, as idiosyncratic in form and style as in subject matter. "I receive my impressions from life and it translates itself into music in a spontaneous natural way," he said. Seeking direct expression of very particular, very private thoughts and feelings, he had no use for received forms: "Every work has its own law."

His music is often surprisingly plain, even simplistic, offering little evidence of sophistication, little subtlety of detail; he was fond of repeated patterns, long-held bass lines and chords, unadorned accompaniments, the most rudimentary harmonic progressions. In long pieces, he does not develop ideas so much as belabour and brood over them. Most of his pieces are static rather than dramatic. His goal seems usually to have been the depiction of a single image or concept or emotional state, at whatever length necessary.[*] (Some of his pieces are less than a page long; others take well over an hour to play.) Harmonically, his music is never as advanced as even the new music of his childhood, sometimes no more so than Schubert,[†] and he did not wield his harmonic vocabulary with much ingenuity or daring.

When asked to name the influences on his music, he tended to cite his pantheon of favourite composers: Liszt, first and foremost; then Grieg, Verdi, and Tchaikovsky; then Berlioz, Bruckner, Debussy, Leoncavallo, Puccini, Strauss. However, given his musical tastes and the proclivities revealed by his performances, the absence of certain traits in his music – singing melody, counterpoint, operatic sensuousness and sentimentality – comes as a surprise. He admitted that his compositions were founded more on harmonic progressions; they are more about *gestures* than tunes. When lyrical, his music can suggest Grieg, or *verismo* opera, or 1920s-era popular song, but often it is devoid of melody. In truth, his music rarely sounds much like that of his putative influences, with one exception: Liszt – the late works especially.

Stylistic features of the later Liszt are pervasive in his music, including the basic harmonic idiom. Liszt's later works, his biographer Alan Walker notes, "frequently collapse into monody, and then into silence. Sometimes the piece is open-ended; that is, it just vanishes." Some of Nyiregyházi's works, too, just vanish, and many include passages in the style of accompanied or unaccompanied recitative. And like the later Liszt, he makes sparing use of virtuosic effects. "Liszt's

---

[*] Géza Révész wrote of the young Nyiregyházi that "a fundamental note of emotion is sustained throughout each of his pieces. This shows, primarily, that each of them is the expression of an individual musical idea."

[†] He seems to have been influenced by two Schubert sonatas in A minor that he admired: Opp. 42 and 143, both of which have a stern, massive, moderately paced first movement. He admired Op. 143, he wrote, because it revealed Schubert's "emotional propensity to concentrate on the dark by-ways of human life."

spiritual style, which was always present in his music, was clouded in the early works by the virtuosity," he said; "its clarity of expression grows as he ages." His own music is often technically simple, and when difficult (or impossible) to play it is never so for the sake of show, but in the service of mass, percussiveness, ferocity, bite.

Like the later Liszt, Nyiregyházi was fond of sonorities in the low register, including massive chords that produce mostly noise. He wrote whole pieces that rarely (or never) require the treble clef, and his music in the high register is more often lacerating than lyrical or glittery. All his life, he liked to add unwritten lower octaves and to transpose certain chords and melodies down an octave or two for greater mass and emotional effect. When he was six, he recalled, he played one of his pieces for Ödön Mihalovich, the principal of the academy, who took the boy's hands and placed them higher up on the keyboard, saying, "Ervin, don't always play in the bass!" Ervin replied, "But I feel it that way." Mihalovich sighed, put Ervin's hands back where they had been, and said, "You are a pessimist." It was not a glib remark. At the bottom of the keyboard Nyiregyházi could express his darkest feelings. As a songwriter he was especially fond of the baritone voice, and he loved the cello; at the keyboard, he said, he was often "playing the cello."

Nyiregyházi did not merely ape Liszt's late style; he felt a temperamental affinity with what he called the "stark" and "tragic" mood of Liszt in his last years. "No matter how triumphant I am, I am still a pessimist," he once declared, and there is little of the positive side of life in his music – optimism, joy, sensuality, wit. Where there is humour, it takes the form of irony or sarcasm. Certain late works of Liszt especially influenced him – brooding, despairing works like *La lugubre gondola, Mosonyis Grabgeleit, Nuages gris, Unstern!*, and particularly the two elegies Liszt wrote upon the death of Wagner, in 1883, *R. W. – Venezia* and *Am Grabe Richard Wagners*. The former "rises from the black depths of the keyboard," Walker writes. "This is the music of catastrophe. It is void and without form.

For thirty-one measures this hopeless keyless music strives to find the light . . . only to collapse and fall back into the abyss." That describes a lot of Nyiregyházi's music.

Most of it is slow and lugubrious; where it is fast, it conveys terrifying rather than cheerful energy. His music is *extreme*. Now solemn, introspective, and despondent, now wild, raging, and explosive, it plumbs both ends of the (negative) emotional spectrum with terrible earnestness.* Both kinds of work tap into the adolescent grandiosity and over-the-top emotionalism that were permanent parts of his psychology. The clangorous *Tragic Victory* No. 1, composed when he was in his early forties, begins and ends triple-forte and never dips below forte, and the music is replete with heavy chords and octaves and searing tremolos. The first page bears the footnote "The entire work to be played in a Titanic manner," yet he insists on trying to quantify the titanism as the work proceeds. As he builds climax upon climax, he asks the pianist to play in a manner that is by turns "cyclopean," "Fatalistic," "*Triumfante*" "Overwhelming," "With tremendous eruptive force" (in another footnote), with "Tremendous conviction and force," "cyclopean" (again), "*Grandioso*," and finally "Torrential." This is music as pure id, from a composer desperate to express outsized emotions that can barely be contained in music for ten fingers.

While Nyiregyházi's manuscripts include only basic dynamic and tempo and expression markings, his published pieces give more

---

* John Lukacs notes that the streak of melancholy in the Hungarian temperament and literature runs alongside a mercurial wildness and a great appetite for life. There is an old saying: the Hungarian "rejoices with tears." This stereotype certainly applies to Nyiregyházi's personality and music.

precise directions to the performer. In the early 1950s, taking one last stab at finding a public for his music, he brought out four piano pieces,* and these scores are littered with fanatically precise directions – conventional symbols for accents, phrasing, dynamics, and such, but also constantly fluctuating tempo and metronome markings, directions for all three pedals, and supplementary verbal instructions and footnotes. He gives finicky directions for normally spontaneous expressive effects like tempo rubato, rhythmic accents, rolled chords, and the "limping" effect that comes from having one hand play slightly behind the other. Three of the pieces include this footnote: "The letter 'R' above or below a note indicates to hold that note longer than its normal time value. A double R 'RR' means to hold the note considerably longer. The sign R-p (or R-poco) is to hold the note very little longer." There is a parallel scheme for holding notes *less* long than indicated.

The goal of all this notational fuss and bother was to capture on paper "the impulsive aspect of my playing," to ensure that anyone who played these pieces exactly as written would, in effect, sound like Ervin Nyiregyházi. These scores resemble transcriptions of Nyiregyházi recordings; in fact, at least some of them *are*. Beginning in the late 1940s, he occasionally made private recordings of new pieces, and notated the scores while listening to slowed-down playbacks. (None of these recordings seem to survive.) His notational scheme, he said, "one day will be considered great." *Eccentric* it certainly is.

---

* They were: *A Soldier of Fortune, Tonal Drama* No. 1, *Tragic Victory* No. 1, and *Checkmate* No. 2. The first two appeared in 1950 from "Bysshe and Barratt Publications," meaning the two wealthy friends who subsidized the printing; the other two appeared in 1951 from "Nyiregyházi Publications" and were printed at his own expense. The first pieces he had published since 1920, and the last he would *ever* publish, they sold mostly among his friends and brought in only a few dollars.

"I consider myself a better composer than a pianist," Nyiregyházi said, and when asked to assess his own stature as a composer, he replied, "I believe I am very great but will remain unrecognized because musicologists cling to the opinion that in the twentieth century one shouldn't compose as they did in the nineteenth century." In his mind, he ranked just below the Bachs and Beethovens – on the level of, say, Rachmaninov. He treated the greatest composers as his colleagues. As a child he already had enough confidence to compare his Ballade in F Minor favourably with Chopin's ballade in the same key – a ludicrous notion. *Checkmate* No. 2 was, he said, "almost in the class with Mahler's Fifth Symphony" and "one of the greatest works of musical history." He had no fear of competing with his heroes, even Liszt. Inspired by Liszt's *Christus*, he composed his own *Liszt Oratorio*; inspired by Liszt's seven *Historical Hungarian Portraits*, he composed his own set of eight; he composed his own symphonic poem *From the Cradle to the Grave*, and his own pair of *St. Francis Legends*.

He did not intend to exaggerate when he spoke of his music as sublime, monumental, important. But then, his standards were not so much aesthetic as emotional. "The value of a work depends on not only how good a work is but to what extent it expresses my feelings," he said. "If it expresses my feelings very well I don't care if the work isn't very good, because I feel that to reveal what one feels is to reveal the truth, and to reveal the truth – my truth – is very good." He cared about the *content* of music, and judged accordingly. To call Liszt's religious music tedious, he said, is to call Catholicism tedious. Music that successfully expressed great feelings – a great soul – was ipso facto great music. This attitude helps to explain the paradox of his simultaneous grandiosity and insecurity as a composer: to reject his music was to reject *him*.

Of course, if great feeling necessarily produces great art, then infant fingerpainters would create masterpieces. While some of Nyiregyházi's music is impressive and original, much seems amateurish; at times, the disparity between the intensity of expression and the simplistic idiom of the music is almost comical. The musical ideas do not measure up to the emotions. For all its evident passion and grandness of thought, the music is tame rather than audacious. To be sure, it is always *honest* – that is never in doubt. But it is not nearly as pleasing or rewarding for others to listen to as it was therapeutic for Nyiregyházi to write and play.

His music has never found many champions among pianists, publishers, and listeners. It probably never will – and not only, as he thought, because it was unabashedly old-fashioned. (Musicians care much less about avant-garde bona fides today than they did fifty or a hundred years ago.) For posterity the primary value of this strange, deeply personal music will probably always be biographical rather than aesthetic, for whatever its artistic limitations it does hold up a mirror to Nyiregyházi's life and personality. And Nyiregyházi, who equated public success with mediocrity and compromise, did not mind being (like the aged Liszt) at best a minority taste. "I'm not trying to impress anyone," he said. "I just want to express myself."

18

Wine, Women, and Song

Through the 1950s and 1960s, Nyiregyházi continued to live quietly, anonymously, mostly in cheap, sparsely furnished rooms. He now earned almost nothing through music – on his 1965 income-tax return, he gave his occupation as "Retired," his income as $785.32 – and enjoyed financial security only when a woman was supporting him (though he bristled when accused of living off women). Among his papers from the 1960s and 1970s are lists of expenses that reveal much about his lifestyle. Here, for instance, are his expenses for a typical month:

85	–	Rent
15	–	Medicine
10	–	Incidentals
9	–	Street Car Pass
6	–	Telephone
8	–	Movies
36	–	Massage
105	–	Home + Staples

```
20   –    Prime Ribs (4)
27   –    (18 meals per $1.50)
4    –    (4  "   per $1.00)
51   –    Drinks
376
```

The $20 spent on four prime-rib dinners recalls his remark that he acted like a millionaire whenever he had $5 in his pocket.

He was by now comfortable in this lifestyle, and in some ways actually preferred living in the tenderloin, not only because it was cheap. "I'm a city man," he said; he enjoyed the hubbub of "real people" in the streets, was never drawn to the suburbs or the country. Moreover, he said, "I need physical ease in living. For a poor man to have ease, you have to live in the tenderloin." Everything he needed – food, liquor, sex – was close by. But he knew the downside of the tenderloin, too. He kept off the streets after dark, having had bitter and frightening experiences of both crime and the police. Among his papers is this note: "A 'poor' man is in 'good taste' if he spits into a policeman's face (what is meant here is, of course, the L.A. police) – down on the poor drunks but not on the rich drunks." He endured many insults to his dignity and sense of entitlement; his sketchbooks, for instance, are full of laments about the indignities of poverty: "A champagne taste with a beer pocketbook," he described himself in 1977. "But I am entitled to a champagne treatment irrespective of the size of my bank account." He rarely got it. In the cheap cafés he was compelled to frequent – he was no cook – he often felt humiliated by waitresses, and hated the Muzak, and he had no recourse but to rage to those close to him, or to his private papers. ("A titan had to eat with a lot of creeps," he lamented after having been forced to sit family-style in a restaurant because he was dining alone.) Still, he carried himself like an aristocrat and was polite and courtly in most situations, and his English remained precise, formal, a little dated, curiously ornate. "I never saw Ervin off-stage other than neatly dressed, in suit and tie," Raymond Lewenthal wrote. "But that black suit was slightly shabby, slightly shiny and looked as though there might not be another."

Nyiregyházi sympathized with the down-and-out, defended the poor and disenfranchised, hated social injustice and the abuse of power, and espoused a curse-the-rich philosophy. He could form genuine friendships with hard-luck cases, and was known to give his last dime to someone worse off than he. But his politics were contradictory and his convictions wavered. Though he had supported FDR, he voted Republican in the 1950s, because Eisenhower "had a nice smile and was friendly." Sometimes he sounded like a liberal-democrat or a socialist, other times seemed (like many intellectuals) to long for a benevolent dictatorship in which *he* got to be the dictator. He claimed not to judge people on the basis of race or religion or nationality; it was the uneducated and uncultured, those who lacked a "noble" temperament, whom he said he deplored. Yet, he had a regrettable tendency to use racial and other epithets ("nigger," "wetback," "yahoo," "baboon") that suggested a disdain bred of his lofty self-image. He did not approve of integrated neighbourhoods where educated people had to live alongside "uneducated niggers," and in a 1961 letter he defined a good neighbourhood as one that was "not located on a dog-street, where the *God-Damn dogs* run around – as though they owned the streets – which they do not – in spite of the underpaid Mexicans –."*

"I live freely," he told an interviewer in 1978. "I live like Liszt composes and Oscar Wilde writes." That was the crucial advantage of life in

---

* On at least a few occasions, he was held up or physically attacked or had his hotel room broken into. In October 1976, according to a police report, he was attacked by a young Mexican woman, a thief, who "beat me savagely, viciously, also bit me several times on both arms," while a black man held his hands – an incident that sheds some light on his use of racial slurs. (It was for reasons of personal safety, he said, that he tried to "avoid blacks and hippies.") Such incidents so terrified him that, in old age, he began to vote for tough-on-crime Republicans like Ronald Reagan. After reading news stories, in late 1984, about the New York subway vigilante Bernard Goetz, he was inspired to compose, in admiration, *Goetz Versus the Punks*.

the tenderloin – freedom. Despite the loss of his career, he did not consider himself a victim: his "failure" freed him to pursue his personal and artistic goals without compromise. But if money does not buy happiness, neither does poverty. His freedom came at an emotional price. Free of commitments, he could indulge his penchant for melancholy. "There is no greater pain than to remember happy times in times of misery," Dante wrote, and Nyiregyházi, living freely, had plenty of time to brood over his accumulated joys and more plentiful sorrows. He knew boredom, too, intimately, defining it as a feeling of "emptiness" or "frustration," an "inability to cope." "My life has been a big bore," he said, except for the periods of "tremendous great love and creative ecstasy" and the other "outstanding moments," like his meetings with great men. And, of course, he was often lonely. He tried to keep the melancholy and boredom and loneliness at bay, to fill the empty hours, by taking long walks, going to movies, getting massages, though he admitted that he could be plain lazy.

He still had creative and intellectual aspirations, however, and his mind remained active. One of his regular haunts was the public library, where he became something of a legend among the staff. He devoured books and scores – he could still learn new pieces by merely reading scores at a table – and among his papers are library call slips that give some idea of his reading habits. He continued to study his favourite composers, above all Liszt, and his interests ranged well beyond those of a typical pianist, even to esoterica like the operas and oratorios of Anton Rubinstein. He read literature and philosophy in several languages, and still wrote on subjects that inspired him.[*] His passion for chess had not dimmed. He collected books and newspaper clippings on chess, tracked

---

[*] He was intrigued by the Kennedy assassination, and composed several pieces about it. He was convinced that Oswald was innocent and that Kennedy had been the victim of a right-wing conspiracy. Stirred by an editorial in the December 2, 1967, issue of the *Saturday Evening Post*, he outlined his theory in a long letter to the editor, and wrote in closing, "For 'obvious' reasons I prefer not to disclose my name." He signed his letter "X."

chess moves on pieces of paper, wrote chess-inspired compositions. He attended the local Piatigorsky Cup tournaments in 1963 and 1966, and travelled to Denver in 1971 to watch Bobby Fischer (whose boldly original style he admired) defeat the Danish contender Bent Larsen in one of the semi-final matches leading up to the following year's legendary World Championship in Reykjavík.

He was not free in *all* respects, however. He was a slave to his desires and, good Wildean that he was, believed that the only way to get rid of a temptation was to yield to it. Increasingly, his life came to be consumed by his appetites for alcohol, sex, and music (the latter now mostly in the form of study and composition). Wine, women, and song – or, as he put it, "I'm addicted to Liszt, oral sex, and alcohol – not necessarily in that order." He recalled one convergence of all three appetites in a revealing 1965 letter to one of his girlfriends: "If you think back how four years ago you sat next to me at the piano, the bottle of vodka on the other side and how this uniting of factors enabled me to undergo an intense creative process, to unfold the deepest and truest in me and compose wonderful musical works." At such a moment, far from the public arena, one can actually imagine him happy. But if these three appetites were balms for his troubled soul, the drinking and womanizing, at least, were also part of the problem.

Theodore Dreiser once wrote of temperamental, artistic people "so open, emotionally, to every breath of mood and the whips and goads of life as to necessitate a refuge of some sort." Drunkenness was Nyíregyházi's refuge. By the late 1930s, he had come to rely on alcohol. Any sort of interpersonal activity – playing the piano, going to a party, expounding in conversation, making love – now required liquid courage, to loosen the crushing inhibitions that had been bred into him as a child and amplified by years of criticism and failure. Alcohol unlocked his memory and imagination; it "gave a *roseate hue* over the otherwise *bleak landscape. Nothing succeeds like imagination when reality is rotten.*" Alcohol, as he wrote in the early 1960s, became "my Religion," and he equated giving it up with giving up "the joyful experiencing of life." In 1972, on a Bank of America envelope, he scrawled a solemn credo that reads in part: "Right now, *after* starting drinking it seems that I can handle everything marvelously. One sip did it. The otherwise insurmountable difficulties, or so they seem in a sober state, can be overcome easily or at least with not much difficulty."

Like many drinkers, he thought he was a better person when drunk, and drinking did help him to overcome fear and shyness, to express feelings like love, to get his creative juices to flow. "When I am under the influence of Alcohol, I am more logical, less apprehensive and hope is extant that Life wouldn't be that cruel to me," he wrote in 1961. He cheerfully folded his addiction into his creative life – witness such compositions as *Victory for Whiskey, Whiplash of the Alcohol, Beer – A Poor Man's Champagne, It's Nice to Be Soused*. But alcohol also exaggerated both his grandiosity and his insecurity. Drunk, he could express the purplest adoration for a loved one, turn on him or her cruelly and viciously, then apologize extravagantly. Alcohol unleashed his accumulated anger and hurt, self-doubt and paranoia, leading him to lash out with the most wounding venom, even at those dearest to him, and it could induce towering rages over the slightest annoyances. Drinking hurt his career, too, though he hardly cared, since "alcohol made me happier than giving concerts."

After the war, more and more of Nyiregyházi's friends and colleagues dropped out of his life, including supporters like Father Lani and Bela Lugosi.[*] He found it increasingly difficult to maintain a social life; his shyness could be paralyzing when he faced strangers, particularly in groups. But despite his demanding and difficult personality, he always had some friends, and enjoyed conversation (though not small talk – he

---

[*] Father Lani died in 1954. Lugosi became increasingly withdrawn in the face of crippling professional and personal problems, spent his last years depressed and almost penniless, drinking heavily, and died in 1956.

hated hearing Americans talking about baseball and such). He still needed companionship and sex. He remained physically attractive, and women were drawn to him even in old age, though he also faced humiliating rejections from women turned off by his poverty and dissolution. He continued to have affairs with women of every type, and the complications of his love life could be amusingly baroque. One tale involved a young, "man-crazy" woman whom he came to know in the early 1950s (she lived across the street). After their affair began, he said, her father threatened to kill him if he did not marry her – and she insisted the threat was serious. The frightened couple hatched a complicated plan involving a trip to Louisville, a fake divorce (from Vivian), a fake marriage licence, a week's sham marriage in a hotel, a contrived separation and "divorce," and a confession to a heartbroken Vivian, who sobbed all night on the kitchen floor. A composition resulted: *Shotgun Wedding*.

Though the marriage was strained by his infidelity, he and Vivian remained devoted to each other, and when she died from a stroke on Valentine's Day 1955, he was devastated. Yet, the next day he had a date, and was thinking anew about marriage. Many relationships followed, one with a black woman who worked as a sexual masseuse. (She said she had formerly worked in the women's cloakroom at the Senate in Washington, D.C., and would sometimes orally gratify senators.) He proposed marriage to her in November, and she agreed on the condition that he let her arrange a concert tour of Alaska through a shady boyfriend of hers, but he declined. The year before Vivian died, he had begun seeing Elsie Swan after twenty years' estrangement. Now they resumed their sexual affair, and she again became his confidante, though was still unwilling to forfeit her government pension by marrying him.

"I believe very much in the institution of marriage," Nyiregyházi once said, with a straight face, "and if I wanted to be with a woman, then I preferred that we be married." That was certainly true of the women he was serious about, but it was also the case that loneliness and sexual attraction led him to marry rashly. In the fall of 1956, he placed a personal ad in the *Los Angeles Daily Mirror*. Mara Heinz responded, saying that she was tall and beautiful and knew all about sex and was not against drinking. The two met on December 19, and on Christmas Eve, in Las Vegas, they married.

No. 7 rivalled No. 1 as his most unfortunate marriage. Born in Düsseldorf in 1919, Mara, like Mary Kelen, was an unsavoury character. According to Nyiregyházi, she was a blackmailer, a prostitute, and a kleptomaniac who would steal even razor blades and toothpicks; he would learn, from the Swiss police, that she had a criminal record in Switzerland, where she was a citizen. He used words like "perverted" and "degenerate" to describe her. Yet it was because she was a "sex-bomb" that he had been drawn to her in the first place. ("She knows her onions!") He said that she would even service johns at home, though his claim of seeing fifteen or twenty men lined up outside their house sounds frankly incredible, and vindictive. (In court papers, she gave her profession as "physical instructor and nurse.") He would later tell a local newspaper about "goings-on involving her staying out until late hours of night and popping into parked cars after mysterious telephone appointments." She was no homemaker, had a cruel streak, often left him alone, and knew nothing about music. She once tried to impress him with her analysis of a symphonic poem by Liszt, but he recognized that it was plagiarized from a book.

The relationship was stormy. As it turned out, she *did* hate his drinking; he replied, "I don't want a woman telling me what to do." In the first week of January 1957, they separated, and Mara sued him for separate maintenance, citing "extreme cruelty" and claiming that he was "able-bodied" and "well able to pay alimony," though she apparently had more money than he did. She eventually withdrew her complaint, but there were other separations; at one point, Nyiregyházi resettled temporarily in Guadalajara. In one of Mara's letters, however, a picture emerges that is not quite so one-sided as the one Nyiregyházi painted (the spelling and usage are hers):

> I thank you for all the beautifull moments with all my heart and
> kiss you as tender and as slow it ever may be. I wish so much you

would have some nice thoughts about me, some happy feelings, about moments, unforgetable for me, and durable in the eternety, in the sphares over the world where is no more human beeing. I wanted your love, like I gave you my love, but I got it only in our first meeting and our first day in Las Vegas, because I was new for you and you expect the most beautifulliest things, which never could be as beautiful as your wishes; (of course.) But I loved you so much, your exciting in your first meetings with me, your trembling and soft unshowiness in your voice. Your eyes, your happiness. I really believe, you have been happy in our beginnings. Now, when your desires are gone, because you have me, and because, I'm so near to you, you need more freedom.

The same needs and insecurities that drove him into relationships obviously made them difficult to sustain. However much he desired companionship and feared abandonment, even a loving, devoted marriage inevitably came to feel like a constraint to be resisted – that is, came to remind him of life with his mother – and his response, often, was flight. Sometimes the smallest offence could motivate that flight; he separated as rashly as he married.

Mara, who was in the United States on a tourist visa, was apparently already being investigated by the government for prostitution when they married, and Nyiregyházi soon discovered that she had married him only in the hope of getting American citizenship. In court papers, he claimed that she "has threatened to have me arrested if I do not sign Immigration papers for her, and she threatens me, through friends of mine, and breaks into my home, using threats that she will constantly harass me until I do as she requests." (He sought a restraining order.) In March 1957, having faced several hearings, she was finally deported, and resettled in Zurich. When she left, she stole copies of his compositions and the text of his book *The Truth at Last* (it is presumably lost). After failing to get an annulment on grounds of fraud (her "secret intention not to be a real spouse"), he was granted a divorce, which became final on November 18, 1958. He was

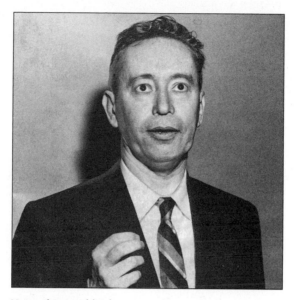

Nyiregyházi at fifty-four, in a photograph that ran in the November 5, 1957, issue of the Los Angeles *Herald-Express*, with an article on his suit for divorce from his seventh wife, Mara. *(Photograph by the* Herald Express. *Herald Examiner Collection, Los Angeles Public Library.)*

happy to see Mara go, yet they kept in touch, until at least the early 1980s, by which time she had moved back to Düsseldorf. She then had at least two children, and still called herself Mara Nyiregyházi.[*]

---

[*] She claimed to have had a son by him, whom she named "Ervin Nyiregyházi," though he denied being the father; the son's whereabouts are unknown. In a 1982 letter, she referred to "Our youngest son" and to "Your son MIKE," who was a musician (trumpet and piano) in Munich. Nyiregyházi once said vaguely, to a friend, that he may have fathered a child somewhere in the eastern U.S., but would not elaborate. No evidence confirms that he fathered any children – a remarkable fact given his sexual career and his admitted refusal to wear a condom.

❧ 19 ❧

Restless (Still)

After divorcing Mara, Nyiregyházi, now fifty-five, began looking yet again for a wife, and continued to place ads in the *Daily Mirror*. He got many replies, which sometimes led to affairs, and he proposed to several women. Finally, he decided to seek a wife in Europe. He had not been there in more than twenty years, but with Vivian gone he was feeling more than usually restless, and yearned to revisit places that had special meaning for him. Now, too, he had the means. Vivian's death in 1955 had left him with a modest pension from the City of Los Angeles, which, eventually augmented by Social Security, was his only source of regular income in the last decades of his life.* (It is no coincidence that he stopped giving concerts almost immediately after beginning to receive Vivian's pension.) Vivian also willed to him her house on Aaron Street, in the Echo Park area.

---

* The pension was worth $83 per month in 1957, $125 by 1965. That same year, at age sixty-two, he began to collect Social Security – at first, $32 per month. Both incomes rose incrementally over time, though in the mid-1970s he reported that his regular income was still only about $250 a month.

He lived in the house with Mara, but sold it to subsidize his trip. In late February 1959, he visited Paris, Vienna, Trieste, and other old haunts, and saw Mara in Zurich. She professed shock when he showed her their divorce decree, but agreed to service him sexually nonetheless. He returned to Europe in September, this time with Elsie. They spent most of that fall in Spain, in Palma de Mallorca and Barcelona, a city he found inspiring. (On Majorca, he played for a group of workmen in a bar.) He had a sentimental hankering to revisit Yugoslavia, too, including Subotica, where he had given a concert when he was fifteen. He visited the concert hall, which still had the same piano, and noted that a string he had broken forty-one years before, while playing Liszt, had never been replaced. At the end of December, Elsie returned home, and he travelled to Vienna, where he remained until the following April. He continued to have affairs, and wrote home proposing marriage to one woman, but there was no new wife in the offing. In the spring and summer of 1961, he returned again to continue the search, but was now finding Europe lonely and discouraging – "a waste." He could not support himself there, still encountered anti-Semitism, and missed the particular comforts (and good steaks) of America.

He and Elsie were now very close, though the relationship could be tempestuous. Her sexuality, like his, may have been ambiguous, to judge from one of his last wife's notes: "1959 Palma Elsie had affair with 2 lesbians & one of them threw out Ervin's pants from Hotel room." Moreover, Elsie was adamantly opposed to his drinking. After one of their quarrels on the subject, he retaliated by proposing to a woman whom he had known since 1946 (she had been his pupil) and who was also a friend of Elsie's: Margaret Benedict. Born Margaret Weil in Cleveland in 1892 to German parents, she had previously been married twice, and though she knew his motive for proposing was first of all vengeance, she accepted him. They married in Las Vegas on November 20, 1961, and when they returned to L.A. as husband and wife, Nyiregyházi had a few drinks and then called up Elsie to gloat.

Margaret was a thin, delicate woman, and he felt tenderly toward her, in part because she had been widowed just six months before their marriage. She had been working as a pianist in a nightclub, but now quit that job, though continued to give some piano lessons. They lived in her house on Duane Street, in the Silver Lake district, and she was a faithful wife and eager homemaker. ("She didn't like Jews," he said, "yet she treated me like a prince.") Her one indulgence was cats, of which she had more than two dozen, including a ferocious white tom whose nickname inspired one of his compositions, *The Killer*. He was frightened by pets, and considered their presence disrespectful. An angry note among his papers was obviously intended for Margaret: "Mischa Elman & Horowitz get a steak without the humiliation of having a cat stand on the table on which they are going to eat." The cats were sometimes a point of furious contention, but he tried to respect Margaret's feelings. When The Killer died, he solemnly played Chopin's funeral march, as though in honour of a fallen hero.

Even life with the devoted Margaret soured. For one thing, as he confided to one of his sketchbooks after her death, "She felt at home in the company of the dregs of humanity. Her associations were remarkably & almost invariably of the lowest." In a letter to Elsie, he accused Margaret of "ill-will and spleen," and continued, "She certainly doesn't offer much in true understanding and intellectual companionship. Therefore, the least one has a right to expect is kindness, consideration, and tenderness. . . . The good in me by far outweighs the bad, as we all know."

In the spring of 1962, after quarrelling with Margaret, he returned to Europe. His problems with her seem to have been mostly of his own making, for she regularly sent him money and, in affectionate letters, wished him well and hoped for his safe, speedy return. Trips to Europe were an expensive way to flee conflicts, and once home he regretted his indulgence, "but when I have a few dollars in my pocket I feel like a millionaire." He soon returned to Margaret, but a year later fled again, this time for a cheaper sanctuary: El Paso, Texas. In a letter to Elsie, he noted Margaret's involvement in "fruitless, picayune" actions against him with "the help of the unenlightened, barbaric Los Angeles Police Department," and added, "I am, fortunately, out of the clutches of that *dastard branch* of the California legal system and of the woman, Margaret, who would employ the help of that system to gain her despicable end." His incorrigible drinking seems to have been at the heart of this conflict. He found out through one of her friends that she seriously entertained the idea of committing him to a psychiatric institution to cure him of it – hence his escape to El Paso. Any check on his well-earned right to drink was in his mind an intolerable intrusion, and the notion of physical confinement must have struck him as the ultimate terror.

He was based in El Paso through the fall of 1963, though spent some weeks in Juarez, where he obtained a divorce on June 8. He hated the desert, the heat and dust and insects, but El Paso had obvious attractions, too: cheap accommodations and proximity to Mexico, where liquor and women were inexpensive and readily available. (Despite everything, Margaret and Elsie continued to send him money.) But he was no happier. He wrote in November, "My stay in El Paso is characterized rather by the absence of the negative than by the presence of the positive." He was lonely, and wanted desperately for Elsie to join him. He declared that "under no circumstances will I go back to Margaret and live with her," but, soon after, wrote that "it would serve no good purpose if I stayed in an apartment of my own (alone)," as though talking himself into returning to her, for food and shelter as well as companionship. Margaret never stopped loving him or wanting to care for him; "you are all I have in this world," she wrote. And so, the Mexican divorce notwithstanding, he returned to her in November – by which time, anyway, the El Paso police, who considered him indigent, had advised him to leave town – and continued to live with her as a husband.

In February 1965, he sailed yet again for Europe, and wrote to Margaret, on the day of his departure, "I don't want to live in a place where my way of life – which is very dear to me – is held over me as a threat. Naturally, I want to live somewhere where I feel free to act and conduct myself as I please. No creative genius or even ordinary human being should settle for less." A note among his papers explains more clearly what he was talking about: "Europe is *definitely* better for drinking but also better for unabashed sex-activity than El Paso (even including Juarez). No dirty coppers in Europe there watching [you] drinking [on the] streets or soliciting street-walkers." Margaret remained patient: "I have an awful lot of butter on hand and no Bitty one to cook for," she wrote, enclosing money. "Please come home very very soon. Please! Please!"

In mid-March, he arrived in Budapest, which he had not visited since 1934. He was there just three days, enough time to make some nostalgic pilgrimages and to see what family remained; he even proposed to his widowed cousin, Edit Rados (it was she who told him the fate of his family and friends during the war). After another week in Vienna and

Paris, he sailed home. Once again, Europe had beckoned, only to prove bitterly disappointing; he hated the people, the hotels, the food, the prices. But he admitted after the fact that his trips to Europe were often motivated by little more than "impulse" – his motivation in so many things – and he wrote to Margaret, with fine understatement, "As you should know by now, I am a highly *volatile* person."

At first he could not face Los Angeles, and so spent that spring in El Paso, where he resumed his usual routine. He did soon return to Margaret, to their pattern of fights and reconciliations, though he resumed advertising for companions too:

Passport photo from the period 1959–70, when Nyir-egyházi, in his late fifties and his sixties, made frequent trips to Europe.

I read your ad in the "Cupid" with great interest. I was especially interested in the statement that many Mexican girls will marry men double their age, and without regard for the man's financial condition or looks.

64 years old retired concert-pianist and composer, feeling very much younger, wishes to meet lady of liberal inclinations who does not object to profusion of cocktails while having intellectual discussions, object, believe it or not, matrimony, but not necessarily.

Despite bitter experiences, he continued to look to Europe. In the spring of 1968, citing "a terrific nostalgia for the past,"[*] he sought out old friends in Oslo, where, for the first time in thirty years, he reconnected with Signy and Astrid Cleve, but was hurt by their cool behaviour. He was back in Europe again in the fall of 1969, after another quarrel with Margaret, and once more in the spring and summer of 1970, but he always returned, restless and unfulfilled, to Los Angeles.

Margaret remained loyal to the end. She died at home, of a heart attack, on November 3, 1970, and Nyiregyházi, offering what was for him his most precious gift, gave a memorial recital for her at the home of one of her pupils. He was devastated by her death, for he had remained deeply attached to her. He had put the Mexican divorce out of his mind and continued to think of himself as her husband. The two may even have planned to remarry formally not long before she died. Such a plan would explain this curious note, dated October 8:

---

[*] Nostalgia was always a factor in these trips. In a letter to Elsie, in the early 1960s, he reported standing in front of a hotel in Palma de Mallorca, "looking up at that little, darling balcony, where through the open window (in 1959) I could see you washing my shorts and *press* them to your darling little face, showing me how much you loved me!"

> I, Margaret Nyiregyházi, hereby solemnly swear, that after marrying
> Ervin Nyiregyházi I will *never* make any move or effort to have him
> committed to Camarillo or any other mental institution to have
> him cured of drinking – or Alcoholism – or any such thing related to
> these. When I put my signature to this, it is understood that I will
> fulfill the convenants of this agreement to the utmost of my capability.

Concealing the Mexican divorce, he assumed the role of widower.
(Among his musical sketches in the months that followed were dirgelike
pieces with heartfelt titles like *Ashes Upon Ashes; Margaret Is Gone*.)
After the house on Duane Street was sold in September 1971, he inherited about $15,000 and cast around once more for a wife. The following
year, he seriously discussed marriage with a sixtyish black chambermaid
who worked in one of the hotels he lived in, but the relationship
foundered. Still, he wanted to marry – someone.

Through his restless fifties and sixties, Nyiregyházi's relationship
with Elsie Swan matured. She continued to support him, as she had
decades before during his first years in Los Angeles, but there were
conflicts over his drinking and promiscuity. She was a stronger, grit-
tier woman than either Vivian or Margaret, and their scraps could
leave him explosive with rage. (His handwritten note: "I hope you
die, you son-of-a-bitch. That's what I said to Elsie Swan. Thursday,
July 11, 1968. 3. P.M.") But she was devoted to him, and had his best
interests at heart. Despite their conflicts, she was still his "Darling
Angel" and "Adored Baby" and "little Monkey Mother." His papers
include many purple but sincere declarations of love for her – like
this one, written in El Paso in May 1963:

> I love you as much as ever. I love you, worship you, adore you. Words
> simply cannot express the intensity, the heart-felt quality of my
> feeling for you. I count the days, the hours, the minutes when I will

again look into your darling, adorable face, touch your darling eyebrows, your forehead, that darling little nose ("Crowds are gathering, a law has been passed") your chin, your bitty toenails, your adorable "Popo" – for which I would give my life – which is worthy of the finest that Liszt has expressed in the Petrarca Sonetta and the musical persuasion which only Oscar Wilde could match in words – *yes, all this* is as dear to me – as inexplicably dear to me – you are the *epitome* to me of all that is ravishing and soul-compelling.

He yearned still to marry her: "There is *nothing* in Life that is as dear to me as you."

By 1972, the year she turned seventy-nine, Elsie was suffering from heart and kidney problems, and perhaps diabetes, and had recently had a stroke. That February, she entered into a legal agreement with Harry F. Holmes, a tenant (and, she thought, friend) who lived with his family on the top floor of a house she owned at 2183 North Argyle Avenue, in the Hollywood Hills. She made Holmes a joint tenant and agreed that the property would become his upon her death; he, in return, promised to manage the building and provide Elsie "with reasonable and proper accommodations within said residence for the remainder of her life" and "with all reasonable care and attention and food while she is alive and residing at said premises." In March, the agreement was expanded to include her grandson Peter M. Hood, a psychiatrist in San Diego, whom Elsie had helped to support and educate after his mother's death. (He and Holmes had known each other since childhood.) With the joint-tenancy agreement, Elsie thought she had ensured that she would be cared for in her own house through her last years.

Within a few months, however, her situation was dire. She later wrote to her lawyer, "Holmes and his wife, Lisa, beat my face black and blue. They locked me in, knowing what terrible effect that would produce upon me. I have closterphobia [sic] and they took advantage of that fact." Elsie reported that Holmes and Hood threatened her, tried to

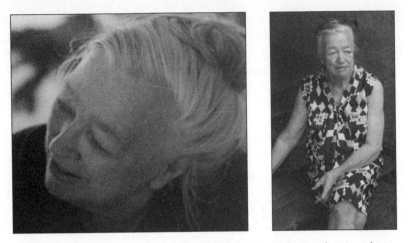

Nyiregyházi's ninth wife, Elsie. *(Left: Photograph by Verix. Right: Ricardo Hernandez.)*

squeeze money from her and drive her from the property, and did not take care of her needs, even as her health deteriorated (claims they later denied). On October 10, she moved out of her house and rented an apartment, but after two days the apartment manager inexplicably called an ambulance, which took her to the hospital (she had suffered no illness or injury). The hospital wanted to send her home, but, according to Nyiregyházi, Holmes prevailed upon the doctors to transfer Elsie to a psychiatric institution and at the same time prodded Hood to have her committed. (He later claimed, in court papers, that Elsie had *requested* to be placed in an institution – though that was a fate she said she had always greatly feared. In the joint-tenancy agreement he had agreed "that if it should be necessary, for any reason, for ELSIE SWAN to go to a hospital for medical treatment, that he shall not permit or consent to her being transferred from said hospital to a rest home or other similar type of home for the aged or disabled.") On October 13, she was sent to the Neurosis and Psychiatric Center in Brea, in Orange County. As she later claimed in court papers, Holmes sought to "deceive and defraud" her in order to "induce" her to transfer the property to him. (Nyiregyházi discovered that the property had been rezoned for development, and so could be sold for a large profit.) Elsie had not been committed or declared incompetent, and no one had her power of attorney, but she was old and ill and mentally weak, and lacked the strength to resist.

Nyiregyházi had planned to go to Europe with the money he had inherited from Margaret, but when apprised of Elsie's situation he acted with remarkable devotion and tenacity on her behalf. He even travelled to San Diego to intercede with Hood, but was rebuffed. As he was only her friend, with no legal standing, he determined to marry her. This meant that she had finally to give up the pension she had been getting for almost fifty years (by 1972, it was worth $272 per month), but now it was imperative that someone sympathetic have the legal authority to make decisions for her. On October 24, he retained a lawyer, who, on November 10, sweet-talked the institution's staff into allowing Elsie to go for a drive; the lawyer then conveyed her to a friend's house, where Nyiregyházi was waiting, and there she signed a statement declaring that she did not want to return to the institution. The couple travelled to Las Vegas, where, on November 11, with money from friends and a borrowed dress – she had left the institution wearing pants, which he would not countenance even in an emergency – Elsie Swan became Nyiregyházi's ninth wife, more than forty years after he had first proposed to her. He was not motivated merely by pity. He married Elsie, he later wrote, "because I love her profoundly and because I was determined to rescue her from a truly precarious position." A year after they married, he paid tribute to her in terms that meant much to him: he loved her, he said, "even more than I love Liszt."

When he married Elsie, Nyiregyházi was almost seventy years old and had been effectively retired as a professional musician for two decades. In 1959, he had written a piece titled *The Last Act of the Tragedy Commences*, and had had every reason then to think that he was playing out the final scenes of his strange story. Yet, it was precisely in 1972 that his professional fortunes began – first gradually, then spectacularly – to change.

Opposite: Nyiregyházi in his mid-seventies. *(Photograph by Caroline Crawford.)*

PART FOUR

THE PIANIST WHO CAME IN
FROM THE COLD

1972–1980

Crescendo

Nyiregyházi's name came up, early in 1972, when the San Francisco Bay Area chapter of the Automatic Musical Instrument Collectors' Association (AMICA) sought to invite a former piano-roll artist to one of its monthly meetings. By this time he was largely a rumour – many people thought he was dead – but the local AMICA president, Alf E. Werolin, finally tracked him down simply by checking the Los Angeles phone book and invited him to the March 25 meeting at his home in Hillsborough, south of San Francisco. Nyiregyházi was flown to San Francisco at AMICA's expense and treated with great deference, and he responded graciously at the meeting, listening to and commenting on his rolls, talking about his career, signing autographs, even agreeing to perform. He chose to play Liszt's stormy Ballade No. 2 in B Minor, because, he later said, "I wanted to express the chaos of life," and though he had not planned to play or practised or warmed up, he gave a performance of such overwhelming power that it is still remembered with astonishment by members who were present. (Of this performance, he wrote, later that day, in a sketchbook, "There is no doubt, I was bold & I succeeded.") Grateful for the respect he had been shown, he retained close ties for years with AMICA and made friends among its members. One of them was Ricardo Hernandez, a San Francisco–based pianist and teacher who was exhilarated and profoundly stirred by Nyiregyházi's "thermal" lyricism and "volcanic upheavals," and found himself reconsidering everything he knew about playing the piano. He became Nyiregyházi's closest friend, and Elsie encouraged the relationship – Ervin needed friends, she said.

Elsie was now almost eighty years old, her health was failing, and her medical expenses were mounting. Nyiregyházi, though hardly eager to revive his career at this late date, considered giving a concert in order to raise money – his devotion to Elsie being stronger than his stage fright – and, through AMICA, he once again had champions keen to put him before the public, including Bill Knorp, a concert promoter. Knorp, Hernandez, and one of Nyiregyházi's former managers, Harold Bowers,* arranged his first public recital in fifteen years at the Century Club of California, a women's social club in San Francisco, on the afternoon of December 17, 1972. He offered a long program no less musically and technically challenging than those he had played half a century earlier, opening with Brahms's F minor sonata and including substantial Liszt and Chopin groups and shorter works by Brahms and Debussy. Despite a technique that had deteriorated from age and neglect, he had lost none of his power or individuality as a pianist, to judge from his monumental, ferociously impassioned Brahms, his slow, dark, brooding Chopin,† his introspective but vibrant Debussy. Though he found it exhausting, he considered this concert one of the best of his career, but his audience was small, his take just $135.30 – not much help to the failing Elsie.

---

* In the early 1940s, Bowers, a young accountant whom Nyiregyházi had met through his wife Vivian, organized some public and private recitals for him, in Los Angeles and Denver.

† Nyiregyházi disapproved of the way most pianists – even giants like Josef Hofmann – played Chopin, "with lack of respect, poking fun at his bleeding heart."

Nyiregyházi with (left to right) Marjorie Werolin, Bill Knorp, and Alf E. Werolin, performing for AMICA members at the Werolins' home in Hillsborough, California, March 25, 1972 – the performance that launched the Nyiregyházi "renaissance" of the 1970s. *(Photograph by Jarod Clark. Bill Knorp.)*

After the recital, he and Elsie decided to move in order to take advantage of his new network of admirers in the Bay Area, and by the end of 1972 they were living in a hotel in San Francisco's Tenderloin. (They lived on little more than Vivian's pension and Social Security; he earned less than $3,000 a year.) Elsie was now mostly bedridden, and Nyiregyházi was ill suited to meeting her practical needs. Hernandez encountered a pitiable sight in their room one day: Elsie, dishevelled and unwashed, sitting up in bed amid rumpled sheets, with urine trickling down her leg, complaining of hunger, while Nyiregyházi stood by concerned but helpless. Hernandez says that he once brought the couple some steak, and that Elsie later complained that Nyiregyházi had eaten it all himself.

Still saddled with medical bills, and the expenses of Elsie's lawsuit against her former tenant and her grandson, which had been filed in January 1973 in Los Angeles, he arranged to give another recital, this time at the Old First Church (Presbyterian) in downtown San Francisco, on the afternoon of May 6. (No admission was charged; an "offering" was collected at intermission.) Before and after the concert, and during the intermission, he sat, his feet and ankles visible, in a curtained enclosure that he had requested be put up next to the piano, because he was embarrassed at the prospect of walking unsteadily from the wings, fearing that the audience might laugh at him. Once settled at the keyboard, he offered another ambitious program that began with a thunderous and extraordinarily vivid account of Schubert's "Wanderer" Fantasy and included Liszt's two *Légendes*. He felt inspired that day, and described this concert, too, as one of his best – a "triumph over adversity." He was beginning to be noticed. Alexander Fried wrote perceptively of this "remarkable, or even startling, recital," in the *Examiner*:

> In a style of playing entirely different from what is standard today, he boldly and tempestuously recalled 19th century romantic traditions.
>
> When he wanted to create thunderous sonorities he smashed them out with a tremendous sense of sound. He meditated over the keyboard with a lingering, personal absorption, slowing his pace rapturously or bestirring it in extremely free variations of pace and rhythm.
>
> When he chose to be lyrical, his melodic touch was tenderly beautiful.
>
> At all times he was as uninhibited as he was individual. His playing involved fantastic broad colorations and messes of wrong notes such as neither ordinary teachers nor students would accept today.
>
> The startling fact is that with all his chunks and clusters of freely attacked sound, he often created a spell of wild physical excitement.

He performed again on May 24, at the clubhouse of the Forest Hill neighbourhood association, his program including the *Légendes* again and some obscure late works by Liszt, and concluding with Scriabin's Sonata No. 4. (His audience, sixty or seventy mostly professional people, apparently found it all heavy going.) Hernandez arranged the event, provided the piano, paid Nyiregyházi a modest fee, and recorded the performance, though at his friend's request he turned off the tape recorder during the *Légendes*. Nyiregyházi insisted that he had never played – never could play – those pieces better than he had done at the Old First Church.* Elsie agreed, and predicted that the Old First Church recital would bring him great fame. In fact, she was right.

The rediscovery of Nyiregyházi began in earnest with the innocent push of a button by a young man named Terry McNeill, who, intrigued by an announcement of the Old First Church recital, attended and taped the performance on a small recorder. He then shared the recording with Gregor Benko, vice-president (and later president) of the International Piano Library (IPL) in New York,† of which McNeill was a research associate. "Nyiregyházi's playing came as a revelation," Benko later wrote. "Although the tape was a miserable recording, it had captured enough to suggest that Nyiregyházi possessed a bigger tone than either Hofmann or Horowitz. I was stunned. I had read dozens of accounts of how Liszt and Henselt, Busoni and Rubinstein had played, but never before had I heard a living pianist who played entirely with that 19th century sense of rhetoric which the old writers had described: the true 'Romantic

---

* When he was fifteen, he played the second *Légende* for Joseph Lhévinne; afterward, he claimed, Lhévinne said he would never play the piece again.

† The IPL was founded in 1965 in Cleveland by Albert Petrak and a twenty-one-year-old Benko, to preserve and disseminate new and historical material relating to the piano and pianists. Shortly thereafter, it was moved to New York.

Style'." Benko and McNeill met Nyiregyházi in San Francisco that summer, and Benko later set down his impressions:

> Mr. Nyiregyházi, a tall man of seventy, paradoxically appeared both strong and frail. His threadbare clothes, his stoic visage and slight stoop conveyed a strong impression: here was a man whose life had been a long, arduous trial. But the years had not depleted his spirit. A few words are insufficient to describe him, for he radiates an aura of aristocratic vulnerability as well as spirituality and a quixotic stubbornness, all combined in one uniquely attractive personality. . . . He answered all our questions in a courtly, old-fashioned way, telling us part of his amazing story without once revealing a trace of bitterness or egotism. It was apparent that he was still, at seventy, the most innocent of idealists, and that he must have suffered greatly because of it. . . . This and everything else he said during that interview and later was related with genuine modesty and humility which quite surprised me, a veteran of many skirmishes with pianistic egos. It is not that Nyiregyházi has ever lacked confidence or pride in his own intellectual and musical abilities. But he does seem capable of a much greater philosophical perspective than most other musicians I have met.

Benko got to hear Nyiregyházi play live on July 29, in a private recital before an invited audience in the home of Ronald Antonioli, a building contractor and piano-roll enthusiast in Novato, north of San Francisco. Antonioli, impressed by Nyiregyházi's concerts and moved by his plight, had befriended him and was helping him financially. In the secluded Antonioli home, he found a harmonious setting and sympathetic listeners. At informal gatherings there, he could be uncharacteristically relaxed, and, when a little drink had brought him out of his shell, could be a genial, articulate, witty guest, might even offer to play encores by request (he liked to show off his memory) or his own compositions – evidence of special trust. (In a recital there on April 30, 1978, he played Liszt's entire *Faust Symphony.*)

Word of the rediscovery of a great pianist began to spread within piano circles (a young Garrick Ohlsson played for him and sought his advice in February 1974), and Benko considered it imperative to record Nyiregyházi's playing for posterity. But while the IPL had issued some albums of historical pianists, it had no budget or facilities for making new recordings; Benko effectively ran the operation out of his home. Still, he set about looking for a way to realize his plan. Meanwhile, in September 1973, Nyiregyházi and Elsie moved back to Los Angeles, because, he said, "Harold Bowers was through with me." Benko, believing Nyiregyházi was "starving" at this time, secured a grant for him through the Musicians Emergency Fund in New York, and, beginning in April 1974, he received $1,000 over ten months from them.

Through several sources, Benko raised enough money to hold a recording session in a Los Angeles church in September 1974.

Nyiregyházi relaxing with (left to right) Pamela Antonioli, Ricardo Hernandez, Ronald Antonioli, and Bill Knorp, at the Antoniolis' home in Novato, California, around 1974. *(Photograph by Rob Thomas. Ronald Antonioli.)*

Nyiregyházi was terrified at the prospect of making his first commercial recordings, and several times sought to pull out of the project; only with much coaxing and reassurance was he able to go through with it. "The great pianist's hands shook noticeably throughout the session," Benko wrote. "He closed his eyes as if in a trance; it seemed as if he had self-protectively withdrawn into a 'piano world' of sound greater than himself. Retakes were hardly necessary, for Nyiregyházi's hands became sure as they touched the keys, shaking once again whenever they left them." He recorded four works by Liszt that would eventually fill up one side of an LP: the nocturne *En rêve*, the B-minor ballade, "Sunt lacrymae rerum," and "Abschied."

Nyiregyházi's relationship with Elsie, despite her illness and their mutual devotion, could still be fractious. Not long after the recording session, Benko was privy to one of their fights. Nyiregyházi called him late at night, in a rage, insisting that he tell Elsie that her husband was a great pianist and, more important, a great *man*, while she, in the background, urged Benko to pay no attention as he was drunk. Benko hung up, and when they next met Nyiregyházi did not even acknowledge the incident. Perhaps he was rebelling, for his efforts to care for Elsie exhausted him. ("It is really not for me to cope with the most brutal and crass of everyday problems," he wrote to Ronald Antonioli.) Sometimes he fled the sickroom; occasionally he paid a stranger to sit with Elsie while he attended to his own needs. Still sexually active, he continued to see other women, even as Elsie lay in the hospital. For a time in the early 1970s, he enjoyed what were advertised as the "Healing Hands of Evelyn." Still, when Elsie died of a heart attack on November 23, 1974, in a convalescent home in Torrance, Nyiregyházi, who could only "kiss her cold cheeks," was hit hard. A few days later, visiting a friend, he became so depressed and intoxicated that he wound up lying on a lawn and was briefly jailed for drunkenness. Nevertheless, he soon began searching anew for companionship.

The International Piano Archives (as the IPL became known in 1974) contracted with Desmar Records in New York to release an all-Liszt album including Nyiregyházi's studio recordings and the *Légendes* from the Old First Church recital, which Nyiregyházi had asked to be included. He considered them quintessential documents of his art, interpretations capturing the "true spirit" of Liszt, and, moreover, performances wrapped up with his feelings for Elsie. They are among the most astonishing piano performances ever recorded. In the first *Légende*, his evocation of birdsong is luminous, his rendering of St. Francis of Assisi's sermon to the birds profoundly stirring. The second *Légende*, which depicts St. Francis of Paola crossing the sea during a storm, he considered "a symbol of my own life – and especially as it was in the context of my circumstances at that time," as he wrote to Marcos Klorman, the president of Desmar. The storm music, in particular, provoked a pianistic cataclysm that stunned listeners in the church and comes across even in the deficient recording. In a program note from 1936, he summarized the piece as "the triumph of 'Faith' over adversity," and in the Old First Church performance he expressed through it his own "almost fanatical desire and determination to succeed – to overcome by sheer indomitable force, all mundane obstacles."

The IPA was eager to bring out the Nyiregyházi album quickly, but its release was delayed for more than two years by technical problems. For one thing, the source Desmar used for the *Légendes* – a second tape that had been recorded by the church – was wretched by commercial standards: the sound was distant and thin, marred by hiss and rumble, by audience and traffic noises, to say nothing of the poor piano and poor church acoustics. The studio recordings, too, presented a challenge, for in the transfer from tape to vinyl it was almost impossible to reproduce Nyiregyházi's huge dynamic range without compression or distortion, and Klorman recalls that the sides had to be mastered again and again. The result, *Nyiregyházi Plays Liszt* (IPA 111), was an album of very high quality, though by the time Desmar released it, early in 1977, the long delay had upset and offended Nyiregyházi.

"I live under almost impossible conditions," he wrote to Benko that May. "And my numerous so-called friends would offer me scant help." In fact, his friends struggled vainly on his behalf. After he had complained of having no music, Ricardo Hernandez brought him some scores, but heard later that he had thrown them down the garbage chute, raging that he wanted money, not charity. By 1977, Hernandez, who had become a de facto amanuensis, supporting him and acting on his behalf in social and business matters, was feeling "saturated," exhausted by the constant telephone calls and personal and professional crises. Nyiregyházi could dominate friends' lives, and those closest to him invariably received, in addition to gratitude and friendship, all manner of abuse, to their faces and behind their backs. Hernandez chose to break with him, at least temporarily, and left for Europe that summer. Feeling abject, "desperate and despondent," Nyiregyházi followed him there in September, despite the cost. The two reconciled in Stuttgart and Nyiregyházi returned to Los Angeles, to a life that was about to become much more complicated.

A Troubled Renaissance

The first major review of the Desmar album was published in the *Boston Globe* on Sunday, August 28, 1977. "What is hard to describe, and inimitable," the *Globe*'s music critic, Richard Dyer, wrote, "is the unfailing splendor and beauty of the sound, the legato, the dynamic range, the sense of grandeur and spaciousness that coexists with something that is abrupt and personal and granitic, and most of all the sense, now so rare, of total identification between performer and music. It is not like anything you've ever heard before – only like what you've read about in the accounts of Liszt's own playing." One of Dyer's readers that day was the pianist and conductor Richard Kapp, who was in the Boston airport on his way home to New York, where he worked as a program officer in the Office of the Arts at the Ford Foundation. Kapp, who knew Dyer as a critic not given to hyperbole, was intrigued by Nyiregyházi's story, and when he returned to the office on Monday he called Marcos Klorman at Desmar, who messengered over a copy of the album. It moved him to tears. "[W]hat I heard on that disc was totally unlike any other music-making in my experience," he later wrote. "The impact of Nyiregyházi's playing upon me was immediately and overwhelmingly emotional." Later that day, Gregor Benko called and introduced himself. He dropped into Kapp's office, and the two placed a call to Nyiregyházi.

It was not the Ford Foundation's business to support individual artists or to provide operating grants to non-performance arts organizations like the IPA, but that is what it did. Kapp became convinced of the importance of preserving Nyiregyházi's art before it was too late and lobbied tenaciously on behalf of the cause. "I wore out numerous copies of the Desmar record playing it for colleagues, superiors, musician friends and anybody else I could cajole into my office," he recalled, and many at the foundation, were astounded and moved by it. The IPA, stressing that here was "a *living* representative of a lost culture," made a formal request for a Ford Foundation grant to subsidize new recordings and provide "a modest but comfortable environment where the pianist can live." A grant was quickly approved for a two-year project officially beginning October 1, to be administered through the IPA.

Of the $38,000 awarded, $14,000 was for recording expenses, $14,000 for other expenses; the remaining $10,000 was to provide a monthly stipend for Nyiregyházi, who was amused to note that *his* share of the spoils was the smallest. But the intent had been to supplement his meagre income without altering his lifestyle, which, Kapp thought, he might have construed as judgmental and presumptuous. Indeed, Nyiregyházi turned down offers of a better apartment, a practice piano, and a maid, even though, as he complained to Ricardo Hernandez, he did not even have a writing desk or a chair in his room, and had to write sitting up in bed bent over a phone book. (He declined a copy of the Desmar album; he had nothing to play it on.) Moreover, the lawsuit over Elsie's joint-tenancy agreement, though finally dismissed in her favour in April 1978, left him with thousands of dollars in legal bills.

Kapp met Nyiregyházi in Los Angeles in October 1977, and they developed a warm friendship. Back in New York, the foundation was anxious to see what Nyiregyházi would do, and he, typically, did what he so often did when something was expected of him: he fled – back to San Francisco. Friends had been concerned about his well-being and safety in Los Angeles, especially as he now had trouble walking alone, even with a cane, and would not go out at night, having "a mortal fear of being *held up and mugged*." (Hence his fondness for hotels: he liked the security of personnel in the lobby.) That summer, Benko offered to help him move to San Francisco, where admirers like Hernandez (who had returned from Europe) and Terry McNeill could attend to his day-to-day needs. He accepted the offer, then backed out. Finally, in December, Kapp reported, "he gathered his belongings and took the bus up, then took a cab around town until he found the hotel he wanted to live in." He chose it, he later said, because it was on the same side of the street as the area prostitutes.

The move was a test, too: were his new champions devoted enough to court and indulge him – to work with him on *his* terms? They were, and Benko set about making new arrangements to record in San Francisco. He was hoping for as much as eighty hours' worth of recordings – perhaps Nyiregyházi's whole repertoire – but Nyiregyházi was now painfully insecure about playing, and would do so only when his mood and the circumstances were just right. The pressure of the upcoming sessions terrified him, and everyone came to wonder whether he would really record at all. But in the end, he agreed to sessions in January 1978 and despite his fears was actually excited at the prospect of working with sympathetic people to preserve his artistic legacy and bring it before the public.

Once the Ford Foundation came on board, word of Nyiregyházi's rediscovery spread quickly. The Desmar album had at first been a difficult sell – Marcos Klorman had trouble getting it reviewed and recalls begging a Sam Goody store to stock just one copy – but with the publicity generated by the foundation, record critics belatedly discovered it. The reviews were overwhelmingly positive – only a few skeptics scoffed at the growing hype around Nyiregyházi – and Benko secured glowing testimonials from some major pianists. Benko considered Nyiregyházi one of the greatest and most important pianists in history, and said that "his playing at the piano has the power to move people in a way no other living musician I know of has." Nyiregyházi's own comments about his work were never modest. Of his recording of the *Légendes*, he said, "my accomplishment in the way I transmit the true spiritual message of Liszt to the world really becomes a major achievement, one of the milestones in musical history." And many listeners heard him in just such elevated terms.

The unanimity of the Desmar reviews attested to the impact of his playing. Critics were moved, astonished, mesmerized – by, first of all, "a level of sonic grandeur almost symphonic in its amplitude." (Some assumed that piano tone on the album had been artificially enhanced.) His skill as a "great colorist" and "great orchestrator" (he was dubbed "the Stokowski of the piano") were still admired despite his deteriorated technique. He was placed among "the greatest living Liszt interpreters," and a British Liszt specialist praised "some of the most vivid, unforgettable and convincing musical experiences I have ever had." Others wrote of "the sense of span" and of "rhetoric in the grand manner," of a "bottomless profundity of feeling" and a "miraculous power of evocation." Some heard not self-indulgence but "aural imagination" and "courage," not idiosyncrasy but "poetry" and "truth." Harris Goldsmith, in *High Fidelity*, heard "a towering figure in the annals of Romantic pianism, a precious and wonderful interpretive voice – a voice, in its way, as distinctive as Rachmaninoff's."

To the general public, though, Nyiregyházi's bizarre story, of which Benko gave an account in his liner notes, proved as intriguing as his playing, and much of the publicity had a sensationalistic air that Nyiregyházi found demeaning. Success quickly became a problem for him. Many people (particularly young people) who were overwhelmed by his playing and moved by his story felt a spiritual connection with him and sought him out. "Since he has become famous again, Mr. Nyiregyházi has been the object of requests for lessons, master-classes, autographs, advice, auditions, interviews, et cetera et cetera et cetera," Benko wrote in a letter circulated by the IPA in late 1977. "While Mr. Nyiregyházi appreciates the good wishes and thoughts of his many admirers, he has always told all of us who have been involved with the project to record his playing that he would make recordings and consider playing again only if he were left strictly alone, and that neither we nor anyone do anything to interrupt his lifestyle."

Benko and Nyiregyházi scoured the Bay Area for a recording venue and settled finally on the Scottish Rite Temple on Nineteenth Avenue at Sloat Boulevard. Nyiregyházi insisted on using the aged Baldwin piano from the Old First Church, which was in wretched condition. It would not stay in tune, its soundboard had lost its "crown" (that is, its slight upward curve), and it had very little sustaining power in the upper register. No matter. This was the piano on which he had played to raise money for his beloved Elsie, and, he insisted, tone production had more to do with emotions than mechanics. "It is not the piano that makes the sound," he told Kapp. "It is *I* who make the sound."

Before the first session, on January 8, 1978, a technician ministered to the knackered instrument, while everyone else ministered to the anxious artist. Kapp later wrote: "Mr. N. was in a state of hysterical terror at the prospect of having to play and it took more than an hour's consoling by Mr. Hernandez before he touched the piano." He did not drink before or during the sessions, only afterward, for he did not want people to be able to point to alcohol consumption as a factor when assessing his playing. In the end, he recorded fourteen pieces that first day – a little over ninety minutes of music – playing each piece only once, without retakes or inserts.

JANUARY 8, 1978*

Liszt: "Funérailles," from *Harmonies poètiques et religieuses*; "Il penseroso," from *Années de pèlerinage*, Deuxième année: Italie; *Hamlet*;* *Nuages gris*;* *Mephisto Waltz* No. 2.

Grieg: *Lyric Pieces*: "Vals" [waltz], Op. 12/No. 2;* "Vaegtersang" [watchman's song], Op. 12/No. 3; "Ensom vandrer" [lonely wanderer], Op. 43/No. 2; "Scherzo," Op. 54/No. 5; "Fransk serenade" [French serenade], Op. 62/No. 3; "Fra ungdomsdagene" [from days of youth], Op. 65/No. 1; "Salon", Op. 65/No. 4.

Rachmaninov: Prelude in B Minor, Op. 32/No. 10.

Liszt: "Vallée d'Obermann," from *Années de pèlerinage*, Première année: Suisse.

His nervousness showed when he began, but, typically, he found more physical and spiritual strength as he played and entered a kind of trance. The music had a nourishing, even intoxicating effect on him (that happened in his concerts, too). "I never get tired when I'm inspired," he declared, and the frail old man transforming himself into a superman at the keyboard became part of the Nyiregyházi legend. But there were limits. As the bravura passages in "Vallée d'Obermann" reveal, by the end of the session he was exhausted.

No one really knew what or how long he would play. He and Benko had discussed repertoire beforehand, though in the end he allowed the feelings generated by one piece to determine what he would play next. Mostly, especially when it came to Liszt, he drew on his capacious memory, sometimes resurrecting music he had not played or studied

---

* In all lists of repertoire from the 1978 recording sessions, an asterisk indicates a recording later released on a Columbia Masterworks album. Nyiregyházi performed all orchestral and vocal works in his own improvised arrangement, even where the composer left a piano version. (He criticized most piano transcriptions, including those of Liszt, for allowing too many pianistic compromises.)

The seventy-five-year-old Nyiregyházi in San Francisco's notorious Tenderloin, August 9, 1978. *(Photograph by Joe Rosenthal. San Francisco Chronicle.)*

for decades. But he also studied some scores in advance, and practised some of the music he planned to play. At his request, certain scores were placed on a table near the piano, and for some pieces (like Grieg's) he used the music. He also occasionally consulted pieces of paper on which he had written down some harmonic progressions and musical highlights – his own shorthand – as *aides-mémoires* for certain works.

As the first session showed, he had no intention of limiting himself to piano music – orchestral, operatic, choral, and solo-vocal works would all figure in his recordings – and even with piano music he favoured relatively obscure works. "It is easier for me to play something with no established tradition of playing," he said; he feared being compared with other performers, because "people would not understand my approach." Still, he was playing music that he was close to emotionally and that was representative of him. "I will record what I want to record," he insisted from the start, and after the first session, listening to the playbacks, he liked what he heard.

While musically the first session was a success, personal conflicts behind the scenes were complicating and even threatening to scuttle the whole project. There had been tension between Nyiregyházi and Benko since at least the recording session in 1974. "At that session he lost all confidence when I quite insensitively opened a score of the Ballade and followed it right in front of him while he played," Benko wrote. "He did not know the ways of recording sessions, and could not have known that producers mark the score at spots which might need retakes." The oversensitive Nyiregyházi thought Benko was checking up on him, seeing if he was rewriting the music; later he claimed that he had played the ballade "well but not too well" for this reason. This incident became a permanent sore spot. He brought it up again and again for the rest of his life, magnifying the slight in the retelling. ("He watches me like a *hawk*! He has no *right*!") Once, he described Benko as a man who "sits with the score in his hand like my mother" – the ultimate insult.

A seed of doubt was now planted: Benko was *judging* him, *disapproving* of him. He once said that in his view the tip of the branch went down to the root – that is, the single act revealed the whole man, and so one slip was crime enough – an unforgiving philosophy founded on his inability to let go of anything that rankled. Once planted, the seed sprouted; his catalogue of complaints about Benko grew. As Benko told a television interviewer in 1978, Nyiregyházi disapproved of Benko's beard and of Benko's home state, Ohio, and even insisted that

Benko pronounced his own name wrong.* As the first recording sessions approached, Nyiregyházi was often "in foment over having to meet B's demands," Ricardo Hernandez wrote – claiming, for instance, that Benko was insisting that he record only from memory. "One or the other party is going to blow this entire enterprise." Nyiregyházi was making Benko a scapegoat, using him to focus and vent the anxieties he felt about recording and seeing in him another force that sought to coerce and restrain and judge him – though Benko, like everyone else, was trying hard to cater to his whims.

The accumulated tension came to a head after the January 8 session, which left Nyiregyházi physically drained and emotionally stirred. Afterward, he met for a long interview with the critic Michael Walsh, of the *San Francisco Examiner*. Spurred by drink, he became, Kapp recalled, "increasingly agitated about Benko," who was not present. "There was absolutely no calming him, and both Walsh and I were in the position of defending Benko, his motives and his behavior in the face of what became an overpowering onslaught." He now raged that Benko had not given him enough praise or encouragement during the session.† He told Kapp "that he needed compliments, that we must provide him with unremitting support since the strain on him was so great and since, regardless of how he had played, the terrors he imposed upon himself were almost too much to bear." The rage, it emerged, had begun as Benko and Terry McNeill drove him to the interview from the session. In the car they tried, as they had in the past, to discuss other pianists with him, something he resented. "I am not a pianist and I will not be put in the position of being com-pared to pianists," he thundered, "because then I am always made the

_____

* Benko – sometimes spelled Benkö – is a fairly common surname in Hungary, and Nyiregyházi liked to spell it with an umlaut and pronounce it accordingly, even after Benko, annoyed, assured him he was of Slovakian ancestry.
† There is a sarcastic note among Nyiregyházi's papers: "Benko: the Apostle of Spirituality: The Piano was out of tune. I would give more praise to a dog."

loser!"* (He pegged Benko and his friends as mere piano buffs uninterested in the larger world of music.) Worse, he claimed that Benko questioned him about his mother, which he interpreted as a tactless effort to discern whether he was Jewish, something he was still at pains to deny.

The next day, taking a break from recording, he continued his interview with Walsh – and continued to rage. He now refused to make any more recordings in Benko's presence and wanted nothing more to do with the IPA. Benko, though hurt, thought it imperative that the sessions continue, and volunteered to absent himself from the process; in the sessions that followed, he observed incognito from the back of the darkened balcony. All of which drew Nyiregyházi closer to Kapp, who he now decided was the only person who could be trusted to share his vision. Kapp proved more adept at giving Nyiregyházi the confidence he needed, overcoming his crippling insecurities with flattery, and passing the "tests" he was always throwing up in conversation, though Kapp also now had the difficult task of juggling the interests of two parties who were no longer on speaking terms. Among Nyiregyházi's papers is a note in which he reported that "Kapp was 'sick' of my diatribe against Benko."

Nyiregyházi always insisted that he liked Benko personally and was moved by his championship, but an old pattern was reasserting itself, and, predictably, someone instrumental in resurrecting his career felt the brunt of his wrath. Embittered by having been (as he thought) so often wronged and let down, he *expected* people to disappoint and betray him. Benko had shown much consideration and respect for Nyiregyházi's artistic standards and personal dignity during their collaboration and had done much to support him artistically, financially,

---

* In this he was hardly consistent: in letters and conversations he often compared himself (favourably, of course) with other pianists. And he did not mind when others ranked him with giants like Liszt and Rachmaninov, Busoni and Paderewski; he objected only to being compared with "nonentities" like André Watts or Jorge Bolet – or Horowitz, with whom he said he was "not too much impressed."

and emotionally. In a 1974 letter, he mentioned his passion to "further your cause," but for Nyiregyházi being a "cause" meant new demands on him, new attempts to control him. Like so many earlier champions, Benko discovered that his devotion and tenacity could be repaid with resentment as well as gratitude.

The upheavals after the January 8·session renewed Nyiregyházi's anxiety about recording. On the morning of January 10, as Kapp wrote: "A most overwhelming and generalized panic, rooted in the profound suffering that playing can cause him, led to a period of an hour or more during which Mr. N., already upon the stage of the auditorium, went through the fires of a personal hell before somehow reaching a state of calm that allowed him to seat himself at the piano and begin to play." He had agreed to allow a second piano – a mint-condition Steinway – on the stage, and it became available at the second session, sitting alongside the battered Baldwin, which, according to Kapp, was "threatening to self-destruct." He used this or that piano according to his whim ("Each piano has a character," he said); in two cases (including his first recording on January 10), he played a piece twice, once on each.

JANUARY 10, 1978
Debussy: "La terrasse des audiences du clair de lune," from *Préludes*, Book Two (two versions: Steinway, then Baldwin).
Liszt: "Abendglocken,"[*] "Ungarisch," and "Polnisch,"[*] from *Weihnachtsbaum*; "Le mal du pays," "Les cloches de Genève," and "Pastorale," from *Années de pèlerinage*, Première année: Suisse; *Mosonyis Grabgeleit*;[*] Benedictus, from the *Missa coronationalis* [Hungarian Coronation Mass].

"If anything, his playing was stronger and more assured than it had been on the first day," Kapp wrote, and Nyiregyházi was evidently pleased with the results, though he had again endured much stress.

His thumbs, which he had injured in the first session, were now in great pain; he left blood on the keys. But he intended to honour his commitment to record for three days, and continued the next morning, this time with much less pre-show turmoil.

JANUARY 11, 1978

Liszt: "Aux cyprès de la Villa d'Este" No. 1* and "Angelus!," from *Années de pèlerinage*, Troisième année; "Invocations" and "Miserere, d'après Palestrina,"* from *Harmonies poétiques et religieuses.*

Grieg: *Lyric Pieces*: "Hun danser" [she dances], Op. 57/No. 5;* "Hjemad" [homeward], Op. 62/No. 6 (two versions: Steinway, then Baldwin*); "Der var engang" [once upon a time], Op. 71/No. 1.

Liszt: Hungarian Rhapsody No. 3 in B-flat Major;* No. 5, "The Three Holy Kings: March," from *Christus.* *

Schumann: "Eintritt," "Jäger auf der Lauer," "Einsame Blumen," and "Verrufene Stelle," from *Waldscenen*, Op. 82/Nos. 1–4; Overture to *Szenen aus Goethes Faust.*

It was an intense week for all concerned, yielding more than four hours' worth of extraordinary recordings. Nyiregyházi was happy with his work, but the personal problems he had provoked continued to worsen. On January 20, over drinks at the St. Francis Hotel, he met with Benko in an attempt at reconciliation. As Ricardo Hernandez recalled in a letter the next day, Benko happened to remark, "Your transcendental recordings are unsuitable for the commercial market" – an intended compliment, at worst a statement of fact, but it enraged Nyiregyházi. Reviving a suspicion planted during the long delay of the Desmar album, he now espoused the view (absurd on its face, as everyone told him) that Benko sought to prevent his recordings from entering the marketplace because they would be more profitable after his death. Now, in his mind, Benko wanted to deprive an old man of the belated opportunity to profit by putting his life's work before the public. "The Benko issue, I fear," Hernandez wrote, "will never be resolved."

Nyiregyházi demanded at least two months' rest before recording again, and in that interval the Desmar album was widely publicized, and word of the new recordings, not yet released, generated buzz. Kapp organized a private audition of the tapes on January 27, in the Ford Foundation's auditorium, for an audience that included record-company executives, pianists, and critics. Harold C. Schonberg, chief music critic of the *New York Times*, despite reservations about Nyiregyházi's technique and interpretations, declared that he heard "an authentic nineteenth-century pianist." CBS Records, which had one of the world's oldest, largest, and most prestigious classical labels, expressed keen interest in the recordings and was soon negotiating to release them. Nyiregyházi's story now reached a national audience through articles in the *Christian Science Monitor, Billboard,* and other publications; especially influential were Schonberg's articles in the *Times* on February 13 and March 5, and a short feature, on February 14, on the CBS *Morning News* – Nyiregyházi's first television interview.

He made a triumphant return to the scene of his ruin when, on February 21, he flew to New York as the guest of Jack Romann, a concert representative for the Baldwin piano company. Romann had been troubled by the Baldwin on which Nyiregyházi had been recording and invited him to look for a new piano for his next sessions. With Kapp as his chaperone, Nyiregyházi spent several busy days in New York. He tried out pianos in the Baldwin showroom, visited the Ford Foundation, and was photographed at Carnegie Hall, Steinway & Sons, CBS. He lunched at the Russian Tea Room with Schonberg and others and spent an afternoon at Schonberg's home for drinks, conversation, and chess. He was in great spirits throughout; he even talked of moving back to New York. Suddenly he was a hot commodity, and media outlets competed for access to him. Through the spring and summer, profiles and interviews continued to appear in major newspapers and national magazines.

Though delighted to be getting the recognition he felt he deserved, Nyiregyházi still wanted his privacy, and continued to live as he always had. A list of his expenses from around this time shows him living on little more than $500 per month, with only his usual modest indulgences: drinks, massages, movies, newspapers, taxis, a few prime-rib dinners. He lived in the Garland Hotel in San Francisco's Tenderloin, in a dingy, barely furnished room littered with dirty glasses and rusty razor blades, with few possessions beyond a beat-up suitcase, a change of clothes, a few scores and library books, the odd bits of paper on which he sketched compositions, and bottle upon bottle of whisky.

With publicity mounting and a major record label on board, everyone associated with Nyiregyházi was eager to get as much of his playing as possible on tape and before the public quickly, and he, rejuvenated, agreed to four more recording sessions at the Scottish Rite Temple, in March. He had found a "friendly" Baldwin piano in New York, and it was duly shipped to San Francisco to sit alongside the Steinway. Jack Romann and two executives from CBS Records now joined the contingent at the sessions, though Benko was still forced to observe incognito. Present, too, was a camera crew under the direction of Karen Lerner, who was producing a television documentary about Nyiregyházi for the newsmagazine *Weekend*, NBC's answer to CBS's *60 Minutes*. "The sessions went smoothly (relatively speaking of course)," Kapp wrote. "There were the inevitable small details and the major issue of N.'s spirits and moods but all in all the March sessions, which I 'produced' for lack of a better word, were much less traumatic than those in January." The result, again, was more than four hours' worth of recordings. In good form, feeling inspired, Nyiregyházi now played some of his own "paraphrases" – improvised potpourris of themes from operas and choral works.

MARCH 19, 1978
Liszt: *R. W. – Venezia; Am Grabe Richard Wagners; Unstern!; Festmarsch zur Saekularfeier von Goethes Geburtstag*; No. 11, "Tristis est anima mea," from *Christus*; "Ehemals! – Jadis," from *Weihnachtsbaum*.

Liszt: Paraphrase on *The Legend of Saint Elizabeth,* based on excerpts ("Prayer," "Dream and Thoughts of Home," and "Chorus of the Poor, Deeds of Charity") from No. 5, "Elizabeth," and the Orchestral Interlude from No. 6, "Solemn Burial of Elizabeth."

Grieg: *Lyric Pieces:* "Gjaetergut" [shepherd boy], Op. 54/No. 1.*

Tchaikovsky: "Juillet: Chant de faucheur," from *Les Saisons,* Op. 37b; "Valse" in A-flat Major, Op. 40/No. 8; *Romance* in F Minor, Op. 5.*

Blanchet: "Au jardin du vieux Sérail (Adrinople)," from *Turquie: Trois morceaux de piano,* Op. 18/No. 3.*

MARCH 20, 1978

* Liszt: "Die drei Zigeuner."

Bartók: "Este a székelyeknél" [evening in Transylvania], from *Ten Easy Pieces.*

Dohnányi: Rhapsody in G Minor, Op. 11/No. 1.

Liszt: Kyrie, from the *Missa solennis zur Einweihung der Basilika in Gran* [Gran Mass], closing with the final bars of the Agnus Dei; *Tasso.*

Schoenberg: *Klavierstück,* Op. 11/No. 2.

Liszt: *Bülow-Marsch.*

MARCH 21, 1978

Verdi: Paraphrase on *Il trovatore,* based on the male chorus and duet of Leonora and the Troubadour (Act 4/No. 19, "D'amor, sull' ali rosee").

Liszt: "La chapelle de Guillaume Tell," from *Années de pèlerinage,* Première Année: Suisse.

Bortkiewicz: "In Polen,"* "Venedig (Gondellied),"* and "Spanien (Serenade),"* from *Der kleine Wanderer,* Op. 21/Nos. 6, 7, and 10.

Granados: "Coloquio en la reja" [love duet], from *Goyescas.*

Verdi: Paraphrase on *Otello,* based on the close of Act 4 and the Drinking Song from Act 1, with Leoncavallo's song "Sérénade française" interpolated.

Wagner: Paraphrase on *Rienzi* (based on the "Chor der Friedensboten" from No. 5, the Introduction to Act 2) and *Lohengrin* (based on the bridal procession and chorus from the opening of Act 2/Scene 4).

MARCH 22, 1978

Medley of popular tunes: the opening of Act One of Puccini's *La fanciulla del West* [the girl of the golden West], "Alexander's Ragtime Band" (with quotations from "Swanee"), "Smiles," "Do It Again," "Charlie My Boy," "Lena," "Dapper Dan/Pullman Porter," "Alcoholic Blues," "Smiles" (reprise), "Rose of Washington Square," "Jabberwocky Town (Newark, NJ)," the closing "Apotheosis" (Easter Hymn) from Gounod's *Faust*, and "When Buddha Smiles."

Schubert: "Der Wanderer"; "Der Doppelgänger," from *Schwanengesang*.

Tchaikovsky: "Otchevo?" [why?], Op. 6/No. 5.*

Verdi: Paraphrase on *Un ballo in maschera*, based on the Preludio; "Volta la terrea fronte alle stelle" (Scena e Ballata), from Act 1; and "Ah! dessa è là" (Festa da ballo e Coro), from the finale of Act 3.

Leoncavallo: Paraphrase on *Pagliacci*, based on "E allor perchè, di'" (*Andante appassionato*), from the duet of Nedda and Silvio in Act 1/Scene 3; and the close of "Vesti la giubba," from Act 1/Scene 4.

Liszt: *From the Cradle to the Grave.*

After the March sessions, Nyiregyházi returned to New York for several days and visited Kapp's country house in nearby Chappaqua, where he talked and performed on camera for another television documentary: *The Reluctant Prodigy*, directed by Les Rose for the Canadian network CTV. This program actually scooped the NBC documentary, making it to air on April 23; the NBC documentary, *The Lost Genius*, aired on June 3. CBS Records and the Ford Foundation again previewed the new recordings for invited listeners, and anticipation continued to build.

Nyiregyházi's disputes with Benko quickly evolved into hostility between Benko and Kapp, souring relations between the IPA and the Ford Foundation. Because of the bad blood, the IPA, the owner of the new Nyiregyházi recordings and a signatory to any contract involving them,* was effectively shut out of the negotiations between CBS Records, the foundation, and Nyiregyházi. Benko, feeling increasingly marginalized from the whole project, resented being presented with a contract as a fait accompli. Matters became more complicated in early April, when Benko managed to re-establish cordial relations with Nyiregyházi and, afterward, reported that Nyiregyházi had agreed to allow him to renegotiate parts of his recording contract. Nyiregyházi had agreed to a deal whereby he would receive a $10,000 advance, with royalties to be split 75/25 between him and the IPA. Benko now made new demands, the most significant of which was reconsideration of advances and royalties.

CBS executives were upset. According to Thomas A. Frost, director of Artists and Repertoire for CBS's Columbia Masterworks label, Benko's new claims would have increased the IPA's share of royalties and reduced Nyiregyházi's advance. Increasingly strained relations between Benko and Kapp exploded in an angry telephone call on April 4. Benko said he was merely exercising the right Nyiregyházi had given him to renegotiate on his behalf; Kapp, in turn, accused him of jeopardizing the project and working to Nyiregyházi's detriment. Soon afterward, Nyiregyházi told Kapp that he had given Benko authorization only to negotiate business relating to the Desmar album, from which he had still received no money;† moreover, he often complained around this time

---

* In the summer of 1977, the IPA was acquired by the University of Maryland, College Park, and thus became the IPAM, but Benko remained (and remains) the president of the IPA, the separate, non-profit corporation that controls the rights to Nyiregyházi's recordings.

† A Desmar spokesman told *Billboard* in June that the album was "one of the hottest items we've ever had," and the company reported in November that some 10,000 copies had been sold; however, according to the IPA's lawyer, Desmar had not paid any money to

that he had no formal agreement with the IPA as to their business relationship, even though such an agreement was supposed to have been a condition of the Ford Foundation's original grant. Nyiregyházi expressed dismay at Benko's new terms, and became angry at being made (as he saw it) a pawn in a personal battle.

Benko soon withdrew his demands, but there were other conflicts. His account of expenses through April showed that he had already spent more than $42,000, though Nyiregyházi had received only $4,000 of his $10,000 stipend. Benko noted that Kapp had verbally authorized spending in excess of original estimates; indeed, William J. del Valle (né Santaella), then vice-president of the IPA (and for some years Benko's companion), says that Kapp *insisted* that they spend more money and was not himself frugal. Regardless, Kapp, already annoyed by what he saw as the IPA's loose corporate structure and slow, lax accounting, expressed shock and wrote of "the very close identification between the IPA's so-called administration and the costs of keeping Benko and Santaella alive." Outraged foundation executives were loath to give more money to the IPA, but in May they permitted Nyiregyházi to apply for an individual grant to cover the outstanding stipend money, which they doled out in monthly instalments over the next year. When Benko received the CBS contracts that month, he made new demands, including that the IPA be paid $5,000 prior to signing. A busy correspondence ensued between the various parties, delaying the first record release and reheating Nyiregyházi's paranoia about Benko's motives. Increasingly enraged over the stalemate, he considered suing Benko to recover his master tapes, and turned on Kapp, too, even on the loyal Ricardo Hernandez – he accused everyone of being "in cahoots" against him. The IPA's lawyer, in turn, wrote that "at least one member of the Ford Foundation staff has persistently and repeatedly

---

the IPA. Marcos Klorman says the album was financially "a disaster," because "I spent a fortune putting it together." Desmar lost as much as $20,000 on it and eventually went out of business. Nyiregyházi claimed that he never received any money from the album.

defamed our client and its personnel by the making of false and derogatory statements of various kinds." (The feud became public in *Billboard* magazine.) Finally, on July 7, the foundation approved a grant of $7,500 to cover outstanding expenses, and on July 10 a financial accounting of the original grant was settled in a meeting in New York, at which Benko presented the foundation with executed copies of the CBS contract, along with a general release from all actions. On July 13, Nyiregyházi was paid his $10,000 advance by CBS (the IPA also received an advance, of $3,333.33).

No one's behaviour in this affair was without stain, not with Nyiregyházi's popularity offering everyone around him tempting opportunities to further their own interests. Genuine commitment to him became petty wrangling over money and turf; hurt feelings and mistrust turned small business disagreements into ugly personal battles. And with the volatile Nyiregyházi at the centre of things, stirring up in others the intense and turbulent emotions he felt, and people on all sides whispering in his ear, no easy solution was possible, only exacerbation of every problem. The formal resolution of business matters did nothing to heal the animosity among the principals. They could no longer work together, potential recordings were lost (sessions tentatively planned for July were cancelled), and a feeling of bitterness was shared all round.

Just as behind-the-scenes warfare was jeopardizing Nyiregyházi's renaissance, his newfound fame was reaching its pinnacle. He was enjoying it enough to make some uncharacteristic public appearances, signing albums in Bay Area shops and, in June, appearing as guest of honour at the opening of a new Baldwin store in Palo Alto. He was puzzled by some of the trappings of celebrity, though, as when, in Palo Alto, a young girl, an aspiring singer, presented him with her drawing of a cat playing the piano, bearing the title "Meow-stro." He accepted it and smiled politely.

Nyiregyházi's first Columbia Masterworks album, released in 1978, with a cover photograph by Don Hunstein.

The CBS release finally appeared in the first week of August 1978, on its Columbia Masterworks label: *Nyiregyházi Plays Liszt* (M2 34598), a handsomely packaged two-record set of recordings drawn from the January sessions, favouring, at Nyiregyházi's insistence, the more "transcendental" works. It received much more attention than the Desmar album, because CBS Records had a stronger presence in the marketplace and because the album's delay had heightened expectation. Within a week of release, CBS had sold 15,000 sets. The set entered *Billboard's* monthly published chart of the top forty classical releases in October, at No. 27, and reached No. 3 – behind two Pavarotti albums –

in December, before sales gradually fell off.* In all, it spent some twenty-two weeks on the chart. As with the Desmar album, the critical response was mostly positive and followed similar lines. "Next to him," James Goodfriend wrote in *Stereo Review*, "Horowitz sounds like he is playing a toy piano. There is such a sense of *mass* present in his fortissimos."

This time, however, the chorus of naysayers was louder, as the hype had provoked considerable backlash. Now there were detractors, like Samuel Lipman, in the *Times Literary Supplement*, lamenting the "crass way Mr Nyiregyházi is being merchandised as both musician and man." More critics now noted the damaged state of Nyiregyházi's technique. "[A]fter all the ballyhoo, if you're expecting fine pianism, you're in for a shock," Dean Elder wrote in *Clavier*. "The technique is incredibly slipshod, the memory poor, the soft playing pulled out of musical flow, the loud ridiculously amateurish." Skeptical of the idea that Nyiregyházi represented a "lost style," he added, "Exemplary pianists have never played as badly as this no matter what the century." More critics were now prepared to hear self-indulgence rather than Romanticism, lugubriousness and pretentiousness rather than the "grand manner." Lipman heard only "a steady progression downhill from the mock-sublime to the really ridiculous," "theatrical" effects with shock value but without musical logic, and "a tendency to superficiality, spurious religiosity and cloying sentimentality." The latter complaints were aimed not only at Nyiregyházi. Many lamented his choice of unfamiliar and (it was said) third-rate repertoire – this view of Liszt was still widespread. Some well-known pianists weighed in negatively on the album, including Abbey Simon ("He sounds as if he hadn't practised for fifty years and should have") and Earl Wild ("It's the biggest piece of baloney"). Vladimir Ashkenazy, in an interview, dismissed Nyiregyházi as a manufactured sensation, "an amateur," "a joke." It was just the sort of ridicule and rejection that he always dreaded.

---

* According to Nyiregyházi's last wife, there was one week that fall in which *Nyiregyházi Plays Liszt* actually reached No. 1.

The controversy only generated more publicity, though, and opened up musical opportunities for him – created a whole cottage industry, in fact. He was solicited for recitals, including one at Carnegie Hall, and Kapp tried to lure him into the concert hall with promises of personal and professional vindication, money, women. He also lobbied to perform and record concertos with Nyiregyházi, and there were a few concertos – by Bortkiewicz, Brahms, Busoni, and Liszt – that did tempt him. Kapp suggested that Nyiregyházi perform his own compositions, and offered to show them to publishers; he also proposed that they collaborate on a book that would "reflect your philosophy and thinking about matters musical and about life in general." Joan Peyser, the editor of the *Musical Quarterly* and the author of a biography of Pierre Boulez, had the backing of a New York publisher for a Nyiregyházi book, and she spent a day in July interviewing him in San Francisco. That month, however, he entered into a contract with Martin Erlichman Productions, in Culver City, with respect to a book and a feature film about him, and was paid an advance of $5,000. (Erlichman's credits included producing the films *For Pete's Sake* and *Coma*. He was also – and still is – Barbra Streisand's manager.)

To be sure, many listeners and critics "got" Nyiregyházi – understood his intentions, shared his values, saw what was admirable in his playing, realized his importance – but he was not always well served by the over-heated rhetoric of his admirers. Benko placed him "in the same category with Beethoven and Chopin and Liszt and the very few elect musicians in history," and claimed that "he was the most extraordinary prodigy in history after Mozart and Saint-Saëns and Josef Hofmann – the four of them were about equal." He added that "some people have said they've seen flashes of light come out of his hands," and believed there was an "occult" aspect to his art. Kapp claimed to have seen Nyiregyházi's tone make vu meters behave in contradiction to the laws of physics, though the recording engineer for the 1978 sessions, John Kilgore, dismisses this as "plain hogwash." The facts of Nyiregyházi's life and talent and personality were strange enough, yet he still provoked tall tales. It was claimed, for instance, that he had not even touched a piano for twenty years – or thirty, or forty, or fifty – before he was rediscovered.*

A British reviewer twitted "the American critics, who have fallen over themselves to write about him in prose so purple as to be almost apoplectic." One reviewer of the Desmar album called him "a prophet of the human condition whose piano playing, like that of Liszt more than a century earlier, has the power to transfigure the listener." Fans often spoke of him in such terms. A professor of English at Berkeley wrote to Benko of "Lazarus come back from the grave to tell us of things hidden and lost," and a fan from Montreal wrote: "What you bring to mankind is nothing less than a reminder of the vast importance of the human spirit." With the release of the CBS set, more and more admirers sought him out, expecting spiritual nourishment through contact with him.

While these responses were genuine, they were bound to fuel the scoffing of Nyiregyházi's critics. The more he was revered as a guru, a second Mozart, the last voice of a lost art, the more he was dismissed as a has-been, a charlatan, a hoax, and his detractors resented the suggestion that anyone who criticized him lacked the depth to perceive his "message." He was a sponge for flattery, and accepted the loftiest encomiums as his due, but he was not so naive that he did not realize that his celebrity, for most of the public, had more to do with the sensationalistic appeal of his story than with his artistic ideals, and so was often suspicious of the motives of those who sought to befriend or collaborate with him. In the end, the hype surrounding his rediscovery and recordings sabotaged his long-term prospects. He was fated to be, for most of the public, a passing fad.

---

* Every aspect of his life was mythologized. Harold Schonberg, a chess aficionado, recalled that Nyiregyházi's skills had been greatly exaggerated. "Greg [Benko] said, 'He's a great chess player, a grandmaster.' Oh, for God's sake, he wasn't a grandmaster; he was no stronger than I was, and I was never a grandmaster," Schonberg told me in 1997. As for the game they played in 1978, "We agreed on a draw. He knew I had a better position, but I said, 'How about a draw?' He gave me a funny look and said, 'Okay.'"

22

Plus beau que la beauté

The Nyiregyházi who re-emerged in 1972 was pushing seventy, had not given a concert for fifteen years, and had done nothing to maintain his pianistic technique. His late performances were flawed by wrong notes, uneven passagework, unbalanced textures, little staggers and stumbles and other symptoms of age and neglect. So much had his technique deteriorated that nearly every virtuosic demand – every fortissimo and allegro marking, every octave and chordal passage, every scale and arpeggio – carried with it the promise of error. Sometimes the damage was insignificant; sometimes it was decisive. On occasion he did precisely what his detractors accused him of doing: put the pedal to the floor and made enough clatter to bluff his way through music he could no longer command. Listeners not inclined to look past the flaws heard a pitiable, embarrassing spectacle, a desperate, broken old man who, as Vladimir Ashkenazy said, "can't play the instrument."

Ever the idealist, Nyiregyházi told an interviewer, "I don't pay undue attention to getting all the notes right because that's not the heart of the matter." Of his recording of "The Three Holy Kings," he quipped, "So I hit a few wrong notes. So what? They lost a few men in the Crusades, didn't they?" For him, the accuracy of the overall conception mattered more than the details. "They play the right notes the wrong way!" he said of other pianists. "I play the wrong notes the right way!" He had a point: in a correct but banal performance, all the notes may be right, but who cares? Of course, there are limits. There are passages among his late recordings – especially in bravura piano works, or transcriptions of grandiose orchestral or vocal music (like "The Three Holy Kings") – so marred that the basic musical ideas scarcely register – the music hardly "speaks" – and only the raw emotions come across. In such cases, "the accuracy of the overall conception" comes at a steep price.

But then, even in old age he was a fearless pianist, rarely compromising his musical ideas in deference to his aged fingers – like an athlete pressing on through injury and pain. He pushed himself to his technical limits, often making difficult pieces more difficult in search of massive, "orchestral" textures, adding octaves and chord tones or animating static accompaniments and so further courting wrong notes. In the bass register wrong notes were especially troublesome, producing riots of overtones – as much noise as music. (Sometimes, however, noise was his intent, as when he sought to imitate percussion instruments. He invested Liszt's cymbal crashes, especially, with a great deal of emotional and even spiritual significance.)

If one listens past the (admittedly grave) technical shortcomings of the late recordings, however, as one looks past the layers of grime on an Old Master, one realizes how much of Nyiregyházi's technique still remained impressive; otherwise, he could hardly have captivated so many informed listeners with the force of his musical personality. He still had an unrivalled command of the dynamic resources of the piano, for instance. He was still The Loudest Pianist in the World, yet also produced pianissimo sonorities of extraordinary richness and vibrancy. What he had lost, mostly, was merely full command of certain kinds of digital gymnastics. For all his flaws, Nyiregyházi in his seventies was still a great – and unique – pianist.

Nyiregyházi's digital technique was strange, even uncanny, and was "not a conscious or taught one," he said. "My fingers move according to the dictates of the music and my subconscious." His fingers, long and willowy though slightly more spatulate at the tips, were both delicate and strong,[*] and his unusually long thumbs and pinkies gave him an immense span. His fingers were never far from the keys, over which they often seemed to glide, and he made no great movements of the arms or hands, even in treacherous and torrential passages.

His goal, it appears, was not to strike the keys but to *press* them. At low and moderate volumes, he kept his wrists low (sometimes below the level of the keys) and "tented" his hands – the fingers diagonal relative to the keys, the first set of knuckles forming the peak of the "tent." (Imagine cupping a hand as though to pick up a golf ball with the palm.) This position allowed him to press the whole pad of the fingertip onto the key. To increase the volume, he pressed harder: rather than bring the hand down onto the keys from a greater height, he raised the wrist and elbow and shoulder higher to increase the force of the pressing, drawing power from the back and groin, as though to *squeeze* more sound out of the piano.[†] It sounds absurd, yet the result was unparalleled volume and mass of sound.

From Nyiregyházi's strange technique emerged a broad, deep, robust tone of unsurpassed intensity and luminosity, as well as unusually smooth legato phrasing[**] and impressive sustaining power, even in the

---

[*] The elder Nyiregyházi's hands and fingers betrayed no signs of age, remaining unlined, hairless, pink – "like a child's hands grown up," as Richard Kapp put it – and he was apparently not plagued by ailments like arthritis. In April 1968, according to one of his letters, he fractured his right hand, though he never mentioned any lingering effects of this injury.

[†] In a program note for Liszt's "Sursum corda," he wrote of one passage, "The left hand must here veritably 'imprint' itself upon the piano."

[**] Ricardo Hernandez observed him using a lot of "organ fingering," changing fingers on depressed keys to achieve a more fluid connection between successive notes.

upper register, even on a clunker like the old Baldwin. Whether in "orchestral" or lyrical playing, his tone had a melancholy beauty and a sometimes overwhelming emotional impact; it could suggest both the depth and sustaining power of an organ and an operatic voice throbbing with emotion. (He commanded a variety of *détaché* and staccato effects, too, which he used sparingly but to great effect.) He tended to project melodies unusually powerfully; for him, a potent, ravishing lyricism was the primary carrier of his emotional message.

His command of the sustaining pedal contributed much to his tone and phrasing, but he pedalled for other reasons, too: to "develop" a sonority after the strings had been struck (he could make the piano's tone seem to swell rather than decay), to create walls of sound in emotionally charged passages. In his youth, some critics complained of overpedalling, and in his seventies pedal-blurred textures were put down to old age, but he intentionally cultivated dissonant washes for expressive reasons. "Harmonically it may not be distinct," he said of one such passage, "but emotionally it is right!" The pervasive sheen of pedalled sonority in his performances often has the effect of a vocal vibrato, and he had a remarkable ability to bring out a melody through a haze of accompanying harmony. Like Liszt, moreover, he often sought a particular quality of gesture for which precision and clarity were detrimental. At the beginning of Liszt's B-minor ballade, he creates an amorphous growling in the left-hand part out of which melody emerges as though from trombones,[*] and Alan Walker might have been referring to Nyiregyházi's recording when he wrote, of the opening of "Funérailles": "The player who lacks the courage to keep the pedal down may produce a 'cleaner' sound, but he will lose the noise and clangour of funeral bells which build up to a deafening roar. If he loses that, he loses the piece."

---

[*] Liszt himself, according to his pupil August Göllerich, "played the passage in the left hand very broadly and thunderously with a lot of sound and pedal, not as a 'brilliant' run as it is usually done."

Nyiregyházi's playing was the ultimate expression of a cliché of Romantic pianism: that one should make up for the "neutral" tone of the piano by trying to evoke other instruments and human voices. He claimed to have no special fondness for the piano; it just happened to be his instrument. "In reality, I am a conductor and a singer," he said. He commanded a huge range of tone colours – one hears brass, woodwinds, harps, bells, organs, solo voices, choirs, percussion – and he "orchestrated" even the most pianistic works. He could make simple octaves and sixths and thirds sound as though scored for two different instruments; nothing was ever just an interval or just a chord to him. The result was extraordinary contrapuntal tension. Glenn Gould once defined counterpoint at its best as an "explosion of simultaneous ideas," but not even under his hands was pianistic counterpoint ever quite so explosive as under Nyiregyházi's, whose playing was fundamentally, ecstatically "three-dimensional." His textures vibrate with life, and to keep them alive he brought out inner voices (and added some of his own), staggered intervals, rolled chords, and cultivated rhythmic dislocation of the hands, as nineteenth-century pianists did to underscore counterpoint and intensify expression (the effect mimics the *portamento* of a string instrument or voice). He liked to delay melody notes slightly, the way a singer or instrumentalist will expressively lag a little behind the accompaniment. He indulged in such devices to a degree that startled his contemporaries and might have made even Paderewski blush, yet his ardent Romanticism could be deeply affecting.

Rhythmically, his playing was flexible and fluctuating, often devoid of a prevailing pulse. He did not mark time, treated barlines as mere notational conveniences, played phrases and periods rather than bars and beats, and fudged rhythmic details in order to let the music "breathe" and "speak." This, again, was the approach of Liszt, who hated the metronome and, influenced by Gypsy musicians, espoused "free declamation." "While playing, Liszt seemed barely preoccupied with keeping in time," his pupil Carl Lachmund observed, and Liszt himself once said that "for me no one can play freely enough." For Nyiregyházi, rhythmic precision deferred to the expressive needs of the moment; he cultivated an atmosphere of improvisation.

His tempos tended to be slow, sometimes glacial; there are recordings of his literally twice as long as those of other performers. For the first movement of his D-minor concerto, Brahms suggested a tempo of 58 for the dotted half-note; the tempo with which Gould caused a scandal when he performed the concerto in New York in 1962 was about 40; Nyiregyházi's tempo, in an excerpt he played on television in 1978, was about 30. The massive tone, rich textures, and rhythmic flexibility he sought demanded slower tempos: in order to be *bigger* and still "speak," the music had to move more slowly. He thought like a singer, who must slow down if he wishes to deepen and vibrate each note. When making a crescendo, he said, one should play slower, not (like most people) faster. This was advice from someone who cared more about mass than drive.

Heightening expression, obviously, was Nyiregyházi's goal. He played every piece as though it was the most important thing in the world. He lingered and savoured and italicized in search of the most profound depths of emotion. He was opposed to "good taste," to that critical cliché "admirable restraint," which he considered an oxymoron. "The more gushing, the better" was his motto. He cultivated extremes at the piano, in tempo and dynamics and everything else, veering (as in his compositions) between brooding and wildness. Whether the music was intimate or grandiose, his tone and gestures were bold and full-blooded. His Debussy, for instance, though introspective and achingly expressive, was never diffident or watery. ("Why should Debussy always sound so effete anyway?" he wondered.) As a performer he was a maximalist, believing, with Wilde, that moderation is fatal and that nothing succeeds like excess.

To some ears, his style was more than a little *de trop*. His detractors heard coarseness and bombast, grotesque exaggeration and swooning sentimentality, but in his mind he was simply being true to his unusually vivid and volatile emotional life. Others, he believed, lacked the insight or courage to probe the music fully and dredge up all that was in it. "Pianists today are so lacking in expressiveness that I don't feel very much when I hear them play," he said in 1978. Other performers can sound pale, reticent, decorous next to him, or he can sound over-wrought next to them – it depends on one's definition of "too much." Certainly he was intent on raising the bar in terms of expression. And, in his defence, what *does* Blanchet mean when, at the climax of "In the Garden of the Old Seraglio," he writes *fff* and *tutta forza* and *Sontuoso* [sumptuous], if not that the performer should give everything he can?

Though his performances and comments reveal a grasp of musical architecture, his approach to interpretation was more intuitive than intellectual. As Melville wrote of Ahab, he "never thinks; he only feels, feels, feels." For him, as for Liszt, music was about feeling before any-thing else – usually elevated, epical feelings. He heard a great deal in the music he loved, and when he played it he grappled with matters of life and death. In his program note for Liszt's "Sunt lacrymae rerum," a lament Liszt wrote for Hungary's defeat in the revolution of 1848–49, Nyiregyházi referred to "a pain that is almost unmeasurable" and "a tragic consciousness, but so stark, stern and forebidding as, indeed, to shut out the light of what could be called the softer human emotion." He described the opening as "titanic, heroic – the sorrows of a superman"; of a later passage he wrote of "darkness enveloping the World in a sinister shroud." "Technically the work is easy," he said, "but spiritually it is not easy at all."

Nyiregyházi was no mere sentimentalist; emotionally, he paid dearly at the piano. In his recording – by turns despairing, searing, resigned – of "Tristis est anima mea," from Liszt's *Christus*, he was not only interpreting Christ's words in the Garden of Gethsemane ("My soul is exceeding sorrowful, even unto death"), but working through a lifetime's melancholy, hurt, and rage. His libido, too, fed his playing – "That's where all the fortissimos come from," he said. He never acquired the kind of musical superego that tames the free expression of feeling. He once wrote that he sought, regardless of what he was playing, to express "the turmoil of my soul, its infinite *indulgence* in the expression of triumph, Joy, Sadness, Defeat[,] Bacchanalian proclivities, transcendental mysticism, Despair, the groping for the unknown and *unknowable*, all the seemingly, but, perhaps, not really, heterogenous elements that form the integral entity of my individuality." That was what performing meant to him – exposing himself. No wonder he found it agonizing. And no wonder his interpretations were larger than life, never conventional, respectful, or restrained. Giving a sort of private masterclass on Liszt's sonata, he advised Ricardo Hernandez, at one climactic passage, to "ruin your hands," and at another to leave "blood on the keys."

Nyiregyházi was an unrepentant Romantic who rejected "objectivity" in interpretation. The conductor Arturo Toscanini, an influential champion of such "objectivity," famously said of the first movement of Beethoven's *Eroica* Symphony, "To some it is Napoleon, to some it is Alexander the Great, to some it is philosophical struggle; to me it is *Allegro con brio.*" Now compare Liszt, who ridiculed the just-the-notes approach. Of the bravura middle section of Chopin's Polonaise in A-flat Major, he told a pupil, "Do I care how fast you can play your octaves? What I wish to hear is the canter of the horses of the Polish cavalry before they gather force and destroy the enemy." For Nyiregyházi, too, a performance (like a composition) had to have a "story," something to provide emotional content and a dramatic trajectory.[*] (In Liszt's sonata, he heard, at various points, "the wrath of God," "the last gasp of Lothario," "a Gypsy's heartbreak," "a murderer's fury," "Gregorian solemnity," "Catholic incense," "sexual idealism," "lightning strikes," "storms," "Hell," and more.) His preparation for a performance did not involve musical analysis or even practice so much as getting in the right mood.

---

[*] Even as a child, he had a "picture" in mind when he played – in the case of Chopin's *Berceuse,* "a very beautiful woman with a madonna-like face." According to Frederic Lamond, Liszt always had some image in mind when he played.

The performer's first duty, he said, was not to the composer but to his own life and personality, his own thoughts and feelings. As he put it, "I want that my dirty Alcoholic heart should *shit* itself out on the piano." (Thus his performances, like his compositions, amount to a diary of his life.) He cheerfully confessed that he heard things in pieces that their composers could not have intended, and played them as though he had composed them himself. He did not feel bound by the composer's own program or professed intention where it conflicted with his own "story" for a piece. A natural contrarian, he sometimes heard resonances in a piece that contradicted its ostensible meaning – undercurrents of discontent in peaceful music, for instance. This was not mere perversity or attention seeking, but a genuine effort to convey how *he* felt about the music.[*] "I am an artist of life, and I express myself at the piano," he said. "I have confidence in my own instincts and I don't worry about the purists."

Nyiregyházi took liberties with the scores he played that scandalized many listeners. Some have assumed that his liberties were merely memory slips, and certainly there were cases in which he spontaneously filled in improperly remembered music. But he took liberties as a matter

---

[*] Consider his startlingly monumental readings of some of Grieg's miniatures. The *Lyric Pieces* are "small in size but very emotional and even tragic," he said. "There is tremendous drama in those little pieces." *Lyric Pieces* of a nostalgic bent tapped his bitter feelings about his own early years. In "From Days of Youth," as he heard it, "the more the music becomes seemingly boisterous, reminiscent of the 'pranks' of youth, the more evident is the tragedy, because it rests on the memory of things of the past irretrievably lost"; his recording of it is deeply melancholy, hardly *Allegro moderato*. Playing "Homeward," he envisioned a sexually charged adolescent returning to his home from school, feeling depressed and confined by his life, emotionally confused and rebelling against a world that forces him to keep his true feelings – his soul – hidden. "Grieg gives me the blueprint upon which I express my feelings," he said; he believed that such music was great enough to absorb his point of view.

of principle; even the recordings he made with music in front of him are full of them. In this, too, he was a genuine Romantic. And he had *always* thought of performance as a fundamentally creative act. His own memories, his early reviews, his first Ampico piano roll, and his few minutes' playing on the soundtrack of *The Lost Zeppelin* suffice to reveal that even in his childhood, teens, and twenties he had a propensity for tinkering with scores.

He could be remarkably casual about notes and rests, stretching or contracting their value at will. He rendered regularly notated figuration imprecisely, rewrote passagework, altered accompaniments and even melodies and harmonies. He doubled melodies and basslines at the octave, fleshed out thin textures, sometimes moved a whole passage up or down an octave. Occasionally he made a sort of photographic negative of a score: up became down, loud became soft, fast became slow. His changes extended to matters of form, too. He might cut or add bars here and there, reorder some phrases, telescope a sequence of events, cut a whole section, repeat a whole section that he especially liked, craft a new ending.

And, yes, he did so in the music of his beloved Liszt – with Liszt more than any other composer, in fact.* Liszt's own practice was the best witness in his defence, for among composers there was no more passionate advocate for creativity in interpretation. Liszt did not see performers as passive vessels for the thoughts of others. "We are pilots, not mechanics," he said. "We are helmsmen, not oarsmen." He was an inveterate, ruthless reviser of other people's music, always stamping his own personality onto it.† (Chopin, after hearing one of

---

* By his standards, even pianists like Lamond and Hofmann and Arrau – all, to modern ears, dyed-in-the-wool Romantics – qualified as (respectively) "scholastic" and "objective" and insufficiently "extreme" interpreters.

† Liszt's ability to play music with complete fidelity when he wanted to was also witnessed, as was Nyiregyházi's. But for both of them, playing "straight" was merely one valid option.

his nocturnes performed by Liszt, dryly asked who had composed the piece.) And Liszt was just as liberal with his own music; as Alan Walker observed, to speak of a final form of a work is "to misunderstand Liszt's art." Nyiregyházi's indulgences were sometimes as radical as Liszt's. Raymond Lewenthal recalled a concert in the 1940s that included Scriabin's Sonata No. 5, "plumb in the middle of which" Nyiregyházi interpolated part of Scriabin's *Poème tragique*, "probably for no other reason than that he liked the tune."*

"It is no sin to change a score, but you can't do it in a frivolous way," Nyiregyházi said. "An artist has to impose a sense of responsibility on the music. He must never violate the faith of the composer. That is a matter of artistic honor." In his mind, he was not abusing scores but bringing their essence to life. "Actually I'm in good company," he said. "Liszt himself wrote that the most important thing is what is *not* in the score." Sometimes, he insisted, it was essential to betray a composer's notation to properly project his underlying message. "It would be illusory to believe that one can put down in black and white everything that gives a performance character and beauty." This was most true of Liszt: "What Liszt put down on paper is only a fair approximation of his inner intent, less apt to be right than with other composers, not because of an inability to write down the notes, but because of the force of his vision."

In his recording of Liszt's Hungarian Rhapsody No. 3, for instance, he takes an unmarked repeat of the whole first section, doubles some notes at the octave, adds his own ornamentation and figuration, freely

---

* He applied Romantic principles of interpretation even to much earlier music; for instance, he usually played Bach in nineteenth-century arrangements. "The way I play Mozart would be even a greater revelation to you than the way I play Liszt," he said in a 1980 interview. That is easy to believe. He was "terribly *sincere* about Mozart," whose music, he said, is more substantial, intense, and dramatic than most people realize. "The *real* Mozart is very close to Liszt," he said, and, "to be done right, *should* be played like Liszt." He left no recordings of music by Mozart.

adapts some accompaniments, repeats some bars and cuts others – to say nothing of the freedom he takes with rhythm and dynamics and texture throughout. An appropriate spirit of Gypsy-style improvisation is palpable. And in his recording of Bartók's "Evening in Transylvania," he effectively improvises the left-hand part (adding and dropping chords, moving chords from weak to strong beats or vice versa), changes some harmonies, embellishes the melody – yet he forges an appropriate atmosphere of melancholy and nostalgia and creates a vivid palette of tone colours. It is a great and moving performance precisely because of those features that, by the standards of his and our day, make it utterly aberrant. Such playing, as Harold Schonberg wrote, "is a kind of madness, but a divine madness."

Nyiregyházi liked to say that he had the misfortune to live in the wrong century, and hearing him for the first time in the 1970s was a little like coming across a videotape of David Garrick on stage – an unexpected glimpse into a distant past. His strange, provocative recordings challenged his contemporaries' fundamental assumptions about musical interpretation. And yet, if we take nineteenth-century sources on performance practice – especially Liszt – at their word, there is every reason to believe that he was not a mere aberration but an authentic holdover from a lost musical tradition, and as such a figure of real historical importance.

But the wrong notes, the ragged runs, the stumbling chords – they remain, and complicate our appreciation. A correction must be entered: Nyiregyházi in his seventies was not a great pianist but the *ruin* of a great pianist – a ruin in the prosaic sense, something that time and fortune have left damaged and incomplete, but a ruin in the elevated sense, too. A ruin is not the same thing as a pile of rubble, after all; it can be magnificent and affecting, in its own ways. Ruin fanciers speak of feelings that ruins evoke more intensely than intact structures: mystery, romance, nostalgia, wistfulness, melancholy, regret. Ruins, moreover, evoke the distinction – crucial to Romantic aesthetics – between the beautiful and the sublime. That which is sublime is not pretty or delicate or orderly, but powerful, massive, and monumental, suprahuman, dark and rugged, possibly ugly, but also bold, perhaps wild or violent, and emotionally overwhelming, provoking astonishment, awe, even terror. Kant, in his *Critique of Judgement*, defined the sublime as "that which makes everything else seem small in comparison with it." A butterfly is beautiful; a mountain is sublime. The elder Nyiregyházi was a *sublime* ruin – grand, lofty, noble, solemn, strange, ecstatic, in some ways repellent, in other ways marvellous, something *plus beau que la beauté*.

One who heard greatness in the ruin of Nyiregyházi was Raymond Lewenthal, who was deeply moved by the IPA recordings. "I listened for over an hour as he sang his sad songs with incomparable grandeur," Lewenthal wrote. "He was like a great bard shouting into a void, as Liszt himself was when he wrote those late black pieces, so sadly grand and so grandly sad. Nyiregyházi's is the playing of a man completely *der Welt abhunden gekommen* [lost to the world], who cares not one whit for what people think of him and who plays the way he does because he must."

Lewenthal related a historical anecdote that deserves to be repeated, about the last performance of the great soprano Giuditta Pasta, who had been persuaded to sing in a benefit concert in London, in 1850, though she was past fifty, long retired, and had all but lost her voice years earlier. "Its state of utter ruin on the night in question passes description," the English critic Henry F. Chorley wrote. "A more painful and disastrous spectacle could hardly be looked on." Some of those present were derisive, questioning the great singer's reputation, but one of her renowned younger colleagues, the mezzo-soprano Pauline Viardot, who was seeing Pasta for the first time, still heard *something*. "Dismal as was the spectacle, broken, hoarse, and destroyed as was the voice, the great style of the singer spoke to the [other] great singer," Chorley wrote. When the concert was over, Viardot, in tears, turned to a friend and exclaimed, "You are right! It is like the *Cenacolo*" – the *Last Supper* – "of da Vinci at Milan – a wreck of a picture, but the picture is the greatest picture in the world!"

23

Adored Baby

Nyiregyházi remained sexually active in his seventies, still needing sex at least three or four times a week and describing himself as a "good-time Charlie" who played the piano "to get girls." Prostitutes and masseuses provided some satisfaction, and he turned to his new friends and colleagues to help him meet his needs. One of them remembers going, rather absurdly, from one bar to another in search of someone willing to give his friend a "Frenchie," and Ronald Antonioli remembers Nyiregyházi calling him up to ask, politely, "Do you think you can procure me some commercial sex?"

While in New York in February 1978, he struck up a brief romance with a woman who worked at the Ford Foundation and aspired to a career as a soprano. She had written worshipfully to him after being moved by his recordings, and Richard Kapp, who wanted to see the old man "back into circulation," set him up on dates with her. (She attests to his virility in old age: "everything still worked.") Back in San Francisco, Nyiregyházi sent ardent letters to his "Darling, Adored Angel." They shared, he wrote, "two most wonderful things in life: Passion for Sex and Passion for Music, the two inextricably interwoven and organically connected," and he commended her beauty, speech, and "impeccable taste and breeding" – for she put out a butter knife at meals. He wrote that "I love you the way I play," and, less loftily, that "Mr. KNOB *yearns* for your wonderful, incomparable touch." He proposed marriage, and wanted to move to New York to be with her, but she, intent on her career, soon broke off the relationship.

He did need a wife, as always, to offer deeper companionship – the loss of Elsie still hurt – and to manage his domestic life. One day in the early summer of 1978, when he was feeling particularly depressed, he was given a detective magazine by a friend in his hotel, and he opened it to the back looking for massage ads. He found instead a long personal ad that an unnamed woman had placed with the "Have a Friend Club." On July 3, he replied to Miss X: "I read your ad with absolute amazement. It seems we share just about everything that makes life worth-while, even wonderful, to me. Classical music, *Gustav Mahler, Opera, chess,* Pleasure, Massage, socialism etc."

Miss X was born Doris Jean Holcomb in 1935, into a well-off family in Miami, though she eventually renounced the family's privilege and took an active interest in political and social causes.* In 1955, she married her childhood sweetheart, August Charles Churchill, Jr., and two years later they settled in Chicago. They had four children, but divorced in 1974. She and Nyiregyházi exchanged letters and phone calls, he sent her clippings about his recent fame, she praised his recordings, and a serious relationship quickly formed.

Doris, who claimed to have psychic feelings and took astrology seriously, spoke of their having known each other in past lives, and of having fallen in love with his hands while watching one of the movies he had worked on; he, though not prone to superstition, said that as early as 1930 he had had a "vision" of her face, which gave him "a great

---

* While I was reading one of her datebooks from 1981, a small, bright-red paper card fell out from behind the vinyl cover flap: her membership card from the Socialist Labor Party of America, for which she once ran for a political office.

feeling of tenderness." On September 5, he declared, "I am heart and soul with you. I love you intensely." On September 9, he proposed, over the phone, and on September 23, they married in Las Vegas. It was the first time they saw each other.

They decided to live in Los Angeles, and Doris, then forty-three, joined him there after settling her affairs in Chicago. She worked at first at the Bank of America's Word Processing Center, and later for the post office, though they lived as Nyiregyházi always had, in cheap hotels. He claimed a taxable income of a little over $25,000 for 1978, though the expenses involved with the marriage and move claimed most of what remained of his record royalties, and he still had little regular income besides Vivian's pension and Social Security. The sale of property Elsie had owned left him with some savings – he deposited nearly $18,000 in the bank in November 1975 – and he was careful with it. Though he still liked to boast about having no money for necessities, only for luxuries, Doris told a reporter, "I find Ervin quite frugal. His only extravagances are usually a fifth of vodka a day and a bottle of wine or whatever for me when I want it, plus eating out sometimes in expensive restaurants. He doesn't even wish to pay to have a 2nd suit he owns cleaned and will absolutely not spend a cent himself on clothing or even for a newspaper." She was still trying to support her children in Chicago, and he gave her what money he could.

Sensitive and soft-spoken, with a great capacity for empathy and compassion, Doris was also an intense, determined, and focused woman, acutely aware of her husband's frailties and fiercely protective of him. She became wife and mother, guardian and muse to him, utterly devoted to his daily needs as well as his artistic and intellectual and spiritual ambitions. In a 1979 letter to her daughter Mary, she wrote that he

> is super insecure and some of the simplist [*sic*] matters cause great confusion in him. . . . Ervin is VERY uptight. Slow service, slow elevators and the like upset him. He feels it lacks dignity and insults

him. He feels people don't like him or he would get quick service 'like President Carter'. He was pouring out to me all these aggravations and worries about which he even has nightmares, to me. To hint he should relax only upsets him more, makes him feel I am unsympathetic, so I listen to his upsets. . . . Ervin is a combination of one of the most sublime intellects and souls there is and one of the most petty and almost subintelligent. . . . I must protect a very delicate man, a very easily hurt man and confused man.

Doris liked classical music, sang, and played the piano. While she and Nyiregyházi were courting by letter, she sent him a list of her favourite music, and it aligned well with his own tastes – almost exclusively nineteenth-century fare, including many operas and everything by Chopin, Liszt, and Mahler (her favourite). During the marriage, to improve herself as a companion, she read about music, chess, and other subjects, frequented the public library, took correspondence courses, listened to the radio, joined book and record clubs. Nyiregyházi did not consider her musically sophisticated, though she did understand what distinguished him as a pianist and composer.

When she moved to Los Angeles, she brought along her youngest son, Robert, who was then just shy of sixteen, but he was given his own room in the hotel. "I never see him," Nyiregyházi said. "I get along." (Robert moved out on his own after about a year.) Seeing that he was clumsy with his hands and too embarrassed to ask for help, Doris found ways to make dressing and shaving and other tasks easier for him. Strangers made him nervous and upset him; he would go out or hide if the maid was expected or the bellman was bringing up ice. Doris encouraged people to contact her at work rather than at home, because he was shy to the point of panic about answering the phone and talking to strangers, and anyway she did not want to risk upsetting him by talking to her family or to others in his presence.

Mostly they kept to themselves; he was, she said, "almost a recluse," and she was reluctant to leave him alone. Sometimes she *had* to leave to stave off cabin fever, and then he would complain of being "abandoned." He complained that she worked too much, particularly evenings and nights, when he was afraid to go out. She had to handle all of the problems endemic to their lifestyle – bad plumbing, employee strikes, thefts, inadequate maid service. Meals were always complicated – finding restaurants with acceptable fare and good service and no Muzak – and he would go hungry rather than compromise his standards. He was upset when a waitress pushed the daily special too eagerly, or when Doris got more gravy than he. Once he told a friend that Doris was letting him "starve" because she went to work knowing that he refused to go to the hotel's coffee shop and face a waitress who "hates my guts."

They were not married long before Doris, like Vivian before her, found herself run ragged struggling to reconcile a full-time job with the demands of her needy but helpless husband. She reported health problems – exhaustion, depression, high blood pressure, dizzy spells, swollen glands, problems with her eyes, thyroid, and stomach – took many sick days, and had many medical tests, but mostly she kept her problems to herself. She was patient with him, because his frailties, though they burdened her, also moved her. According to her daughter Mary, he declared, after the marriage, "I'm guilty of a crime: I'm Jewish," and Doris felt terrible that he should be so frightened to admit this. (She, incidentally, was a devout Christian.) She sometimes wept just talking about him – so strong were her feelings for him.

He returned her love and devotion, but the marriage was far from idyllic. Her continued contact with her family in Chicago stoked his paranoia. She had effectively abandoned three of her children for him (her daughter Mary, for a time, was homeless), and, though she gave what support she could from afar, the breach caused a great deal of pain and hardship on both sides. She tried to shield Nyiregyházi from her other life, but it was not always possible, as when she took her annual two-week holiday in Chicago. Moreover, her ex-husband Charles was mentally ill, and occasionally threatening. Early in 1979,

Ervin and Doris Nyiregyházi, in a photograph that accompanied an article in the *San Francisco Examiner*, January 9, 1979. Later that year, Doris purchased a large print of the photograph as a gift for her husband, and inscribed it, "Precious Ervin, I hold the deepest love for the *most wonderful man – YOU*. Happy 1st Anniver[s]ary, from your Doris." *(Photograph by Rob Brown. Herald Examiner Collection, Los Angeles Public Library.)*

he travelled to Los Angeles with the avowed intent of killing Doris, Robert, and perhaps Nyiregyházi; only a religious conversion en route stopped him. In L.A., he began to see Robert regularly, and Nyiregyházi was deeply upset by his presence in town. In a letter, shortly before proposing to Doris, he had written that he was "*deadly afraid of suffering physical harm*" at the hands of a jealous ex, and needed to be assured "that there will be no violence on the part of a man 'left behind.'"

A month after their wedding, Doris wrote to him:

> Precious Ervin,
> This is just a little note of mine to thank you for the precious love you give to me. How very beautiful it has been these past brief weeks to have your dear love, your depth, tenderous [*sic*] and affection. What a wonderful thing for you to do to play for me today and the other time such beautiful loving music and for you to give me your love as you were doing so and as you do every day of our lives. Thank you for your precious love. God is very good to me to give me you who I love and adore and belong to to the depth of my being. You have my love completely.
>> Your loving property,
>> Your adoring wife,
>> Doris

Yet he could still ask others, "Do you *really* think she loves me?" In 1980, he told a friend that Doris said "I love you" to him "every five minutes" and that he believed it less the more she said it. But she couldn't win: *not* worshipping him insistently enough she would also have courted suspicion. He was jealous, too, convinced that Doris would leave him and return to Charles, yet despite his own pledge of faith during their epistolary courtship he was not immune to the charms of other women.

He was still drinking prodigiously. Friends report seeing him imbibe a dozen or sixteen or more drinks – doubles – at one sitting, and Harold Schonberg saw him down three-quarters of a bottle of Bourbon in a single afternoon without showing any ill effects. He was occasionally falling-down drunk, though Doris insisted that he now drank less than he had in the 1940s, 1950s, and 1960s: "He is not an alcoholic but has to drink quite a bit before he can overcome his shyness even enough to talk to me." According to her, he drank heavily only when upset, agitated, or inhibited; otherwise, a bottle of hard liquor usually lasted him two or three days. But she herself was not always patient with his drinking. Gregor Benko, in January 1979, reported that "Terry McNeill saw him six weeks ago and his new wife had hit him in the head with a whiskey bottle and he had a black eye and a gash on his forehead." (This incident was reported in the press.) When drink unleashed his demons, he could be cruel, attacking Doris where it hurt most – deriding her children, her "white trash" habits (she embarrassed him by taking doggie bags from restaurants), her "ungrammatical" speech, her appearance. (She fretted about her weight, which her personal ad gave as 260 pounds, and her stressful life made dieting difficult.) During one particularly nasty spat, he said he did not love her, and threatened divorce – a threat she had reason to take seriously.

In the end, both were able to put such incidents behind them. When thinking clearly, he appreciated how much Doris brought to his life. He called her his favourite wife – tenth time lucky – and, though theirs was the greatest age difference (thirty-two years) in any of his marriages, he felt as secure and supported with her as he ever had. He paid tribute to her in compositions with titles like *Adored Baby*, *Doris' Hands*, *From the Other World I'll Call You . . . Doris*, *Prayer for Doris's Protection*, *Prayer of Gratitude for Meeting Doris*.

She, for her part, was convinced that he was a great artist, and became a tenacious champion, quick to anger where she perceived someone demeaning or trivializing or cheating him. "I believe a higher force has meant me to be with Ervin in this period of his life," she wrote, "to love him, guard him, protect him." She said she felt honoured to be loved by such a great man and proudly jotted down his endearments, which were as effusive as his abuse was venomous. ("Nyiregyházi adores his wife. He worships her. He has no words to tell his adoration. May 6, 1984.") In 1980, asked by an acquaintance if he was happy, he replied, "I am *moderately* happy," and, for an aged, embittered melancholic who had experienced more disappointment than joy and had been "pushed around by ladies all my life," that was saying a great deal.

24

Diminuendo

Nyiregyházi's fame continued into 1979, and, helped by the international distribution of CBS Records, spread overseas, particularly to Europe and Japan. In Germany, where the Desmar LP was distributed by Telefunken, he was the subject of two short television programs, and a writer in *Der Spiegel* opined that Horowitz, who was celebrating the Golden Jubilee of his American debut in 1978, had been several times "the piano-man of the hour" but that Nyiregyházi was the "pianist of the year." The long-awaited second Columbia Masterworks release appeared in March 1979, a single album titled *Nyiregyházi* (M 35125) and featuring music by Grieg, Tchaikovsky, Blanchet, and Bortkiewicz. By this time, however, he was getting less attention in the press, and sales of the new album were more modest. By June 30, 1979, according to his CBS statements, about 22,500 copies of the Liszt set had sold in the United States, but only half as many copies of the second release, which did not break into *Billboard*'s classical top-forty list. (There were some modest additional sales overseas.) Nyiregyházi received two royalty payments in 1979, totalling $17,600, but thereafter saw only negative balances on his statements. Returns outnumbered sales to such an extent that by the end of 1982 he actually owed CBS about $3,600. Figuring in that debt, his take from his albums amounted, in the end, to little more than Doris's salary for a year. "If a man of idealism doesn't starve to death," he groused, "it is a miracle."

CBS Records had originally promised to release four albums culled from the 1978 recording sessions, the fourth probably to feature symphonic and operatic transcriptions. CBS had also negotiated for options to release recordings of past and future concert performances, and any future studio recordings – everyone had high hopes in the spring of 1978. But it became clear a year later that, from a commercial standpoint, the Nyiregyházi fad was over. A fourth album never materialized, and Nyiregyházi resented what he perceived as the company's sudden indifference. In the spring of 1980, he sought to terminate their agreement, but CBS would not surrender its licence on the IPA recordings unless given a financial incentive to do so.

Hurt and angry, Nyiregyházi's paranoia took over, abetted by his uncertain grasp of the complex artistic, economic, and legal issues involved.* He came to believe that CBS – and Gregor Benko – "disapproved" of his interpretations; he saw a conspiracy of materialistic people working to keep his spiritual message from the public. He even threatened to take legal action for "emotional suffering and for loss of income because of CBS's unwillingness to be fair to the recording artist." He seemed unable to accept that People magazine and NBC and most of the public had not been truly committed to his art but merely briefly titillated by (as he was called) the "skidrow pianist," the "hobo pianist," "the Franz Liszt of the Tenderloin," "the pianist who came in from the cold." And so he had to believe that CBS and Benko were suppressing his recordings for selfish and nefarious reasons. (In letters to CBS, he went as far as speculating as to Benko's psychological motivations.) He stewed and complained for the rest of

---

* He naively believed that CBS Records could cull a popular "jazz album" from the twenty minutes' worth of improvisations on old songs he had taped in 1978.

his life about CBS's "dropping him" and treating him "like a dog." He believed that CBS should have released his recordings more quickly, though in fact rapid saturation of the market was part of the problem. Had he been permitted to re-emerge more gradually with less hype, he might have sustained a longer, if less noisy, comeback. Instead, he experienced the rapid backlash that often follows hype. For this his champions deserve some blame, though he was fundamentally incompatible with the kind of celebrity that was being offered him. Both CBS and the Ford Foundation worried about his insistence on recording dour and esoteric pieces, and during the financial squabbles in the spring of 1978 some foundation executives felt that there was little point in subsidizing more recordings if he was going to play "unknown repertoire and transcriptions" rather than "the major piano literature." But he stubbornly thought of himself as advancing "the understanding and appreciation of Liszt's music," and envisioned recording all of the symphonies, symphonic poems, oratorios, and masses. "[W]hen I embraced the cause and glory of Liszt it was not in order to enrich commercial people," he wrote. "All they want to do is to make money. They don't care a damn about Liszt."

The cottage industry folded. In August 1979, he terminated his agreement with Martin Erlichman, who had lost interest in him, and awarded exclusive rights to his story to another producer, Jacob Zilberg. In 1981, Zilberg managed to interest a major writer in a Nyiregyházi biography: William Hoffer, who had recently had success with *Midnight Express* and *Saved!: The Story of the Andrea Doria, the Greatest Sea Rescue in History*. Hoffer interviewed his subject and produced an outline, but no book or film ever appeared, for there was no longer an audience for this story. Naively, and pitiably, Nyiregyházi wrote to Joan Peyser in 1983, expecting that she might still want to write, as they had once discussed, a book about his "musical concepts": "If you, Mrs. Peyser, thought in 1978 that I would be a worthwhile subject to write a serious treatise about, wouldn't I be just as worthwhile a subject to write a serious treatise about today?"

His own personality undermined his renaissance. He wanted what celebrity offered – attention, praise, vindication, self-expression, money, companionship, sex – but found the price in anxiety too high. He had lived too long, suffered too much to begin compromising now, he said, and he was too idealistic, too stubbornly independent, too accustomed to privacy to play the celebrity game properly or be wholly at ease with his new fame and latest saviours. For one thing, he was far too particular about where and when and under what conditions he would play to sustain even a recording career, never mind the concert career he was being offered. He turned down $15,000 to play in Carnegie Hall because he did not want to feel "on trial," sitting before "those malicious hawks, sticklers who would follow in their scores, eager to see me sweat, taking some kind of sadistic delight in my pain." In the end, his nerves simply could not tolerate all this, and he declared, "I'd really rather stay in my hotel."

He seemed constitutionally bound to turn off people and institutions that could help him, to complicate or sabotage every opportunity. It was often obvious in his behaviour at this time that he was rebelling against the pressures of celebrity. He could be petulant and offensive in social situations he did not find congenial, when he felt that something was expected of him. In Stuttgart, at dinner in the home of a friend of Ricardo Hernandez's, he childishly refused to eat, seemingly *because* the hostess had prepared goulash especially for him, though he drank heavily, and at one point announced darkly, to a young man among the company, "There is one person in this room who is against me, and that is *you*." Not long after the last IPA session, he arranged, on a whim, to make some new recordings at the San Francisco studio of Richard Wahlberg. He arrived at the studio late, and drunk. "He was in a very shaken-up state, literally," Wahlberg recalls, "because he had just been dangled outside the window of his flophouse by a black whore whom he hadn't paid for her services." (Nyiregyházi said so on arrival.) Over the next few hours, he drank most of a bottle of whisky, recorded several major works by Liszt (not well), and grew increasingly belligerent and abusive.

Nyiregyházi's friends became enemies, his enemies friends, with dizzying speed, and his obsessiveness and paranoia only increased in the last decade of his life.* To Benko he complained about CBS, to CBS he complained about Benko, to others he complained about both. In the few years after 1978, he continued to fulminate against Benko, refused to meet with him in person, lamented his "animosity," and still insisted that he did not want his recordings released because he "hates my playing." At the same time, he addressed Benko directly in a different vein: "I wish you to know that I *am* convinced that you believe in my idealism as much as I do," he wrote, and talked of the two of them as kindred spirits standing together against commercialism and materialism. He never had trouble weathering the contradictions that came of following his emotional whims.

Clearly, it was exhausting and frustrating to be Nyiregyházi's champion. For those close to it, his renaissance was an emotionally fraught experience that left much disappointment and bitterness in its wake and created personal rifts, some of which fester to this day. Of those involved with him, there are reports of nervous breakdown, illness, financial crisis, and divorce for which the Nyiregyházi affair was at least partly to blame. It was the major factor in Kapp's leaving the Ford Foundation in early July 1978, and his relationship with Nyiregyházi cooled that summer. Other

---

* He could never forgive the critic Martin Bernheimer for one or two unflattering remarks about Liszt. His letter to the editor of the *Los Angeles Times* in February 1981 says much about his thinking in his later years: "Bernheimer, your music critic, should be fired, because he doesn't like Liszt because Liszt isn't a Jew and Bernheimer has race prejudice against non Jews. I hope you will discharge this phony no good [*sic*]. I believe in the greatness of the Jewish race but Bernheimer contradicts the greatness." The following year, Bernheimer won the Pulitzer Prize for criticism.

friendships, too, were strained. In July 1980, Nyiregyházi wrote to Ricardo Hernandez complaining that he had not heard from him since marrying Doris and moving back to Los Angeles, adding that Kapp had "also discontinued communicating with me after I ceased to be in the limelight." He insisted that he still thought highly of Kapp, yet soon was raging that Kapp was a "dirty dog" who "doesn't give a damn about me" and "chooses to treat me like dirt." The precipitous fall of his star inspired such rhetoric from him for the rest of his life.

The many unreleased IPA recordings became a sore spot, for he had recorded them under "great emotional strain," and placed some of them among "the greatest musical renditions that have ever taken place in the history of the world." With some urgency he looked into various ways of releasing them, soliciting help from friends. He even threatened to use his own copies of the tapes, in defiance of CBS's licence, to release them under his own auspices. But it was an empty threat, for he had no resources. Despite his resentment over the recordings that languished unreleased, he was not opposed to making new ones, under the right conditions, and among his papers are several lists of works (almost two hundred in all) that he considered recording in the late 1970s and early 1980s. The lists make mouthwatering reading, though one wonders how much of this music he was really fit to play technically as he approached eighty.*

---

* These lists include reams of Liszt; many works by Brahms, Chopin, Debussy, Grieg, Rachmaninov, Schubert, Scriabin, and Tchaikovsky; Romantic novelties (mostly Russian, French, and Spanish, plus works by Dohnányi, Godowsky, MacDowell, and others); a little Bach, Mozart, and Beethoven; orchestral works (Berlioz's *Symphonie fantastique*, Bruckner's Ninth, Rachmaninov's symphonic poem *Isle of the Dead*); solo versions of concertos (Rachmaninov, Brahms, Bortkiewicz); and whole repertories of nineteenth-century opera.

One opportunity came about through Neil Levenson, an audio and electronics technician who had contributed several articles on Nyiregyházi to *Fanfare* magazine and had recently moved to Los Angeles. In April 1980, he approached Nyiregyházi on behalf of two small, independent record companies interested in making new solo recordings. He formed a limited partnership, and brought Robert Fulton, a maverick audio engineer based in Minneapolis, to L.A. They were to record that summer in the home of a retired surgeon in Bel Air, whose large living room had two pianos and good acoustics. Nyiregyházi made it clear that he did not want the homeowner or his various pets anywhere nearby while he recorded, but, when he arrived for the session, the surgeon was not only present but, according to Levenson, "made a horse's ass of himself" with brusque and arrogant behaviour; moreover, there were cats and dogs about – one cat sitting on a piano. Nyiregyházi was unnerved, the atmosphere was poisoned, and without playing a note he quietly asked to be taken home. Fulton returned to Minnesota, and Levenson's investors lost their money.

Benko, meanwhile, far from opposing the release of Nyiregyházi's recordings, envisioned a seven- or eight-disc set, *The Ervin Nyiregyházi Story*, including concert, film, and studio performances as well as piano rolls, and perhaps some of Nyiregyházi's compositions, with a companion book that he would write. Unfortunately, neither he nor the IPA had the financial resources for such a project; indeed the IPA had come close to folding in the wake of its Nyiregyházi adventure.

In April 1980, Michael Kellman, marketing director for the Telarc label, reported that Telarc was considering a new digital recording project with Nyiregyházi, but nothing came of it. A few other major labels considered making new recordings if he agreed to record more popular repertoire – Mozart, say, or Liszt's sonata – but he refused. Benko sought private backing from wealthy sponsors, too, for new recordings or new releases of the IPA tapes and, in the mid-1980s, tried to make Nyiregyházi's recordings accessible through an educational organization affiliated with the University of Maryland. None of these projects materialized, and Nyiregyházi, typically, accused Benko of not following through on promises – as though record companies were still in bidding wars over him. Benko's patience finally wore thin, and the tone of his letters became chillier, though he continued (as late as 2005) to make efforts to release Nyiregyházi's recordings.

Though bitter at losing his public yet again, Nyiregyházi was also relieved. He considered composition his *real* legacy anyway. When he wrote a final report to the Ford Foundation, in the spring of 1979, he emphasized that their grants had helped him greatly as a composer, since "the actual *writing down* of music requires a high degree of peace of mind." The mandate of the original grant had been "to save a legacy and to try to keep a genius alive," and in that sense the project had been a success. Though Nyiregyházi's renaissance was troubled and controversial and fleeting, the recordings and compositions it yielded remain – his footprint in the sand.

Opposite: The seventy-nine-year-old Nyiregyházi in concert at Dai-ichi Seimei Hall in Tokyo, January 21, 1982. *(Photograph by Yoshimasa Hatano.)*

PART FIVE

A GREAT ANTITHESIS

1980–1987

Teacher, Father

By 1980, there was every reason to believe that Nyiregyházi's career was finished. Asked in 1978 if he would ever give concerts again, he had said, "It is most unlikely unless some miraculous event takes place, which I doubt very much." But the miraculous event did take place, in an unlikely location: Japan.

His story, playing, and ideas deeply impressed a thirty-two-year-old musician named Tetsuji Koike, vice-president of the newly established Takasaki College of Music, in Takasaki, a city of (today) about a quarter of a million people in the Gunma prefecture, about a hundred kilometres northwest of Tokyo. The college was devoted to a "new concept of music education," which included the teaching of traditional Japanese music. Early in 1980, after Koike was given a small budget to organize an event in celebration of the college's establishment, he and a twenty-four-year-old friend and fellow-musician, Masahiro Sekikawa, determined to bring Nyiregyházi to Takasaki to perform. They envisioned not just a coup for the college but a potentially liberating impact on Japanese musical culture. For them, Nyiregyházi personified an emotional and spiritual rather than commercial and materialistic view of art, and a subjective approach to interpretation that contrasted with what they perceived as the mechanistic, literalistic style prevalent among Japanese performers of Western music.

And so, in March, Koike and Sekikawa flew to Los Angeles. Acting on a tip from a friend in Hawaii, they scoured seedy neighbourhoods until they tracked Nyiregyházi down at the Clark Hotel, on South Hill Street. Dressed in the traditional robes, hats, and straw slippers of mendicant Zen Buddhist monks of the Fuke sect, and speaking broken English, the pair made a bizarre spectacle in downtown L.A., and the hotel's clerk refused to give them Nyiregyházi's room number until he was bribed. They knocked on Nyiregyházi's door and announced that they had come from Japan to see him, but he, home alone, only shouted back in a frightened voice. He called to the lobby to complain, and the visitors were dragged back downstairs. When they explained themselves, the clerk permitted them to telephone Nyiregyházi, who agreed to meet them in the lobby an hour later. When he appeared, he smiled and thanked the two for coming to see him from such a distance. At once they invited him to perform in Japan, and he, who had spurned Carnegie Hall and described giving concerts as "brutal, like someone choking me," simply looked his visitors in the eye and agreed. He said, in fact, "I was waiting for you." Since childhood he had felt a spiritual kinship with Japan – his first composition, recall, was inspired by *Madama Butterfly* – and he seemed to think it his destiny to go there.

Koike and Sekikawa moved into the Clark Hotel and met with Nyiregyházi daily. They worried about his ability to play, having noticed that his hands trembled so badly he could barely put sugar in his coffee, and they asked if he would play for them. When he refused, they offered to play for *him* in their hotel room, Koike on the *shakuhachi* (an end-blown bamboo flute), Sekikawa on the *biwa* (a pear-shaped plucked lute). After a dozen nightly performances, Nyiregyházi was sufficiently enticed to agree to play the next day for his visitors, who lay awake all night in anticipation. In the morning, the three men found a piano at a nearby church, and though contending with an old, battered, out-of-tune instrument that was missing some notes, Nyiregyházi played several pieces with great power, as though transformed, with hands that no longer shook. Koike and Sekikawa were moved to tears.

Nyiregyházi agreed to travel to Japan in late May to give two concerts. Koike and Sekikawa had to work quickly to make the necessary arrangements, and Koike sank a great deal of his own money into the venture. On May 19, Doris Nyiregyházi, without her husband's knowledge, wrote a twenty-six-page letter to his Japanese hosts in order to alert them to his needs and fears, his insecurity and fragility:

> Ervin very much enjoys it when he is able to be cooperative, when things run smoothly. He doesn't want to be uncooperative. Usually, when Ervin reacts in what some people might term a negative manner it is a result of the fact he is very shy, very unsure of himself, very scared of getting into a situation that will humiliate him. Then he either acts gruff or flees the situation altogether. Or it is the result of hurt feelings, of feeling people dislike him or consider him "a punk" or not to be a man of high quality.
>
> Many times a week, after saying nothing at all about a situation that happens to the person involved in it, Ervin will say to me, especially, for instance, concerning a waitress giving slow service, forgetting to bring ice water right away, etc., "Why doesn't she do it for me? What's wrong with me? She'd bring it right away for President Carter or for Horowitz but she thinks I'm 'a punk' so she doesn't do so for me. Why does she hate me? Don't I look masculine enough for her? She never smiles at me but she smiles at a rough-looking truck driver type of man. Why does she hate me? What have I done wrong?" and so on. Sometimes waitresses overcharge Ervin. He is too shy to talk to them about it but he asks me if he looks so dumb that they think they can cheat him. He checks every last cent putting it in an empty pocket so he can do so only after going back to his room so as not to offend the waitress. . . .

The root theme of Ervin's life possibly more even than music is, is [*sic*] the need to feel respected. He needs this even more than he needs to feel he is loved. Every thing that happens to him is weighed in the terms of, not is he liked or loved or appreciated, so much as it is weighed in terms of is he respected.

She warned that he needed help walking, was clumsy with touch-tone phones and shellfish and chopsticks, and should be excused from the Japanese custom of removing shoes. He feared crowds and feared being mugged, so should be driven in a car, not put on a train. He feared being laughed at, so Japanese girls should not giggle in his presence. He should not have children or animals around him. He should be asked twice, *but never three times*, if he wants a drink, and hard liquor should always be on hand because he is too shy to ask for it. He should not be asked to play in private homes, should not be taken to performances by other pianists, should not be told favourable things about other pianists, lest he feel he is "on trial." And so on. One can only imagine the reaction to advice like this:

> He is taking 3 [pairs of] underpants. He is very embarrassed if anyone sees his underware [*sic*] so don't ask to do them. He hides them even from me when they are dirty, puts them in a bag to go to a laundry and makes me promise not to look at them because it would embarrass him. He may let you take them to be laundered but only if you give him a paper bag and come back later to get them. Don't insist.

Doris was right to worry, for Koike and Sekikawa had unwittingly come close to scuttling their plan early on:

> Right now he intends to go but says it is tentative. Why? He felt pushed when you kept insisting he play privately for you and especially when you requested he play the 'Moonlight Sonata'.

He especially fears playing any number people know well . . . When you told him some people opposed him musically you really scared him. He is extremely nervous about going. . . .

He is worried about how long he will stay and he is especially suspicious a long stay will mean "auditions"[,] that he will be like a timid captive forced to play. . . .

Ervin agreed to come to Japan because the request was made *before* you insisted he play for you in private and talked about auditioning for a manager in Japan who didn't think much of Ervin. After that happened he has really wanted to back out due to fear of humiliation.

All his life he has adored Japan, but the old imperial Japan of extreme courteousy [*sic*] in which he felt the people were very soft spoken, meek and not pushy. Now he fears the new Japan which he equates with the non meek which he feels may be pushy which may push him into what he doesn't want to do.

Doris was certain, though, that once he was actually in Japan he would perform except under the direst circumstances. And he was taking the opportunity seriously, making long, ambitious – indeed courageous – lists of possible repertoire that said much about his commitment to these concerts.

He arrived in Tokyo on May 28 – alone. Doris had been invited but did not go, partly because, he later told a friend, he was insecure about how he would play and did not want to disappoint her, actually fearing she would stop loving him if he played badly. In March, his visitors had been surprised by his aged, shabby appearance, but the man who emerged from the plane, Koike recalls, had "dignity and nobility." The concerts, on May 31 and June 1, in the college's small performing space, attracted people from all over Japan. Nyiregyházi would not give out a program in advance, but relied on the inspiration of the moment, playing (from memory) pieces that had special meaning for him. (In the end, he mostly duplicated repertoire he had performed and recorded in the 1970s.) His listeners treated him with respect, sitting still and silent, often with eyes closed; of course, no one laughed (as he had feared) when he was helped to and from the piano by Koike. And though Doris had recommended that he be offered alcohol to loosen his "overwhelming inhibitions," he insisted on playing sober. For once he felt comfortable enough to do without his usual crutches. He was honoured at social events, lavished with gifts, and treated royally, by his hosts, the public, and the press. In return, he was uncharacteristically sociable, and stayed for two weeks after his recitals before returning home.

The concerts made money, and Nyiregyházi was happy with them. He had felt inspired, he said, and had been much less nervous than he had been when recording for the IPA. The transformation of the old man into a musical force at the keyboard moved many listeners. Admittedly, his technique was now in even greater disrepair than it had been in 1978, but he still commanded great emotional and tonal resources. His playing had become more extreme, his interpretations even freer, more expansive and strongly projected. His highly original, very personal interpretations impressed his audiences. In sombre and reflective and lyrical works – Brahms's E-flat-minor intermezzo, Chopin's A-minor mazurka (KK IIb/No. 5), Debussy's "Pagodes" – and in choral and operatic music by Liszt, Verdi, and Wagner, he could still tap into deep wells of dark feeling, and in a simple little song like Schubert's "Heidenröslein," he could find heartbreaking beauty and wistfulness.

Some Japanese listeners – young people especially – admired his uncompromising idealism and anti-establishment stance, and heard nobility and profundity in his playing. Just as Koike and Sekikawa had hoped, some saw him as an aged master, a spiritual or religious figure, even a saint – an artist with an important message to convey, whose contempt for worldly things was evidence of wisdom and integrity. Yet, even in Japan the sensational facts of his life were much discussed, and sometimes exaggerated to self-serving ends: one of the college's publications referred to "his first public appearance in over 50 years" (actually, barely seven). Moreover, as Koike and Sekikawa admit, the positive press he received was to a degree manufactured: the media agreed to suppress dissent in deference to Koike and Sekikawa's aesthetic agenda. And there *was* disapproval of his playing for the usual musical reasons. One witness to the first concert reports sensing discomfort in the audience over Nyiregyházi's technical struggles, and many professional musicians and academics dismissed him outright. But national pride was a factor for the press. The Japanese could boast that only in *their* country could Nyiregyházi find true vindication as an artist.

Nyiregyházi was touched by the respect with which he had been courted and received in Japan, and the airy response of many Japanese fit neatly with his own image of himself. He had always admired the Japanese people, he said, for their dignity and sincerity, their seriousness about music, their aspirations to something higher than American "hot-dog culture"; otherwise, he would hardly have made what was for him the ultimate concession by agreeing to give concerts, or have referred to the experience, later, as "a fulfillment of a childhood dream."

Koike and Sekikawa felt a strong spiritual connection with Nyiregyházi and treated him with great deference. After he left, they kept up a warm correspondence with him. Koike, with whom he developed an especially close, fatherly bond, referred to him as "my teacher" and "my father," to himself as "your disciple" and "your son," and considered him a master on the level of Beethoven and Liszt. A new cottage industry now formed around Nyiregyházi. He gratefully agreed to the founding of a "Nippon Nyiregyházi Kyokai," which had its first meeting on December 7 in Tokyo (in English, it was referred to as "The Ervin Nyiregyházi Institute in Japan"). Its charter praised him loftily: "He opened up a new path in music, which enabled us to glance at the universal and harmonious world of music and made us expect the enlargement of the cosmos. It may safely be said that the essence of his music of full love and peace is the great universe itself. The music of Sir [*sic*] Ervin

Nyiregyházi will keep on washing our soul as a 'Fountain of Eternity.'"

The institute had ambitious goals: recordings, documentary films, published compositions, regular bulletins featuring writings by and about Nyiregyházi (the first appeared in June 1981), regular meetings to discuss his performances, concerts and lectures, and other events inspired by him. It intended to help him financially, too. His interest in performing in Japan had not been financial; he even proudly rejected Koike's offer to buy him some new suits.* He never talked about money with his hosts, or had a contract with them, though they still sought to relieve his burdens. Koike handed him several million yen (a few thousand dollars) in Japan, which he put in his pocket without a glance, and the institute, for a time, sent him money regularly.

The institute wanted to bring him back as early as July 1981, for concerts in celebration of the formal opening of the Takasaki College of Music. Those plans fell through, but the Japanese continued to court him. Koike visited Los Angeles that summer, and after several days' coaxing persuaded him to return in January 1982 to give two concerts in honour of the college's first anniversary; moreover, Koike persuaded him to give a recital devoted to his own music, something he had not done since 1937.† Koike even suggested that he move to Japan and become a professor at the college, to which idea he seemed receptive.

In the fall of 1981, a two-album boxed set appeared on the Japanese market, on the Toshiba-EMI label (LRS-770/71), bearing the title *The*

---

* In 1984, he composed a piece inspired by the old shoes he had insisted on wearing at his Japanese concerts, expressing his contempt for those who "dress up like monkeys and play like shit"; he preferred to dress shabbily and play elegantly. The title: *Like Me, Like My Dog. Like Me, Like My Shoes.*

† In 1980, Koike and Sekikawa sought his permission to bring out his compositions, but he did not want them published while he was alive. He could not face criticism of them, he said; besides, only he could play them properly. He did, however, donate several batches of manuscripts to the college in the 1980s.

Messengers of Peace, Part 1: Revelation of Music by Nyiregyházi, and including eleven recordings from the 1980 concerts,* along with a booklet offering details of Nyiregyházi's visit, photographs, his own liner notes, and an essay by Harold Schonberg. The first pressing of the set sold out quickly, and a second was required to meet demand, as public interest in Nyiregyházi remained strong.

The 1980 concerts, though they received a good deal of media attention, were small and hastily organized. His return visit was a grander affair. Koike's colleagues at the college, who had been among the dissenters in 1980, did not want to sponsor it, however, believing that Nyiregyházi was a "fraud" as a musician and not an appropriate figure to represent them. Koike and Sekikawa were compelled to force the college's hand: they released news of the return visit to the press so that the college could not back down without losing face. Even so, the college refused to take financial responsibility, which Koike and Sekikawa had to assume personally. The two were able to secure sponsorship from Japan's Ministry of Foreign Affairs, the International Communication Foundation, the broadcaster NHK, and the newspapers *Yomiuri Shimbun* and *Jomo Shimbun*, as well as influential individuals whom the institute had attracted from the worlds of politics, literature, journalism, film, music, academia, and broadcasting. Bunta Sugawara, a popular star of Yakuza movies, was a great fan of Nyiregyházi's,

---

* They comprised four works by Liszt ("Sunt lacrymae rerum," "Les jeux d'eau à la Villa d'Este," the "March of the Crusaders" from *The Legend of Saint Elizabeth*, and the "Song of the Shepherds at the Manger" from *Christus*); Tchaikovsky's *Romance* in F Minor and a paraphrase on Lensky's aria from Act 2 of *Eugene Onegin*; Blanchet's "Au jardin du vieux sérail"; Debussy's "Pagodes"; Grieg's "From Days of Youth," one of the *Lyric Pieces*; Schubert's song "Heidenröslein"; and a paraphrase on two numbers by Wagner (the "Chor der Friedensboten" from Act 2 of *Rienzi*, and the bridal procession and chorus from Act 2 of *Lohengrin*).

plugged his recordings on a televised music show, and was instrumental in securing government and media support and overcoming some resistance.

Nyiregyházi arrived in Tokyo on January 4, 1982, to a tumultuous welcome. After two days in Tokyo, he continued on to Maebashi, the capital of the Gunma Prefecture, near Takasaki. In the days leading up to his concerts, he endeared himself to the locals with flattering comments – "I don't want to play anywhere except Japan"; "Japanese audiences are fantastic. I can spiritually relax myself in Japan" – and it was noted with admiration that he spent his downtime in contemplation rather than practising.

On January 10, he offered what his hosts described (wrongly) as the "First Historical Performance in the World" of his own music, at the Gunma Music Centre in Takasaki. His program comprised seven works he had composed in the 1930s and 1940s, two of which, from the war years, had a Japanese connection. The two-thousand-seat hall was significantly overfilled (at Nyiregyházi's request, seats were placed on the stage so he could feel closer to the audience), and again he drew people from all over Japan. But there was a disparity once more between the "official" response and the real feelings of those present, some of whom, despite a native receptivity to serious and meditative fare, were baffled and bored by the unrelentingly slow, gloomy music. (Worried about the response, he had almost backed out of the concert, Sekikawa recalls.) His bloodying the keyboard did, however, convince many of his devotion to the music.

Once again, he was fêted at social functions and appeared uncharacteristically relaxed. At one event, on January 11, a thirteen-year-old girl played some piano music she had composed inspired by his life, and sobbed uncontrollably when he graciously praised it. On January 19, his seventy-ninth birthday was celebrated at the New Otani Hotel, in Tokyo, at a gathering of about seventy people, including several Japanese celebrities. And on January 21, he gave his second recital, in Dai-ichi Seimei Hall, in Tokyo (the seven hundred seats were sold out long in advance, though standing-room places and onstage seats were added at the last minute). This time he returned to a typical recital program heavy with Liszt but including the entire slow movement of Rachmaninov's Piano Concerto No. 2. He later insisted that the Tokyo recital had been *the* greatest of his life, and declared that he would never again perform in public. He never did.

Nyiregyházi was now a national phenomenon in Japan, the subject of dozens of newspaper and magazine articles and news items on radio and television, as well as an NHK documentary, and again the coverage was mostly flattering. He described his own work as "a blow against the blindness of the modern musical world," and many in Japan admired him precisely because he was a culture unto himself, out of step with modern life. The music critic Masami Warashina, after the January 10 concert, said that Nyiregyházi had appeared as though through a "time warp" from the nineteenth century: "He may be the last performer to create his own world without prostituting himself for the public. He possesses something that other modern performers do not. He is a great antithesis to the twentieth century." Of course, with media outlets and media figures among the visit's sponsors, some of the press was self-serving, and again there was some private and published dissent. The composer Toru Takemitsu told Sekikawa that he thought Nyiregyházi was "insane."

Among the dissenters was Harold Schonberg, who had been invited to give lectures during Nyiregyházi's visit and lend his prestige to the events. He was quoted in *Yomiuri Shimbun* making kind remarks about the January 10 concert, but privately he was now entertaining grave doubts about Nyiregyházi's playing and the Nyiregyházi renaissance.*

---

* In April 1979, Nyiregyházi attended a festival in Tucson, Arizona, at which Schonberg lectured on Romantic pianism, and was hurt that Schonberg used no examples of his playing: "I smelled a rat there! He didn't have the courage to put on my recordings." And in the fall of 1981, he was offended by the essay Schonberg submitted for the Toshiba-EMI release. While professing "full admiration of this unique personality,"

In a 1997 interview, he dismissed his hosts' interest in Nyiregyházi as "ancestor worship," and spoke witheringly of the January 21 concert: "By that time, he couldn't play at all, really. But he sat down and sort of stumbled around the piano, and everyone said 'Ooh' and 'Aah.' And I was so shocked, really, that I sort of withdrew." The Rachmaninov, he said, "was overwhelmingly bad." At intermission, he and his wife left. "And they never forgave me for walking out. It was a terrible breach of etiquette."

Long-accumulating disenchantment may explain Schonberg's response, for the tape of the Rachmaninov is one of the most moving documents of Nyiregyházi's art. It is not so much a performance as a meditation on the score, with the piano and orchestral parts woven into a single statement. The tempo is astonishingly slow, the melodic tone immense, like that of a great operatic voice, and the expressive potential of every gesture is unashamedly milked. It is a performance unlike any other of this well-known music, and bizarre by any conventional standard, yet strangely compelling, with its own special merits: those big piano chords in the closing pages, for instance, under Nyiregyházi's hands, evoke the slow, sad tolling of great bells. Had Schonberg stuck around after intermission, he would have heard intensely lyrical versions of songs by Schubert and Grieg, a tonally seductive and uncommonly tender reading of Liszt's "Au lac de Wallenstadt," and a performance of the Hungarian Rhapsody No. 13 that, despite some hopeless stumbling through the bravura closing pages, offers a lesson in improvisatory playing in the Gypsy style. Though nearing eighty, Nyiregyházi could still weave a unique and profound emotional spell at the keyboard.

Schonberg addressed the faults as well as the virtues of the playing, and referred to Nyiregyházi as a kind of fossil, valuable more as a historical document than as a model. (He revised the essay when apprised of Nyiregyházi's feelings.) When the second edition of Schonberg's popular book *The Great Pianists* came out in 1987, the year Nyiregyházi died, it bore no mention of him.

A week later, he returned to Los Angeles. At his hotel, shortly before he left, he made a formal farewell to the Japanese people, which was published: "I am deeply grateful to the nation of Japan for the sympathy and understanding shown toward my artistic and spiritual ideas as expressed in my musical performances. Therefore, my two concerts in Takasaki and Tokyo are among my most outstanding spiritual experiences. The nation of Japan represents the hope for idealism and its attainment." He meant it.

Yet, even in Japan his celebrity was short-lived, for there was not enough genuine appreciation of his art to sustain a public once the novelty had worn off. The institute could not realize its ambitious plans, and in fact survived the 1982 visit largely in name only. Those involved in planning it were exhausted, and it had been expensive, leaving a debt that took long to pay down. (For one thing, Koike had

Nyiregyházi, supported by Tetsuji Koike, walking off amid the cheers of the onstage listeners, after his concert at Dai-ichi Seimei Hall in Tokyo, January 21, 1982.

had the concerts and other events filmed, at great expense.) There was no more interest in him among record labels (there would be no Part 2 of *The Messengers of Peace*), and Koike did not have the means to distribute recordings himself. Nyiregyházi, who wanted the Tokyo recital in particular released, was hurt to find that in Japan, too, he was merely a fad, and sometimes, characteristically, he castigated Koike, his greatest supporter, for not prolonging his Japanese fame. Still, Koike visited him in Los Angeles in February 1982, remained an admirer and champion, and retained a strong emotional investment in him. ("His energy changed my life," he recalled in 2004.) And Nyiregyházi, though embittered by another passing comeback, remembered his visits to Japan warmly, and gratefully, for the rest of his life.

26

The Sun Sets

Doris Nyiregyházi continued to minister to her husband with seemingly infinite patience through his last years. In 1984, one of the New Year's resolutions she jotted down in her datebook was "most important be a good wife," and in 1985, a local newspaper carried this Valentine's Day message: "I adore *Ervin Nyiregyházi*, the sweetest, best husband in the world. *Doris.*" Their lifestyle had not changed. Her income from the post office, for 1983, was about $24,000, and he, his income as a recording artist having dried up, was again bringing in little more than a few thousand dollars a year in pensions, barely enough to cover about $300 per month in rent. (Tetsuji Koike sent him periodic gifts of a few hundred dollars through the 1980s.) In 1981, Doris had to stop sending money to her daughter, and she was often exhausted and in poor health, and isolated socially. On March 15, 1985, she wrote in her datebook, "No one sent me a card even on my 50th birthday."

Nyiregyházi himself had only a few friends. Ricardo Hernandez, though living in San Francisco, remained close, through letters and phone calls and occasional visits. But Nyiregyházi was high-maintenance even at a distance. Having been (as he saw it) dropped and betrayed by many people once he was no longer famous, he needed ever-stronger assurances of friendship, and chided even devoted champions for any transgression. Koike sent many letters, birthday greetings, and gifts as well as money, but when there was any lapse in the correspondence – and despite Koike's apologies from a "bad disciple" and "bad son" – Nyiregyházi was quick to bristle.

He still considered performing, had even been amenable to a suggestion, made in Japan in 1982, that he undertake a concert tour of China. In the fall of 1983, he became eager to commemorate his homeland's greatest son by giving an all-Liszt recital in Hungary, and proposed the idea to the Ministry of Culture and Education. Interkoncert (International Concert Management), in Budapest, invited him to perform there the following October, and though they offered no more support than a modest fee and local accommodation, he accepted with gratitude. He and Doris planned a two-week trip to include stops in Barcelona, Palma de Mallorca, Paris, and Vienna – he was nostalgic for his old haunts, and keen to show them to his wife – and he began mulling over repertoire. In the end, however, Interkoncert cancelled, ostensibly because of scheduling problems. All that came of the plan was a work composed in the wake of the cancellation, based on a patriotic poem he had studied as a child and bearing a poignant title: *Cherished Place of My Birth Will I Ever See You Again?*.

He had not entirely lost his pianistic prowess. One stormy day in 1984, while visiting Hernandez in San Francisco, he felt moved to play two works by Liszt, which he allowed Hernandez to record on tape: "Aux cyprès de la Villa d'Este" No. 2, and the "Song of the Shepherds at the Manger" from *Christus*. They are deeply meditative readings – musings – in which a rich, orchestral tone (if not much technique) is still evident. They were his last preserved performances, and it was perhaps fitting that his career should close, at age eighty-one, with those ethereal A-major chords at the end of the shepherds' song, played on an out-of-tune piano for an audience of one.

There were now only glimmers of interest in him. His recordings continued to languish, despite the efforts of Koike, Gregor Benko, Neil Levenson, and others. Benko still entertained the idea of writing a biography, and enlisted the help of Marc Goodman, a piano and piano-roll enthusiast and head of the audio-visual department at Case Western Reserve University in Cleveland (where today he is an antiques dealer). He struck up a friendship with Nyiregyházi by letter and phone and visited him several times. The two became close friends; Goodman even moved to California for two years to be near him. Using questions supplied by Benko, whom he had known since the late 1960s, Goodman taped three interviews with Nyiregyházi in August 1980, but the biography was abandoned soon after. Another prospective biographer appeared in Nyiregyházi's last years: Paul Hartman, a Canadian-born doctor and pianist with far-reaching intellectual and cultural interests. In March 1985, then twenty-six and in a one-year residency in neurosurgery at the University of Toronto, he interviewed Nyiregyházi and established friendly relations with him and Doris. Later there were phone calls and letters, and more interviews in August and September 1986, by which time Hartman had resettled in Australia.

Doris herself considered writing her husband's biography,[*] motivated in part, as she wrote, by disgust at the "ridiculous trash" and "lies and distortions" in so many of the articles about him. Beginning in February 1981, she taped conversations with her husband, some of them hours long, about every aspect of his life and work, took detailed written notes, and did additional research to flesh out his recollections. "The story I shall put together someday of Ervin's life experiences and feelings," she wrote, "will be one of the most moving portraits of a human being and artist that has been told."

---

[*] In the late 1960s, Nyiregyházi's eighth wife, Margaret, had considered writing his biography. She interviewed him about his life and began making notes, though none of this material appears to survive.

Nyiregyházi continued to compose, and Doris, who considered him a "very great" composer, was a real muse to him. With her encouragement and support, he was unusually prolific in his last years, creating many new works and writing down many old ones. During their marriage he composed more than at any other time in his life – almost manically, perhaps feeling the pressure of mortality on a brain still teeming with accumulated feelings and memories that demanded creative expression. At the end of 1985, Doris noted that he was writing an average of fifteen new works per week, sometimes sketching or completing several, perhaps four or five or six, occasionally even more, in a single day. Often he worked into the wee hours of the morning, or rose before dawn to compose, as he had done as a child. Doris helped him to organize and microfilm the completed music and, in her conversations with him, elicited his reflections on composing as well as details about hundreds of individual works.*

Most of his late works are short and undeveloped – emotional snapshots. He was still inspired by a wide range of subjects, though with age his thoughts were increasingly pessimistic; most of his late music is sad and desolate and mystical to a degree unusual even for him, and performance directions like "slow" and "heavy" and "lugubrious" occur frequently. The titles of many of these pieces evoke despair or failure or imagery of death and leave-taking: *Facing the Bleak Future, Ill Forebodings, The Last Farewell, My Life's Work in Vain, The Sinister Shroud, Utter Resignation, Vanishing Hope.* The rare exceptions are mostly works of homage to Doris.

Nyiregyházi enjoyed remarkably good health for most of his life, despite his poverty, and in his later years generally passed for a younger man. His face did not become wizened, and he retained a good

---

* According to one admittedly ambiguous note in her hand, she may have taped him playing some of his works, though I found no such recordings among her effects.

crop of hair. There was little to report until a prostate operation in January 1973. But as he approached eighty, he began to suffer more and more physical problems, and to require medical tests and medication. His stomach was often upset, his appetite poor; he was prescribed a low-salt diet and given supplements for vitamin, mineral, and folic-acid deficiencies; by 1981 at the latest, he was taking medication to control high blood pressure, high uric-acid levels, and anxiety, and taking painkillers as necessary. That April, Doris reported some neurological and other tests on the basis of which some kind of cerebellar abnormality was suspected, though nothing more is recorded on that subject. An EKG taken at the same time indicated that he had apparently had a mild heart attack sometime in the preceding year, without knowing it, and he began to keep nitroglycerin on hand.*

For a proud man who was shy about his body, the decline of his health was deeply upsetting, and when possible he avoided indignities like medical tests. In his later years, he carried a magnifying glass to help him read because he refused to wear glasses. Walking had always been one of his great pleasures, but by about 1984 he was unable to walk on his own without what he called a "walkie," which, he wrote, "causes me real embarrassment." He became reluctant to go out in public and, in letters, warned prospective visitors to expect embarrassment if they wanted to walk with him. He had episodes of weakness and occasional falls. His hands shook worse and worse, too. Doris wrote more and more letters for him, and his signature and musical script became laborious.

Sometime around early 1985, he noticed increasing difficulties with his bowels (he did not eat a lot of roughage, Doris noted; he preferred beef), and he was too shy to seek medical attention until, despite laxatives and enemas, he was unable to defecate. On April 15, he had

---

* The lopsided lips apparent in photographs from his later years have led some people to wonder if he had a small stroke perhaps in his late sixties or early seventies, but I have found no evidence that he did. Perhaps his various missing teeth were to blame.

an operation to remove what Doris described, in her datebook, as an "obstruction 6-9 inches above anus," and was fitted with a semi-permanent colostomy. Two weeks later, he was diagnosed with cancer (adenocarcinoma) of the colon, and told he would die without a second operation – perhaps even with one. On May 3, he endured an abdomino-perineal resection (removal of the rectum and large intestine) and was fitted with a second, permanent colostomy. His doctors were confident that they had removed all of the cancer. Had he been less embarrassed to talk about his bowel problems and have the necessary tests, the cancer might have been detected sooner, his treatment and recovery less traumatic.

He returned home on May 31, much weakened and medicated for pain, nausea, and insomnia. Doris, though profoundly upset by his illness, threw herself into his recovery, and left a detailed record of his treatment. He was not a gracious patient, for his condition made him bitter and resentful. He became enraged when, for instance, Doris tried to get him to read a book on colostomies. All his life, bathrooms and bodily functions had been matters of great embarrassment and anxiety for him. Doris had written to the Japanese: "He is afraid if anyone hears him in the toilet they will look down on him. If possible have a toilet in his own room so he doesn't have to go outside to go to the toilet. It would embarrass him to ask where the toilet is or to use it in the hall." To be stricken with colon cancer was a terrible irony, and the attendant indignities were harrowing for him. From time to time, his colostomy bag broke and spilled, sometimes when Doris was at work, and he was helpless at dealing with such things himself. His illness and treatment had all sorts of side effects: pain, shortness of breath, dry mouth and coughing and difficulty swallowing, nausea and loss of appetite, discomfort and weakness in the arms and legs, difficulty moving, discoloured fingernails. Some side effects he found particularly humiliating: bleeding and foul-smelling discharge in the rectal area, gas and burping and hiccups, episodes of dopiness.

His health became a terrible burden for both of them, physically and emotionally but also financially. In the last two years of his life, he endured many tests and treatments, ambulance trips and hospital stays, and while Medicare and some additional insurance covered most of the expenses, there were still bills to be paid and supplies to be purchased. Doris worked overtime to earn extra money, though also had to take time off to care for her husband. She looked into nursing homes, but he would not hear of it – rules, confinement – and anyway they were too expensive. In letters from this period he wrote of being financially "on the brink of disaster." In one of them, he solicited Paul Hartman to "form some sort of a club or society that would ease my financial burden," a group who, "knowing my musical record throughout my life, will share your belief that the last few weeks or days of this champion for freedom and integrity and musical honesty, Ervin Nyiregyházi, should not be rewarded or punished by physical want but should have the gorgeous satisfaction of eating regularly and even, God forbid, enjoying a few gourmet meals." Illness had not shrunk his ego or sense of entitlement – his needs and wants were someone else's responsibility – and he did not hesitate to play the guilt card: "If, however, contrary to my devote [sic] expectations, you either are not able or possibly not willing to do this for the dying Nyiregyházi, I want you to know I certainly wouldn't hold that against you."

Through 1985 and 1986, his health worsened. His symptoms became more chronic and severe, he took more and more medication, and he had to make frequent trips to the hospital for tests and emergency treatment. By 1986, his weight was down to about 120 pounds (he stood five-eleven, and in more robust days weighed about 170), and he was often dehydrated because he did not eat properly. He could no longer walk and relied on a wheelchair – yet another indignity. He could no longer play the piano, "except pianissimo," and the tumultuous sex life that had so long ruled him now definitively ended. On August 12, 1986, after experiencing coughing, bloating, and pain in his stomach, chest, and back for almost two weeks, he was taken to the hospital, where it was discovered that his left lung had collapsed; almost a gallon of thick fluid and, a few days later, bloody discharge were removed from his lungs. The cancer, he was told, had not only recurred in the bowel area, but had metastasized and spread to the pleural cavity of the lungs. His doctors now held out little hope of recovery. He received chemotherapy beginning in late August, but it did not help and was discontinued after two months. He was spared the embarrassment of losing his hair.

His mind and memory remained intact, only a little blunted by illness and medication, and he continued to compose until two months before his death. He kept in touch with friends like Hartman and Hernandez, but his deterioration and confinement made him lash out, too. On his eighty-third birthday, he picked a fight with Doris because she was late coming home and tore up her birthday card in a rage. That fall, a trivial accounting error caused him to explode at her (he "called me names which hurt me," she noted). In his 1986 interview with Hartman, he talked dispassionately, without self-pity, about his cancer, even about how little time he had left to live. He was almost eighty-four, he said; if not cancer, it would be something else. Still, his constitutional melancholy does seem to have intensified. When he took up composing again the summer after his operations, the titles of many works reflected his depression: *The Grim Reaper Approaches, The Lid Closes, The Light Goes Out, Solemn Introduction to the Hereafter, The Sun Sets, Time is Running Out, With Slow Footsteps Death Approaches.*[*] Moreover, Doris quoted him as saying, "You love me and you want me to keep on suffering. If I live, I suffer." Perhaps, at least in theory, he was tempted by suicide.

---

[*] For the record, he also composed *A New Beginning* in October 1985; perhaps that title was ironic. And his last surviving work, dated February 7, 1987, seems to have been inspired by nothing more profound or pressing than the week's news: *In Memoriam Liberace.*

In his last months, though not in extreme pain, he was very un-comfortable physically no matter what position he was in, and he was in and out of the hospital frequently. His prodigious memory eventually began to haunt him. In the two weeks before his death, Doris later wrote, "off and on, Ervin's mind seemed to wander somewhere else. We never took a cab except to the doctor. One day, he said 'Hurry, you must call a cab.' It wasn't his appointment day, so I asked why. 'I have to get to Carnegie Hall to play.'" On another occasion, "he thought it was the 1950's after Vivian, his librarian wife, had died. He was worrying about having her estate taken away from him." On March 31, 1987, coughing and short of breath, he was taken to the hospital. Found to have pulmonary complications from the lung cancer, he underwent a thoracentesis (draining of pleural fluid through a needle), and was sent home, on April 4, with oxygen and morphine. At about nine o'clock on the morning of April 8, after a night Doris described as "a horror story," he was returned to the hospital. Doris left him in the emergency room and went to the cafeteria to get him some ice water. When she returned, she was told that he had died shortly after arriving. She was relieved. In the previous few weeks, as she wrote, "he had had only misery," and she herself had been physically and emotionally drained by his illness (she had had only a few hours' sleep during his last days). On the death certificate, the cause of death was given as "Carcinoma of Colon, far Advanced."

Opposite: The manuscript of a typical late work by Nyiregyházi, composed less than four months before his death. The title and the unsteady handwriting attest to his deteriorating health, though many stylistic features of the music – its brevity, bleakness, and single-mindedness, the conspicuous absence of melody and of pianistic bravura, the weirdly dissonant chords at the beginning, the mysterious tremolos, the lugubrious "recitative" deep in the bass, the augmented triads at the end – show that the late works of Liszt continued to inspire him to the end of his life. (International Ervin Nyiregyházi Foundation.)

Opposite: Nyiregyházi in Japan, January 1982. *(Photograph by Yoshimasa Hatano.)*

POSTLUDE

THE NYIREGYHÁZI LEGACY

How poor a bargain is this life of man,
And in how mean a market are we sold!
When we are born our mothers weep, but when
We die there is none weep for us. No, not one.
— OSCAR WILDE, *A Florentine Tragedy*

Nyiregyházi loved that quote, and by the time of his own death, there were indeed, if not *none*, certainly few to weep for him. His body was visited in the mortuary only by Doris, Neil Levenson, and Tetsuji Koike, who made a generous contribution toward the funeral expenses. A non-denominational funeral took place on April 17, 1987, at the Little Church of the Flowers in Forest Lawn Memorial-Park, in Glendale, north of L.A., where he was buried. Levenson, who delivered a heartfelt eulogy, speaking of Nyiregyházi's integrity, courage, and idealism, remembers the turnout as "pathetically small": Doris, Koike, two daughters and a son-in-law of Nyiregyházi's cousin Henry Fried, a few others.

Nyiregyházi's estate was valued at little more than about $2,000. (Horowitz's, two years later, would be valued at $6 million to $8 million.) Doris, his sole heir, was convinced that his musical legacy was of great value, artistically and financially, though in truth he no longer had much of a reputation. (There were obituaries in some major newspapers, however.) Doris still hoped to bring his work and story to the public — indeed, considered it her duty and destiny to do so —

despite her precarious financial situation. "I have thousands of hours of taped conversations with Ervin which I will use to write his biography," she wrote to her lawyer in June. "The tapes are in storage and I don't have the money to get them out until I receive the inheritance." By this time, she was already being charged late fees by Forest Lawn.

Her ex-husband, Charles Churchill, with whom she had remained in contact, now re-entered her life. "I have seen [him] over the years, [and] he hasn't done well without me," she wrote to Paul Hartman. "He visited me [in the] late fall [of] 1988 and was so sweet to me, I felt as a result that it was probably my Christian duty to remarry him." They remarried in 1989, and she moved back to Chicago with him, but the relationship was troubled. Charles had assured her that he did not object to her writing a biography of Nyiregyházi, but he soon changed his mind. "He hates Ervin," she wrote to Hartman. "He not only wants me not to write about him but he wants me to throw out everything Ervin ever did etc. He considers my marriage to Ervin to be adultery." He became so paranoid and volatile that she feared seeing or telephoning or writing to people, especially about Nyiregyházi, and felt imprisoned in her home. (She was no longer working.) "My husband is extremely jealous of Ervin and my life I feel may be in danger," she wrote to Marc Goodman in 1991. "My husband is physically ill, mentally depressed & enraged over many things." She was torn by feelings of duty toward both husbands, but finally could tolerate her new life no longer. She separated from Charles in 1993 (he died in 1999), and renewed work on behalf of Nyiregyházi's legacy.

Hartman, for a time, continued to do research for a biography and in 1992 moved to the United States, having developed a new specialty in child and adolescent psychiatry, and an interest in child prodigies. His project, however, fell afoul of Doris's furious devotion to her late husband's memory. In a postcard to Nyiregyházi not long before his death, Hartman had lightly inquired if he was still "in the land of the living," quoting a phrase he had used in Nyiregyházi's presence during their good-natured banter. When Doris came upon the card after his death, she was deeply offended and angered, for it called to mind Nyiregyházi's claim that some people were waiting for him to die in order to profit from his legacy. Now she no longer trusted "the Doctor" (as she called him), and with her withdrawal of cooperation coupled with his own burgeoning medical career, Hartman had to set his research aside.

Meanwhile, Koike, by this time the president of what had become Takasaki Art Center College, remained committed to Nyiregyházi. In the early and mid-1990s, he engaged a Chinese-born businessman named David S. Kung to represent the college in developing Nyiregyházi-related projects. Kung, who undertook business ventures of an artistic and cultural nature and had many contacts internationally, travelled around North America and Europe meeting Nyiregyházi's family, friends, and colleagues, and collecting information and materials. In February 1994, Koike travelled to Sacramento to pick up manuscripts and microfilms and other materials from Nyiregyházi's cousin Henry Fried, who had been holding them on Doris's behalf; more effects were soon added to the archive in Takasaki, some of them that October, when a memorial concert was held in Nyiregyházi's honour. The college also lent his name to a series of music and art competitions for high-school students at Takasaki (the first was held in 1993, the seventh, and last to date, in 2001). In the fall of 1994, Doris entered into an agreement with Koike's Nyiregyházi institute "to assist in the organization, cataloging, transcription and classification of the materials in its possession," and to transcribe her taped interviews, for "the preparation of a biography." The institute agreed to set her up with office space, a computer, and other assistance in Chicago, and to pay her a retainer of $700 per month. But she made only a little progress on this admittedly daunting task, and Koike terminated their agreement the following June.

Such experiences left Doris bitter and touchy, and more stubborn on the subject of Nyiregyházi's legacy, which she feared would be lost. After the relationship with Koike ended, she consented to the forma-tion of the International Ervin Nyiregyházi Foundation in Holland, to administer her husband's posthumous affairs. Based in Krommenie, a town just north of Amsterdam, the foundation was created by Mattheus Smits, a pianist and teacher whom Kung had approached on Doris's behalf. (Smits has a longstanding relationship with the Bechstein piano company in Berlin, and is chairman of the Bechstein Foundation for Piano Education in the Netherlands.) The foundation was legally constituted in March 1996, with Smits as president and Doris as honorary president. At first, there were plans for cooperative projects with Koike's institute – a biography, published compositions, CDs, films – but they proved to be not feasible commercially.

One posthumous effort did bear fruit. In 1992, Video Arts International in New Jersey released a CD on its VAI Audio label: *Nyiregyházi at the Opera* (VAI/IPA 1003), a program of operatic paraphrases drawn from the 1978 IPA recordings and one of the Japanese recitals. VAI initially considered releasing other Nyiregyházi recordings, but the CD, according to the company's president, Ernie Gilbert, was no better than a "slow, but steady, seller." No further CDs followed, though the IPA recording of the Hungarian Rhapsody No. 3 was included in VAI Audio's anthology *Liszt: The 19 Hungarian Rhapsodies Played by 19 Great Pianists* in 1994, permitting Nyiregyházi to take his place, for once, alongside other great pianists.

A promising plan arose to make a feature film based on Nyiregyházi's life – an undeniably movie-worthy story. In 1996, the American playwright William Hauptman was hired by Merchant Ivory Productions, working in cooperation with Sony, to rewrite a script by the director Michael Fields. Titled *Tenderloin Rhapsody*, Fields's script was only loosely based on fact: it told of the rediscovery of the elder Nyiregyházi, in San Francisco, by a woman who is also a down-and-out pianist. "It was an excellent script, and one scene – the 'rediscovery' concert itself – I kept almost intact," Hauptman recalls. "My idea was to re-make Renoir's *Boudou Saved from Drowning* – the story of a genius who had gone beyond critical recognition and become a bohemian; an artist whose rediscovery brought chaos into the lives of everyone concerned; an artist who in the end disappeared again into happy obscurity." Hauptman recalls being "blown away" by the "fading echoes of romantic pianism" in Nyiregyházi's recordings, but the project was shelved after the release of *Shine* – the David Helfgott story – in the fall of 1996. The producers doubted that the market would sustain two movies about an eccentric pianist rescued from obscurity.

Doris, finally, had to abandon her plans to write about Nyiregyházi because of her worsening health: she was suffering the combined effects of high blood pressure, heart disease, diabetes, and arthritis, and struggling still with her weight. Eventually, she packed her Nyiregyházi material away in a closet. Like her late husband, she now felt that she had been mistreated and betrayed by many people, and was suspicious of those who did show an interest in him.[*] She died in July 2001, and the following spring, according to the terms of her will, which stood despite her disenchantment with the Japanese, Koike flew to Chicago to collect those of her effects related to Nyiregyházi.

Over the years, the occasional person has been bitten by the Nyiregyházi bug, though interest in him has never been better than cultish. Until now, the liner notes for the Desmar album counted as the most substantial thing written about him since the Révész book.[†] Recently, a few pianists have offered his compositions in concert, though no major performers. A few Web sites devoted to him have sprung up, but, despite occasional plans in the United States, Japan, and Holland, no major publication or recording projects materialized until the first edition of this book was released, in Canada, in February 2007.

The state of Nyiregyházi's reputation became plain during his centenary. The year 1903 has long been hailed by piano buffs as an *annus*

---

[*] To Smits, she initially questioned my own motives, thinking I might be associated somehow with "the Doctor" because, like Hartman, I am Canadian.

[†] In 1999, the American writer David Leavitt published a short story, "Heaped Earth," inspired by Nyiregyházi. It tells of a great but down-and-out and dissolute Eastern European pianist playing at a Hollywood party in the early 1960s.

mirabilis, because Claudio Arrau, Vladimir Horowitz, and Rudolf Serkin were born that year, and in 2003 the centenaries of all three pianists were duly celebrated. About the other great pianist born in 1903, however, there was scarcely a word.

The story of Ervin Nyiregyházi is many things. A great yarn, to be sure – a picaresque tale, equally astonishing and sad, of the rise and fall and rise and fall of a genuine *monstre sacré* and *musicien maudit*. A cautionary tale, too, about the psychological perils of great talent, the fragility of the gifted child, the fate of idealism in a materialistic world, the high cost of being a maverick. But where it receives any attention at all, the story is most often read as one of failure – failure to realize the promise of prodigious gifts, failure to overcome personal demons in order to flourish as an artist, failure to capitalize on opportunities. The literature (musical and otherwise) is rife with infantilized and exploited prodigies who, feeling unbearably oppressed by high expectations, seek independence as adults by rebelling against their gifts and rejecting the very field for which they are so endowed. Some believe that Nyiregyházi *wanted* (consciously or not) to fail, in order to be revenged on his mother and her values, that he was a classic case of the young man who had it all and threw it all away – in Wildean terms, the spendthrift of his own genius.

If we look more forgivingly at what he actually did rather than what he might have done or failed to do, however, a different perspective becomes possible. After all, Nyiregyházi never rebelled against his gifts or rejected his field; he was simply unfit psychologically for a conventional musical career. He refused to equate success with *public* success. As an adult, far from turning his back on music, he jealously sheltered those spheres – contemplation, private performance, composition – in which he could cultivate his musical ideas without compromise. This, of course, is little consolation to a public that might have wished for him a long, prolific concert and recording career, but it is no reason to minimize what he did achieve, even as a pianist. Praised by Puccini and

Lehár, Dohnányi and Lamond, Nikisch and Monteux, and the greatest fellow-pianists as a child; praised by Schoenberg a decade after he was supposedly washed up; praised as a potent and original musical communicator even in old age, when his technique was in ruins – was this artist really nothing but a failure?

The spectacularly gifted but psychologically cursed artist who seems reluctant to practise his art is a type uncommon but not unknown. Such artists, because of impossibly high standards, implacable demons, disgust with the commercial realities of their field, dread of fame – whatever reason or combination of reasons – end up dropping out, working in isolation, severely restricting their output, drifting into silence or ruin, or otherwise eschewing well-trodden career paths. They are frustrating artists, whose particular species of talent and originality is inseparable from just those neuroses that restrict or even sabotage a career. We must take them as they are; they could be more prolific or less neurotic only by diminishing their art. By these standards, Nyiregyházi was a failure only in that he left little of himself behind, creating an immense, lasting rift between his talent and his reputation. Still, enough evidence survives to suggest that the effort to reconstruct and assimilate his work and ideas – to make room for him in the pantheon of the great pianists – would be worthwhile even were his personality and story not so colourfully bizarre.

To be sure, Nyiregyházi never thought of himself as a failure. When it came to his personal life and career, admittedly, he only shrugged and said that he had done the best he could – and he *was* dealt some bad cards early on. But when it came to his art, he spoke with fierce pride of waging brave, lonely battle against philistines and staying true to his ideals in the face of much adversity and injury. The Nyiregyházi who sat composing in a cheap hotel, whisky at hand, was actually realizing musical ambitions he had cherished since he was five years old. "Ever striving upwards" – that was Liszt's description of himself, and might have been Nyiregyházi's, for though he was forever being dragged down – in his words, "sidetracked" and "derailed" – by forces within and outside him, he insisted that only his "prestige" suffered, never his "inner worth." He was the classic Wildean hero, lying in the gutter but looking at the stars; he could live squalidly and anonymously in the tenderloin yet still fancy himself an aristocrat and a titan – a great artist, a great mind, a great man. "The defeated man triumphs!" he was heard to declare, and while we cannot claim, yet, that he has exactly triumphed, neither can we speak of him as truly defeated. He was a genius not quite wholly lost, and we have perhaps not yet reached the end of his story.

Opposite: The tattered last page – all that survives – of a passionate letter from Nyiregyházi to one of the women in his life (probably Elsie Swan in her later years). His reference to "this planet of grief and sorrow" is characteristic, though his assertion that only "damnable cowardice" kept him from suicide is more surprising – assuming it is literally true. This page is typical of many of the sources that survive among Nyiregyházi's papers: fragile, fragmentary, yet highly revealing. *(International Ervin Nyiregyházi Foundation.)*

> 5
>
> and adoration as imaginable.
> But there is another aspect to it. One against which we are all powerless. I feel, Darling, that one of us will soon depart from this planet of grief and sorrow. Please believe me Darling, that I wish to God that I were the first one to go—and it is only damnable cowardice that prevents me from committing suicide to that end. But no matter who goes first, I want to be near you when that happens. Near to you in Life, but always with an eye on the inevitable final act—my Darling, Adored, Only Baby!!
> I want you to be accessible—within reach. If it took my last penny, I would try to make that possible. But I don't want a fatal surprise to countermand my dream and inmost desire to be near, very near, you in Life and when the Night descends.
> CE

NOTES ON SOURCES
AND ACKNOWLEDGEMENTS

The Papers of Ervin Nyiregyházi
and Doris Nyiregyházi Churchill

I began studying Nyiregyházi in the fall of 1996. My research consisted mostly of tedious detective work – the slow accumulation of nuggets of information from scattered sources – but there was one great exception: the posthumous effects of Nyiregyházi and his last wife. After Doris's death, I contacted her daughter and executor, Mary Shapiro, and both she and Daitetsu (Tetsuji) Koike agreed that I should be permitted to work with these effects before they were removed to Takasaki. I did so during a week-long visit to Chicago in May and June 2002.

This trove comprised fifteen boxes of papers; three boxes of compositions; one box of LPs and reel-to-reel tapes from the 1970s and 1980s; one box of collectibles (odd bits of paper Nyiregyházi had annotated, clippings, fan letters, programs, catalogues, menus, bills, and so on, as well as artifacts – a tie, a watch, a pen, hotel-room keys, an Ampico piano roll); one box of gifts from Japanese admirers; one file-card box full of notes on Nyiregyházi's compositions; one canvas bag full of musical scores; nine of Doris's datebooks (1981, 1984–7); photographs; and 279 audio cassettes of the couple's conversations in 1982 and 1983. The latter, alas, proved useless: Doris's questions were clearly audible, but Nyiregyházi's answers were muffled except during passionate outbursts (most accompanied by the clink of ice against glass). Doris took detailed notes during at least some – perhaps all – of these conversations, however, and during many other conversations that were not taped.

Nyiregyházi claimed to hate books like this one. He railed against biographies of Liszt that concentrated on "gossip" like his concert career and love affairs. "I don't want journalism books on Liszt!" he thundered. "I want a philosophical investigation of Liszt of the most profound character." Yet, by allowing Doris to interview him at great length he made a comprehensive biography of himself possible. He surely wanted his story told; he certainly thought it *deserved* to be told. And just as the aged Liszt once refused to allow a photographer to remove his facial blemishes from a portrait, so Nyiregyházi gave every evidence of wanting to be seen by posterity warts and all.

"Memory is the diary that we all carry about with us," Wilde wrote. In Nyiregyházi's case, the diary was unusually rich and accurate, for he had almost day-by-day recall of his life. He could remember not just people he had met and places he had visited, but quotes from books he had read (with page numbers) and series of moves in chess games he had played as a boy. He could remember the date and day of the week, program, hall, orchestra, conductor, and fee for just about every concert he had ever given, and could usually quote from (or closely paraphrase) the reviews, too, and remember the names of the critics and newspapers. He could remember almost every piece of music he had ever played, composed, or studied.

Géza Révész noted that as a child Nyiregyházi "was intrinsically honest and open-hearted, and he always said frankly what he meant"; in fact, "among all the data I received from various sources, those obtained from Erwin himself were those which corresponded most nearly to the truth." Ninety years later, I found that to be still the case in his conversations with Doris. While in public interviews or with acquaintances he was circumspect and self-protective, with Doris he spoke in great detail, frankly and dispassionately, about his whole life, including sensitive matters (Jewishness, homosexuality) that he refused to discuss, or lied about, in other situations. Wherever I could bring my own research to bear on one of his recollections, he proved almost always to be correct – often precisely so, usually at least substantially so. (He remembered the fee for his work on the 1929 film *Fashions in Love* as $165, and I dutifully jotted down that figure. Years later, I saw a payroll document from Paramount that gave his fee as . . . $165. That sort of thing happened again and again during my research.) He sometimes made small errors about, say, a date, or was uncertain or inconsistent on a point, especially when it came to his very early years, but not often, and he did not make up biographical data out of whole cloth. Where a specific memory could not be documented, it was usually rendered likely or at least plausible by related facts. The *tone* of his recollections, too, proved reliable; he did not, for instance, exaggerate either his successes or his failures (reviews always confirmed his memory of how one of his concerts was received). No evidence emerged that he knowingly misrepresented the facts of his life in his conversations with Doris, and in those cases where documentation stubbornly refused to emerge – the performance he claimed to have given of the Busoni concerto in 1919, for instance – I tended to accept his memory. But I stress that his reliability as a source was never axiomatic with me; it was confirmed again and again as I worked with his memories.

Doris's interview notes, moreover, gave every evidence of being precisely what they purported to be: verbatim records of Nyiregyházi's conversation. She had no need or desire to falsify information about his life, and, to judge from the volume of unflattering material about him recorded in her hand, she did not. (According to her son Robert, she wanted any biography of Nyiregyházi to reveal the *whole* truth.) In letters and datebooks, her handwriting was legible, but in many of her notes it presented real difficulties, suggesting that she wrote them on the fly as Nyiregyházi talked. Also, she often had him clarify dates, spelling, and other details, and explain the historical, musical, literary, and other issues that arose as he reminisced; her notes were all the more reliable and comprehensive for this reason, and among them were no conspicuous gaps in Nyiregyházi's story.

Mark Twain said that writing a biography of Shakespeare was like trying to reconstruct a brontosaurus from "nine bones and six hundred barrels of plaster of Paris"; writing a biography of Nyiregyházi would have been like that, too, had I not had access to his and Doris's papers, which were the most important source of information about and quotes from him in this book. And so my first thanks must go to my subject himself and his last wife. I regret that I was able to exchange letters with Doris only once, in 1997, because of her health, but I was pleased to hear, from Mattheus Smits, president of the International Ervin Nyiregyházi Foundation, that she approved of my project. I am also grateful to Mary Shapiro and Daitetsu (Tetsuji) Koike for allowing me to examine Nyiregyházi's and Doris's effects. Mary and her husband, Ken Shapiro, cared for the material responsibly after Doris's death, and were gracious hosts to me during my stay in Chicago, which was madly productive but also (despite a heat wave) enjoyable. Mary, moreover, helped with the dreary task of photocopying papers both during and after my visit. I also thank her for giving me permission to quote from Doris's papers. From the beginning, she adopted the generous attitude that by helping me she was helping to realize her mother's dream of putting Nyiregyházi's story before the public. Her support was crucial.

Notes on Sources and Acknowledgements

SELECTIVE LIST OF OTHER SOURCES CONSULTED

For ten years, I accumulated information and materials from a huge range of sources, and benefitted from the generosity of many individuals and institutions around the world. In the pages that follow, in which I acknowledge my debts, I spare the reader the constant repetition of words like "thanks" and "gratitude," but I assure all of those named here that they have my deep appreciation. This book could not have been written – or at least, would not have amounted to much – without their contributions. I apologize abjectly to anyone whose name should appear in these pages but does not. Blame some glitch in my memory or my files, not a want of gratitude.

PRELUDE: THE STRANGE CASE OF ERVIN NYIREGYHÁZI
On the Mr. X concert: Joy and Irwin Parnes, *Irwin Parnes Takes the "Bull by the Horns"* (1988); Samuel Will Parnes. Frederick Marvin shared memories by telephone of that concert and of encounters with Nyiregyházi dating back to 1936. Raymond Lewenthal's unpublished essay "Remembrance of Nyiregyházi Past" (1978) was supplied by Gregor Benko.

Schoenberg's two-page letter to Klemperer (© Arnold Schönberg Center, Vienna) was supplied by Therese Muxeneder, who also granted me permission to publish it (the translation is mine).

PART I: MUSICAL WONDER CHILD

1 Beginnings in Budapest
On Nyiregyházi's family background: Imre Szabó, "Zsidó fejek: Nyiregyházi Ervin" [Jewish portraits], published in the January 1918 issue of an unidentified, non-musical Hungarian publication and found among Nyiregyházi's papers; the late Henry and Leah Fried, Aaron Gross, Zoltan Repassy, and Mattheus Smits.

On Hungary and Budapest: *Budapest: A History from Its Beginnings to 1998*, ed. András Gerő and Janós Poór (1997); László Kontler, *A History of Hungary: Millennium in Central Europe* (1999, 2002); Paul Lendvai, *The Hungarians: A Thousand Years of Victory in Defeat* (English ed. 2003); John Lukacs, *Budapest 1900: A Historical Portrait of a City and Its Culture* (1988); Miklós Molnár, *A Concise History of Hungary,* Cambridge Concise Histories

(English ed. 2001); *A History of Hungary,* ed. Peter F. Sugar, Péter Hanák, and Tibor Frank (1990).

On Hungarian Jews: William O. McCagg, Jr., *A History of Habsburg Jews, 1670–1918* (1989) and *Jewish Nobles and Geniuses in Modern Hungary* (1972); Raphael Patai, *Apprentice in Budapest: Memories of a World That Is No More* (1988) and *The Jews of Hungary: History, Culture, Psychology* (1996).

On musical life in Hungary and Budapest: Judit Frigyesi, *Béla Bartók and Turn-of-the-Century Budapest* (1998); Claude Kenneson, *Székely and Bartók: The Story of a Friendship* (1994).

On Nyiregyházi's father and grandfather, the Royal Opera, and Lehár and Puccini in Budapest: Nóra Wellmann (Archives, Opera House, Budapest).

On István Thomán: "About István Thomán" (1927), in *Béla Bartók Essays,* sel. and ed. Benjamin Suchoff (1976), 489–91. (I also drew on Bartók's essays on Liszt and on musical life in Budapest in 1920.)

Máté Mesterházi, a musicologist at what is today the Ferenc Liszt Academy of Music, copied and translated pages from the academy's yearbooks for 1908–9 through 1913–14.

Jurriaan Dijkman, a young Dutch pianist, supplied information, clippings, and photographs during the 2005–6 school year, which he spent studying at the Leó Weiner High School of Music, in Budapest.

2 Under the Microscope

Géza Révész, *Erwin Nyiregyházi: psychologische Analyse eines musikalisch hervorragenden Kindes* (Leipzig: Veit & Company, 1916), 148 pages; *The Psychology of a Musical Prodigy* (no translator named), International Library of Psychology, Philosophy and Scientific Method (London: Kegan Paul, Trench, Trubner & Co., Ltd., and New York: Harcourt, Brace & Company, 1925), 180 pages. The English edition has remained available over the years in reprint editions from a handful of American and British companies, including Reprint Services Corporation (Temecula, California), which sent me a complimentary copy. Nyiregyházi is also discussed in Révész's major work, *Introduction to the Psychology of Music,* first published in 1944 (English ed. 1953, now available as a Dover reprint, 150–6).

On prodigies: Brendan G. Carroll, *The Last Prodigy: A Biography of Erich Wolfgang Korngold* (1997); David Henry Feldman, with Lynn T. Goldsmith, *Nature's Gambit: Child Prodigies and the Development of Human Potential*

(1986); Renee B. Fisher, *Musical Prodigies: Masters at an Early Age* (1973); Joan Freeman, *Gifted Children: Their Identification and Development in a Social Context* (1979); Joseph Horowitz, *Conversations with Arrau* (1982); Michael J. A. Howe, *The Origins of Exceptional Abilities* (1990); C. G. Jung, "The Gifted Child" (1942 lecture), in English in *The Collected Works of C. G. Jung*, ed. Sir Herbert Read, et. al., Vol. 17: *The Development of Personality* (1954), 135–45; Claude Kenneson, *Musical Prodigies: Perilous Journeys, Remarkable Lives* (1998); Joan Peyser, "An Idiosyncratic Balance: Parents and Genius Children" (1984 lecture), in *The Music of My Time* (1995), 399–407; Ruth Slenczynska and Louis Biancolli, *Forbidden Childhood* (1958); Maynard Solomon, *Mozart: A Life* (1995); Norbert Wiener, *Ex-prodigy: My Childhood and Youth* (1953); Ellen Winner, *Gifted Children: Myths and Realities* (1996).

3 Prodigy's Progress

Compositions d'Ervin Nyiregyházi, Opp. 1–3: Katalin Szerzö (Music Collection, National Széchényi Library, Budapest).

The entry in the diary of the Prince of Wales (RA EVIII/Diary/1911: 2 June) was transcribed by Douglas Sulley (Royal Archives, Windsor Castle), and is quoted with the permission of Her Majesty Queen Elizabeth II.

4 To Berlin – and Liszt – and Back

Information about the private recital in Berlin reviewed in the *Börsen-Courier* came from an unsigned article from a Hungarian newspaper, hand-dated November 13, 1913, and found among Nyiregyházi's papers.

On Ernő Dohnányi: Harriette Brower, "Erno von Dohnanyi," in *Modern Masters of the Keyboard* (1926), 104–12; Ilona von Dohnányi, *Ernest von Dohnányi: A Song of Life*, ed. James A. Grymes (2002); Elza Galafrés, "Galafrés and Dohnányi," in *Lives . . . Loves . . . Losses* (1973), 91–409; Boris Goldovsky, "With Dohnányi in Budapest," in *My Road to Opera* (1979), 74–128; *Perspectives on Ernst von Dohnányi*, ed. James A. Grymes (2005); Deborah Kiszely-Papp (Ernő Dohnányi Archives, Institute for Musicology of the Hungarian Academy of Sciences, Budapest).

On Nyiregyházi's concerts in Berlin, 1915–18: Lim M. Lai, "Lilli Lehmann," *The Record Collector*, February 1981, 152–90 (supplied by Larry Lustig); Jutta March (Archive, Berlin Philharmonic).

On Frederic Lamond: Harriette Brower, "Frederic Lamond," in *Modern Masters of the Keyboard* (1926), 94–103; Frederic Lamond, *Beethoven: Notes on the Sonatas* (1944) and *The Memoirs of Frederic Lamond* (1949); Alan Vicat, "Frederic Lamond: A Great Scot," *International Piano Quarterly,* Spring 1998, 54–69.

Reviews of Nyiregyházi's concerts in Budapest, 1916–17: Jurriaan Dijkman.

5 The Wunderkind on Tour

Programs, clippings, contracts, and other materials relating to Nyiregyházi's concerts in Denmark, Norway, and Sweden, 1918–20: Jan Amberg, Inger Johanne Christiansen (National Library of Norway, Oslo), Lars Karlsson (Stockholm Concert Hall Foundation, Royal Stockholm Philharmonic Orchestra), Karin Borgkvist Ljung (Reference Service Department, National Archives, Stockholm), Hans Riben, Andreas Sopart (Archive, Breitkopf und Härtel), Musse Magnussen Svare (Music History Museum and the Carl Claudius Collection, Copenhagen), and Kaisa Vitri (Statistics Sweden). Jörgen Lundmark made queries on my behalf, conducted research in Swedish libraries, archives, and museums, supplied copies of programs and reviews, and translated articles in Swedish and Norwegian.

István P. Korody supplied pages on Nyiregyházi from his unpublished book *Ormándy-Széll-Reiner . . . zenéről és emigráns muzsikussorsról* [on music and Hungarian émigré musicians] (1993), including a review of the 1918 recital in Szeged.

On Nyiregyházi's concerts in The Netherlands, 1919: A. de Wal, *De Pianistenwereld: Beroemde Pianisten van Voorheen en Thans* (1927).

Three letters from Nyiregyházi (1919) and one from his mother (1926) to the Norwegian composer Gerhard Schjelderup, and two letters from Nyiregyházi to Halfdan Cleve (1924 and 1929), were supplied by Sigbjørn Grindheim (Department of Manuscripts, National Library of Norway, Oslo). The Norwegian pianist Jørn Fossheim, who discovered these letters, helped me to translate them and shared some of his own research on Cleve and Schjelderup.

Nyiregyházi's published compositions, 1919–20: Donald Manildi (International Piano Archives at Maryland (IPAM), College Park), the Photoduplication Service of the Library of Congress, and Mattheus Smits.

Notes on Sources and Acknowledgements

PART 2: A YOUNG LISZT OF THE PIANOFORTE

6 A King in New York

Ship's manifests and other data on Nyiregyházi's arrivals at Ellis Island, 1920, 1923, and 1924: www.ellisislandrecords.org.

On musical life in America and New York in the 1920s: Joseph Horowitz, *Classical Music in America: A History of Its Rise and Fall* (2005) and *Understanding Toscanini* (1987); Norman Lebrecht, *When the Music Stops . . . : Managers, Maestros and the Corporate Murder of Classical Music* (1996); R. Allen Lott, *From Paris to Peoria: How European Piano Virtuosos Brought Classical Music to the American Heartland* (2003).

Clippings relating to Nyiregyházi's American activities: Donald Manildi (IPAM), the Music Division of the New York Public Library, and Michael A. Kukral, who loaned me a file of material that had been collected by the late Emmett M. Ford.

7 Under New Management

On R.E. Johnston: *The Accompanist . . . and Friends: An Autobiography of André Benoist*, ed. John Anthony Maltese (1978); Arthur Rubinstein, *My Many Years* (1980); Charles L. Wagner, *Seeing Stars* (1940).

Programs and reviews, 1921–23: Bridget Carr (Boston Symphony Orchestra Archives) and Marilou Carlin (Public Relations, Detroit Symphony Orchestra).

On Nyiregyházi's concerts in Los Angeles, 1923: Merle Armitage, *Accent on America* (1944), 347–8.

8 Re-enacting

On Ampico: Q. David Bowers, *Encyclopedia of Automatic Musical Instruments* (1972); Larry Givens, *Re Enacting the Artist: . . . a story of the Ampico Reproducing Piano* (1970); *The Ampico Reproducing Piano*, ed. Richard J. Howe (1987); Arthur Loesser, "An Instrument that goethe with a whele withoute playinge uppon," in *Men, Women and Pianos: A Social History* (1954), 577–86; Elaine Obenchain, *The Complete Catalog of Ampico Reproducing Piano Rolls* (1977); Arthur W. J. G. Ord-Hume, *Pianola: The History of the Self-Playing Piano* (1984); Larry Sitsky, *The Classical Reproducing Piano Roll: A Catalogue-Index*, Vol. 2: *Pianists* (1990). I also consulted various Ampico catalogues and magazines, and issues of *The AMICA Bulletin*.

On Nyiregyházi's piano rolls: Kenneth C. Caswell, Matthew Caulfield, John Farmer, Richard Groman (Keystone Music Roll Company, Bethlehem, Pennsylvania), Denis Hall, Bill Knorp, Michael A. Kukral (editor and publisher of *The AMICA Bulletin*), Jeffrey Morgan, Robin Pratt, Richard D. Reutlinger, and Mark Starr.

9 Decline and Fall

Clippings relating to Nyiregyházi's concerts in Kristiania, 1923: Inger Johanne Christiansen (National Library of Norway, Oslo).

Reviews of Nyiregyházi's concerts in Montreal, 1923–4: John Kalbfleisch.

Rudolph Valentino and His 88 American Beauties, a short film by a young David O. Selznick about the 1923 pageant in New York (Nyiregyházi does not appear in it).

Filings in the case of *Erwin Nyiregyhazi v. R. E. Johnston* (New York County Clerk Index No. 38068/1924): Bruce Abrams and Joseph Van Nostrand (Division of Old Records, County Clerk and Clerk of the Supreme Court, New York County Court House).

Annals of the Metropolitan Opera: The Complete Chronicle of Performances and Artists, 2 vols., ed. Gerald Fitzgerald (1989).

10 Love and Marriage

On Theodore Dreiser and Helen Richardson: Helen Dreiser, *My Life with Dreiser* (1951); Vera Dreiser, with Brett Howard, *My Uncle Theodore* (1976); Richard Lingeman, *Theodore Dreiser,* Vol. 2: *An American Journey, 1908–1945* (1990); Jerome Loving, *The Last Titan: A Life of Theodore Dreiser* (2005).

Five letters from Nyiregyházi (1927, 1929, 1932, 1946, and one undated fragment) among the Theodore Dreiser Papers were supplied by Nancy M. Shawcross (Rare Book and Manuscript Library, University of Pennsylvania, Philadelphia), and are quoted with permission.

Nyiregyházi's first wife's suit for separation alimony, in the Supreme Court of the State of New York, was filed in October 1927, went to trial in 1928, and was discontinued in 1929. According to Bruce Abrams (Division of Old Records, County Clerk and Clerk of the Supreme Court, New York County Court House), filings in the case of *Mary Nyiregyhazi v. Erwin Nyiregyhazi* survive (New York County Clerk Index No. 37138/1927); however, as the case concerns a separation they are restricted by law until 2027, and can in the meantime be opened only with a court order.

PART 3: A SOLDIER OF FORTUNE

11 Down and Out in L.A. and Abroad

Programs, press releases, and clippings relating to Nyiregyházi's concerts in Los Angeles, 1923–57, and information on the cultural life of the city in those years: Lance Bowling, D. Norman Dupill (Art, Music, and Recreation Department, Los Angeles Public Library), Victor Ledin, Dace Taube (Regional History Collection, Specialized Libraries and Archival Collections, University of Southern California, Los Angeles), and Philip Weyland. I drew on three volumes published in Hollywood by the Bureau of Musical Research: *Who's Who in Music and Dance in Southern California* (1933), *Music and Dance in California* (1940), and *Music and Dance in California and the West* (1948).

On early talkies, Hugo Riesenfeld, and Nyiregyházi's film work: Gillian B. Anderson, *Music for Silent Films, 1894–1929: A Guide* (1988); Ronald Bergan, *The United Artists Story* (1986); Donald Crafton, *The Talkies: American Cinema's Transition to Sound, 1926–1931* (1997); Clifford McCarty, *Film Composers in America: A Filmography, 1911–1970*, 2nd ed. (2000). Clifford McCarty supplied information on the score of *Coquette*. Lance Bowling supplied Paramount documents relating to *Fashions in Love*. Research at U.C.L.A. and at the Academy of Motion Picture Arts and Sciences' Margaret Herrick Library, in Beverly Hills, was conducted on my behalf by Charles Barber.

On Marie Pergain: See the Lingeman and Loving biographies of Dreiser cited above.

A transcript of his unpublished interview with the late György Sándor (New York, June 2002) was supplied by Gregor Benko. István P. Korody's book, cited above, includes a review of Nyiregyházi's 1934 recital of his own works in Budapest.

Interlocutory and final judgments of divorce in the case of *Xandra Lucille Nyiregyházi vs. Ervin Nyiregyházi* (Case No. D141110), filed May 14, 1936, and May 15, 1937, respectively: Executive Officer/Clerk of the Superior Court, State of California, County of Los Angeles.

Clippings relating to Nyiregyházi's wives Xandra, Genevieve, and Olga: Carolyn Kozo Cole (Photograph Collection, Los Angeles Public Library) and Dace Taube (Regional History Collection, University of Southern California, Los Angeles).

12 Pianist for Hire

On the Federal Music Project: Cornelius Baird Canon, *The Federal Music Project of the Works Progress Administration: Music in a Democracy* (Ph.D. diss., University of Minnesota, 1963); Jannelle Jedd Warren Findley, *Of Tears and Need: The Federal Music Project, 1935–1943*, (Ph.D. diss., The George Washington University, 1973); Martin R. Kalfatovic, *The New Deal Fine Arts Projects: A Bibliography, 1933–1992* (1994).

On F.M.P. discs and rumoured Nyiregyházi recordings: Gregor Benko, Nathan Brown, Victor Ledin, Aurora Perez (Archive of Recorded Sound, Stanford University), and Mark Renovitch (Franklin D. Roosevelt Library, Hyde Park, New York).

An excerpt from one of Nyiregyházi's reviews for the *B'nai B'rith Messenger* (June 1937) was supplied by Charles Timbrell.

13 Bela and Gloria

I came across Willy Pogány's eleven-by-thirteen-inch charcoal portrait of Nyiregyházi in 2003, in an eBay auction. The seller told me that the portrait came from an estate sale at a home in San Marino, California, and the buyer, Mark Nicholls, supplied a scan of it.

On Bela Lugosi: Richard Bojarski, *The Films of Bela Lugosi* (1980), which includes a photograph wrongly identified as of Nyiregyházi; Robert Cremer, *Lugosi: The Man Behind the Cape* (1976); Arthur Lennig, *The Immortal Count: The Life and Films of Bela Lugosi* (2003 rev. of *The Count*, 1974). I conducted a telephone interview with Bela G. Lugosi.

On Gloria Swanson: *Swanson on Swanson: An Autobiography* (1980). Eleven letters from Nyiregyházi (1936–8) as well as programs and other items among the Gloria Swanson Papers, and transcriptions of several notes in her hand, were supplied by Steve Wilson (Film Collections, Harry Ransom Humanities Research Center, University of Texas at Austin), and are quoted with permission. (Wilson also searched for the Liszt recording Nyiregyházi made in Swanson's home.) Mary Piznar (William Doyle

Gallery, New York) supplied information about Doyle's 1983 auction of artifacts from Swanson's estate.

14 Restless
Clippings relating to Nyiregyházi's concerts in Oslo, 1938: Inger Johanne Christiansen (National Library of Norway, Oslo). Unsigned English translations of various reviews were found among the Gloria Swanson Papers.

The producer's log for, and clippings relating to, Nyiregyházi's 1939 recital for Norwegian radio were supplied by Elisabeth Bredeg (Radio Archive, Norwegian Broadcasting Corporation, Oslo).

15 That Strange Romance
Elizabeth Carr, *Shura Cherkassky: The Piano's Last Czar* (2006), 106.

16 Swan Songs
Clippings relating to Nyiregyházi's tour of Nevada, 1942: Gregor Benko.

Raymond Lewenthal's comments are from the unpublished essay cited above, and from a recorded interview (September 21, 1978) with Donald Manildi, who supplied a dub of the relevant portion.

Two letters from Nyiregyházi to Ayn Rand (1944) were supplied by Jeff Britting (Ayn Rand Archives, Marina Del Rey, California).

17 An Uncompromising Rebel
I studied all of the published compositions known to survive (those in the Révész book and the others cited here), all of the unpublished compositions among Doris Nyiregyházi Churchill's effects (hundreds of pages of music, photocopied from Nyiregyházi's manuscripts, most of it from the years of their marriage but including a representative sampling of works from throughout his life), nine sketchbooks from the 1950s, 1960s, and 1970s, and many sketches on loose bits of paper. (I was not able to visit Takasaki, and was not permitted to have photocopies of any of the unpublished compositions on paper and microfilm there.) I also consulted several long lists of compositions that survived among Doris's effects, some in Nyiregyházi's hand, some in that of a Japanese archivist. Doris's file-card box and other notes provided me with Nyiregyházi's comments about hundreds of his compositions. As of the spring of 2008, the German music publisher Schott had plans to bring out at least one volume of Nyiregyházi's compositions.

18 Wine, Women, and Song
Nyiregyházi's published compositions, 1950–1: Donald Manildi (IPAM).
Filings in the cases of *Mara Nyiregyhazi v. Ervin Nyiregyhazi* (Case No.
D514330, complaint for separate maintenance filed January 10, 1957) and *Ervin Nyiregyhazi v. Mara Nyiregyhazi* (Case No. D520409, complaint for annulment-divorce filed May 15, 1957): Executive Officer/Clerk of the Superior Court, State of California, County of Los Angeles. Information relating to Mara's deportation was supplied, at my request under the Freedom of Information Act, by U.S. Citizenship and Immigration Services, U.S. Department of Homeland Security, through the F.O.I.A. Division of the National Records Center (Lee's Summit, Missouri). Other research and clippings relating to Mara: Carolyn Kozo Cole (Photograph Collection, Los Angeles Public Library) and Kelly Haigh (Department of Special Collections, Charles E. Young Research Library, University of California at Los Angeles).

19 Restless (Still)
Filings in the case of *Elsie Swan Nyiregyhazi v. Harry F. Holmes, Peter M. Hood, Does I through X, Inclusive* (Case No. C48608, filed January 29, 1973): Executive Officer/Clerk of the Superior Court, State of California, County of Los Angeles.

PART 4: THE PIANIST WHO CAME IN FROM THE COLD

20 Crescendo
On the Nyiregyházi renaissance in the 1970s, I conducted telephone interviews with Ronald Antonioli, William J. del Valle (né Santaella), Ernie Gilbert, Marc Goodman, the late Richard Kapp, John Kilgore, Marcos Klorman, Bill Knorp, Neil Levenson, Garrick Ohlsson, the late Harold C. Schonberg, Wayne Stahnke, Mark Starr, and Richard Wahlberg. In many cases, I also had follow-up correspondence and received copies of documents, recordings, and other materials. I had many long conversations with Ricardo Hernandez, who visited me several times and supplied copies and transcriptions of notebooks and loose pages in which he recorded conversations with Nyiregyházi, in San Francisco and Stuttgart, between late 1976 and the spring of 1978. Ronald Antonioli loaned me his Nyiregyházi file, which included published articles, letters, concert programs, and photographs. I also received information and materials from Gregor Benko, Bill Boles and Richard Pennington (*Boston Globe* Library), Christiana Duranczyk (Library Express, San Francisco Public Library), Richard Dyer, Daniel Greenhouse, Foster Grimm, Paul

Hartman, Steven Heliotes, Lois Jermyn (*San Francisco Chronicle* Library), Michael Kellman, James Kreger, Michael A. Kukral, Karen Lerner, Larry Lobel, Donald Manildi (IPAM), Terry McNeill, and Andrew Thayer.

21 A Troubled Renaissance
The late Richard Kapp loaned me his large file of correspondence, memoranda, recording data, and other Nyiregyházi-related papers, as well as four cassettes of conversations with Nyiregyházi (New York, February 21, 23, and 24, 1978).

The Ford Foundation's Nyiregyházi file was supplied by Idelle Nissila-Stone, of the foundation's archives, and permission to quote from it was given by Alan S. Divack, of its Research Services office.

A transcript of Nyiregyházi's appearance on the *CBS Morning News*, February 14, 1978, was supplied by Robert Tomlin (CBS News Archives, New York).

Carl Loeffelhardt, who sold pianos for Baldwin in the Bay Area at the time, supplied recorded reminiscences of a day he spent with Nyiregyházi in San Francisco in June 1978.

Mark Starr supplied dubs of "The Art of Ervin Nyiregyházi," two one-hour programs, featuring interviews and piano rolls, that aired in his weekly series *Speaking of Music* (KQED, San Francisco, mid-1978).

On the Nyiregyházi renaissance – published articles based on original interviews with Nyiregyházi (in chronological order): Gregor Benko, liner notes to *Nyiregyházi Plays Liszt* (Desmar IPA 111, 1977); Michael Walsh, "Recluse piano genius emerges in The City," *San Francisco Examiner,* January 9, 1978, 1, 8; Michael Walsh, "2 passions of genius," *San Francisco Examiner,* January 10, 1978, 15, 21; Michael Walsh, "Return of the eccentric," *San Francisco Sunday Examiner and Chronicle,* January 29, 1978, Scene, 6; Harold C. Schonberg, "After 50 Years (and 9 Wives), Erwin Nyiregyházi Is Back at the Piano," *New York Times,* February 13, 1978, C20; Harold C. Schonberg, "The Case of The Vanishing Pianist," *New York Times,* March 5, 1978, D15–16; unsigned, "For pianist Nyiregyházi, fame, unjustly, is nine wives and ten photographed fingers," *People Weekly,* March 13, 1978, 71–2, 74; Donna Perlmutter, "The pianist who came in from the cold," *Los Angeles Herald Examiner,* March 21, 1978, B1, 5; Dave Smith, "Tribute to Ervin Nyiregyházi: A Genius in Seclusion," *Los Angeles Times,* April 2, 1978, Calendar, 50; Mary Ann Hogan, "The Prodigy Who Wanted a Good Time," *Washington Post,* April 22, 1978, C1–2; Annalyn Swan, "Nine Wives and 700 Works Later: Nyiregyházi returns from out of the past," *Time,* May 29, 1978, 43–4; Michael Walsh, "Ervin Nyiregyházi," *Stereo Review,* July

1978, 58–63; "Recording with Ervin Nyiregyházi: A Chronicle by Richard Kapp" and liner notes by Michael Walsh, both in *Nyiregyházi Plays Liszt* (Columbia M2 34598, 1978); Warren Hinckle, "The Franz Liszt of the Tenderloin," *San Francisco Chronicle*, August 10, 1978, 4; Michael Walsh, "A late brush with fame," *San Francisco Examiner*, January 9, 1979, 15, 18; "Nyiregyhazi's rise, fall, rise," by Kenneth LaFave, *The Arizona Daily Star*, ca. April 1979; Bill Zakariasen, "Curmudgeon of the Keyboard," *Sunday News Magazine* [New York], April 22, 1979, 26–7, 34, 39–40; Neil G. Levenson, "One Sunday in Southern California" [interview], *Fanfare*, March-April 1980, 12–13, 221; Robert J. Silverman, "A Candid Talk with Erwin Nyiregyházi," *The Piano Quarterly*, Spring 1982, 18, 20–21.

On the Nyiregyházi renaissance – other published articles (in chronological order): Robert Jones, "In Key: Horowitz? Forget him," *Sunday News* [New York], June 13, 1976, 14; Brad Knickerbocker, "'Rediscovery' of an elusive pianist prodigy," *Christian Science Monitor*, February 7, 1978, 1, 30; unsigned, "A 'lost' prodigy is rediscovered: Marin man [Ronald Antonioli] recalls friendship with piano genius," *Independent-Journal* [Marin County], February 17, 1978; *Billboard*, several short articles March 4 through July 22, 1978; Robert Commanday, "The Surfacing of an Instant Cult Figure," *San Francisco Sunday Examiner and Chronicle*, March 12, 1978, 48–9; Blaik Kirby, "A forgotten genius comes out of hiding," *Globe and Mail* [Toronto], April 22, 1978, 17; Irving Kolodin, "The reappearance of a powerful pianist," *Newsday*, May 28, 1978; Frank Cooper, "Play it again," *Inquiry*, July 24, 1978, 29–30; Samuel Lipman, "The prodigy in old age," *The Times Literary Supplement*, September 22, 1978, 1052 (reprinted in his book *Music After Modernism*, 214–17); Richard Dyer, "A Bizarre Story Updated," *Boston Globe*, October 1978; unsigned, "Gewitter in der Kirche," *Der Spiegel*, October 9, 1978, 236, 238; R. T. Kahn, "The Triumphant Return of a 'Lost' Pianist, 75," *50plus*, December 1978, 44–5; Carol Mont Parker, "Nyiregyházi: A Puzzling Phenomenon," *Clavier*, January 1979, 32–4; Carsten Stroud, "Divine Madness," *Fugue*, January 1979, 20–1, 23; Alan Sanders, "Here and There: Ervin Nyiregyházi," *Gramophone*, July 1979, 175–6.

Reviews of the Desmar and Columbia Masterworks albums (in chronological order): Richard Dyer, "Nyiregyházi: Like nothing you've heard," *Boston Globe*, August 28, 1977, A9; Neil G. Levenson, "Nyiregyházi," *Fanfare*, November-December 1977, 33–4; Levering Bronston, *The New Records*, December 1977, 11–12; Keith Fagan, "The Incredible Nyiregyházi," typescript, late 1977; Richard Freed, "The Boy Who Was Obsessed with Liszt," *Stereo Review*, January 1978,

104; Harris Goldsmith, "Gems and Curios from the International Piano Archives," *High Fidelity Magazine,* February 1978, 82–3; Rafael Kammerer, "A Feast for Pianophiles," *American Record Guide,* February 1978, 8; Neil G. Levenson, "The Synoptic Vision of Ervin Nyiregyházi," *Fanfare,* May-June 1978, 4–5, 128; Frank Cooper, *Journal of the American Liszt Society,* June 1978, 30–2; Derrick Henry, "Nyiregyházi's Liszt," *Record Review Magazine,* August 1978, 40–1; Michael Walsh, "Nyiregyházi's album," *San Francisco Examiner,* August 8, 1978, 18; James Goodfriend, "The Return of Nyiregyházi," *Stereo Review,* October 1978, 156; Dean Elder, "Recent Records" *Clavier,* January 1979, 14–15; Margaret Daugherty, "Nyiregyházi Revisited," *Record Review Magazine,* February 1979, 42–3; Charlotte Greenspan, "Nyiregyházi's Liszt," *19th Century Music,* July 1979, 72–5; James Methuen-Campbell, *Records and Recording,* July 1979, 96; L.S. [Lionel Salter], *Gramophone,* July 1979, 230; F. E. Kirby, "Quarterly Review of Recordings," *The Piano Quarterly,* Spring 1982, 17.

22 *Plus beau que la beauté*

On performance practices in the music of Liszt: *Remembering Franz Liszt* (1986), comprising *Life and Liszt: The Recollections of a Concert Pianist,* by Arthur Friedheim, and *My Memories of Liszt,* by Alexander Siloti; *The Cambridge Companion to Liszt,* ed. Kenneth Hamilton (2005); *The Piano Master Classes of Franz Liszt, 1884–1886: Diary Notes of August Göllerich,* ed. Wilhelm Jerger, trans. and ed. Richard Louis Zimdars (1996); Richard Hudson, *Stolen Time: The History of Tempo Rubato* (1994); Charles Rosen, "Liszt: On Creation in Performance," in *The Romantic Generation* (1995), 472–541; Harold C. Schonberg's chapters on Liszt in *The Great Conductors* (1967), 156–62, and *The Great Pianists* (1963, 1987), 161–82; Alan Walker, *Franz Liszt,* 3 vols. (1983, 1988, 1996; reprinted 1987 (revised), 1993, 1997); Adrian Williams, *Portrait of Liszt: By Himself and His Contemporaries* (1990).

Two sources offered a kind of "masterclass" on Liszt's sonata: a taped interview with Paul Hartman (March 1985) in which Nyiregyházi went through the sonata, bar by bar, and discussed his interpretive ideas; and a score in which Ricardo Hernandez noted (ca. 1974–5) Nyiregyházi's performance suggestions.

On ruins: Rose Macauley, *Pleasure of Ruins* (1953, 1984); Christopher Woodward, *In Ruins* (2001).

Henry F. Chorley, "Madame Pasta," *Thirty Years' Musical Recollections,* ed. Ernest Newman (1926), 92–3.

23 Adored Baby
I conducted telephone and in-person interviews with Mary Shapiro, and telephone interviews with Robert Churchill and Virginia Brobyn, who also supplied three letters from Nyiregyházi (1978).

24 Diminuendo
The two German television programs, both featuring interviews and performances filmed in Los Angeles, were: "Wenn die Andern feiern," a segment in the series *Kultur*, broadcast December 24, 1978, on ZDF (Zweites Deutsches Fernsehen), Munich; and a segment in the music-magazine show *Notenschlüssel*, produced by Christoph Winter and broadcast in September 1981 on SWR (Südwestrundfunk), Baden-Baden.

Marc Goodman supplied dubs of his three interviews with Nyiregyházi (Los Angeles, August 16, 18, and 20, 1980).

Peter Brügger supplied recollections of his family's dinner with Nyiregyházi in Stuttgart, in September 1977.

PART 5: A GREAT ANTITHESIS

25 Teacher, Father
My most important source of information about Nyiregyházi and Japan was Tomoyuki Sawado. On my behalf, in 2004 and 2005, he visited the University of Creation: Art, Music, and Social Work (the former Takasaki College of Music and Takasaki Art Center College), where he copied clippings, photographs, and recordings, and interviewed Daitetsu (Tetsuji) Koike and Kakuyu (Masahiro) Sekikawa. Later, he served as my liaison with the Japanese, translated many sources, and provided me with a great deal of other information and advice. I could not have written this section of the book without his extraordinary efforts.

At Takasaki, I am also grateful to Satoru Kambe, who sent me the college's 1996 booklet on Nyiregyházi and the *Messengers of Peace* albums. Sadako Nguyen contacted the college on my behalf on a trip to Japan in 2000, translated documents, and helped in other ways with Japanese-related matters.

Recollections of Nyiregyházi in Japan: Christopher Yohmei Blasdel, Janos Cegledy, Riley Lee, and the late Harold C. Schonberg, whom I interviewed by telephone in 1997.

The booklet enclosed with *The Messengers of Peace* includes two items in English: "The Letter from Ervin Nyiregyházi" (his own program notes for the recordings), and Schonberg's article "Lofty Pianist Nyiregyházi."

26. The Sun Sets

Paul Hartman loaned me eight cassettes of his conversations with Nyiregyházi (March 1985 and September 1986). Coincidentally, he is today a child and adolescent psychiatrist at the Kaiser Permanente Los Angeles Medical Center, formerly Kaiser Foundation Hospital – the hospital at which Nyiregyházi received his medical care. On my behalf, he examined the one medical chart that survives at the hospital, on Nyiregyházi's hospitalization from April 1 to 4, 1987, just before his death. Hartman also gave me many insights into Nyiregyházi's psychology (it was he who suggested a diagnosis of Borderline Personality Disorder).

POSTLUDE: THE NYIREGYHÁZI LEGACY

On Nyiregyházi's posthumous "life": Gregor Benko, C. H. Freeman, the late Henry and Leah Fried, "ie Gilbert, Aaron Gross, William Hauptman, Peter Jermyn, David S. Kung, Neil Levenson, Ward Marston, Mark Mitchell, Gordon Rumson, and Mattheus Smits.

Web sites devoted to Nyiregyházi: www.nyiregyhazi.org, maintained by Aaron Gross, son-in-law of Nyiregyházi's late cousin Henry Fried; "The Ervin Nyiregyházi Appreciation Page" (www.marymaclane.com/nyiregyhazi), which includes scores and MIDI transcriptions of some of the childhood compositions in the Révész book; www.michaelsayers.com/ervinnyiregyhazi.html; Tomoyuki Sawado's personal Web site, which includes a section on Nyiregyházi in Japanese and English (www.fugue.us/Ervin.html); and the official site of the International Ervin Nyiregyházi Foundation (www.ervinnyiregyhazi.net). Sawado's site, just being established as this book first went to press early in 2007, now already includes biographical data, recordings, scores, photographs, facsimiles, and other material that significantly supplements this book.

AUDIO AND VIDEO RECORDINGS

I studied all of the audio and video recordings known to me of Nyiregyházi playing, with the following exceptions: the films *Fashions in Love* and *Lummox* (they survive in the Film and Television Archives at the University of California at Los Angeles, the former in a shrunken print, the latter as a set of five Vitaphone soundtrack discs); outtakes from the 1978 NBC documentary; the German program "Wenn die Andern feiern"; his private performance, for Koike and Sekikawa, at Los Angeles Temple Church (March 1980); a few pieces from the Takasaki concert of June 1, 1980; and the short test-recording of Liszt that he made (May 1981) for Wayne Stahnke on the Bösendorfer 290SE, Stahnke's then new, computer-assisted update of the reproducing piano.

Only one of Nyiregyházi's piano rolls, "Mazeppa," has ever been released as a commercial recording. It appeared on LP, in 1966, in *The Golden Age of Piano Virtuosi: Ampico Piano Rolls – Record III*, on the British label Argo (DA 43), and on CD, in 1986, in *The Performing Piano*, on the American label Newport Classic (NC 6002). The VAI Audio CD *Nyiregyházi at the Opera* is still available, and secondhand copies of the Desmar and Columbia Masterworks albums can sometimes be found on eBay and elsewhere. The two-CD set *Ervin Nyiregyházi in Performance: Live Recordings, 1972–1982*, released on the American label Music & Arts (CD-1202) late in 2007, includes performances from the public and private recitals in San Francisco, Novato, Takasaki, and Tokyo, as well as the Federal Music Project's 1936 Macpherson recording. The films *The Lost Zeppelin, The Soul of a Monster, A Song to Remember, Song of Love,* and *The Beast with Five Fingers* can all be purchased commercially; relevant scenes from some of them have also been placed on YouTube and on some Nyiregyházi-related Web sites.

For supplying copies of and information about audio and video recordings, I am grateful to Albert Frantz, Marc Goodman, Daniel Greenhouse, Christine Hahn (Zuschauerservice, Bayerischer Rundfunk, Munich), Steven Heliotes, Ricardo Hernandez, Ron Hutchinson (The Vitaphone Project), Satoru Kambe (Takasaki Art Center College), the late Richard Kapp, Marco Lenssen and Silke Rönspies (Mitschnittdienst, SWR Media, Baden-Baden), Donald Manildi (IPAM), Tomoyuki Sawado, Kakuyu (Masahiro) Sekikawa, Mattheus Smits, Wayne Stahnke, Mark Starr, Rob Stone (Film and Television Archives, UCLA), and Nathaniel Yangco. I am also grateful to Kenneth C. Caswell and John Farmer, who made recordings especially for me of Nyiregyházi piano rolls in their collections; to Terry Smythe, who supplied MIDI files made from computer scans of six of the rolls; and to Gordon Rumson and Michael Sayers, who made private recordings of themselves playing piano works composed by Nyiregyházi.

Notes on Sources and Acknowledgements

Photographs and Facsimiles

For providing photographs and facsimiles, information about them, or permission to reproduce them, I am grateful to the following individuals and institutions: Ronald Antonioli; Gordon Bazzana; Bill Blair (Music and Media Librarian, McPherson Library, University of Victoria); Jarod Clark; Carolyn Kozo Cole (Photograph Collection, Los Angeles Public Library); Gary Fong (Photo Sales, *San Francisco Chronicle*); Jørn Fossheim; Yoshimasa Hatano; Ricardo Hernandez; Bill Knorp; Junichi Miyazawa; Joel Moran; Mark Nicholls; Nicole M. Pace (*Musical America*, New York); Joy Parnes and Samuel Will Parnes; John Pollack and Nancy M. Shawcross (Rare Book and Manuscript Library, University of Pennsylvania, Philadelphia); Tomoyuki Sawado; Michael Sayers; Mattheus Smits (International Ervin Nyiregyházi Foundation); Sven Oluf Auguste Cleve Sørensen; Katalin Szerzö (Music Collection, National Széchényi Library, Budapest); Dace Taube (Regional History Collection, Specialized Libraries and Archival Collections, University of Southern California, Los Angeles); Nóra Wellmann (Archives, Budapest Opera House); World University Press (Benson, Arizona).

The reproductions on the jacket and title page, and on pages 73, 187, 213, 240, 244 (left), 247, 300, 311, 324, 335, 337, and 347, are from items found among the papers of Nyiregyházi and his wife Doris.

Acknowledgements

My research was generously supported by awards, in 1998 and 2003, from the Grants for Professional Writers program of the Canada Council for the Arts.

In addition to all those persons mentioned above, my thanks, for help of various kinds, to Lloyd Arriola, Leon Bahn, Jonathan Bellman, Michael Brown, János Kárpáti, Gregor Klenz, Andras Nagy, Jeremy Nicholas, Ray Osnato, Melvin Rosenberg, Mária Biro Watts, and the *New York Review of Books*, which printed an author's query from me in October 2002. I am grateful to the McPherson Library at the University of Victoria, in particular its Interlibrary Loan, Microforms, and Music, Audio, and Media Services. For translating sources in Hungarian, my thanks to Anett Barkóczi, Jurriaan Dijkman, Dorottya Fabian, Laszlo Gombos, and Fred Maroth.

Mattheus Smits shared information, copied recordings, scores, and articles, found research assistants, contributed financially to my trip to Chicago, and helped me in many other ways over the years. As president of the International Ervin Nyiregyházi Foundation, which has the authority to act on behalf of Nyiregyházi's estate, he gave me permission to copy archival materials, quote from unpublished writings, and publish photographs and facsimiles, and offered to use his Web site to promote and supplement this book. I greatly appreciate his crucial efforts on my behalf.

Many of those mentioned in the pages above, especially those who knew Nyiregyházi personally, read parts (in some cases all) of the manuscript in draft form and made helpful comments; so, too, did my friends Polly Holliday, Marguerite Mousseau, Janet Munsil, Neil Reimer, Jayne Stephenson, and Les Stephenson.

McClelland & Stewart, in Toronto, took an interest early on in this book, and shepherded it through publication with an enthusiasm for which I am very grateful. For their hard work, professionalism, and good humour, I am indebted particularly to my editors, Jenny Bradshaw and Alex Schultz, and to Heather Sangster (copy editor), Susan Renouf (Vice-President, Associate Publisher, Non-Fiction), and Marilyn Biderman (Vice-President, Director, Rights and Contracts).

My thanks also to the Saturday Breakfast Club, to all the other friends who encouraged my work, and to those local cafés that made such pleasant surrogate offices.

My deepest gratitude goes to my partner, Sharon Bristow – my own "adored baby" – who gave me much emotional and practical support while I wrote this book, and commented insightfully on the text. For the second time, I am dedicating a book to her and to the loyal companions who have shared our home. I could not do otherwise.

Brentwood Bay, B.C.
December 10, 2006/May 2, 2008

Index

The abbreviation *N* stands for *Nyiregyházi*. A page number in italic (e.g., *100*) indicates a reference to a photograph or facsimile. The italic letter *n* following a page number (e.g., 100*n*) indicates that the information is in a footnote.

Index

Budapest Opera *see* Royal Hungarian
   Opera
Bülow, Hans von, 57, 65
Busoni, Ferruccio: Bach arrangements,
   57, 75, 84; N compared with, 29,
   103*n*, 252, 267*n*; N's views on, 58,
   61, 103*n*, 164—*Works:* Piano
   Concerto, 74, 279
Bysshe, Ernie, 205*n*, 223

Caplin, Xandra Lucille (second wife),
   160-2, *161*, 177, 180, 190, 216
Capone, Al, 122
Capra, Frank, 175, 176
Carnegie Hall (New York), 83, 88, 89, 93,
   95*n*, 98, 122, 144, 146, 150, 163, 169,
   270, 279, 306, 313, 334
Carroll, Adam, 106
Carter, Jimmy, 217
CBS Morning News (television program),
   270
CBS Records (record label), 270, 273, 274-6,
   277, 280, 303-5, 307, 308
Century Club of California (San
   Francisco), 249
Chaplin, Charles, 170
Cherkassky, Shura, 195, 196
Chicago (Illinois), 94, 145, 296-7, 299,
   339, 342
China, 327
Chopin, Fryderyk Franciszek (Frédéric
   François): 22, 42*n*, 75, 122, 204, 290-1,
   298, 308*n*; compositions inspired by,
   218; N as interpreter of, 88, 134, 249,
   317; N compared with, 30, 129*n*, 224,
   279; N's views on, 249*n*—*Works:*
   ballades, 22, 224; Barcarolle, 84;
   Berceuse, 288*n*; Étude in G-flat
   Major ("Black-Key"), 151; Mazurka
   in A Minor, KK IIb/No. 5, 317; Piano
   Sonata No. 2 in B-flat Minor, 11, 75,
   160, 205*n*, 238; Piano Sonata No. 3
   in B Minor, 11, 68, 75; Polonaise in
   A-flat Major, 204, 288; Polonaise-

Fantaisie, 133; Waltz in D-flat Major
   ("Minute"), 69; Waltz
   in E Minor, KK IVa/No. 15, 50
Chorley, Henry F., 293-4
Churchill, August Charles, Jr., 296,
   299-301, 339
Churchill, Doris (tenth wife): after N's
   death, 338-42; as champion of N, 302,
   328, 338-41; compositions inspired by,
   302, 329; death, 342; health, 299, 326,
   334, 342; interviews N, 328, 339;
   marriage to N, 297-302, 304,
   316, 326-34; marriages to Charles
   Churchill, 296, 339; on N's personality, 297-8, 301, 314-16, 317, 331,
   326; personality, 296, 297-9, 302,
   340, 342; physical appearance, *300*,
   302, 342; plans to write N's biography,
   328, 338-40, 342
Churchill, Mary *see* Shapiro, Mary
Churchill, Robert, 298, 300
Clark Hotel (Los Angeles), 313
Cleve, Astrid (girlfriend), 77, 126, 181-2,
   241
Cleve, Halfdan: compositions inspired by,
   218; friendship with N, 75, 77, 118,
   126, 181—*Works:* Ballade, 108, 110
Cleve, Signy (girlfriend), 77, 126, *127*,
   181, 241
Cliburn, Van, 204*n*
Cohn, Harry, 203
Columbia (film studio), 203, 204
Columbia Masterworks (record label),
   263*n*, 274, 277, 303
Compositions d'Ervin Nyiregyházi,
   Opp. 1-3 (publication), *vi*, 42
Conan Doyle, Sir Arthur, 55
Constantinople *see* Istanbul
Copenhagen (Denmark), 72, 74
Coquette (film), 150
Cremer, Robert, 174
Cross, Mildred (sister-in-law, girlfriend),
   184
Crown, John, 9-10

Index

Index

Index

194, 210, 223, 253, 321; compositions by, published, 42, 76-7, 95, 223; compositions by, recordings of, 223, 321, 329n; as conductor, 24, 50-1; death, 334; dress habits, 55, 69, 73, 78, 92, 122, 142-3, 227-8, 253, 271, 297, 315, 319n; drinking, 72, 84, 132, 145, 159n, 163, 173-4, 181, 184, 194, 195, 196, 205n, 211, 214, 227, 230-1, 233, 237, 239-40, 242, 253, 255, 266, 271, 297, 301-2, 306-7, 315, 317; eating habits, 35, 39n, 51-2, 90-1, 95, 121, 123, 142, 152, 184, 227, 237, 250, 297, 299, 330, 332; education, non-musical, 19, 35, 58, 66-7; family holidays, 45-6, 50, 51, 54, 66; family life, 17, 35-41, 50, 51-3; film enjoyed by, 30, 96, 93n, 123, 149n, 211; film work, 149-51, 158, 202-5; financial situation and income, 8, 44, 50, 56, 74, 78, 79n, 82, 95, 97, 106-7, 114, 117-19, 120-3, 123-4, 131, 143-5, 146, 149-51, 158, 165, 166, 176, 177, 179, 180, 182, 190, 195, 196-7, 205, 212n, 223n, 226-7, 233, 236-7, 239, 242, 249-51, 252, 254, 255, 271, 274-6, 297, 303-4, 319, 326, 332, 338; funeral, 338; gangsters befriended by, 122, 157; genealogy, 16-17; hair styles, 36, 55, 83, 90, 97-8, 99, 104, 330, 333; hands and fingers, 22, 39, 83, 91, 203-5, 255, 283, 313, 330; health, 45-6, 67-8, 153, 155-6, 260, 283n, 329-34; and Hollywood society, 104-5, 175-8, 202; and homosexuality, 130-1, 132, 195; and Hungarian and Gypsy music, 30, 103, 292, 323; and Hungarian literature, 25, 218; Hungarian temperament, 11-12, 85, 87-8, 222n; I.Q., 28; jailed, 184, 255; as Jew, 16-19, 44, 58n, 88, 118, 267, 299, 307n; jobs, non-musical, 124; languages read and spoken, 18, 25, 58, 66, 74, 91, 95-6; lifestyle, 4, 12, 123, 151, 175, 183, 193-4, 212n, 226-31,

250, 257, 260, 262, 270-1, 297; literary interests, 25, 55, 229; memory, 28-9, 75, 91, 211, 216, 263-4, 289, 316, 333, 334; as Mr. X, 5-8, 205, *206*; muggings, 228n, 260, 315; musical gifts, 20-3, 28-34, 48-9, 75, 91, 150, 229; "MY MUSICAL CREDO," 208-9; name, 3-4n, 16-17, 82, 98; and opera, 21, 24, 37, 122, 296, 341; personality and psychology, 7-8, 12-13, 19, 25, 32, 35-42, 47, 51-3, 54-5, 62-4, 68-71, 77-8, 83-4, 93, 95-6, 104, 105, 119, 121-2, 123, 126n, 128, 138-40, 152-4, 159, 164-5, 168, 169-70, 173-4, 176, 179, 183-4, 187, 189-94, 200-1, 207, 214, 215-16, 218, 221-2, 227-31, 234, 239-41, 253, 260, 265-8, 269, 275-6, 280, 287-8, 297-9, 301-2, 304, 306-8, 314-16, 327, 331-3, 343-7, *347*; philosophical interests, 25, 104, 169, 218, 229; photographs, *vi, 1, 15, 49, 73, 81, 83, 99, 109, 114, 132 147, 162, 172, 206, 235, 240, 247, 250, 254, 264, 277, 300, 311, 324, 337*; physical appearance, 22, 36, 48, 76, 83, 90-2, 125n, 128, 141, 168, 173, 203, 205, 232, 253, 316, 329-30, 332; as pianist and interpreter, 6-7, 9-11, 20, 22, 29, 57, 63, 66, 73-4, 76, 77, 85-9, 90, 92, 98, 102-3, 107, 110-11, 112-13, 115, 120, 128, 130, 133-4, 149, 151, 155-6, 164, 167, 181-2, 199-200, 221, 248, 249, 251-2, 256, 258, 261, 262, 263, 270, 278, 279-80, 281-94, 314, 317-18, 323, 327, 332; piano studies of, 21-2, 30n, 37-8, 47, 56-7, 61, 65-6, 72; pianos used by, 50, 86n, 97n, 262, 268, 284; political and social views, 228, 296; and popular music, 93-4, 104, 144, 219, 220, 273, 304n; posthumous "life," 338-43; and racism, 228; radio appearances, 149n, 158-9, 166n, 182, 322; recordings, concert, 166n, 249, 251-2, 253, 256, 309, 316-17, 319-20, 321-2, 325, 341;